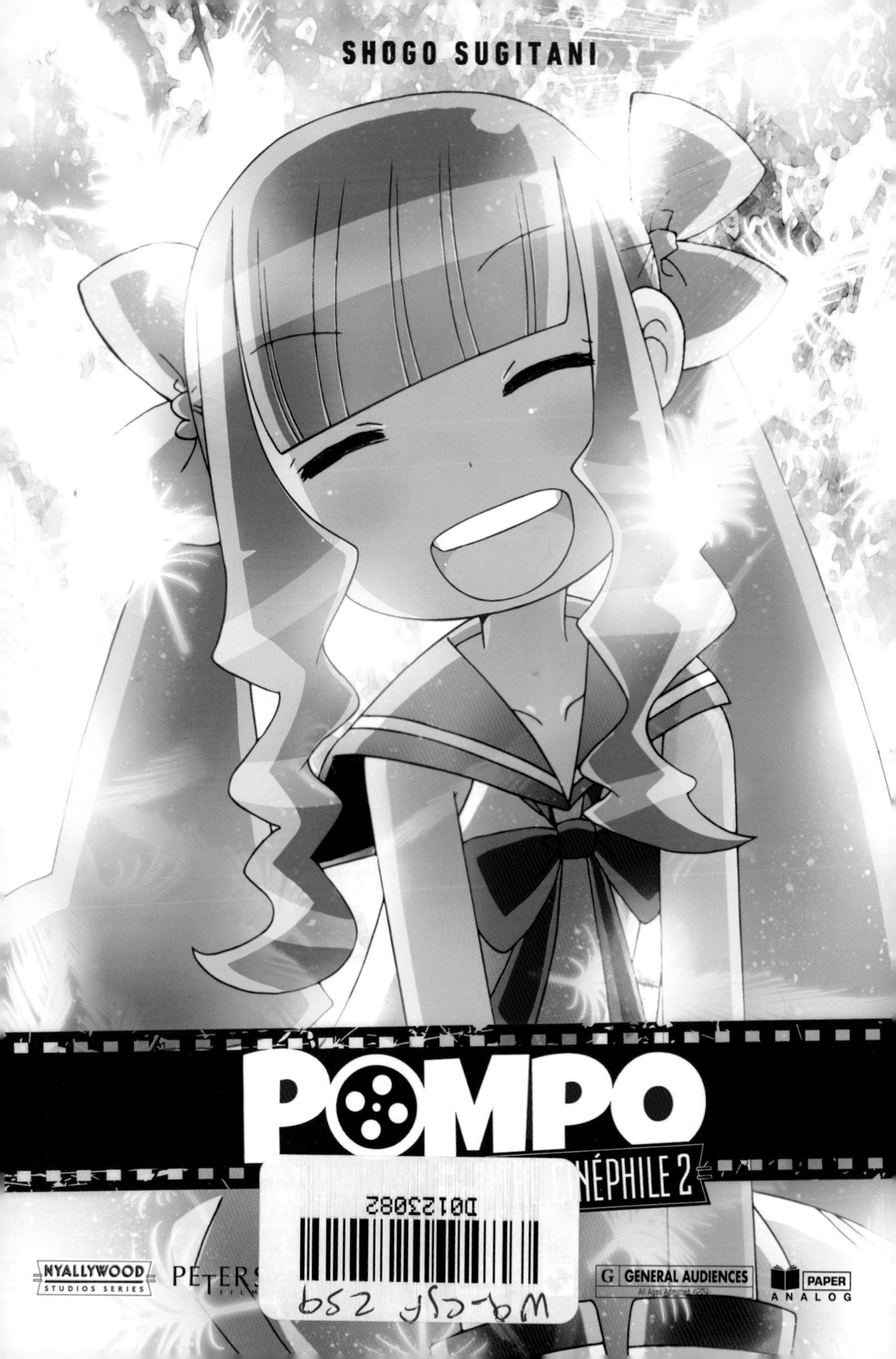
SHOGO SUGITANI
POMPO
NÉPHILE 2
NYALLYWOOD
STUDIOS SERIES
G GENERAL AUDIENCES
All Ages Admitted
PAPER
ANALOG

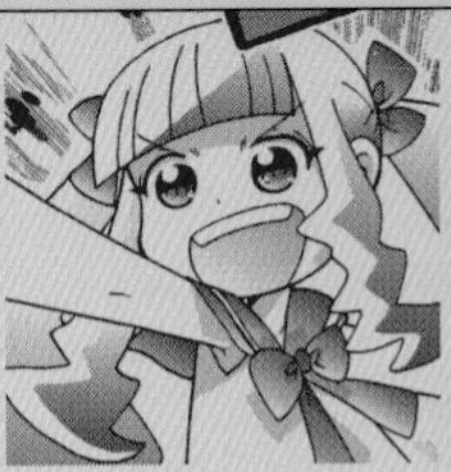

Joelle Davidovich "Pompo" Pomponette

Film Producer

TOP 3 FILMS

Whiplash
Death Proof (as part of *Grindhouse*)
Frankenweenie

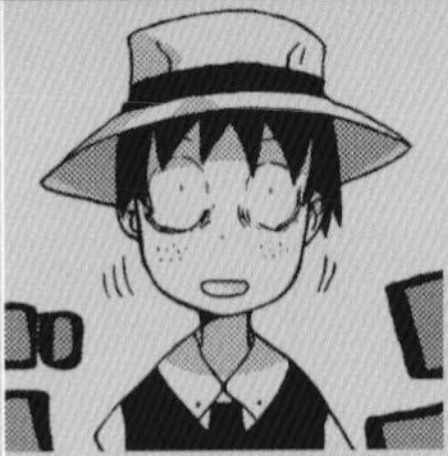

Gene Fini

Emerging Film Director

TOP 3 FILMS

The Sting
Fight Club
Taxi Driver

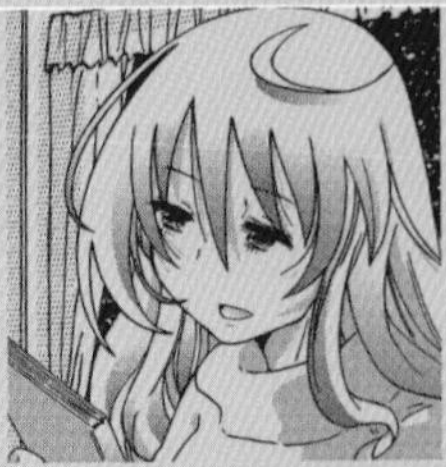

Mystia

Rising Young Star

TOP 3 FILMS

Camille Claudel
The Story of Adele H.
The Brontë Sisters

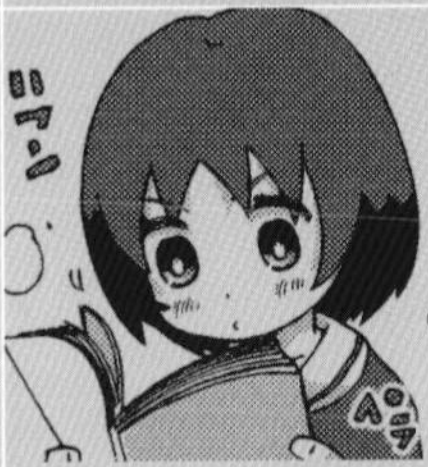

Nathalie Woodward

Emerging Actor

TOP 3 FILMS

My Mother's Castle
The Secret Garden
Babette's Feast

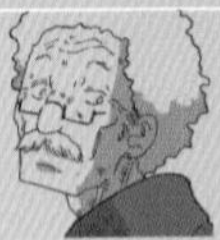

Joel Davidovich Petersen

Retired Film Producer

TOP 3 FILMS

Paper Moon
The Seventh Seal
The Night of the Hunter

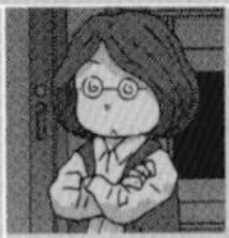

Corvette

Predictable and Reliable Director-for-Hire

TOP 3 FILMS

Go! Anpanman: Nanda and Runda of the Toy Star
Kirakira Pretty Cure a la Mode the Movie: Crispy! The Memory of Mille-feuille!
Girls und Panzer der Film

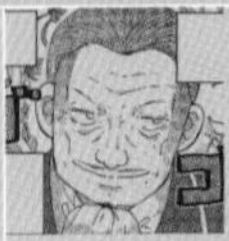

Martin Braddock

Living Legend and World's Greatest Actor

TOP 3 FILMS

A Streetcar Named Desire
The Godfather
Apocalypse Now

← PROGRAM

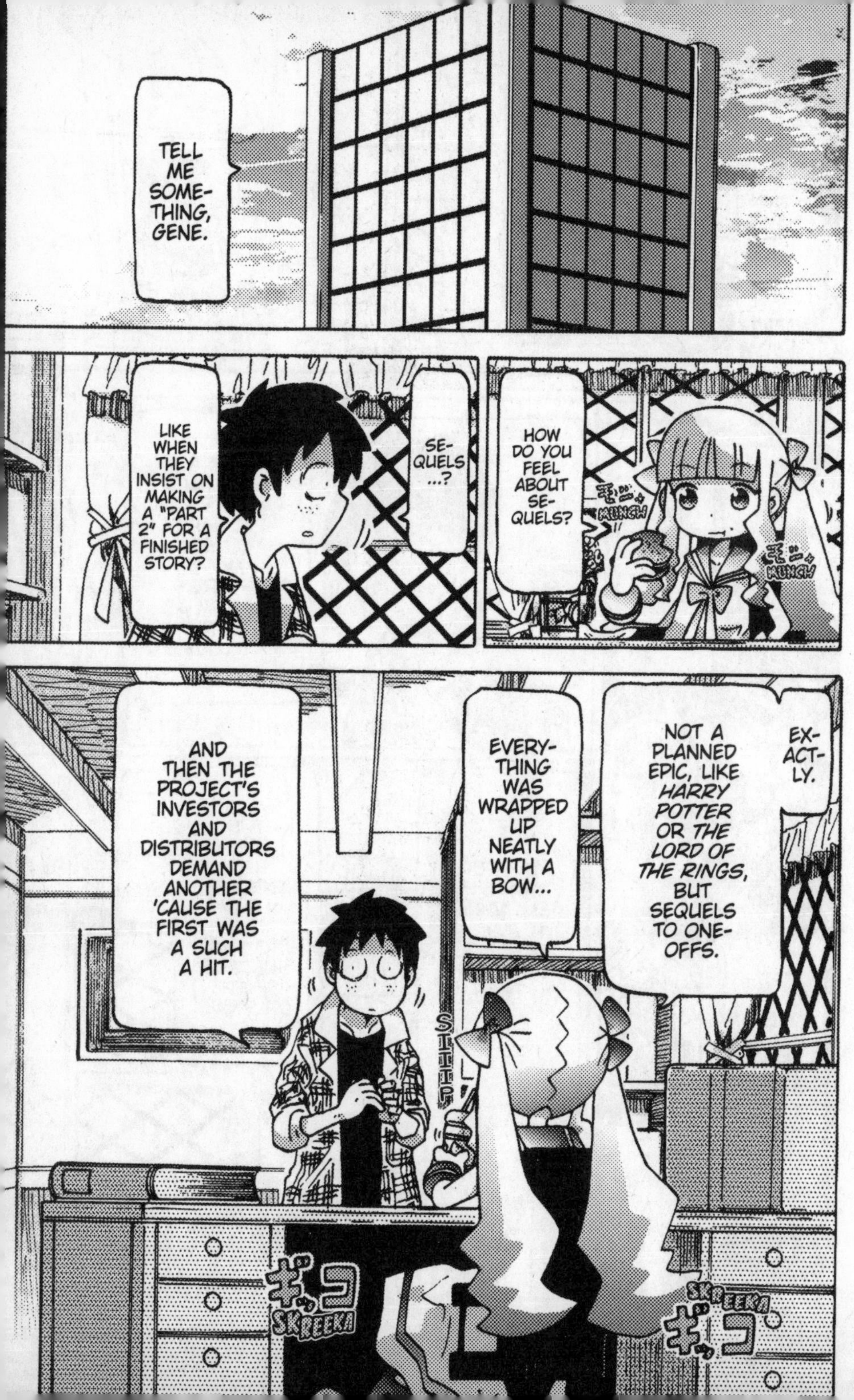
TELL ME SOME-THING, GENE.
HOW DO YOU FEEL ABOUT SE-QUELS?
MUNCH
MUNCH
SE-QUELS ...?
LIKE WHEN THEY INSIST ON MAKING A "PART 2" FOR A FINISHED STORY?
EX-ACT-LY.
NOT A PLANNED EPIC, LIKE *HARRY POTTER* OR *THE LORD OF THE RINGS*, BUT SEQUELS TO ONE-OFFS.
EVERY-THING WAS WRAPPED UP NEATLY WITH A BOW...
AND THEN THE PROJECT'S INVESTORS AND DISTRIBUTORS DEMAND ANOTHER 'CAUSE THE FIRST WAS A SUCH A HIT.
SLIIIP
SKREEKA
SKREEKA

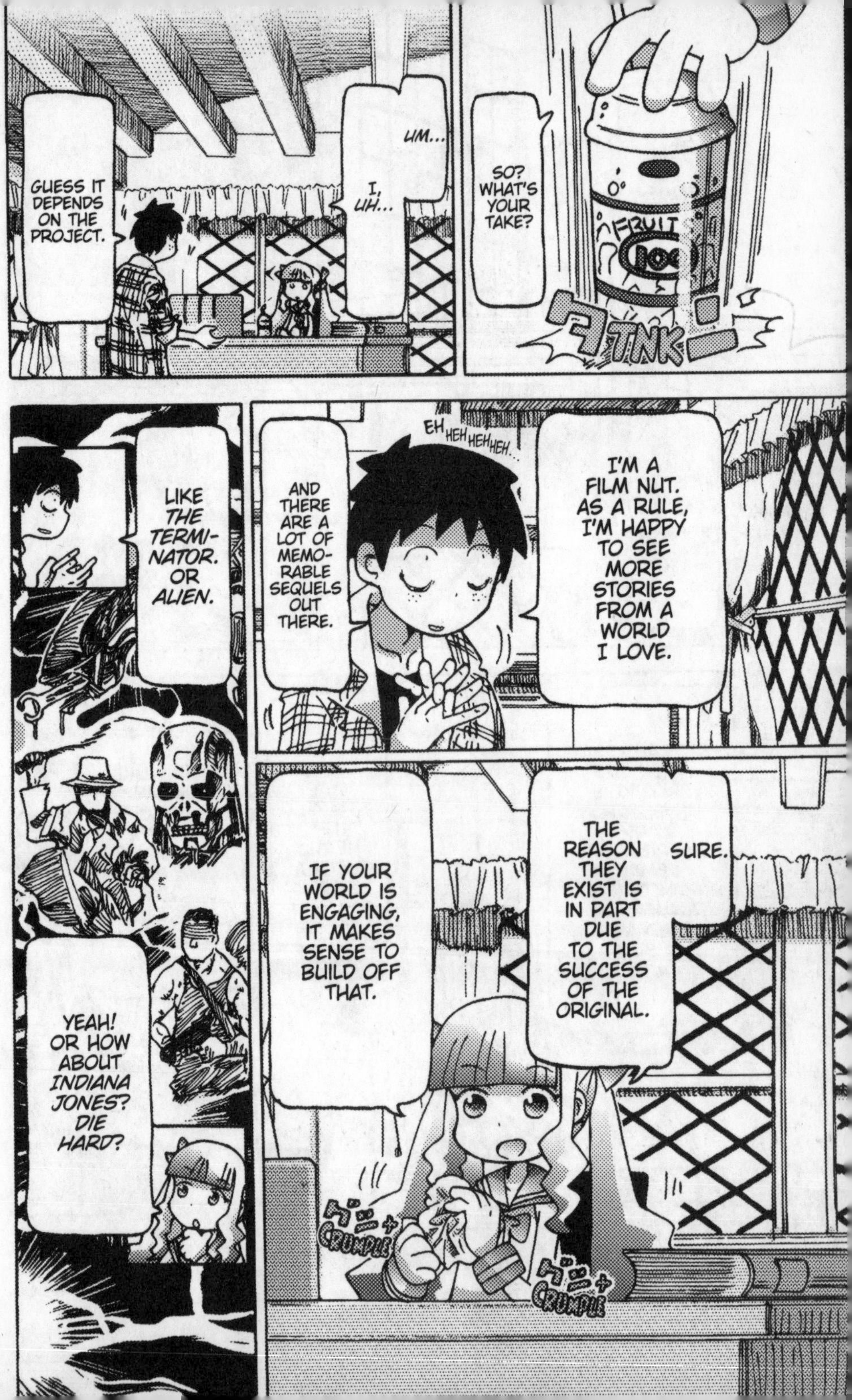
SO? WHAT'S YOUR TAKE?
TINK
UM...
I, UH...
GUESS IT DEPENDS ON THE PROJECT.
EH HEH HEH HEH...
I'M A FILM NUT. AS A RULE, I'M HAPPY TO SEE MORE STORIES FROM A WORLD I LOVE.
AND THERE ARE A LOT OF MEMORABLE SEQUELS OUT THERE.
SURE.
THE REASON THEY EXIST IS IN PART DUE TO THE SUCCESS OF THE ORIGINAL.
IF YOUR WORLD IS ENGAGING, IT MAKES SENSE TO BUILD OFF THAT.
CRUMPLE
CRUMPLE
LIKE THE TERMINATOR. OR ALIEN.
YEAH! OR HOW ABOUT INDIANA JONES? DIE HARD?

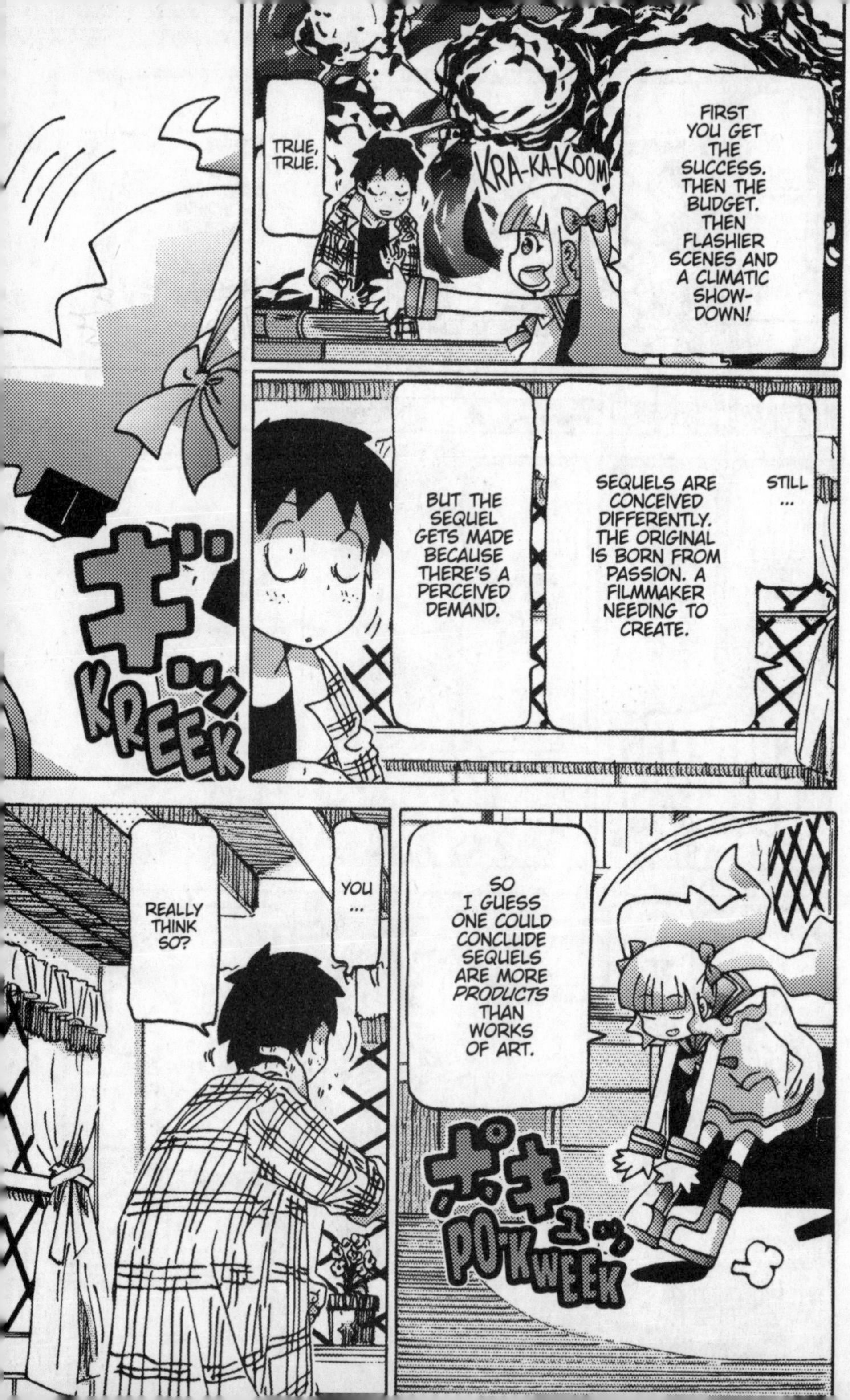
FIRST YOU GET THE SUCCESS. THEN THE BUDGET. THEN FLASHIER SCENES AND A CLIMATIC SHOW-DOWN!
KRA-KA-KOOM
TRUE, TRUE.
STILL ...
SEQUELS ARE CONCEIVED DIFFERENTLY. THE ORIGINAL IS BORN FROM PASSION. A FILMMAKER NEEDING TO CREATE.
BUT THE SEQUEL GETS MADE BECAUSE THERE'S A PERCEIVED DEMAND.
KREEK
SO I GUESS ONE COULD CONCLUDE SEQUELS ARE MORE *PRODUCTS* THAN WORKS OF ART.
POKWEEK
YOU ...
REALLY THINK SO?

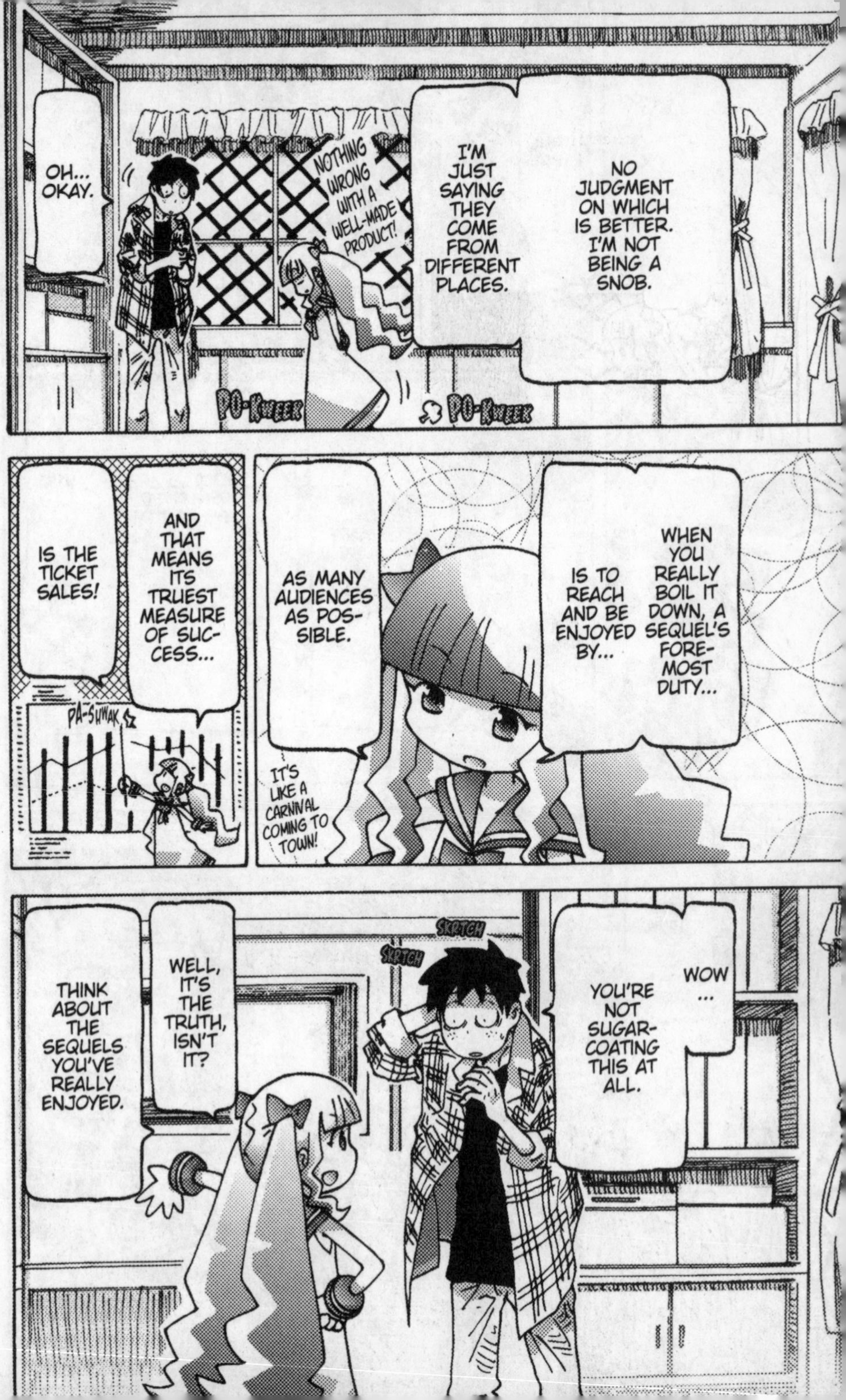

NO JUDGMENT ON WHICH IS BETTER. I'M NOT BEING A SNOB.
I'M JUST SAYING THEY COME FROM DIFFERENT PLACES.
NOTHING WRONG WITH A WELL-MADE PRODUCT!
PO-KWEEK
PO-KWEEK
OH... OKAY.
WHEN YOU REALLY BOIL IT DOWN, A SEQUEL'S FORE-MOST DUTY...
IS TO REACH AND BE ENJOYED BY...
AS MANY AUDIENCES AS POS-SIBLE.
IT'S LIKE A CARNIVAL COMING TO TOWN!
AND THAT MEANS ITS TRUEST MEASURE OF SUC-CESS...
IS THE TICKET SALES!
PA-SHWAK
WOW...
YOU'RE NOT SUGAR-COATING THIS AT ALL.
SKRTCH
SKRTCH
WELL, IT'S THE TRUTH, ISN'T IT?
THINK ABOUT THE SEQUELS YOU'VE REALLY ENJOYED.

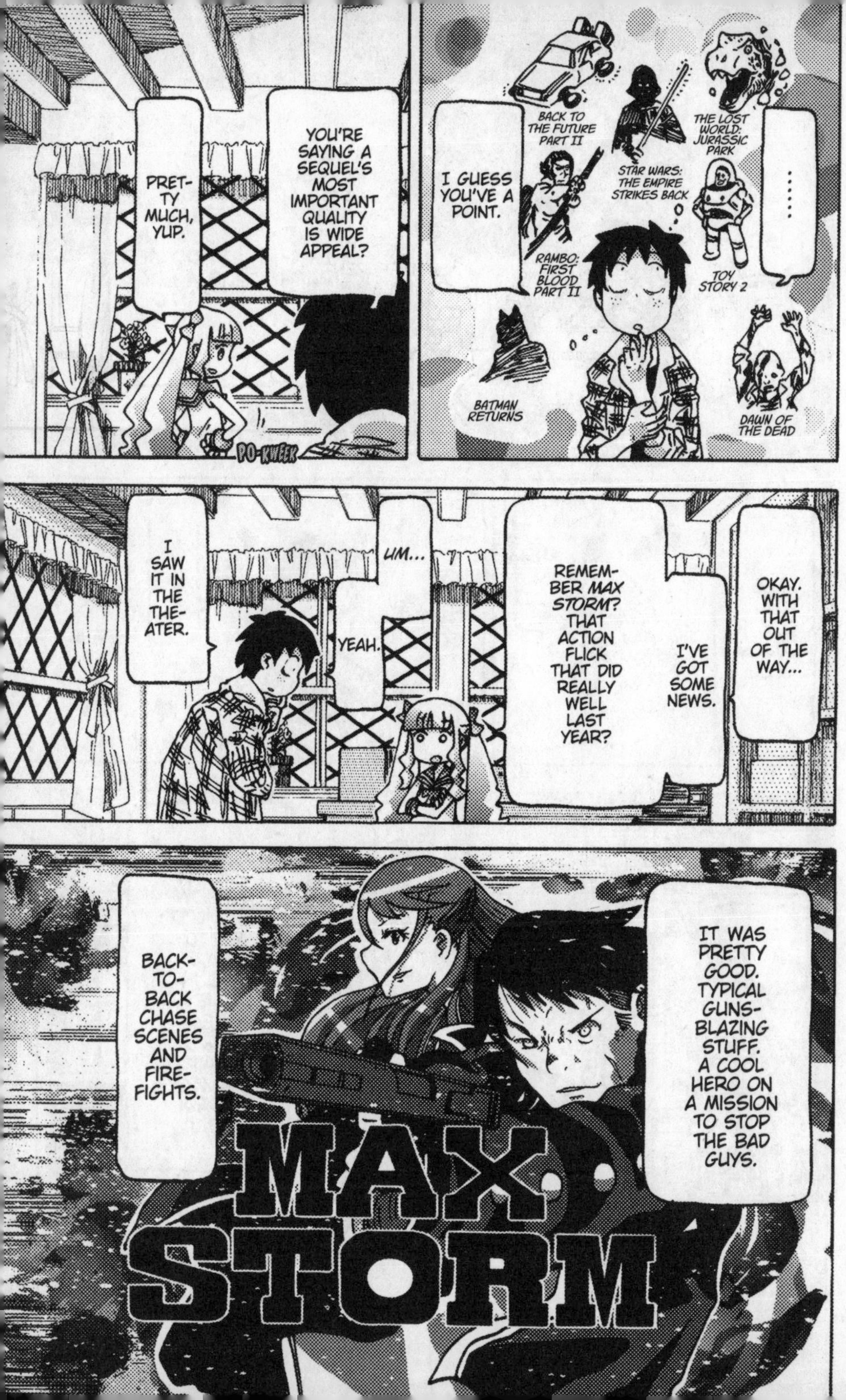

......
THE LOST WORLD: JURASSIC PARK
BACK TO THE FUTURE PART II
STAR WARS: THE EMPIRE STRIKES BACK
I GUESS YOU'VE A POINT.
TOY STORY 2
RAMBO: FIRST BLOOD PART II
DAWN OF THE DEAD
BATMAN RETURNS
YOU'RE SAYING A SEQUEL'S MOST IMPORTANT QUALITY IS WIDE APPEAL?
PRET-TY MUCH, YUP.
PO-KWEEK
OKAY. WITH THAT OUT OF THE WAY...
I'VE GOT SOME NEWS.
REMEM-BER *MAX STORM*? THAT ACTION FLICK THAT DID REALLY WELL LAST YEAR?
UM...
YEAH.
I SAW IT IN THE THE-ATER.
IT WAS PRETTY GOOD. TYPICAL GUNS-BLAZING STUFF. A COOL HERO ON A MISSION TO STOP THE BAD GUYS.
BACK-TO-BACK CHASE SCENES AND FIRE-FIGHTS.
MAX STORM

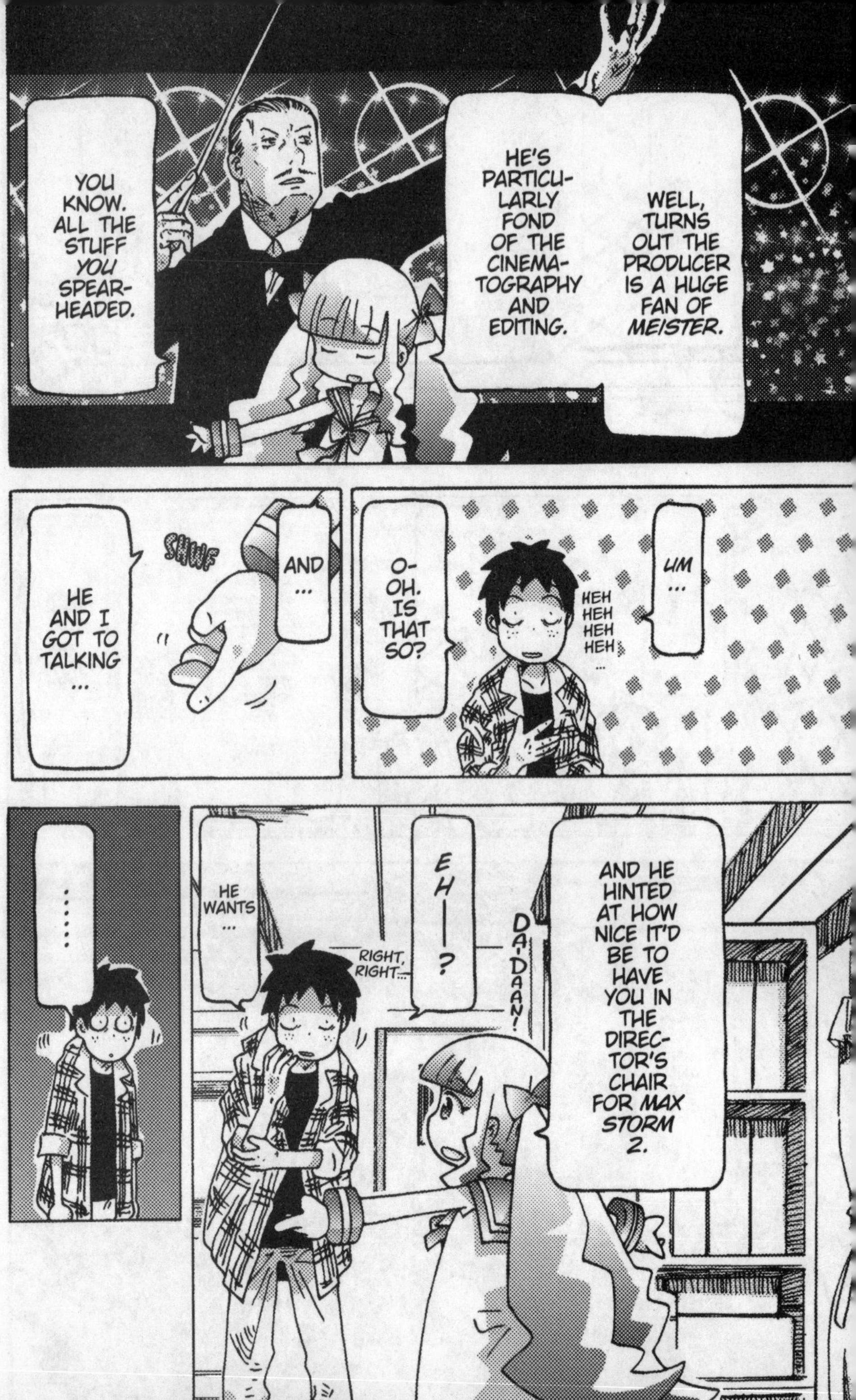
WELL, TURNS OUT THE PRODUCER IS A HUGE FAN OF *MEISTER*.
HE'S PARTICU-LARLY FOND OF THE CINEMA-TOGRAPHY AND EDITING.
YOU KNOW. ALL THE STUFF *YOU* SPEAR-HEADED.
UM ...
HEH HEH HEH HEH ...
O-OH. IS THAT SO?
AND ...
SHUF
HE AND I GOT TO TALKING ...
AND HE HINTED AT HOW NICE IT'D BE TO HAVE YOU IN THE DIREC-TOR'S CHAIR FOR *MAX STORM 2*.
DA-DAAN!
EH—?
RIGHT, RIGHT...
HE WANTS ...
......

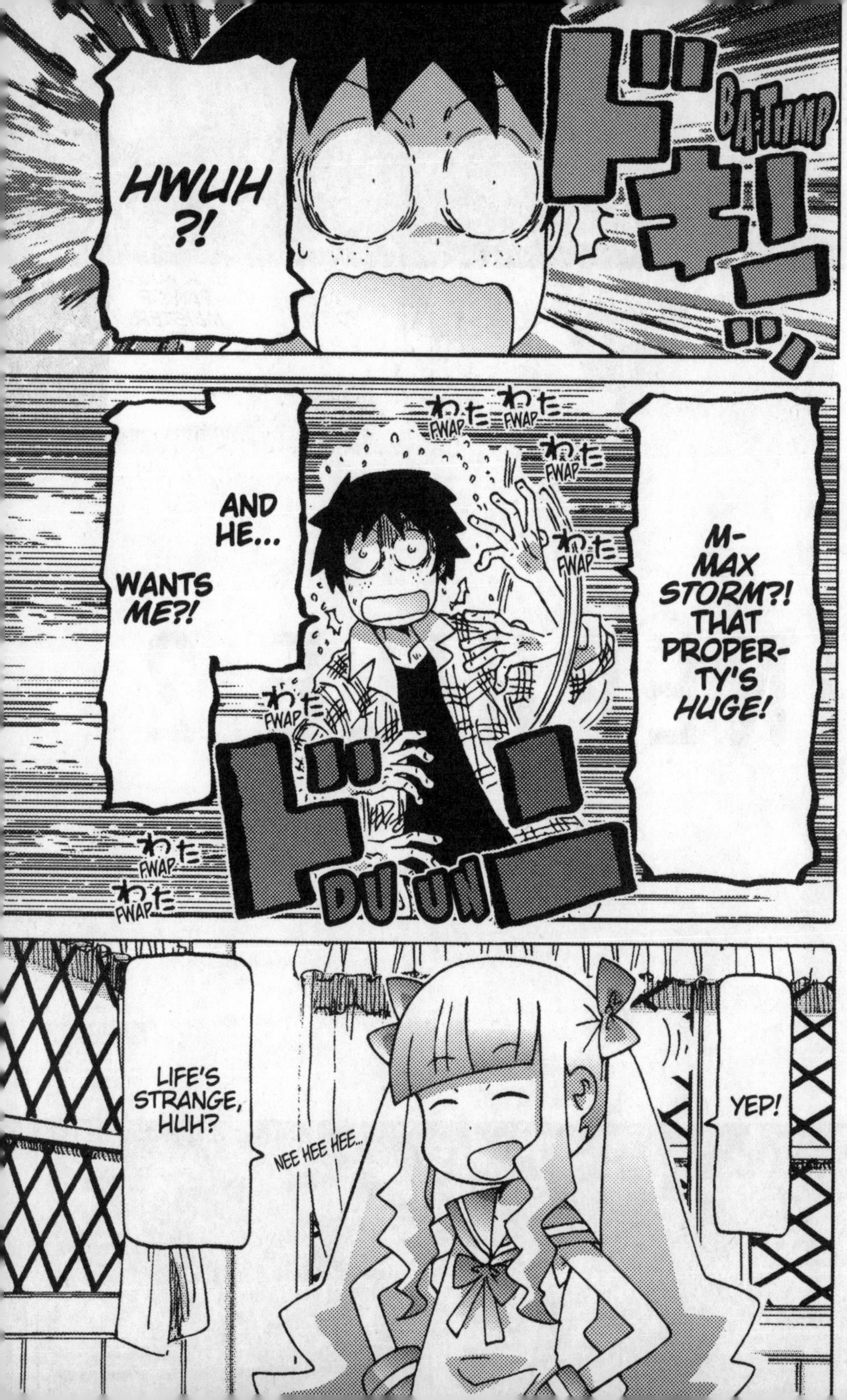
BA-THUMP
HWUH ?!
M-MAX STORM?! THAT PROPER-TY'S HUGE!
FWAP
FWAP
FWAP
FWAP
FWAP
DU UN
FWAP
FWAP
AND HE... WANTS ME?!
YEP!
NEE HEE HEE...
LIFE'S STRANGE, HUH?

CINÉPHILE 2

MANGA
SHOGO SUGITANI
PTCP02

POMPO: THE

Production GoodBook   PETERSEN FILMS

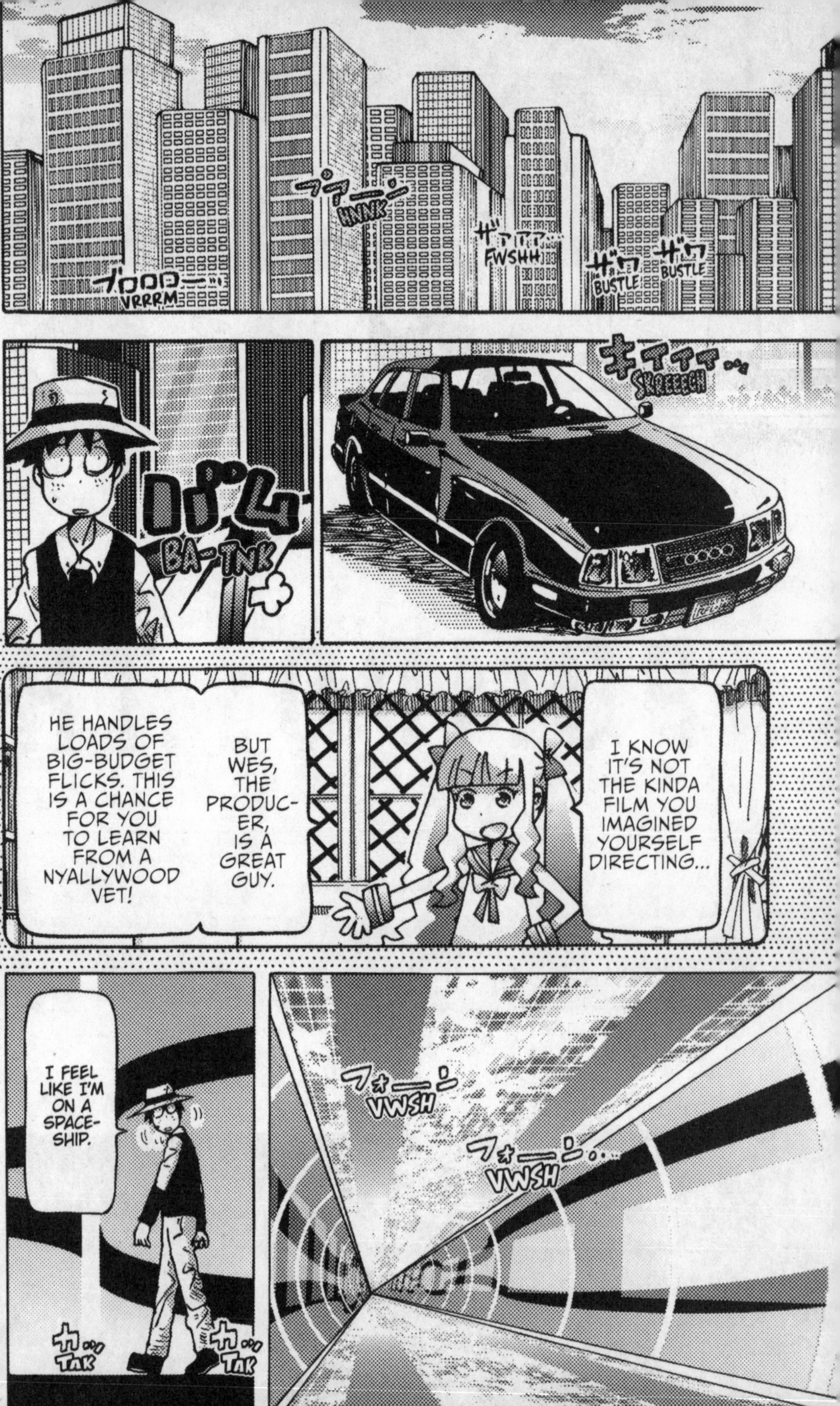
BUSTLE
BUSTLE
FWSHH
HNNK
VRRRM
SKREEECH
BA-TNK
I KNOW IT'S NOT THE KINDA FILM YOU IMAGINED YOURSELF DIRECTING...
BUT WES, THE PRODUCER, IS A GREAT GUY.
HE HANDLES LOADS OF BIG-BUDGET FLICKS. THIS IS A CHANCE FOR YOU TO LEARN FROM A NYALLYWOOD VET!
VWSH
VWSH
I FEEL LIKE I'M ON A SPACESHIP.
TAK
TAK

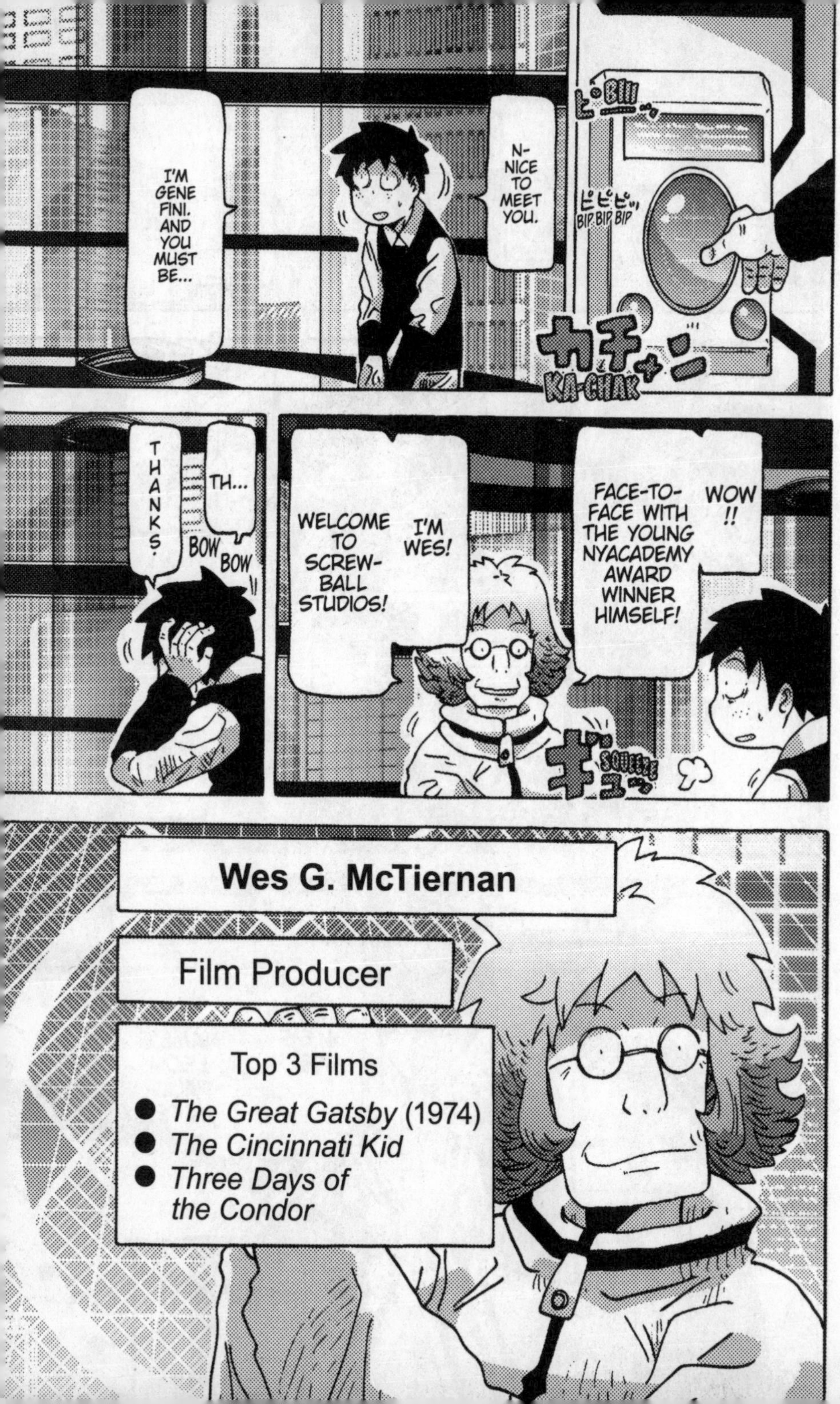

BIII
BIP BIP BIP
KA-CHAK
N-NICE TO MEET YOU.
I'M GENE FINI. AND YOU MUST BE...
WOW !!
FACE-TO-FACE WITH THE YOUNG NYACADEMY AWARD WINNER HIMSELF!
I'M WES!
WELCOME TO SCREW-BALL STUDIOS!
SQUEEZE
TH...
BOW BOW
THANKS.
Wes G. McTiernan
Film Producer
Top 3 Films
● The Great Gatsby (1974)
● The Cincinnati Kid
● Three Days of the Condor

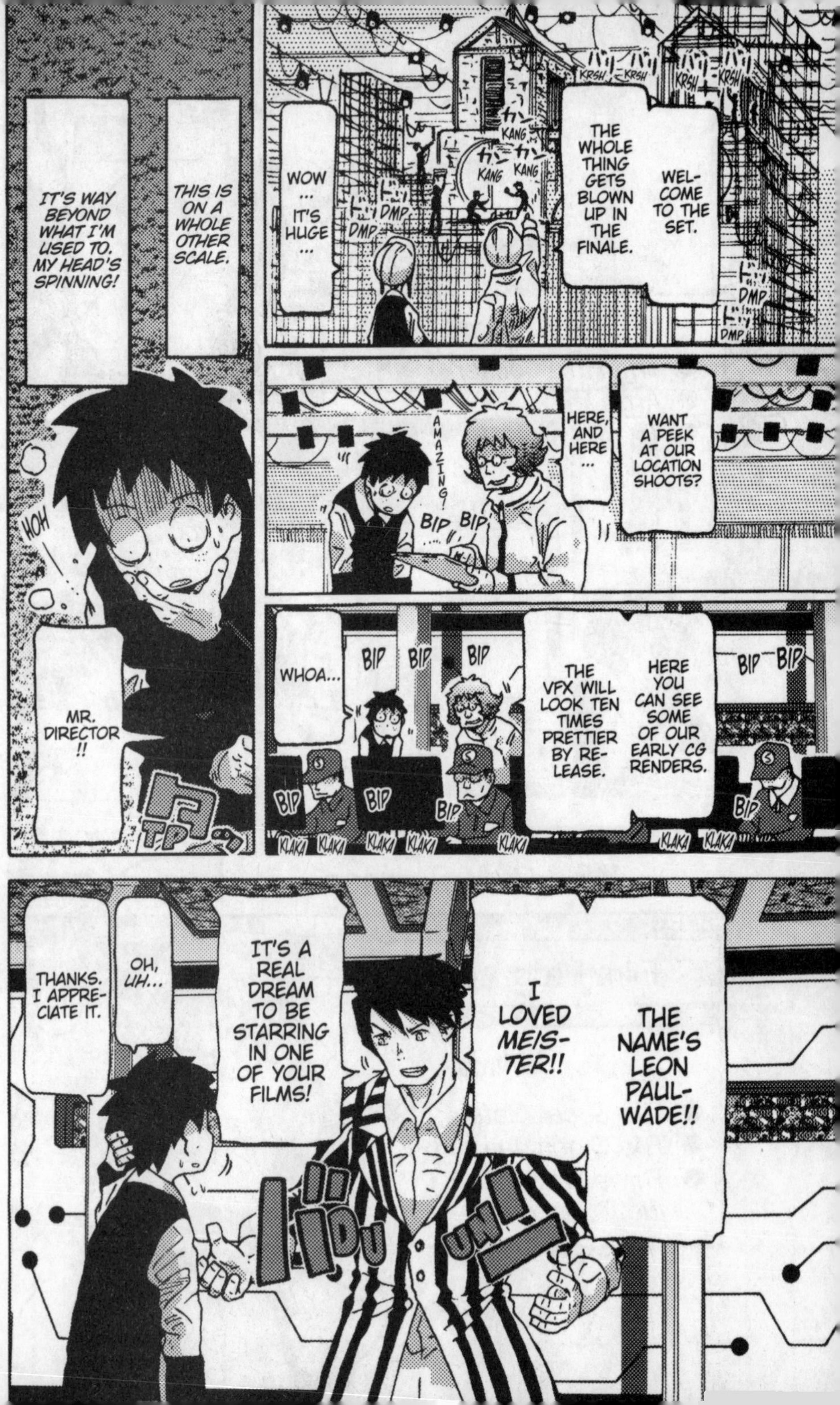
KRSH KRSH
KRSH KRSH
WEL-COME TO THE SET.
THE WHOLE THING GETS BLOWN UP IN THE FINALE.
KANG
KANG KANG
DMP
DMP
WOW ... IT'S HUGE ...
DMP
DMP
WANT A PEEK AT OUR LOCATION SHOOTS?
HERE, AND HERE ...
AMAZING!
BIP BIP
BIP BIP
HERE YOU CAN SEE SOME OF OUR EARLY CG RENDERS.
THE VFX WILL LOOK TEN TIMES PRETTIER BY RE-LEASE.
BIP BIP BIP
WHOA...
BIP BIP BIP BIP
KLAKA KLAKA KLAKA KLAKA KLAKA KLAKA KLAKA
THIS IS ON A WHOLE OTHER SCALE.
IT'S WAY BEYOND WHAT I'M USED TO. MY HEAD'S SPINNING!
HOH
MR. DIRECTOR !!
TP
THE NAME'S LEON PAUL-WADE!!
I LOVED MEIS-TER!!
IT'S A REAL DREAM TO BE STARRING IN ONE OF YOUR FILMS!
OH, UH...
THANKS. I APPRECIATE IT.

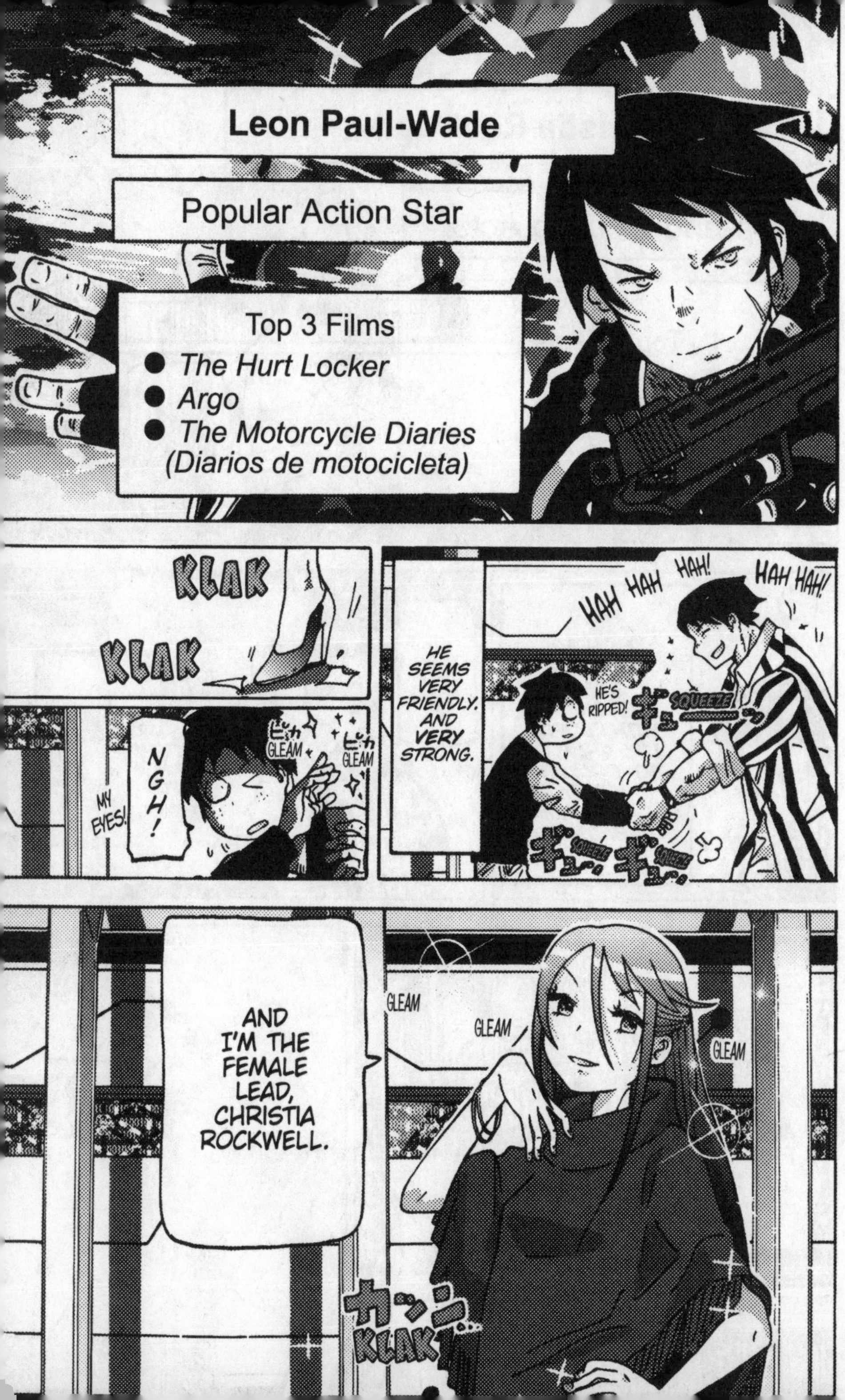
Leon Paul-Wade
Popular Action Star
Top 3 Films
● The Hurt Locker
● Argo
● The Motorcycle Diaries (Diarios de motocicleta)
HAH HAH HAH! HAH HAH!
HE SEEMS VERY FRIENDLY. AND VERY STRONG.
HE'S RIPPED!
SQUEEZE
SQUEEZE
SQUEEZE
KLAK
KLAK
GLEAM
GLEAM
NGH!
MY EYES!
AND I'M THE FEMALE LEAD, CHRISTIA ROCKWELL.
GLEAM
GLEAM
GLEAM
KLAK

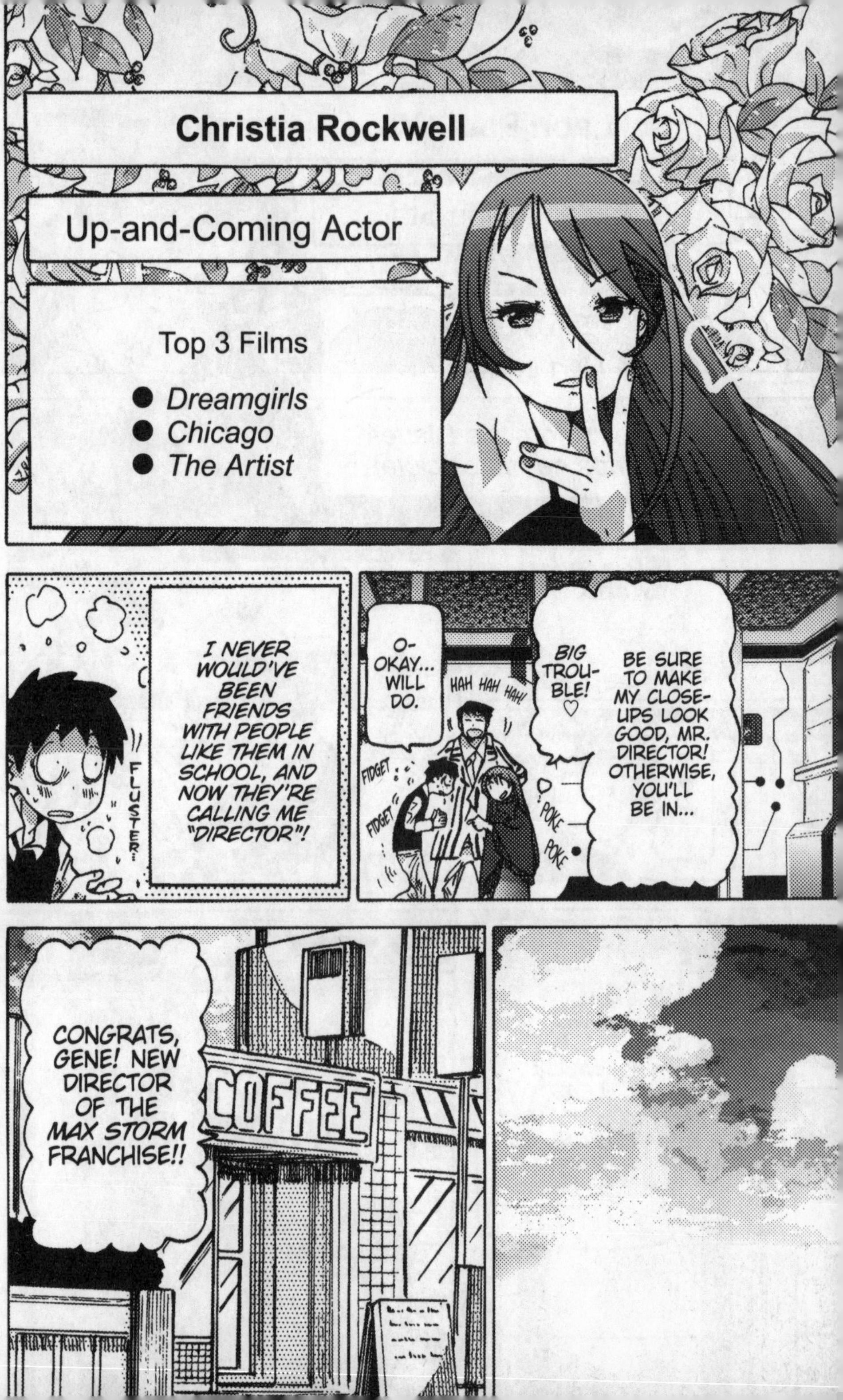

Christia Rockwell
Up-and-Coming Actor
Top 3 Films
● *Dreamgirls*
● *Chicago*
● *The Artist*
BE SURE TO MAKE MY CLOSE-UPS LOOK GOOD, MR. DIRECTOR! OTHERWISE, YOU'LL BE IN...
BIG TROUBLE! ♡
O-OKAY... WILL DO.
HAH HAH HAH!
FIDGET
FIDGET
POKE
POKE
I NEVER WOULD'VE BEEN FRIENDS WITH PEOPLE LIKE THEM IN SCHOOL, AND NOW THEY'RE CALLING ME "DIRECTOR"!
FLUSTER
CONGRATS, GENE! NEW DIRECTOR OF THE *MAX STORM* FRANCHISE!!
COFFEE

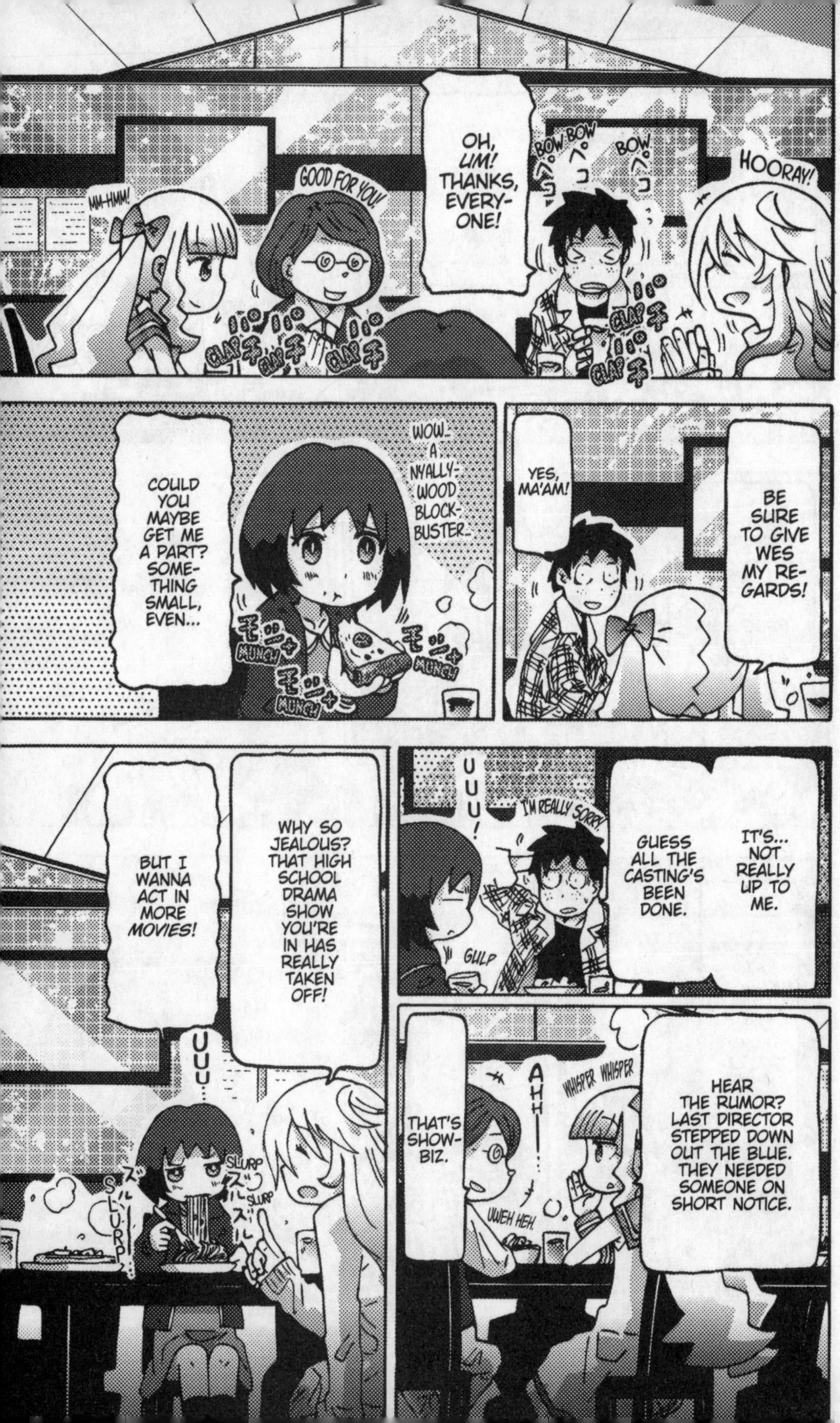
HOORAY!
BOW BOW
BOW
OH, UM! THANKS, EVERYONE!
GOOD FOR YOU!
MM-HMM!
CLAP CLAP CLAP CLAP CLAP
BE SURE TO GIVE WES MY REGARDS!
YES, MA'AM!
WOW... A NYALLY-WOOD BLOCKBUSTER...
COULD YOU MAYBE GET ME A PART? SOMETHING SMALL, EVEN...
MUNCH MUNCH MUNCH
IT'S... NOT REALLY UP TO ME.
GUESS ALL THE CASTING'S BEEN DONE.
I'M REALLY SORRY.
UUU!
GULP
HEAR THE RUMOR? LAST DIRECTOR STEPPED DOWN OUT THE BLUE. THEY NEEDED SOMEONE ON SHORT NOTICE.
WHISPER WHISPER
AHH...
THAT'S SHOW-BIZ.
UWEH HEH.
WHY SO JEALOUS? THAT HIGH SCHOOL DRAMA SHOW YOU'RE IN HAS REALLY TAKEN OFF!
BUT I WANNA ACT IN MORE MOVIES!
UUU...
SLURP SLURP SLURP

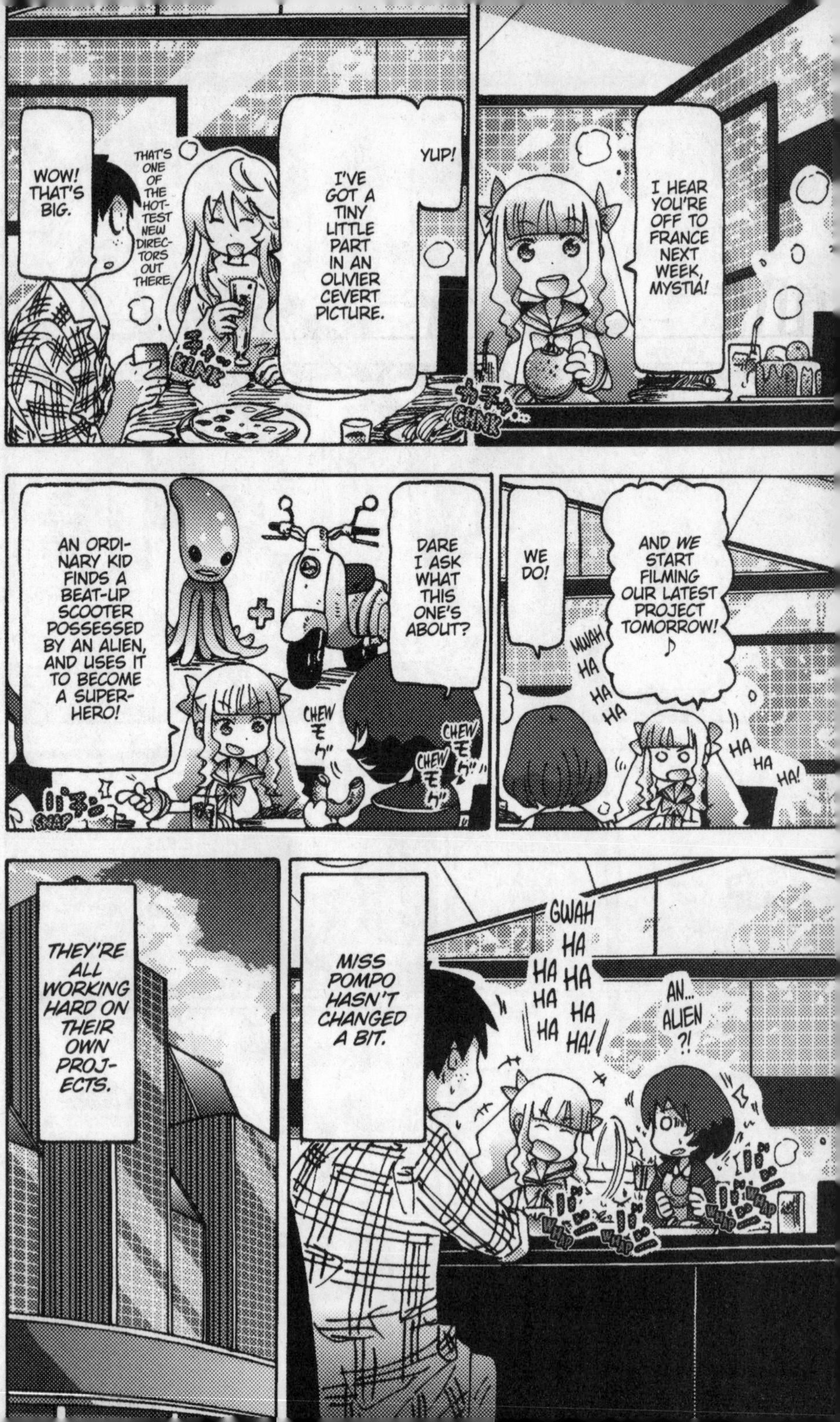
I HEAR YOU'RE OFF TO FRANCE NEXT WEEK, MYSTIA!
CHNK
YUP!
I'VE GOT A TINY LITTLE PART IN AN OLIVIER CEVERT PICTURE.
THAT'S ONE OF THE HOT-TEST NEW DIREC-TORS OUT THERE.
KLINK
WOW! THAT'S BIG.
AND WE START FILMING OUR LATEST PROJECT TOMORROW! ♪
WE DO!
MWAH HA HA HA
HA HA HA!
DARE I ASK WHAT THIS ONE'S ABOUT?
CHEW
CHEW
CHEW
AN ORDI-NARY KID FINDS A BEAT-UP SCOOTER POSSESSED BY AN ALIEN, AND USES IT TO BECOME A SUPER-HERO!
SNAP
MISS POMPO HASN'T CHANGED A BIT.
GWAH HA HA HA HA HA HA HA HA!
AN... ALIEN ?!
WHAP
WHAP
WHAP
WHAP
THEY'RE ALL WORKING HARD ON THEIR OWN PROJ-ECTS.

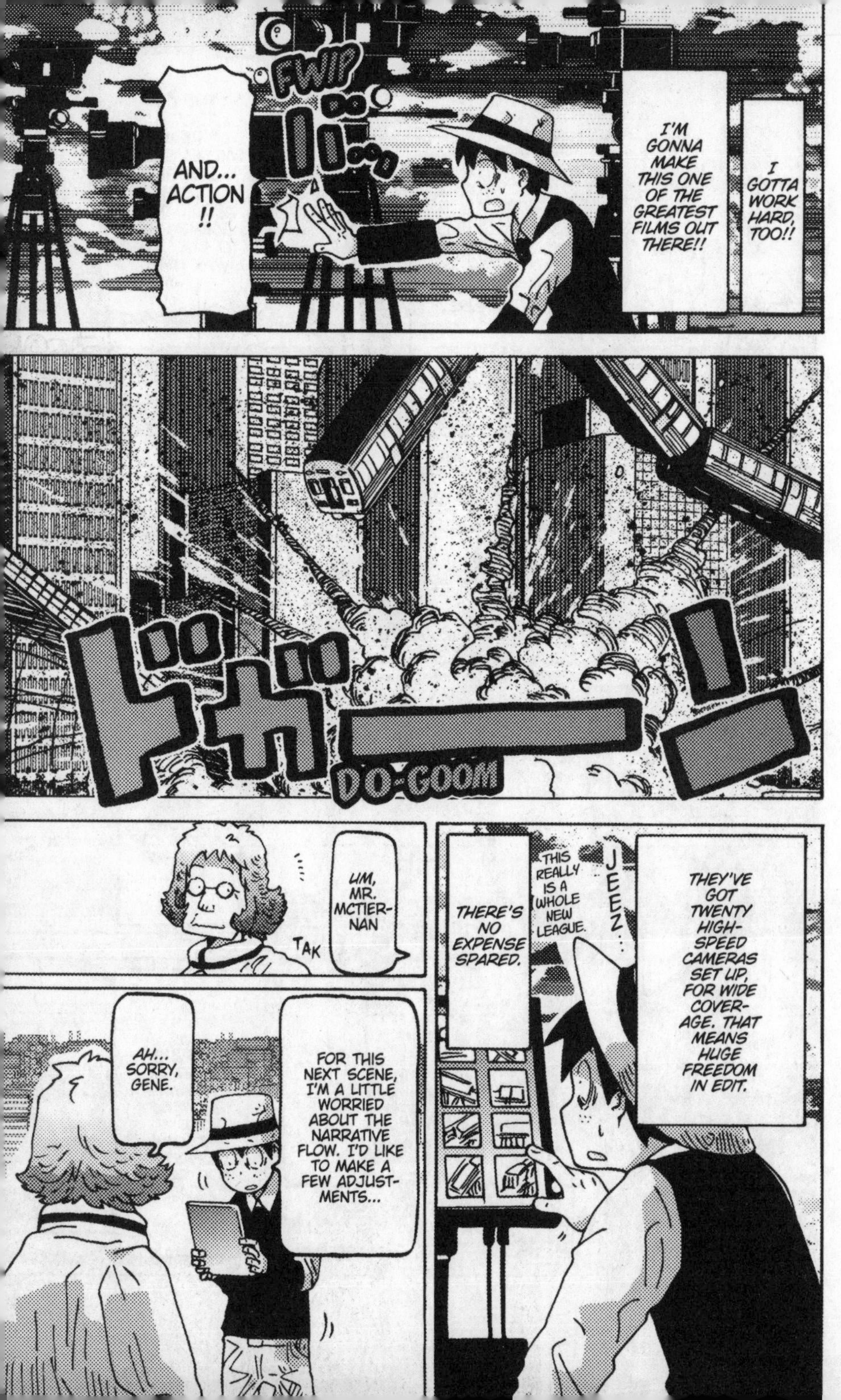

I GOTTA WORK HARD, TOO!!
I'M GONNA MAKE THIS ONE OF THE GREATEST FILMS OUT THERE!!
FWIP
DO
AND... ACTION!!
DO-GOOM
THEY'VE GOT TWENTY HIGH-SPEED CAMERAS SET UP, FOR WIDE COVERAGE. THAT MEANS HUGE FREEDOM IN EDIT.
JEEZ...
THIS REALLY IS A WHOLE NEW LEAGUE.
THERE'S NO EXPENSE SPARED.
UM, MR. MCTIERNAN
TAK
FOR THIS NEXT SCENE, I'M A LITTLE WORRIED ABOUT THE NARRATIVE FLOW. I'D LIKE TO MAKE A FEW ADJUSTMENTS...
AH... SORRY, GENE.

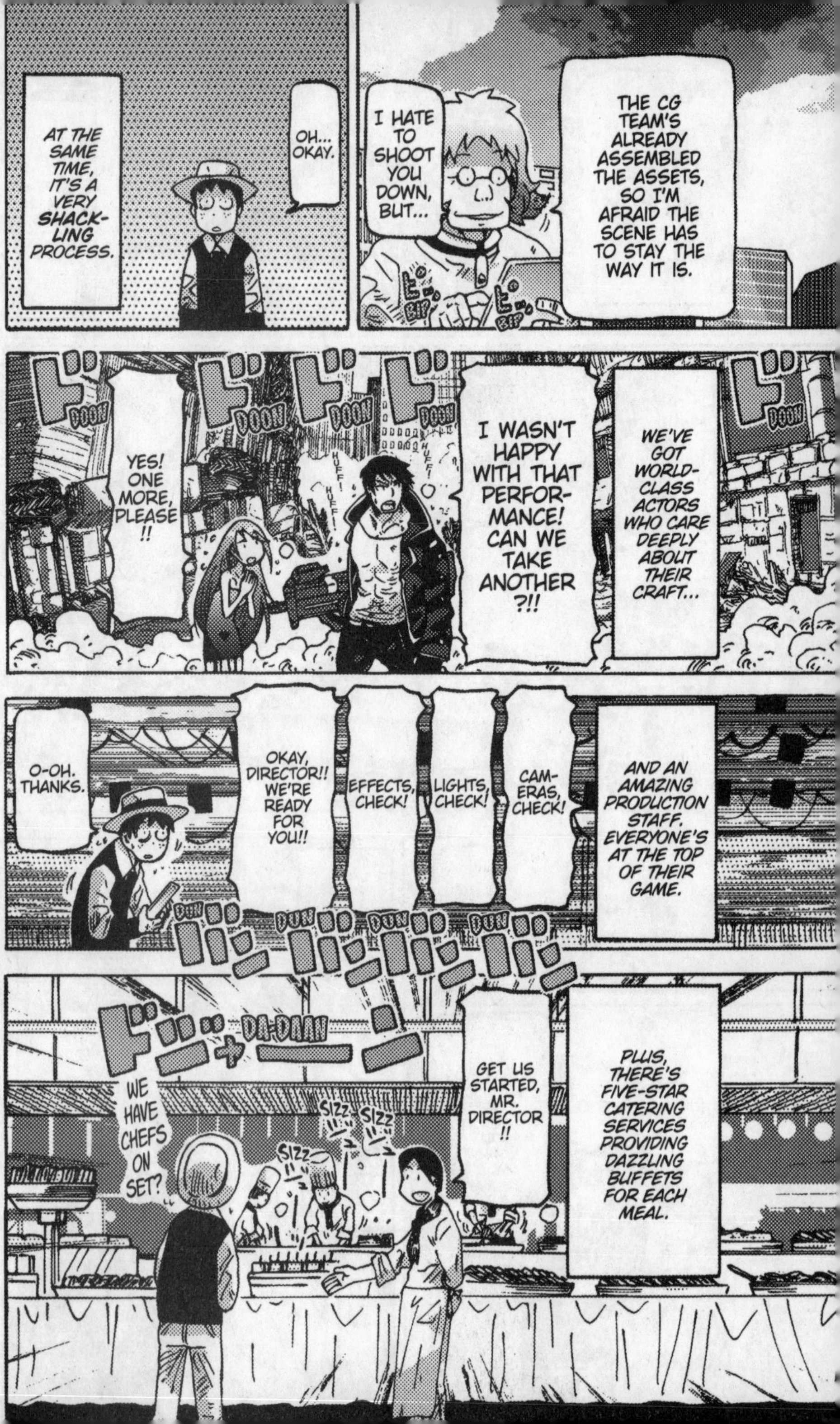
THE CG TEAM'S ALREADY ASSEMBLED THE ASSETS, SO I'M AFRAID THE SCENE HAS TO STAY THE WAY IT IS.
I HATE TO SHOOT YOU DOWN, BUT...
BIP
BIP
OH... OKAY.
AT THE SAME TIME, IT'S A VERY SHACKLING PROCESS.
DOON
WE'VE GOT WORLD-CLASS ACTORS WHO CARE DEEPLY ABOUT THEIR CRAFT...
I WASN'T HAPPY WITH THAT PERFORMANCE! CAN WE TAKE ANOTHER?!!
DOON
HUFF!
HUFF!
DOON
DOON
YES! ONE MORE, PLEASE!!
AND AN AMAZING PRODUCTION STAFF. EVERYONE'S AT THE TOP OF THEIR GAME.
CAMERAS, CHECK!
LIGHTS, CHECK!
EFFECTS, CHECK!
OKAY, DIRECTOR!! WE'RE READY FOR YOU!!
O-OH. THANKS.
DUN
DUN
DUN
DUN
PLUS, THERE'S FIVE-STAR CATERING SERVICES PROVIDING DAZZLING BUFFETS FOR EACH MEAL.
GET US STARTED, MR. DIRECTOR!!
DA-DAAN
SIZZ
SIZZ
SIZZ
WE HAVE CHEFS ON SET?

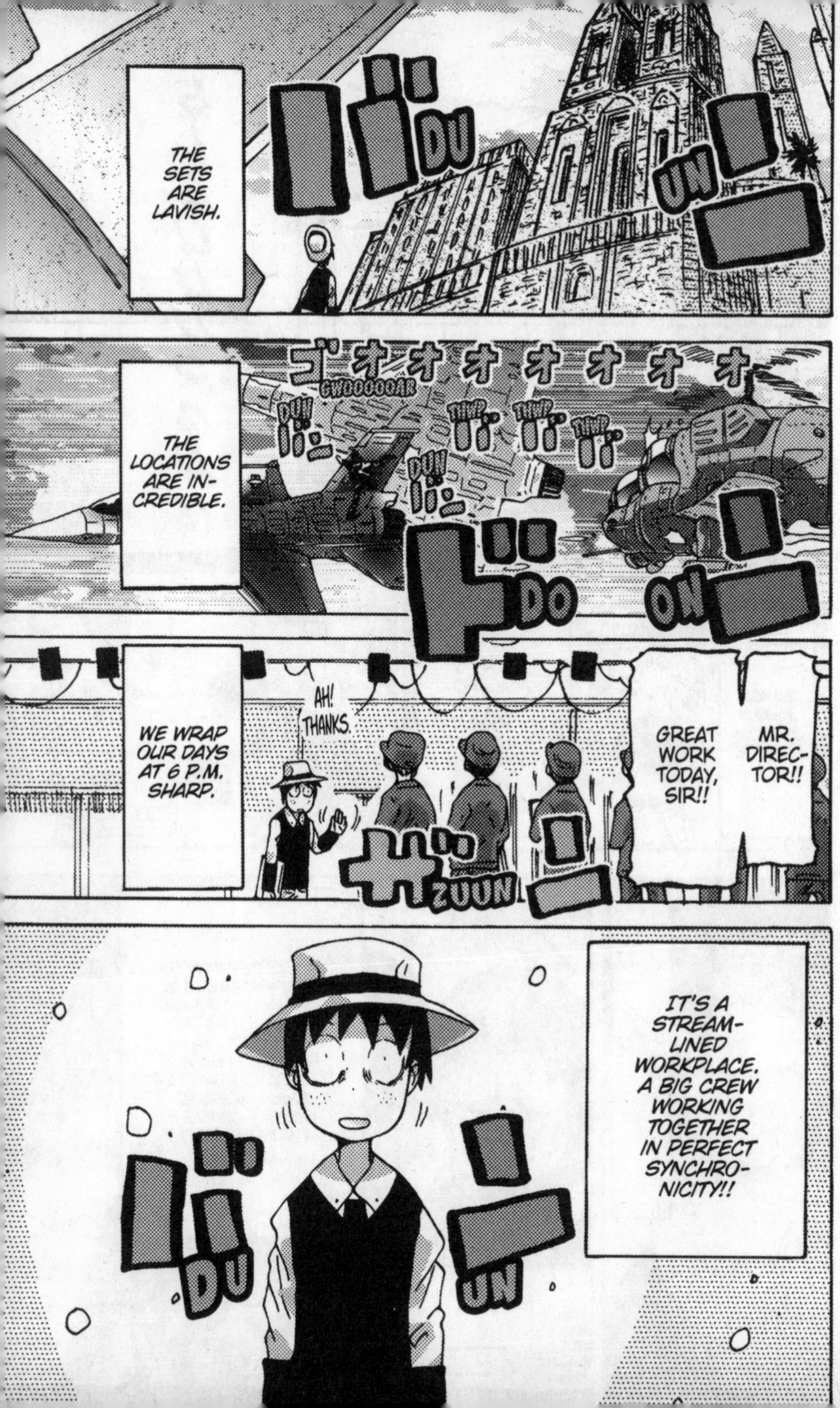
DU UN
THE SETS ARE LAVISH.
GWOOOOOAR
THUMP
THUMP
THUMP
DUN
DUN
DO ON
THE LOCATIONS ARE INCREDIBLE.
MR. DIRECTOR!!
GREAT WORK TODAY, SIR!!
ZUUN
AH! THANKS.
WE WRAP OUR DAYS AT 6 P.M. SHARP.
IT'S A STREAM-LINED WORKPLACE. A BIG CREW WORKING TOGETHER IN PERFECT SYNCHRO-NICITY!!
DU UN

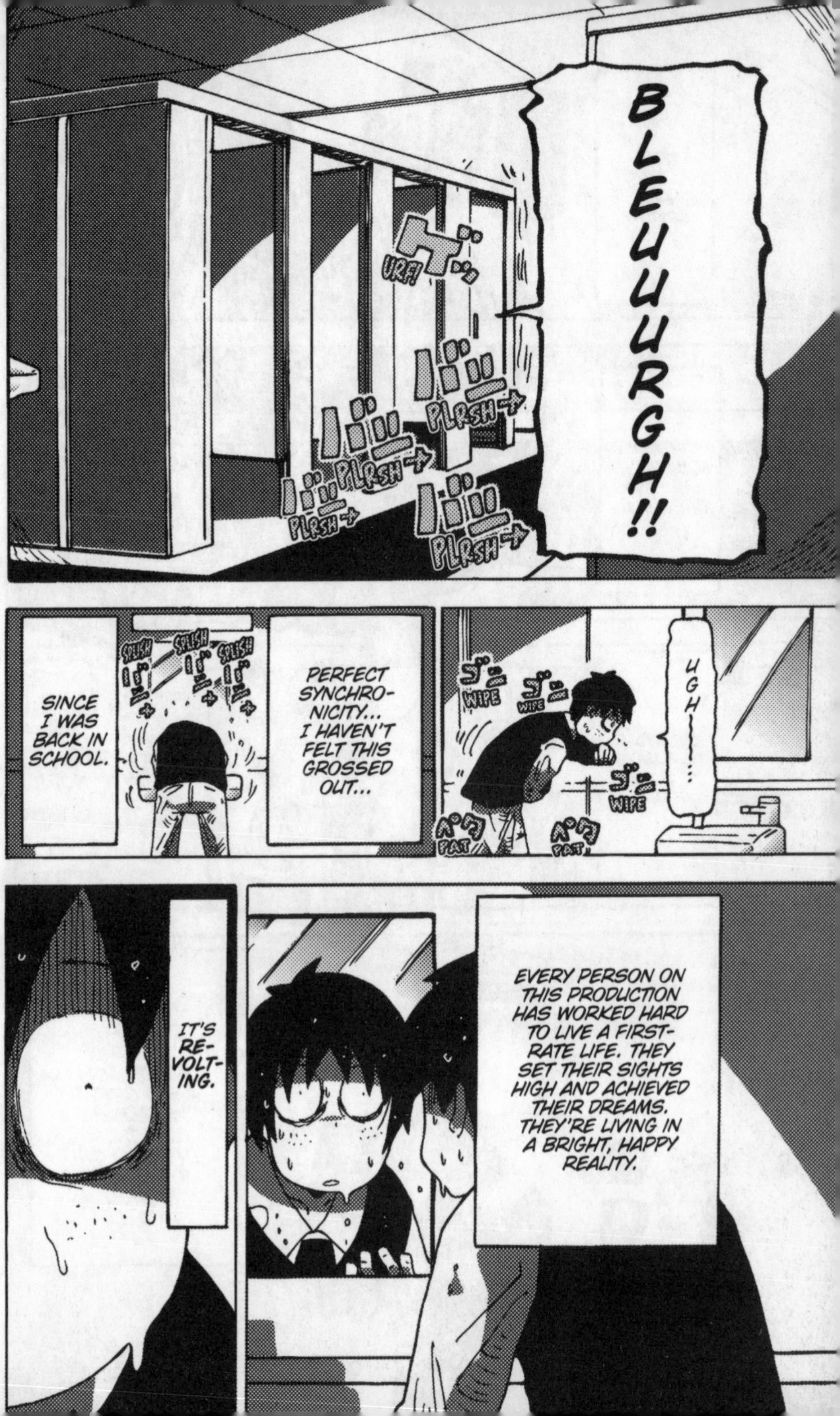
BLEUUURGH!!
URP!
PLRSH
PLRSH
PLRSH
PLRSH
UGH.....
WIPE
WIPE
WIPE
PAT
PAT
PERFECT SYNCHRONICITY... I HAVEN'T FELT THIS GROSSED OUT...
SPLISH
SPLISH
SPLISH
SINCE I WAS BACK IN SCHOOL.
EVERY PERSON ON THIS PRODUCTION HAS WORKED HARD TO LIVE A FIRST-RATE LIFE. THEY SET THEIR SIGHTS HIGH AND ACHIEVED THEIR DREAMS. THEY'RE LIVING IN A BRIGHT, HAPPY REALITY.
IT'S REVOLTING.

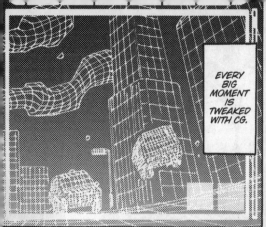

SKRIK
SKRIK
THE CAMERAS ARE ALL HOOKED UP TO COMPUTERS.
UIIN...
EVERY BIG MOMENT IS TWEAKED WITH CG.
THE ACTORS STAND ON GREEN SCREENS, REACTING TO INVISIBLE PROMPTS.
CAMERAS, CHECK!!
OKAY, DIRECTOR! WE'RE READY FOR YOU!!
LIGHTS, CHECK!!
HOW'S A BASIC THIRD-RATE HACK LIKE ME SUPPOSED TO CONTRIBUTE TO SUCH A PRECISE OPERATION?
BLEUUURRGH!!
URF!
PLRCH
PLRCH
PLRCH
PLRCH
URF!

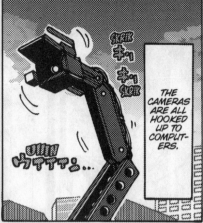

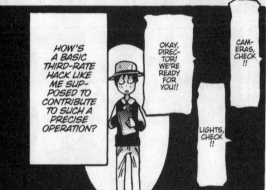

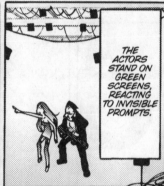

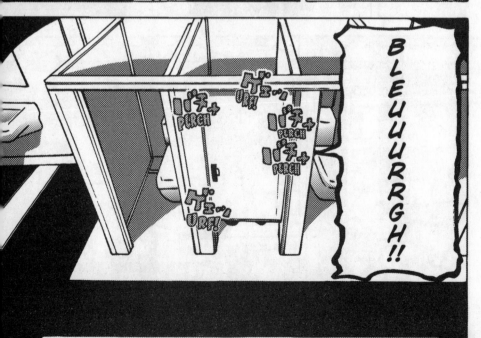

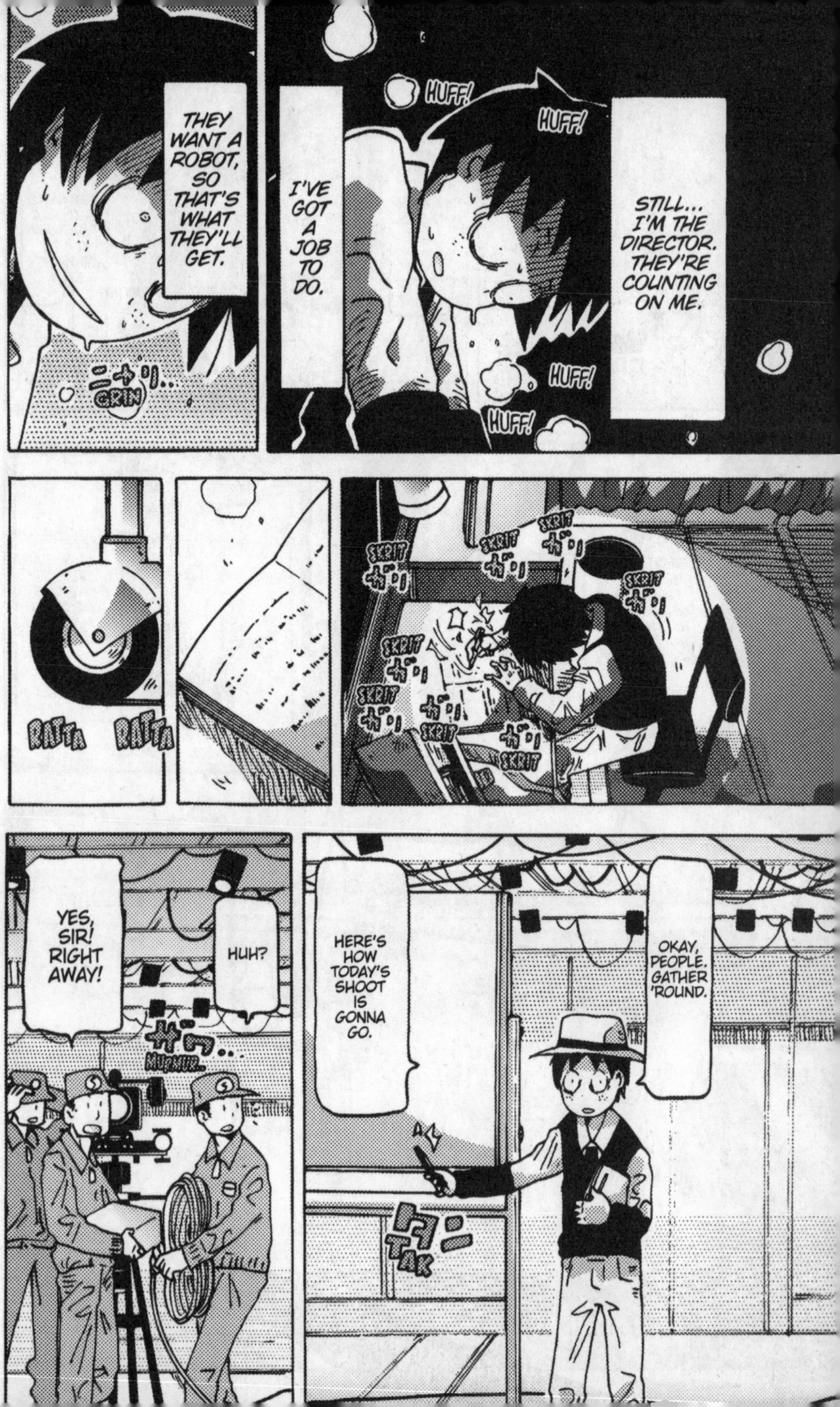
HUFF!
HUFF!
STILL... I'M THE DIRECTOR. THEY'RE COUNTING ON ME.
I'VE GOT A JOB TO DO.
HUFF!
HUFF!
THEY WANT A ROBOT, SO THAT'S WHAT THEY'LL GET.
GRIN
SKRIT
SKRIT
SKRIT
SKRIT
SKRIT
SKRIT
SKRIT
RATTA
RATTA
OKAY, PEOPLE. GATHER 'ROUND.
HERE'S HOW TODAY'S SHOOT IS GONNA GO.
TAK
HUH?
YES, SIR! RIGHT AWAY!

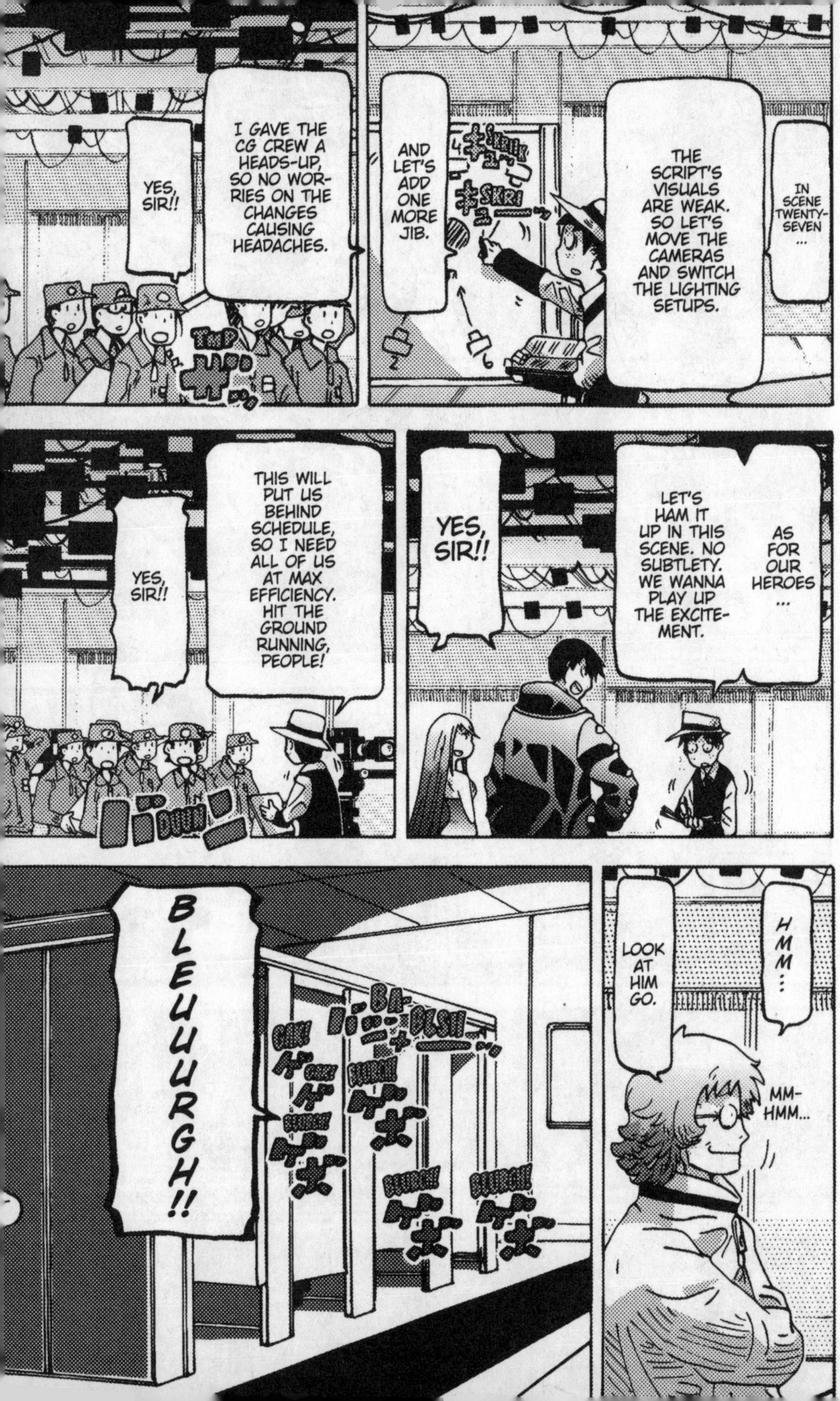
IN SCENE TWENTY-SEVEN ...
THE SCRIPT'S VISUALS ARE WEAK. SO LET'S MOVE THE CAMERAS AND SWITCH THE LIGHTING SETUPS.
AND LET'S ADD ONE MORE JIB.
I GAVE THE CG CREW A HEADS-UP, SO NO WORRIES ON THE CHANGES CAUSING HEADACHES.
YES, SIR!!
AS FOR OUR HEROES ...
LET'S HAM IT UP IN THIS SCENE. NO SUBTLETY. WE WANNA PLAY UP THE EXCITEMENT.
YES, SIR!!
THIS WILL PUT US BEHIND SCHEDULE, SO I NEED ALL OF US AT MAX EFFICIENCY. HIT THE GROUND RUNNING, PEOPLE!
YES, SIR!!
DUUN
HMM...
LOOK AT HIM GO.
MM-HMM...
BLEUUURGH!!

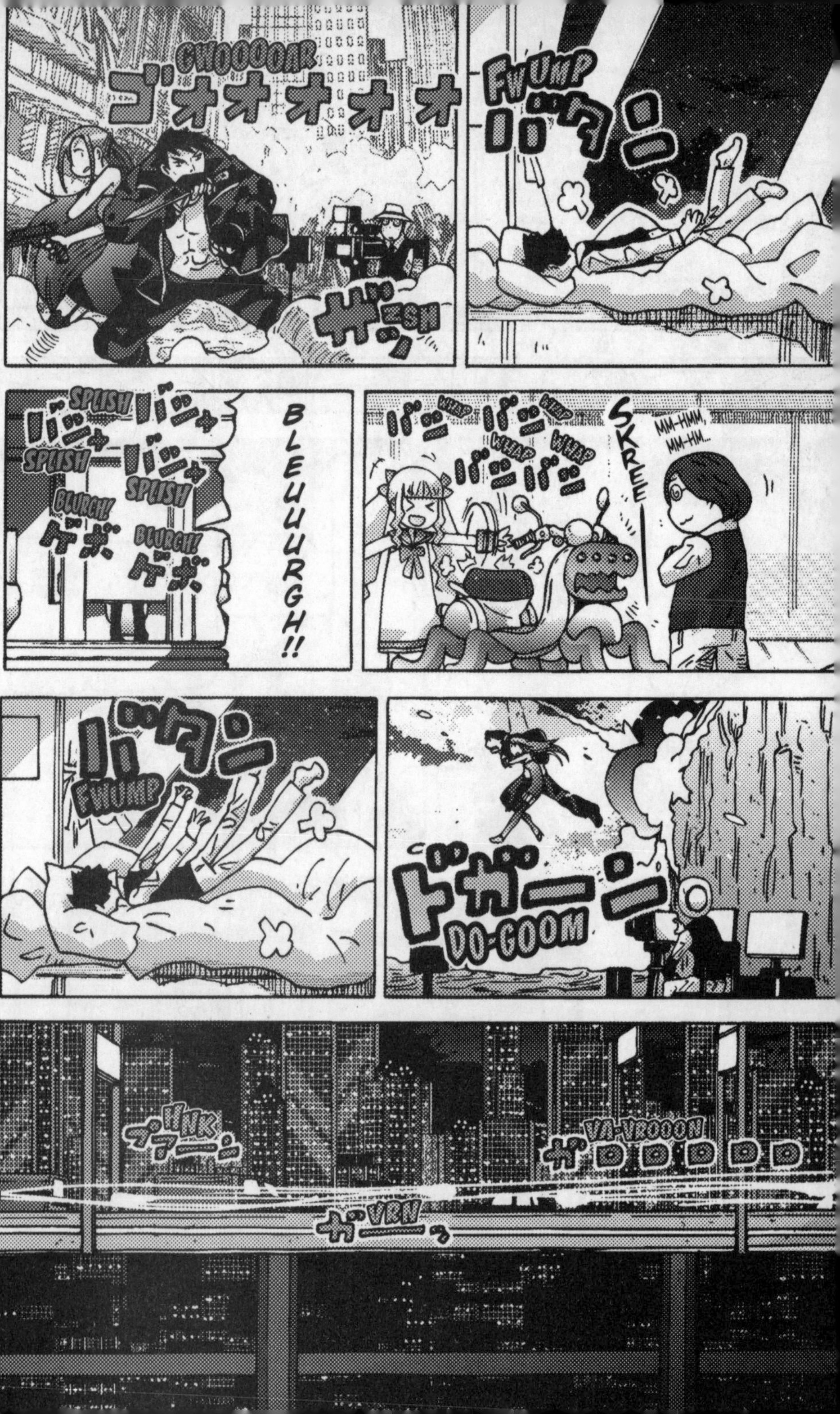
FWUMP
GWOOOOAR
WHAP
WHAP
WHAP
WHAP
SKREE
MM-HMM, MM-HM...
BLEUUUURGH!!
SPLISH
SPLISH
SPLISH
BLURGH!
BLURGH!
DO-GOOM
FWUMP
VA-VROOON
HNK
VRN

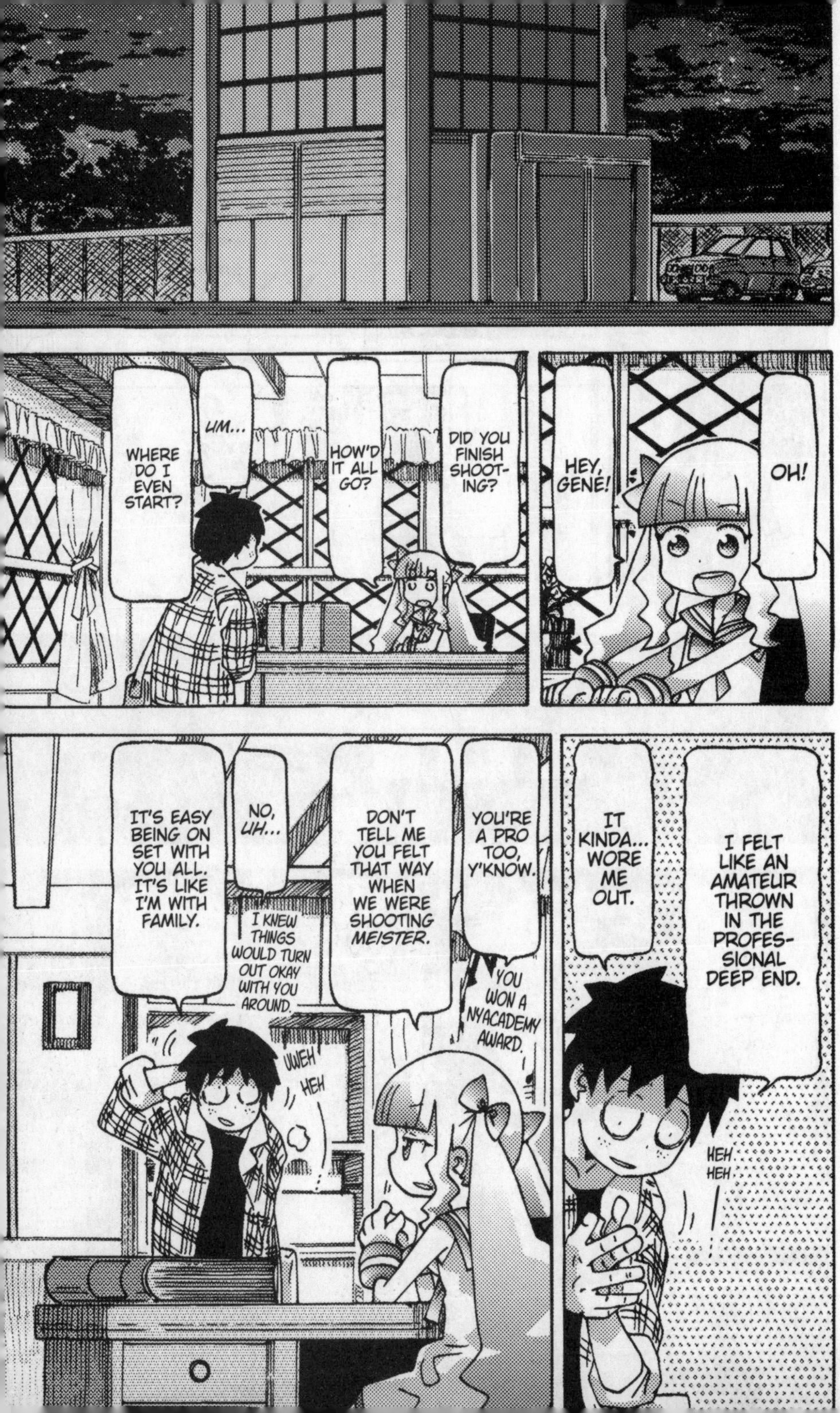
OH!
HEY, GENE!
DID YOU FINISH SHOOT-ING?
HOW'D IT ALL GO?
UM...
WHERE DO I EVEN START?
I FELT LIKE AN AMATEUR THROWN IN THE PROFES-SIONAL DEEP END.
IT KINDA... WORE ME OUT.
HEH HEH
YOU'RE A PRO TOO, Y'KNOW.
YOU WON A NYACADEMY AWARD.
DON'T TELL ME YOU FELT THAT WAY WHEN WE WERE SHOOTING *MEISTER*.
NO, UH...
UWEH HEH
IT'S EASY BEING ON SET WITH YOU ALL. IT'S LIKE I'M WITH FAMILY.
I KNEW THINGS WOULD TURN OUT OKAY WITH YOU AROUND.

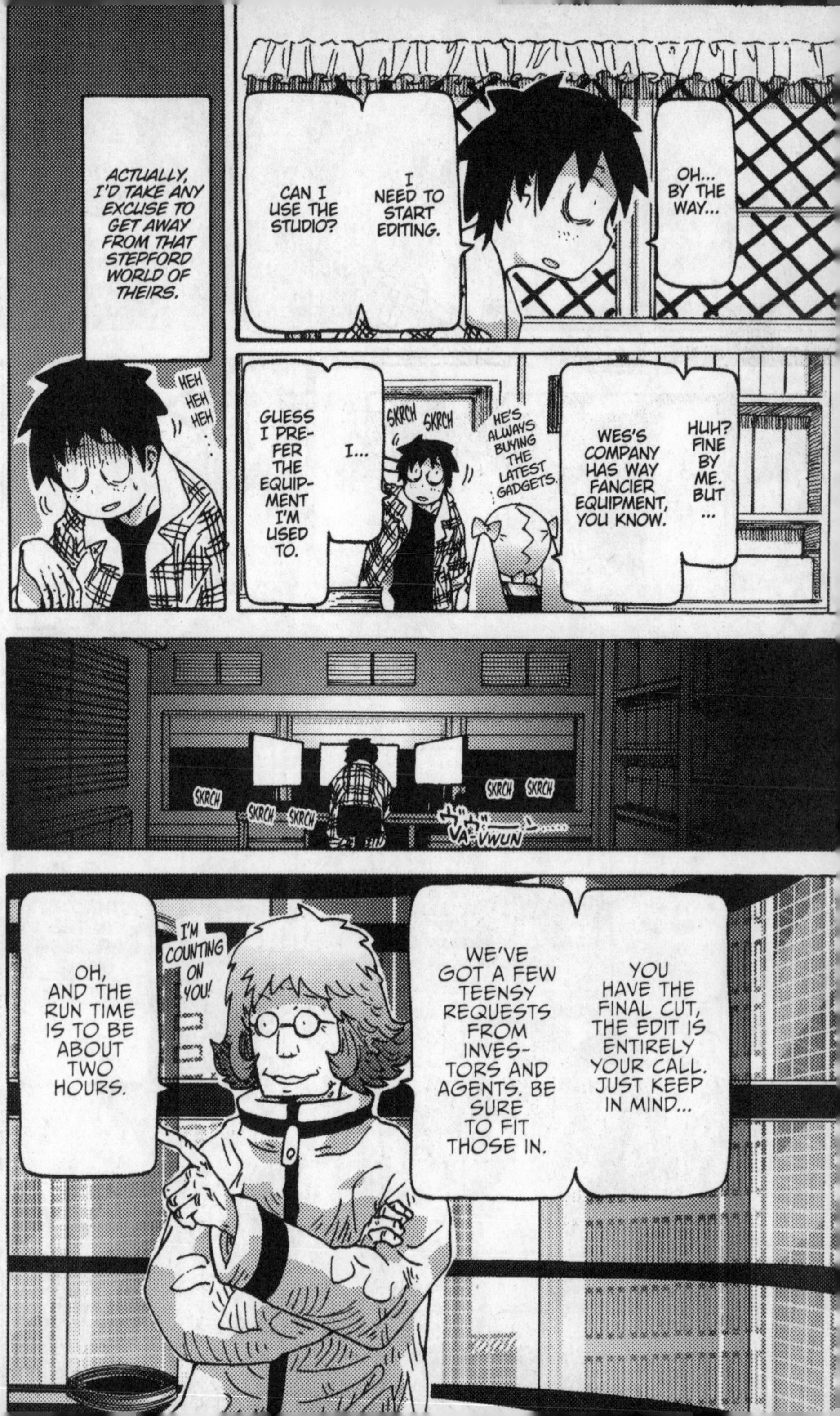

OH... BY THE WAY...
I NEED TO START EDITING.
CAN I USE THE STUDIO?
HUH? FINE BY ME. BUT...
WES'S COMPANY HAS WAY FANCIER EQUIPMENT, YOU KNOW.
HE'S ALWAYS BUYING THE LATEST GADGETS.
SKRCH SKRCH
I...
GUESS I PREFER THE EQUIPMENT I'M USED TO.
ACTUALLY, I'D TAKE ANY EXCUSE TO GET AWAY FROM THAT STEPFORD WORLD OF THEIRS.
HEH HEH HEH...
SKRCH SKRCH
VA-VWUN
SKRCH SKRCH
SKRCH
YOU HAVE THE FINAL CUT, THE EDIT IS ENTIRELY YOUR CALL. JUST KEEP IN MIND...
WE'VE GOT A FEW TEENSY REQUESTS FROM INVESTORS AND AGENTS. BE SURE TO FIT THOSE IN.
I'M COUNTING ON YOU!
OH, AND THE RUN TIME IS TO BE ABOUT TWO HOURS.

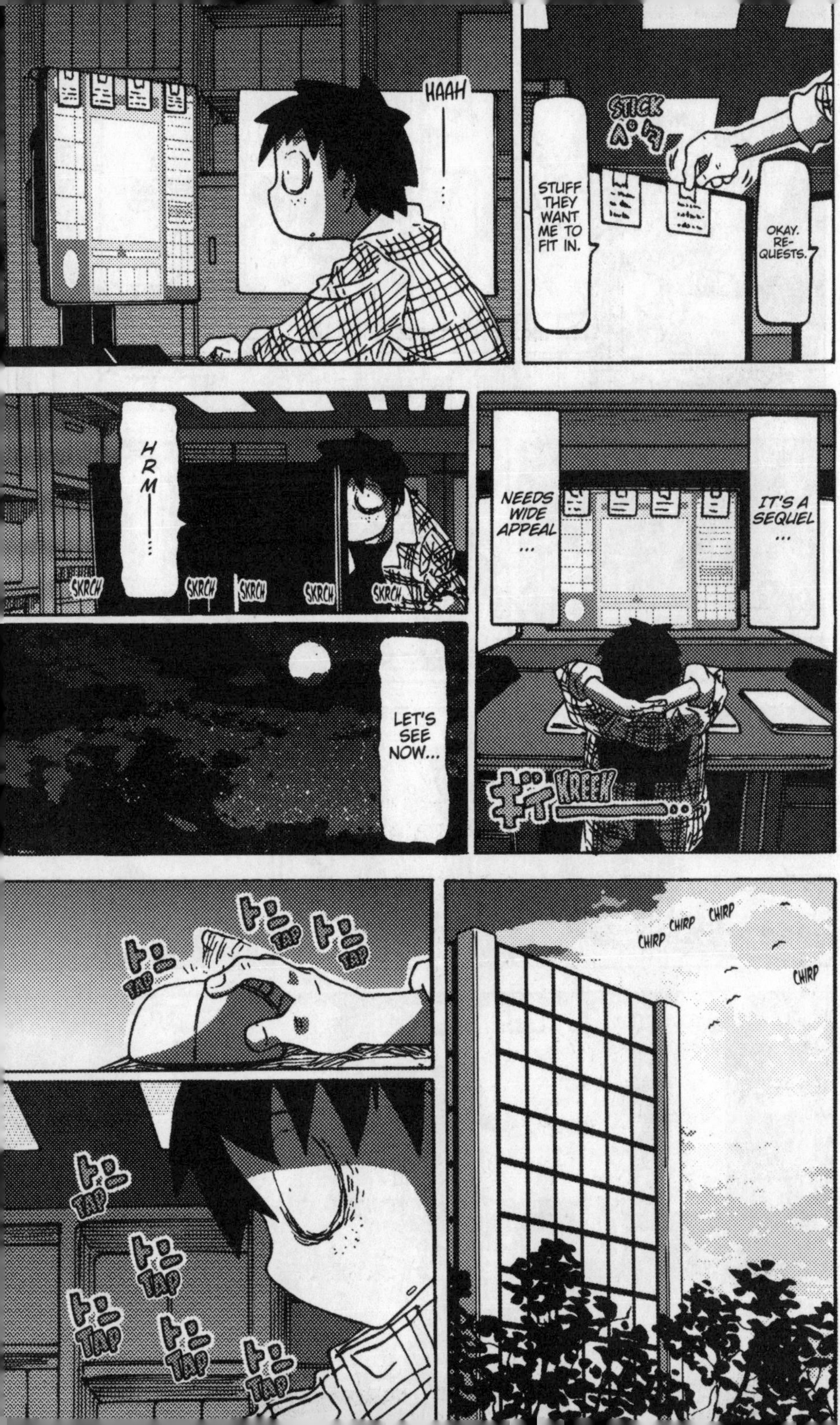
OKAY. RE-QUESTS.
STICK
STUFF THEY WANT ME TO FIT IN.
HAAH ——...
IT'S A SEQUEL ...
NEEDS WIDE APPEAL ...
KREEK ——..
HRM ——...
SKRCH
SKRCH
SKRCH
SKRCH
SKRCH
LET'S SEE NOW...
CHIRP
CHIRP
CHIRP
CHIRP
TAP
TAP
TAP
TAP
TAP
TAP
TAP

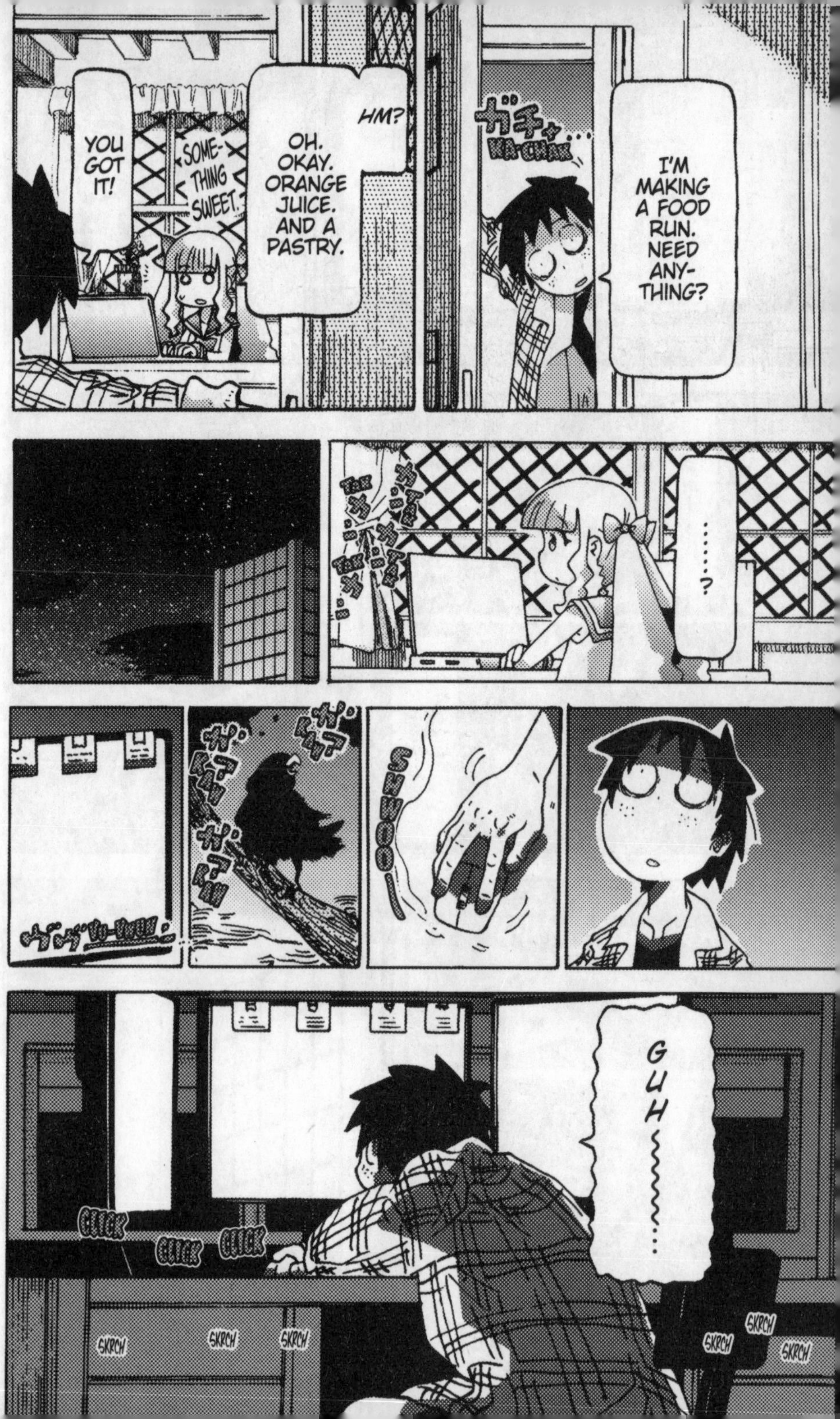

ガチャ…
KA-CHAK…
I'M MAKING A FOOD RUN. NEED ANY-THING?
HM?
OH. OKAY. ORANGE JUICE. AND A PASTRY.
SOME-THING SWEET.
YOU GOT IT!
TAK TAK
......?
SHWOO-
KAW KAW
GUH~~~…
CLICK
CLICK
CLICK
SKRCH
SKRCH
SKRCH
SKRCH
SKRCH
SKRCH

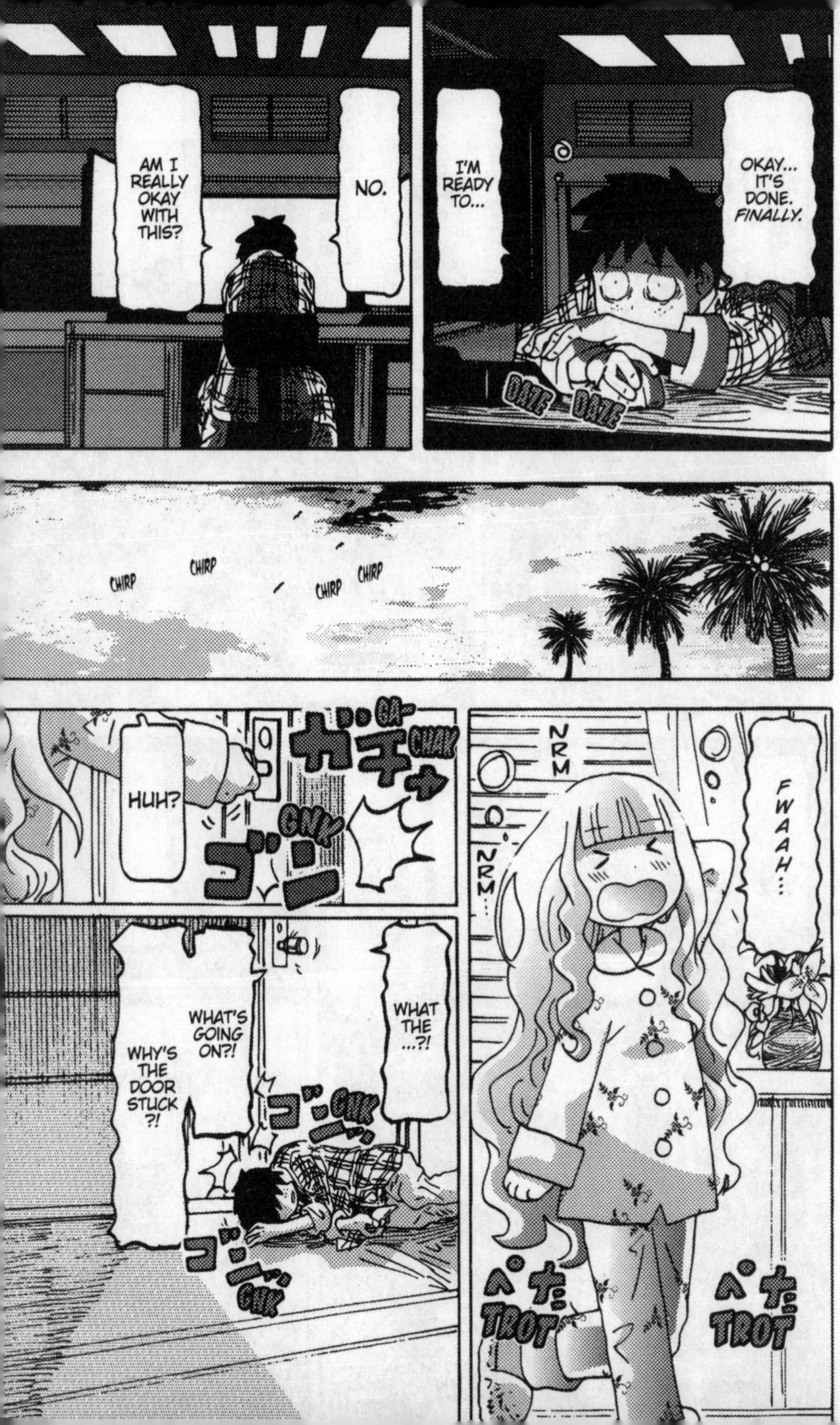
OKAY... IT'S DONE. FINALLY.
I'M READY TO...
DAZE DAZE
NO.
AM I REALLY OKAY WITH THIS?
CHIRP
CHIRP
CHIRP
CHIRP
FWAAH...
NRM
NRM...
TROT
TROT
GA-CHAK
GNK
HUH?
WHAT THE ...?!
WHAT'S GOING ON?!
WHY'S THE DOOR STUCK?!
GNK
GNK

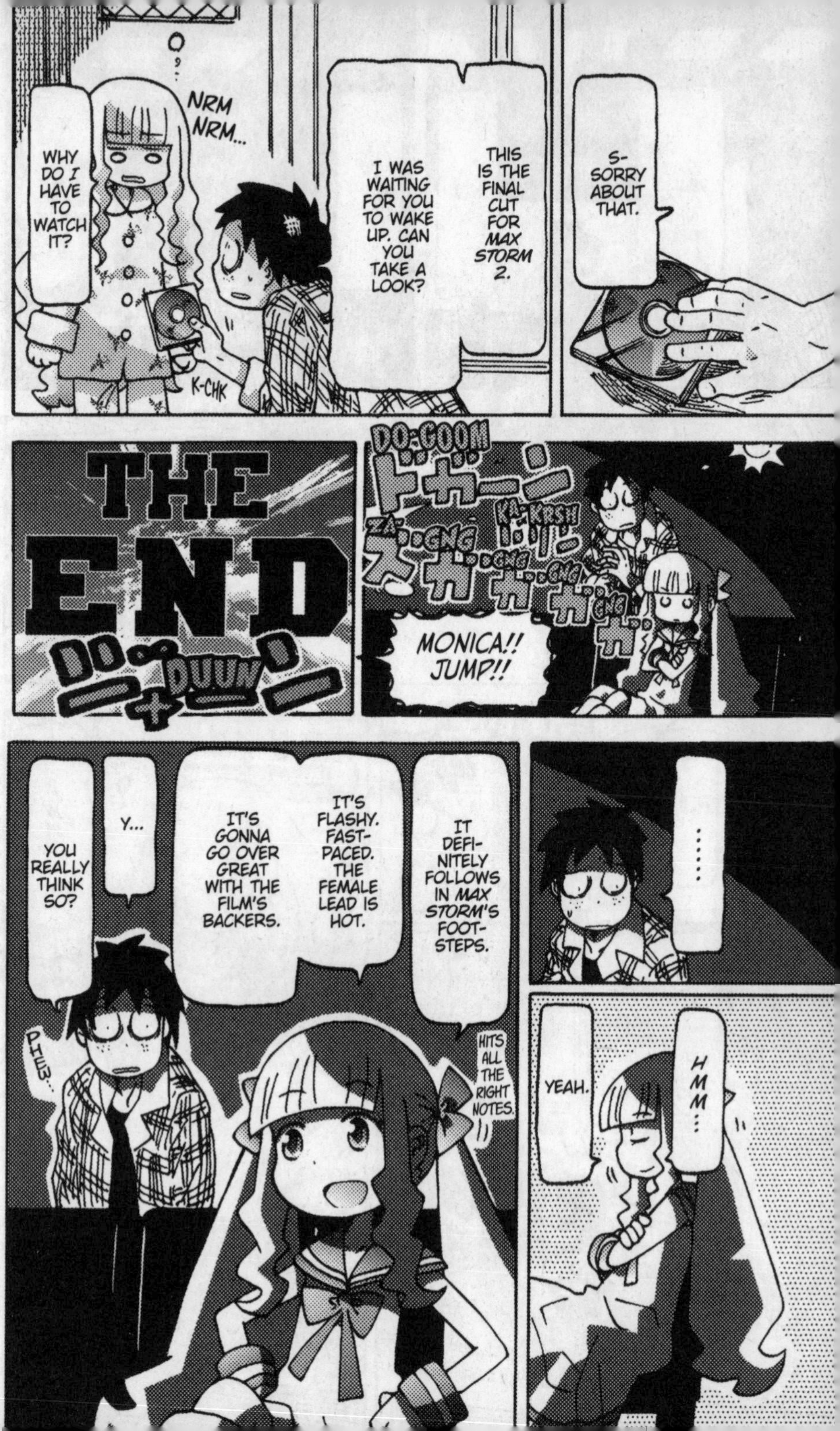
S-SORRY ABOUT THAT.
THIS IS THE FINAL CUT FOR MAX STORM 2.
I WAS WAITING FOR YOU TO WAKE UP. CAN YOU TAKE A LOOK?
NRM NRM...
WHY DO I HAVE TO WATCH IT?
K-CHK
DO-GOOM
ドガーン
ZA-GNG
KA-KRSH
MONICA!! JUMP!!
THE END
DO-DUUN
......
HMM...
YEAH.
IT DEFINITELY FOLLOWS IN MAX STORM'S FOOTSTEPS.
IT'S FLASHY. FAST-PACED. THE FEMALE LEAD IS HOT.
IT'S GONNA GO OVER GREAT WITH THE FILM'S BACKERS.
HITS ALL THE RIGHT NOTES.
Y...
YOU REALLY THINK SO?
PHEW...

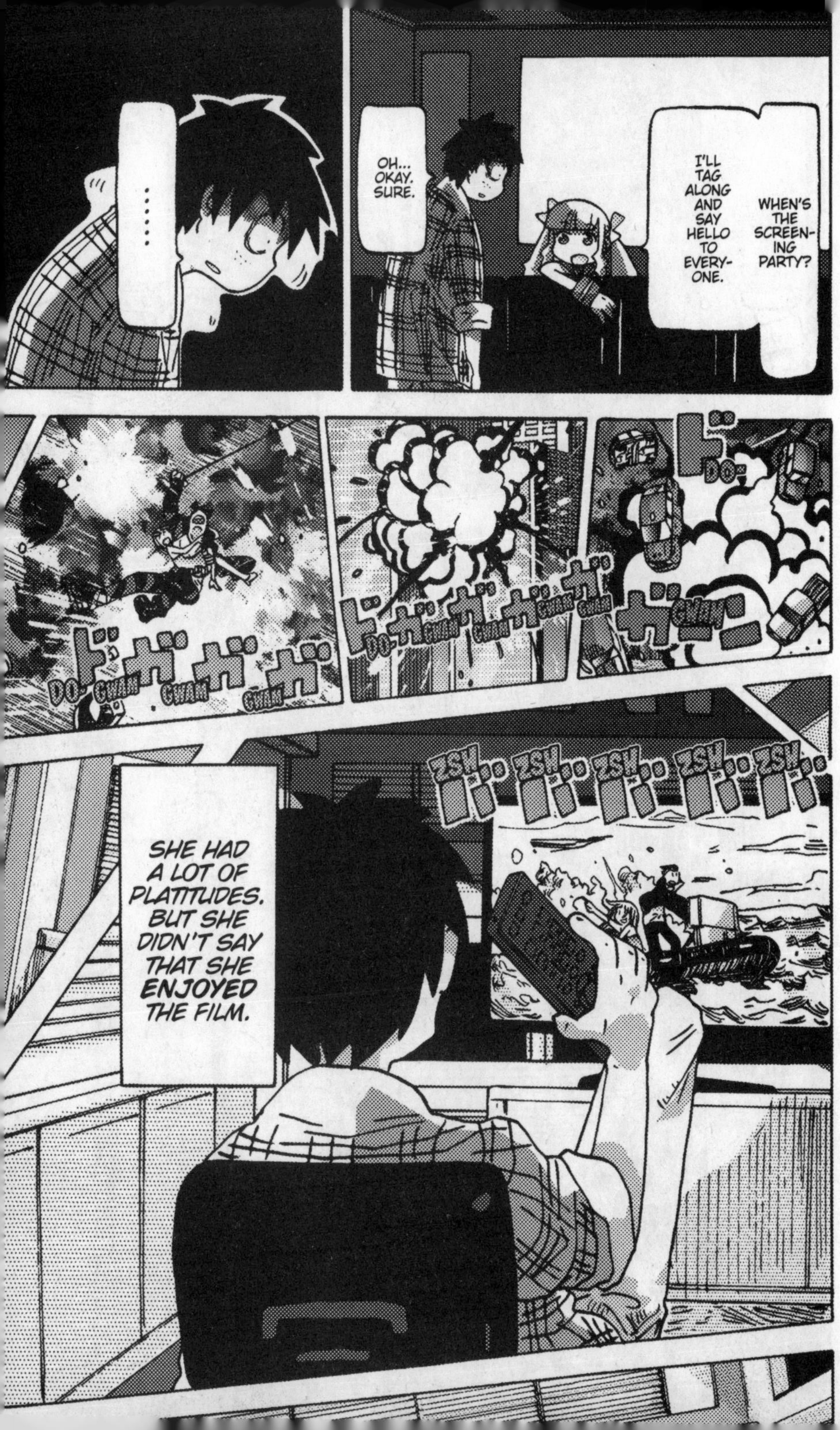
WHEN'S THE SCREENING PARTY?
I'LL TAG ALONG AND SAY HELLO TO EVERYONE.
OH... OKAY. SURE.
......
DO- GWAN
DO- GWAN GWAN GWAN
DO- GWAN GWAN GWAN
ZSH.. ZSH.. ZSH.. ZSH.. ZSH..
SHE HAD A LOT OF PLATITUDES. BUT SHE DIDN'T SAY THAT SHE **ENJOYED** THE FILM.

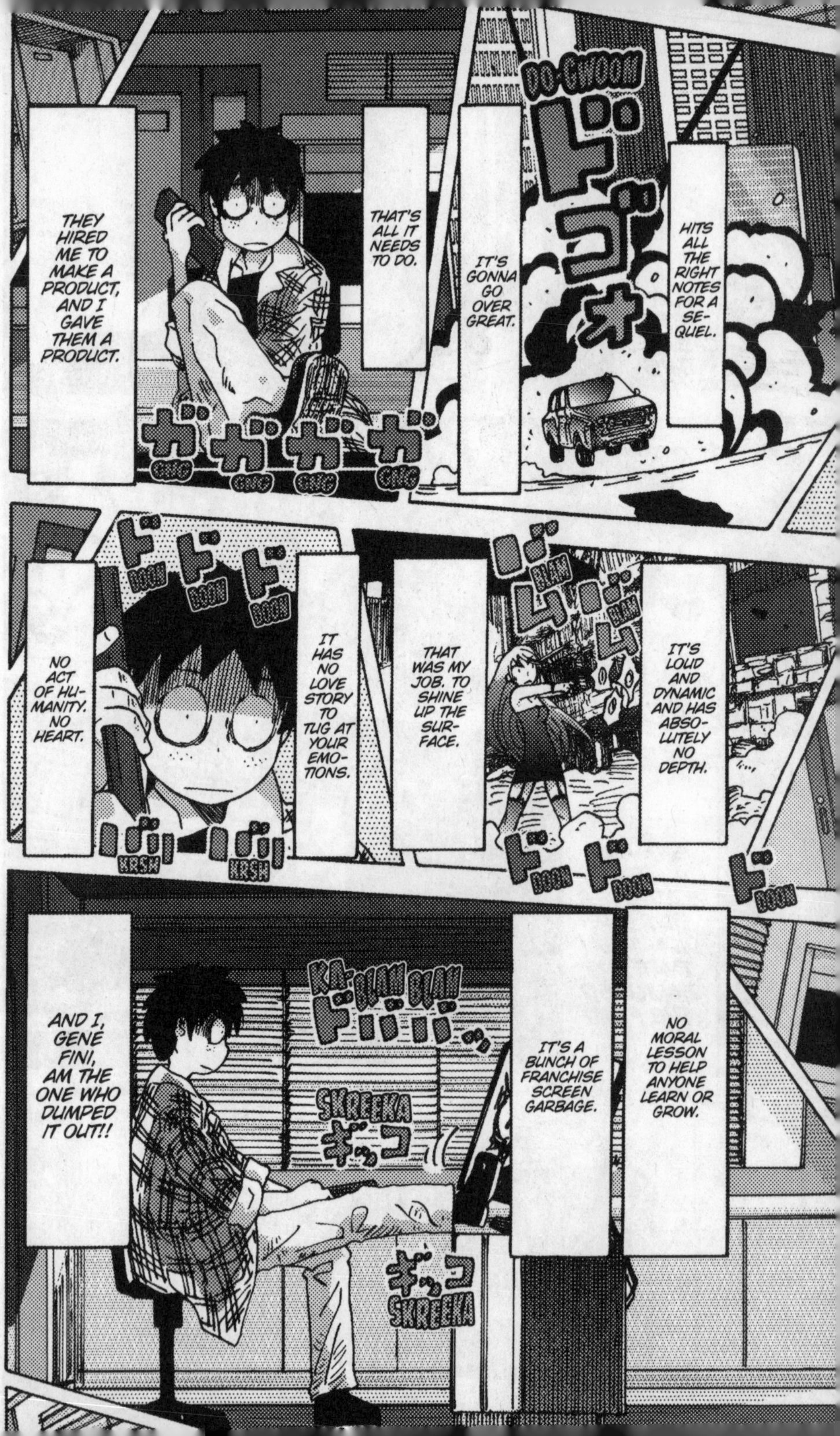

HITS ALL THE RIGHT NOTES FOR A SEQUEL.
DO-GWOON
IT'S GONNA GO OVER GREAT.
THAT'S ALL IT NEEDS TO DO.
THEY HIRED ME TO MAKE A PRODUCT, AND I GAVE THEM A PRODUCT.
GAG GAG GAG GAG
IT'S LOUD AND DYNAMIC AND HAS ABSOLUTELY NO DEPTH.
BLAM BLAM
THAT WAS MY JOB. TO SHINE UP THE SURFACE.
DOON DOON DOON
IT HAS NO LOVE STORY TO TUG AT YOUR EMOTIONS.
DOON DOON DOON
NO ACT OF HUMANITY. NO HEART.
KRSH KRSH
NO MORAL LESSON TO HELP ANYONE LEARN OR GROW.
IT'S A BUNCH OF FRANCHISE SCREEN GARBAGE.
KA-BLAM BLAM
SKREEKA
SKREEKA
AND I, GENE FINI, AM THE ONE WHO DUMPED IT OUT!!

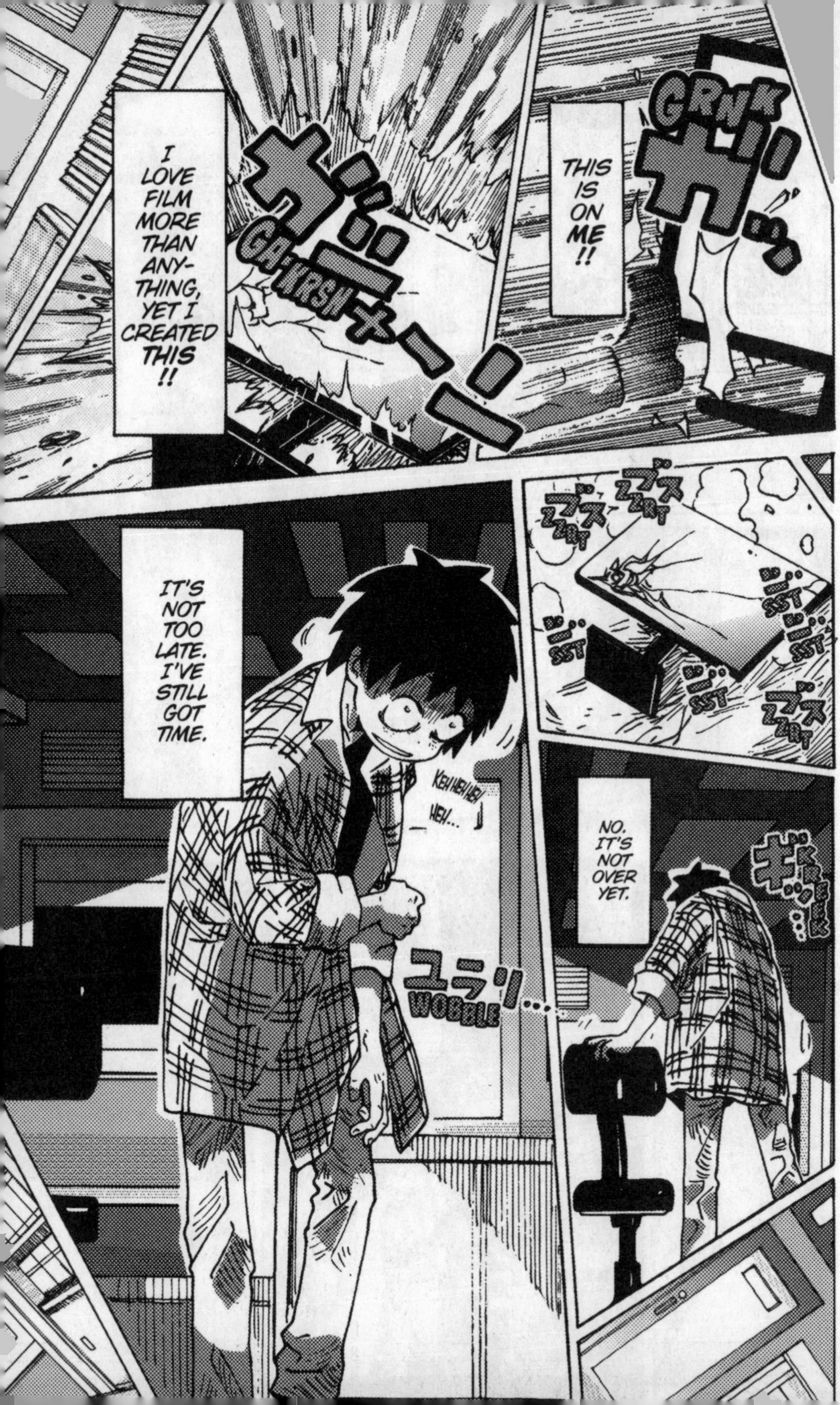

GRNK
THIS IS ON ME!!
GA-KRSH
I LOVE FILM MORE THAN ANYTHING, YET I CREATED THIS!!
ZZRT
ZZRT
SST
SST
SST
SST
ZZRT
NO. IT'S NOT OVER YET.
KREEK
IT'S NOT TOO LATE. I'VE STILL GOT TIME.
KEH HEH HEH HEH...
WOBBLE...

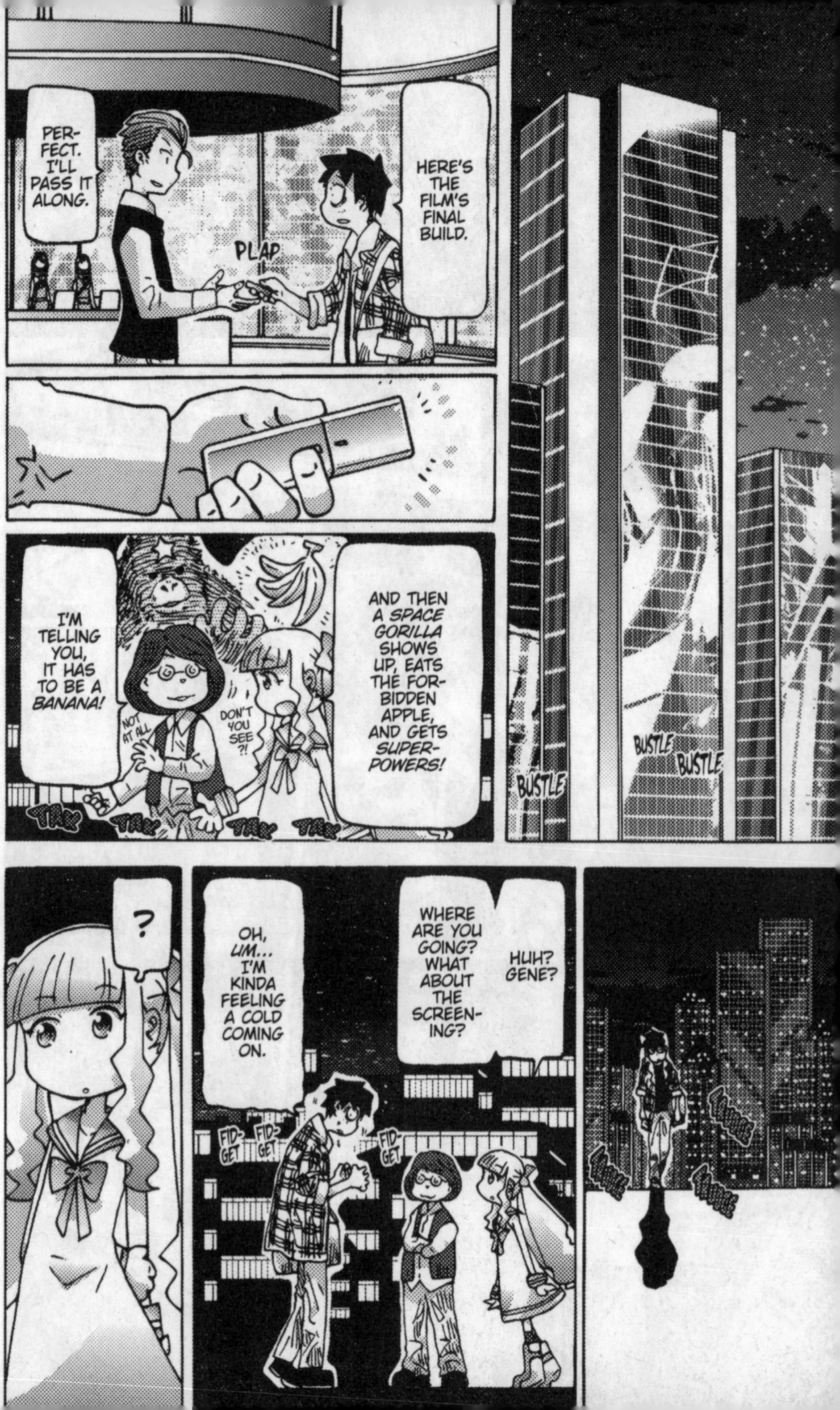
BUSTLE
BUSTLE
BUSTLE
HERE'S THE FILM'S FINAL BUILD.
PLAP
PER-FECT. I'LL PASS IT ALONG.
AND THEN A *SPACE GORILLA* SHOWS UP, EATS THE FOR-BIDDEN APPLE, AND GETS *SUPER-POWERS!*
DON'T YOU SEE?!
NOT AT ALL
I'M TELLING YOU, IT HAS TO BE A *BANANA!*
HUH? GENE?
WHERE ARE YOU GOING? WHAT ABOUT THE SCREEN-ING?
OH, *UM*... I'M KINDA FEELING A COLD COMING ON.
FID-GET
FID-GET
FID-GET
?

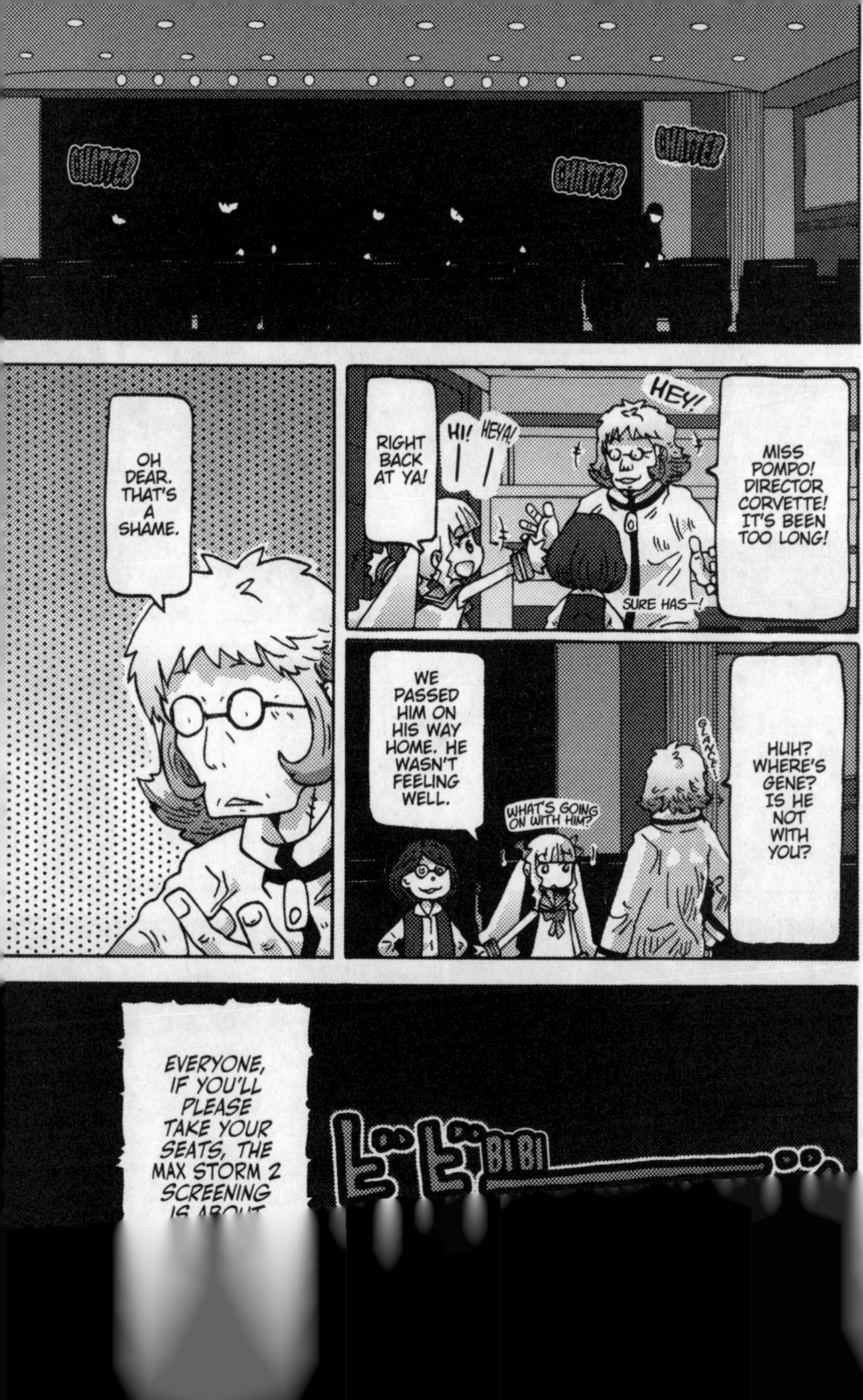
CHATTER
CHATTER
CHATTER
HEY!
MISS POMPO! DIRECTOR CORVETTE! IT'S BEEN TOO LONG!
HEYA!
HI!
RIGHT BACK AT YA!
SURE HAS—!
HUH? WHERE'S GENE? IS HE NOT WITH YOU?
GLANCE...
WHAT'S GOING ON WITH HIM?
WE PASSED HIM ON HIS WAY HOME. HE WASN'T FEELING WELL.
OH DEAR. THAT'S A SHAME.
EVERYONE, IF YOU'LL PLEASE TAKE YOUR SEATS, THE MAX STORM 2 SCREENING IS ABOUT

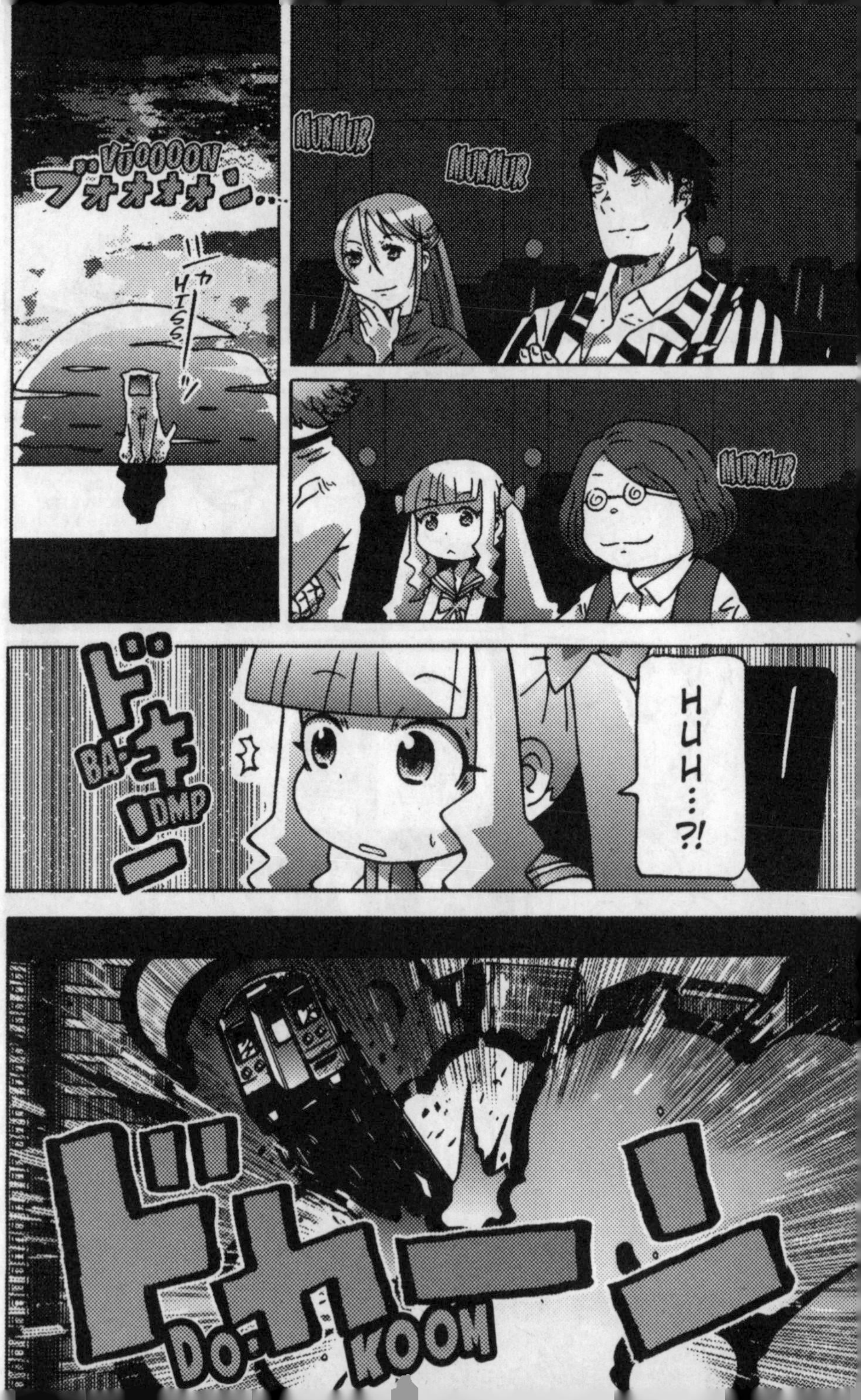

MURMUR
MURMUR
MURMUR
ブオオオオン…
VOOOOON
ヒヤッ
HISS
ドキーン
BA-DMP
HUH…?!
ドカーン
DO-KOON

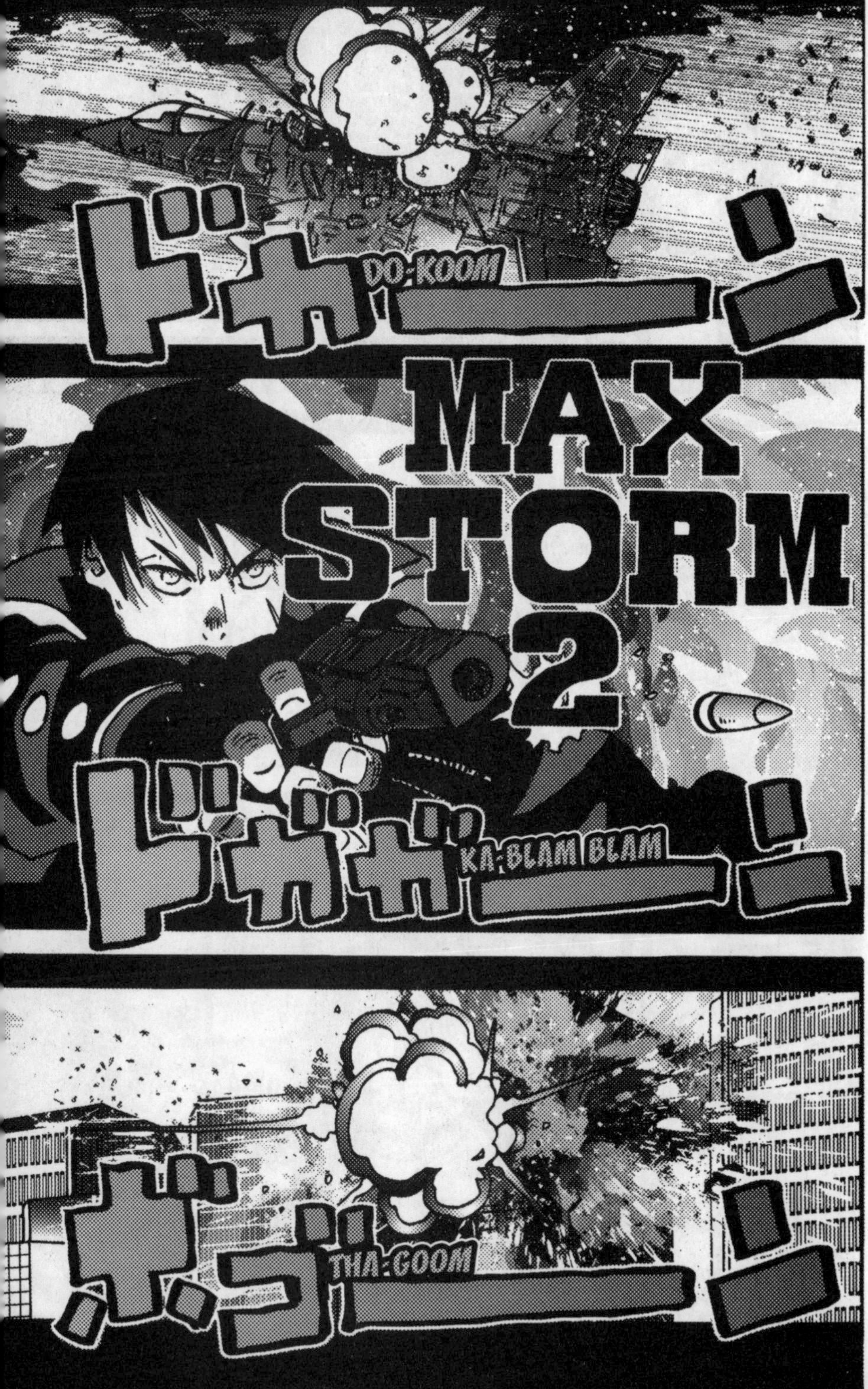

DO-KOOM
MAX STORM 2
KA-BLAM BLAM
THA-GOOM

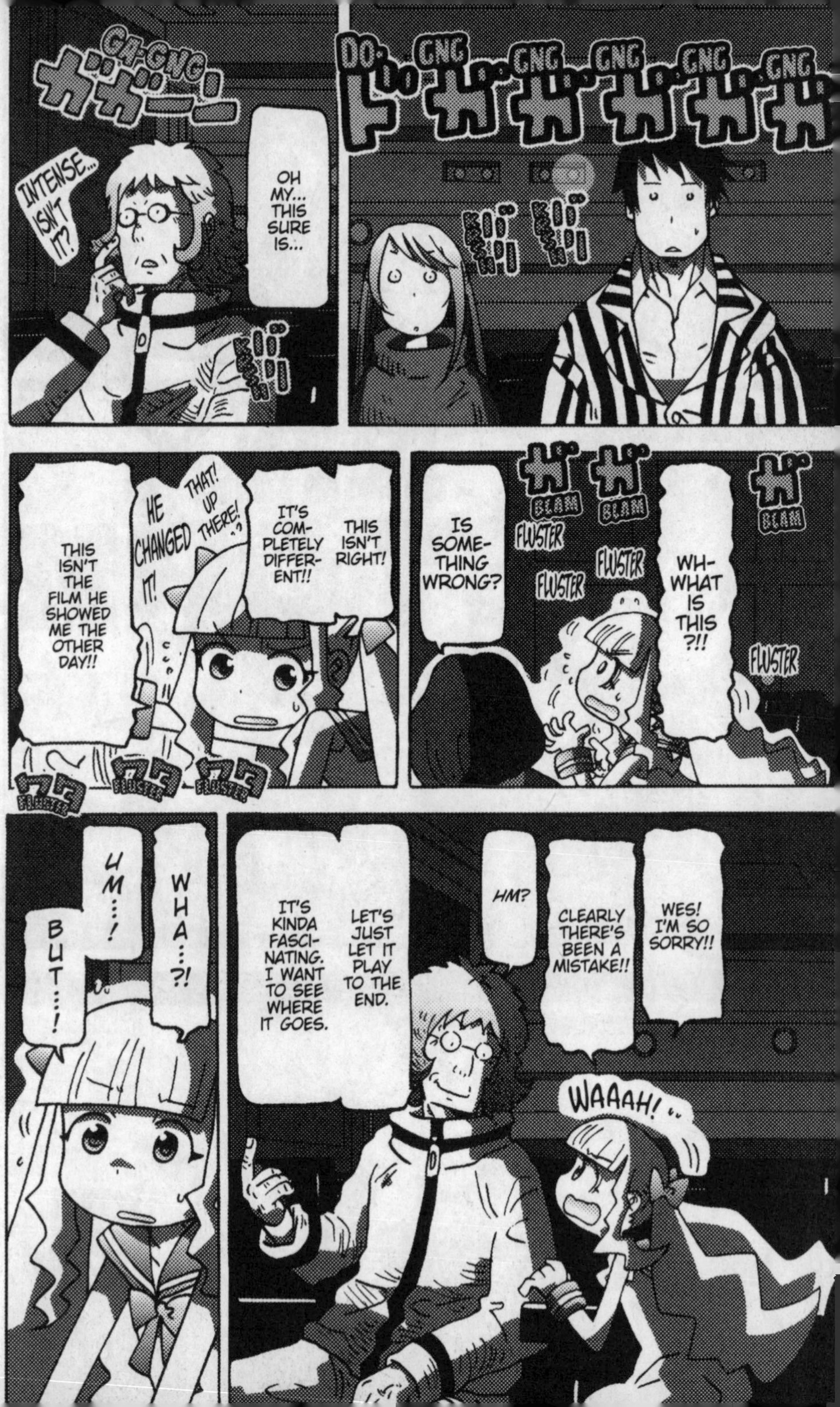
DO GNG GNG GNG GNG GNG
ドガガガガガ
KII KRSHH
KII KRSHH
GA-GNG
ガガーン
OH MY... THIS SURE IS...
INTENSE... ISN'T IT?
KII KRSHH
WH-WHAT IS THIS?!!
BLAM
BLAM
BLAM
FLUSTER
FLUSTER
FLUSTER
FLUSTER
IS SOME-THING WRONG?
THIS ISN'T RIGHT!
IT'S COM-PLETELY DIFFER-ENT!!
THAT! UP THERE!
HE CHANGED IT!
THIS ISN'T THE FILM HE SHOWED ME THE OTHER DAY!!
FLUSTER
FLUSTER
FLUSTER
WES! I'M SO SORRY!!
CLEARLY THERE'S BEEN A MISTAKE!!
HM?
WAAAH!
LET'S JUST LET IT PLAY TO THE END.
IT'S KINDA FASCI-NATING. I WANT TO SEE WHERE IT GOES.
WHA...?!
UM...!
BUT...!

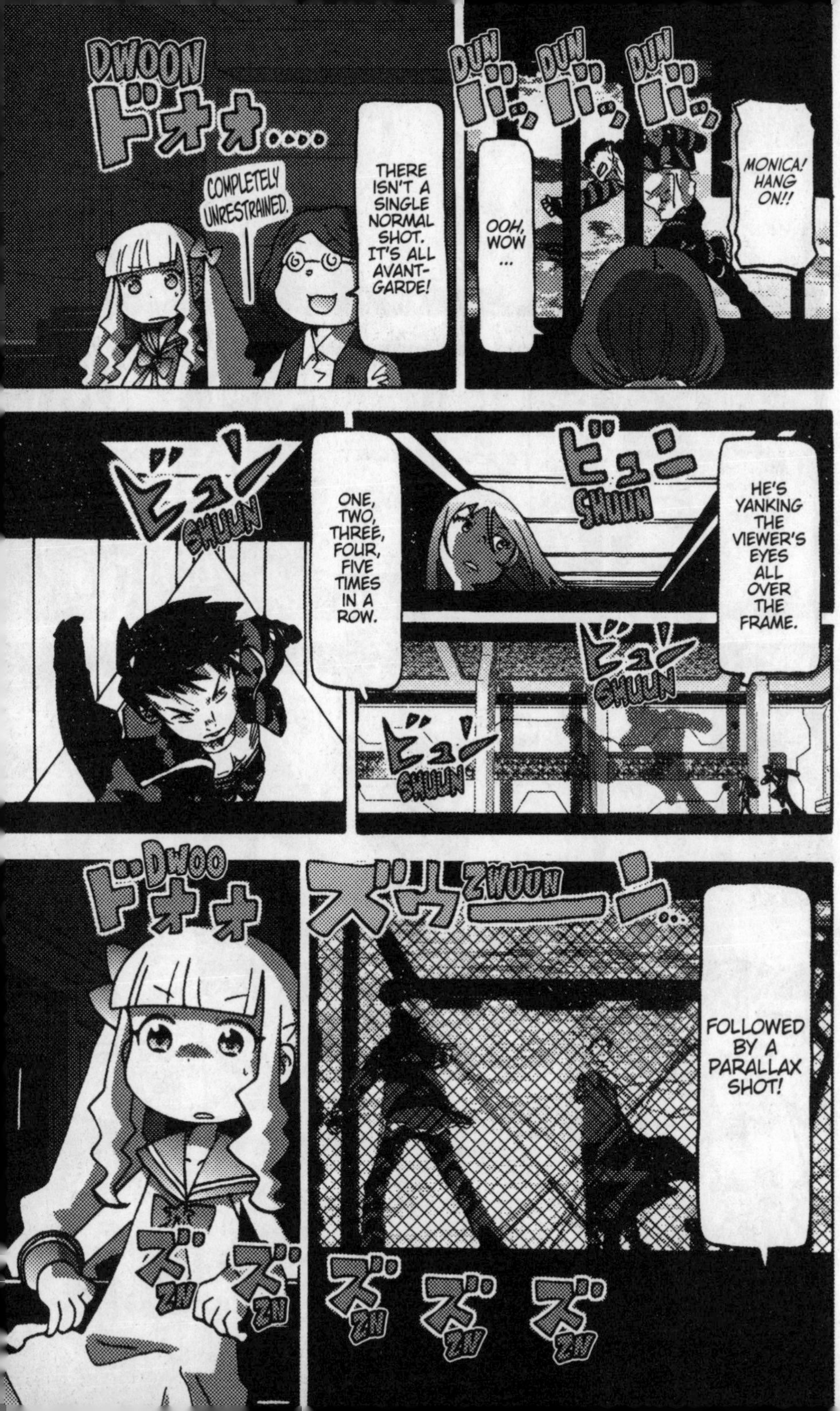
DUN
DUN
DUN
MONICA! HANG ON!!
OOH, WOW ...
DWOON
THERE ISN'T A SINGLE NORMAL SHOT. IT'S ALL AVANT-GARDE!
COMPLETELY UNRESTRAINED.
SHUUN
HE'S YANKING THE VIEWER'S EYES ALL OVER THE FRAME.
SHUUN
SHUUN
SHUUN
ONE, TWO, THREE, FOUR, FIVE TIMES IN A ROW.
ZWOON
FOLLOWED BY A PARALLAX SHOT!
ZN
ZN
ZN
DWOO
ZN
ZN

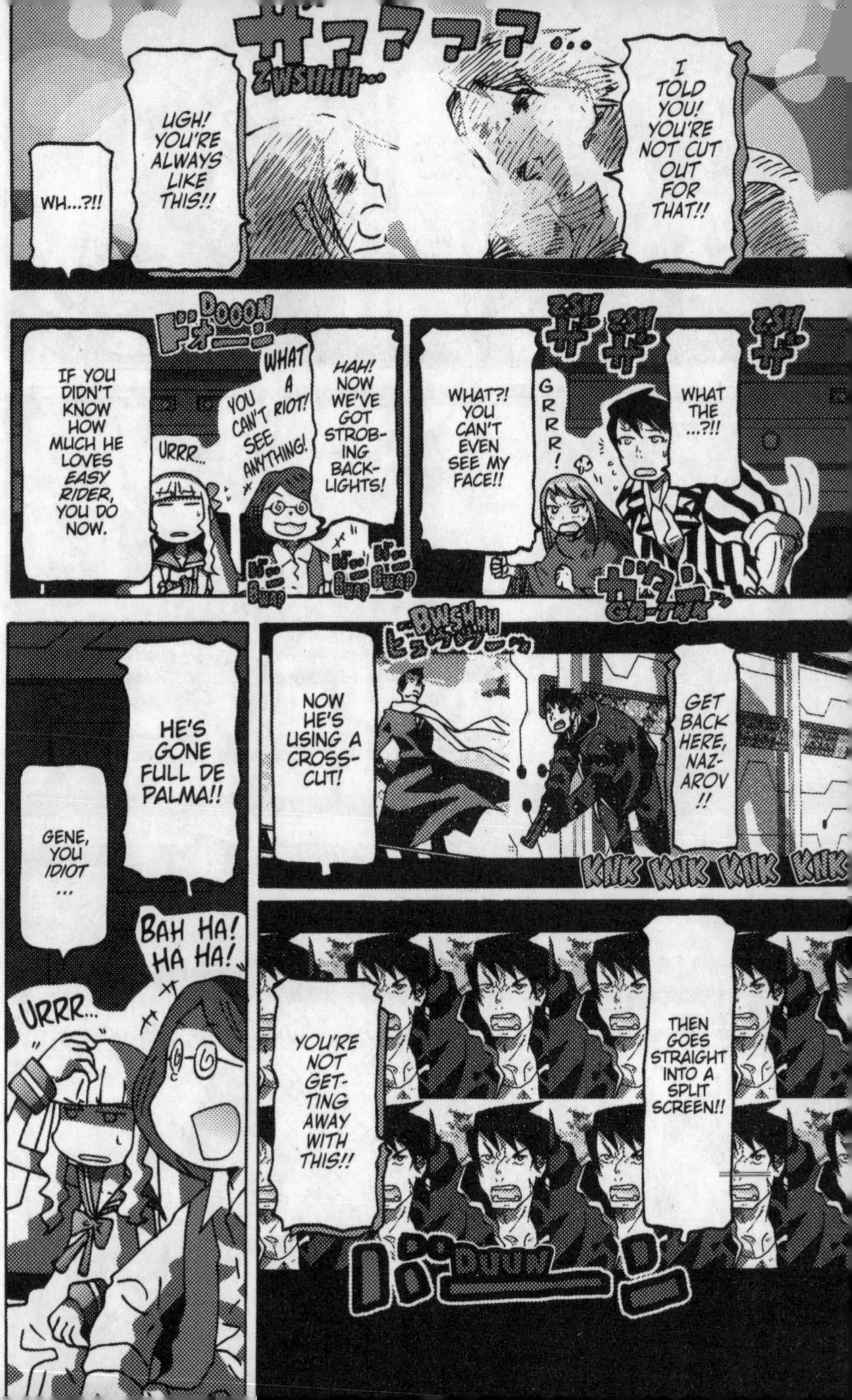
I TOLD YOU! YOU'RE NOT CUT OUT FOR THAT!!
ZWSHHH...
UGH! YOU'RE ALWAYS LIKE THIS!!
WH...?!!
WHAT THE ...?!!
GRRR!
WHAT?! YOU CAN'T EVEN SEE MY FACE!!
DOOON
HAH! NOW WE'VE GOT STROBING BACKLIGHTS!
WHAT A RIOT! YOU CAN'T SEE ANYTHING!
URRR...
IF YOU DIDN'T KNOW HOW MUCH HE LOVES EASY RIDER, YOU DO NOW.
BWSHHH
GET BACK HERE, NAZAROV!!
NOW HE'S USING A CROSS-CUT!
KNK KNK KNK KNK
THEN GOES STRAIGHT INTO A SPLIT SCREEN!!
YOU'RE NOT GETTING AWAY WITH THIS!!
DO-DUUN
HE'S GONE FULL DE PALMA!!
GENE, YOU IDIOT ...
BAH HA! HA HA!
URRR...

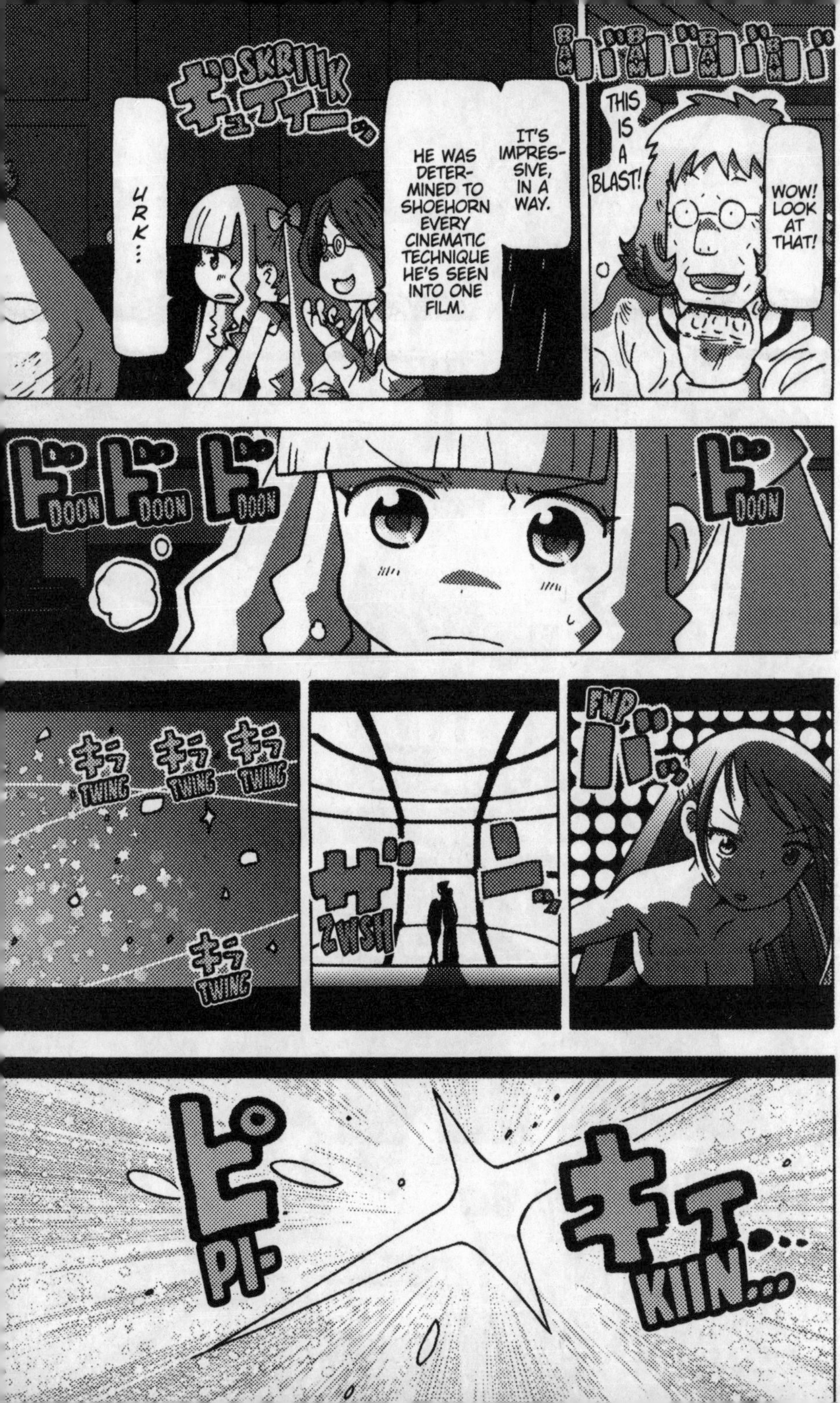
BAM BAM BAM BAM
WOW! LOOK AT THAT!
THIS IS A BLAST!
IT'S IMPRESSIVE, IN A WAY.
HE WAS DETERMINED TO SHOEHORN EVERY CINEMATIC TECHNIQUE HE'S SEEN INTO ONE FILM.
SKRIIIK
URK...
DOON
DOON
DOON
DOON
FWP
ZWSH
TWING
TWING
TWING
TWING
PI-
KIIN...

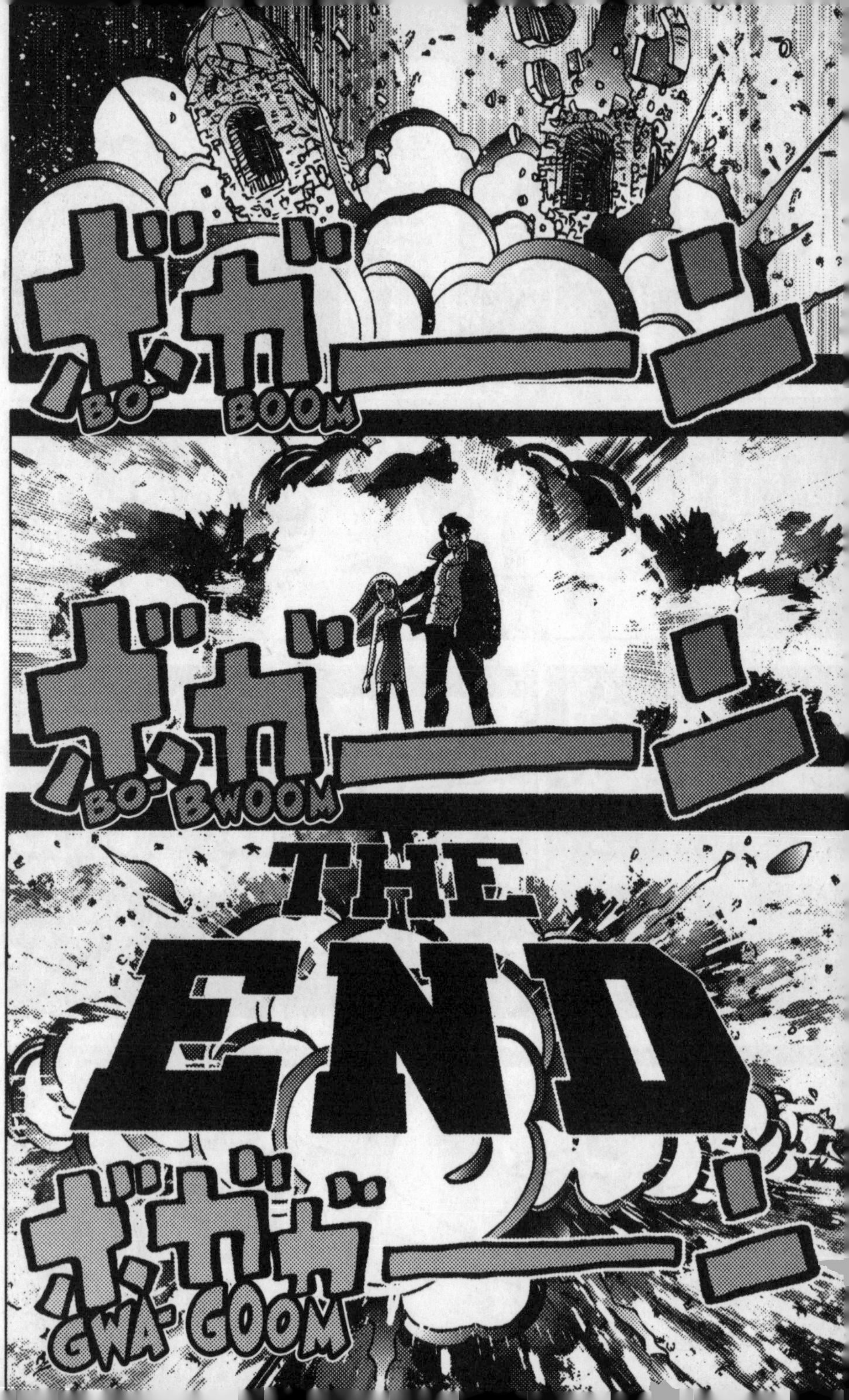
BO-BOOM
BO-BWOOM
THE END
GWA-GOOM

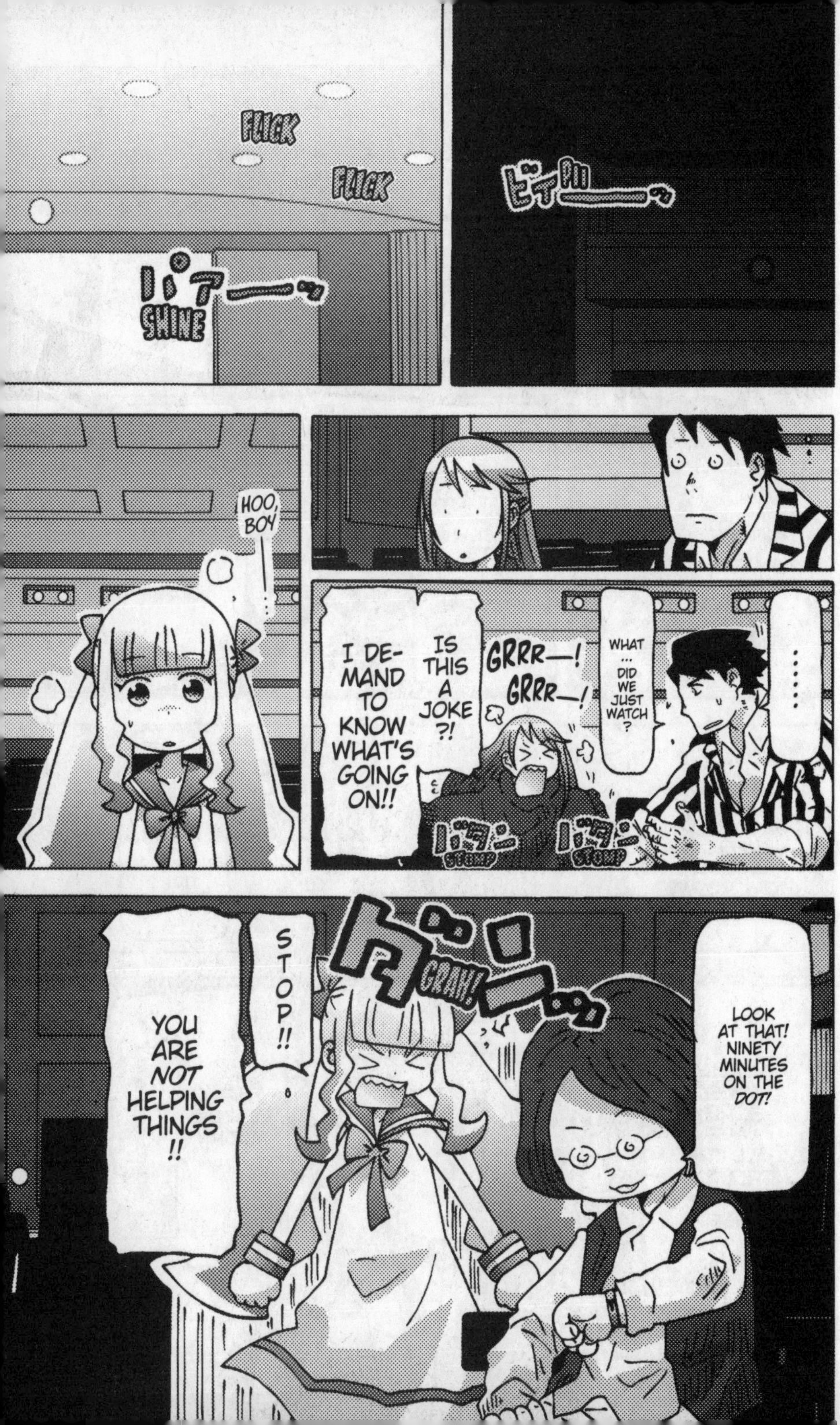
ビィ!!!―――ッ
FLICK
FLICK
パアーーッ
SHINE
......
WHAT... DID WE JUST WATCH?
GRRR—!
GRRR—!
IS THIS A JOKE?!
I DEMAND TO KNOW WHAT'S GOING ON!!
STOMP
STOMP
HOO, BOY...
LOOK AT THAT! NINETY MINUTES ON THE DOT!
CRASH!
STOP!!
YOU ARE NOT HELPING THINGS!!

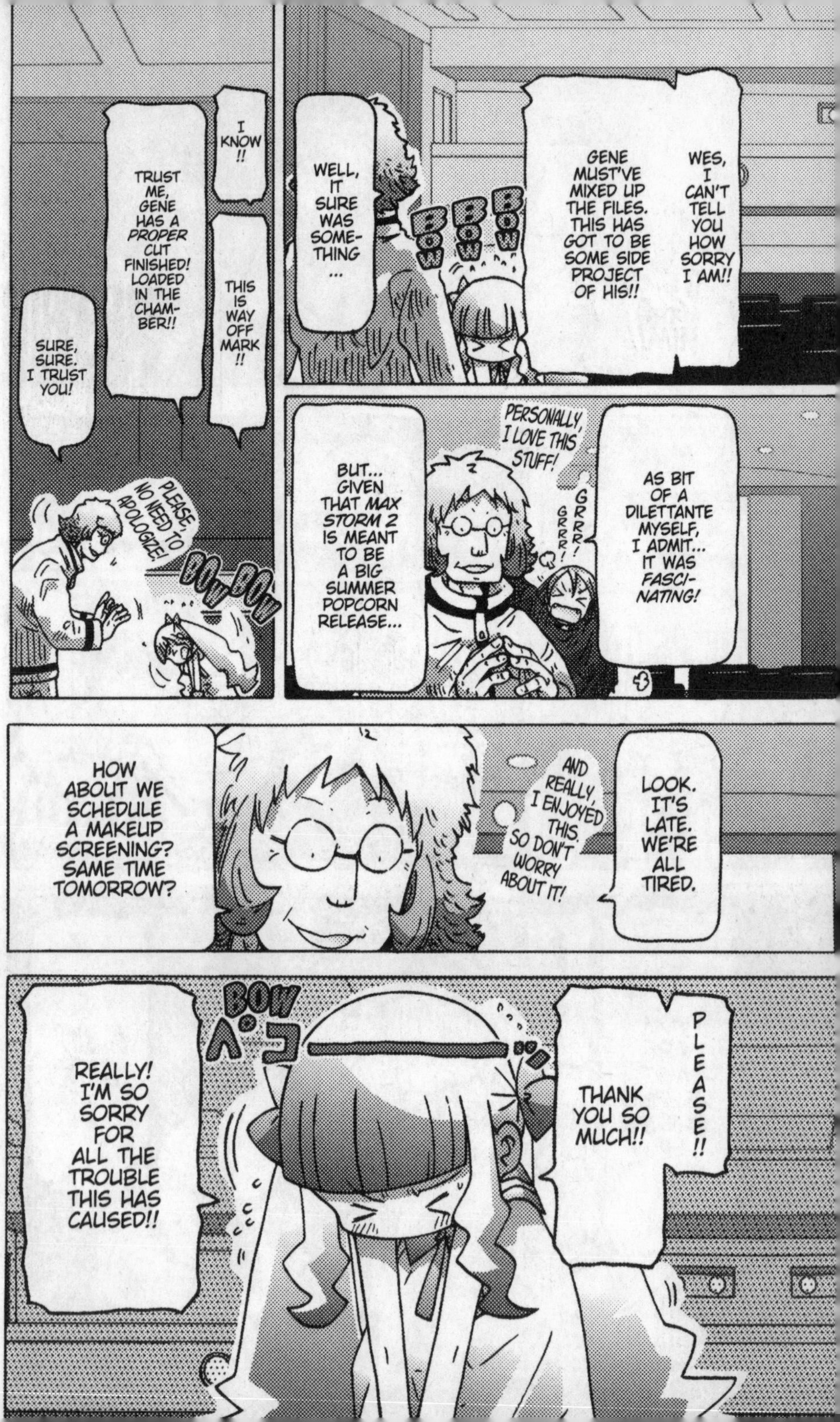
WES, I CAN'T TELL YOU HOW SORRY I AM!!
GENE MUST'VE MIXED UP THE FILES. THIS HAS GOT TO BE SOME SIDE PROJECT OF HIS!!
BOW BOW BOW
WELL, IT SURE WAS SOMETHING...
AS BIT OF A DILETTANTE MYSELF, I ADMIT... IT WAS FASCINATING!
GRRR! GRRR!
PERSONALLY, I LOVE THIS STUFF!
BUT... GIVEN THAT MAX STORM 2 IS MEANT TO BE A BIG SUMMER POPCORN RELEASE...
I KNOW!!
THIS IS WAY OFF MARK!!
TRUST ME, GENE HAS A PROPER CUT FINISHED! LOADED IN THE CHAMBER!!
SURE, SURE. I TRUST YOU!
PLEASE, NO NEED TO APOLOGIZE!
BOW BOW
LOOK. IT'S LATE. WE'RE ALL TIRED.
AND REALLY, I ENJOYED THIS. SO DON'T WORRY ABOUT IT!
HOW ABOUT WE SCHEDULE A MAKEUP SCREENING? SAME TIME TOMORROW?
PLEASE!!
THANK YOU SO MUCH!!
BOW
REALLY! I'M SO SORRY FOR ALL THE TROUBLE THIS HAS CAUSED!!

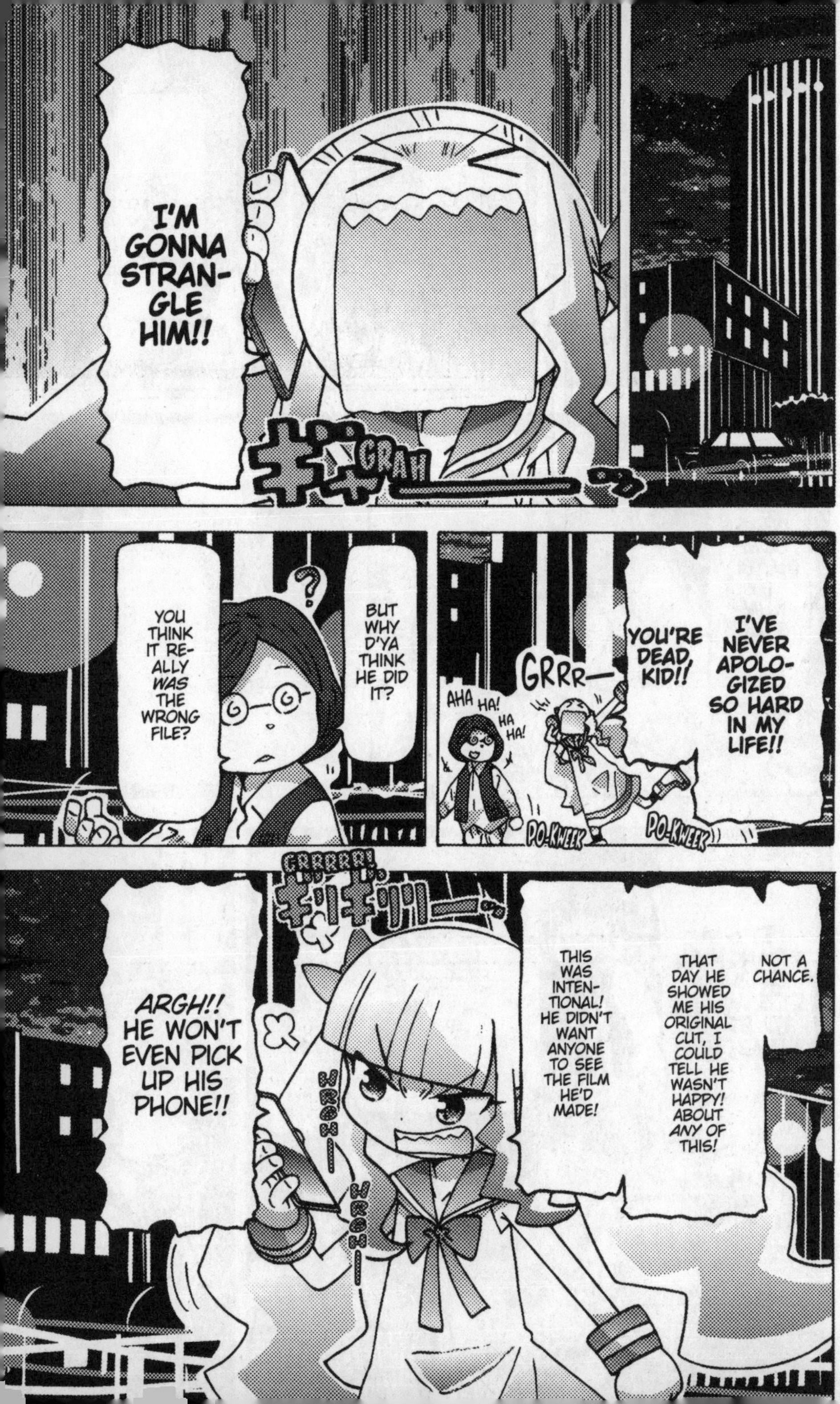
I'M GONNA STRANGLE HIM!!
GRAH
I'VE NEVER APOLOGIZED SO HARD IN MY LIFE!!
YOU'RE DEAD, KID!!
GRRR—
AHA HA! HA HA!
PO-KWEEK
PO-KWEEK
BUT WHY D'YA THINK HE DID IT?
YOU THINK IT REALLY WAS THE WRONG FILE?
NOT A CHANCE.
THAT DAY HE SHOWED ME HIS ORIGINAL CUT, I COULD TELL HE WASN'T HAPPY! ABOUT ANY OF THIS!
THIS WAS INTENTIONAL! HE DIDN'T WANT ANYONE TO SEE THE FILM HE'D MADE!
GRRRRR!
ARGH!! HE WON'T EVEN PICK UP HIS PHONE!!

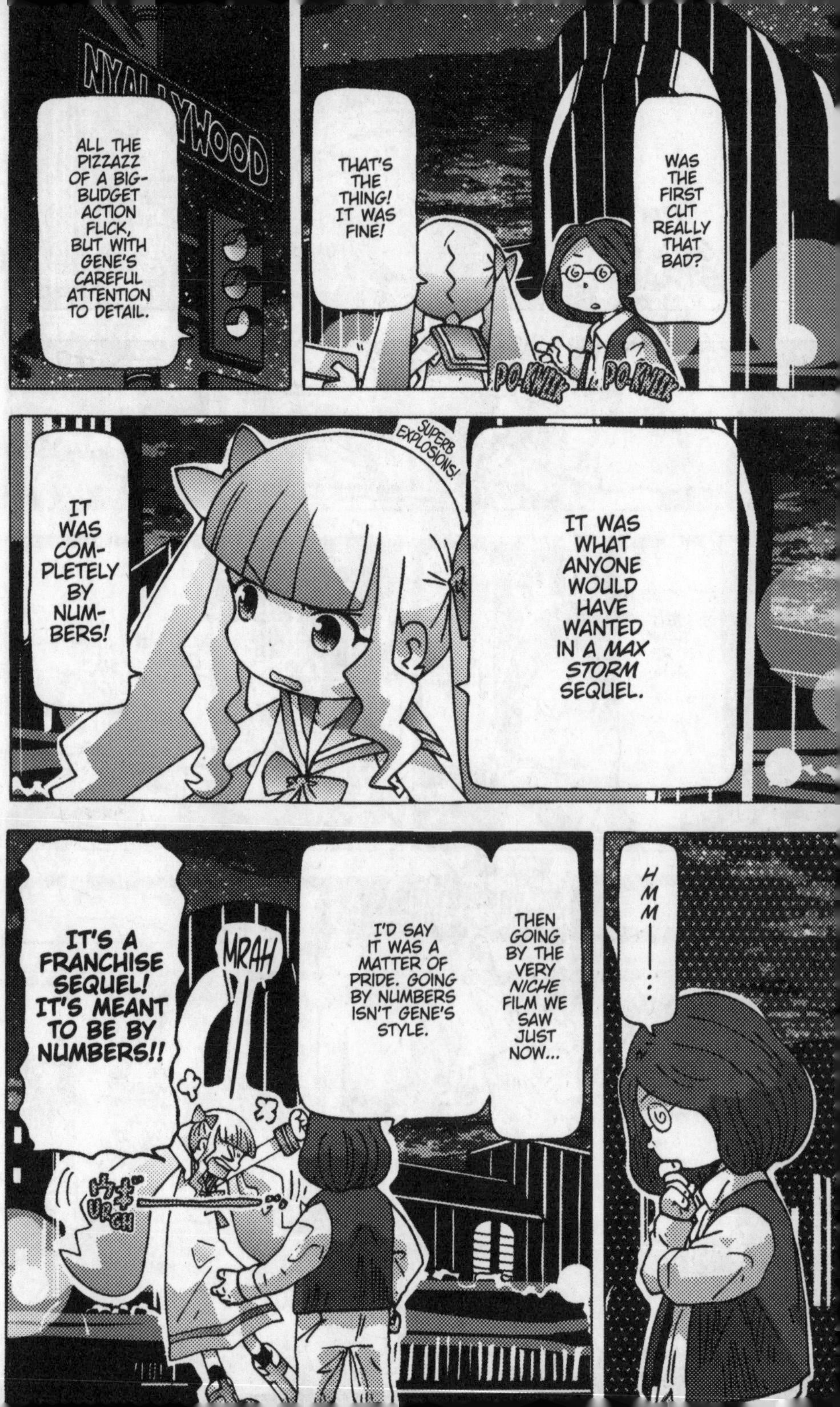
WAS THE FIRST CUT REALLY THAT BAD?
PO-KNIIK
PO-KNIIK
THAT'S THE THING! IT WAS FINE!
NYALLYWOOD
ALL THE PIZZAZZ OF A BIG-BUDGET ACTION FLICK, BUT WITH GENE'S CAREFUL ATTENTION TO DETAIL.
IT WAS WHAT ANYONE WOULD HAVE WANTED IN A *MAX STORM* SEQUEL.
SUPERB EXPLOSIONS!
IT WAS COM-PLETELY BY NUM-BERS!
HMM———...
THEN GOING BY THE VERY *NICHE* FILM WE SAW JUST NOW...
I'D SAY IT WAS A MATTER OF PRIDE. GOING BY NUMBERS ISN'T GENE'S STYLE.
MRAH
IT'S A FRANCHISE SEQUEL! IT'S MEANT TO BE BY NUMBERS!!
URGH

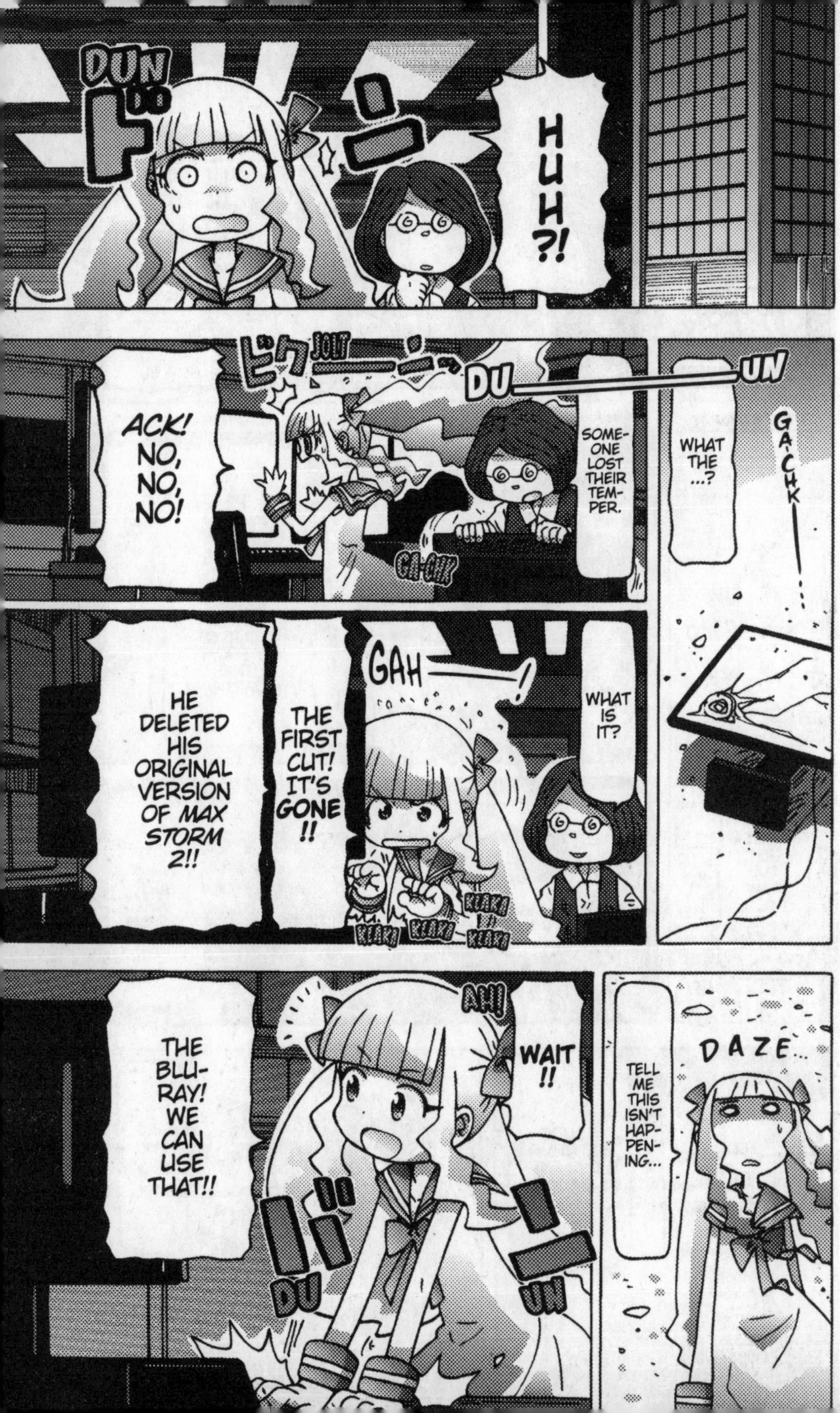

HUH?!
DUN
DO
DU—UN
WHAT THE ...?
GA-CHK
SOME-ONE LOST THEIR TEM-PER.
JOLT
ACK! NO, NO, NO!
GA-CHK
WHAT IS IT?
GAH
THE FIRST CUT! IT'S GONE!!
HE DELETED HIS ORIGINAL VERSION OF MAX STORM 2!!
DAZE...
TELL ME THIS ISN'T HAP-PEN-ING...
AH!
WAIT!!
THE BLU-RAY! WE CAN USE THAT!!
DU
UN

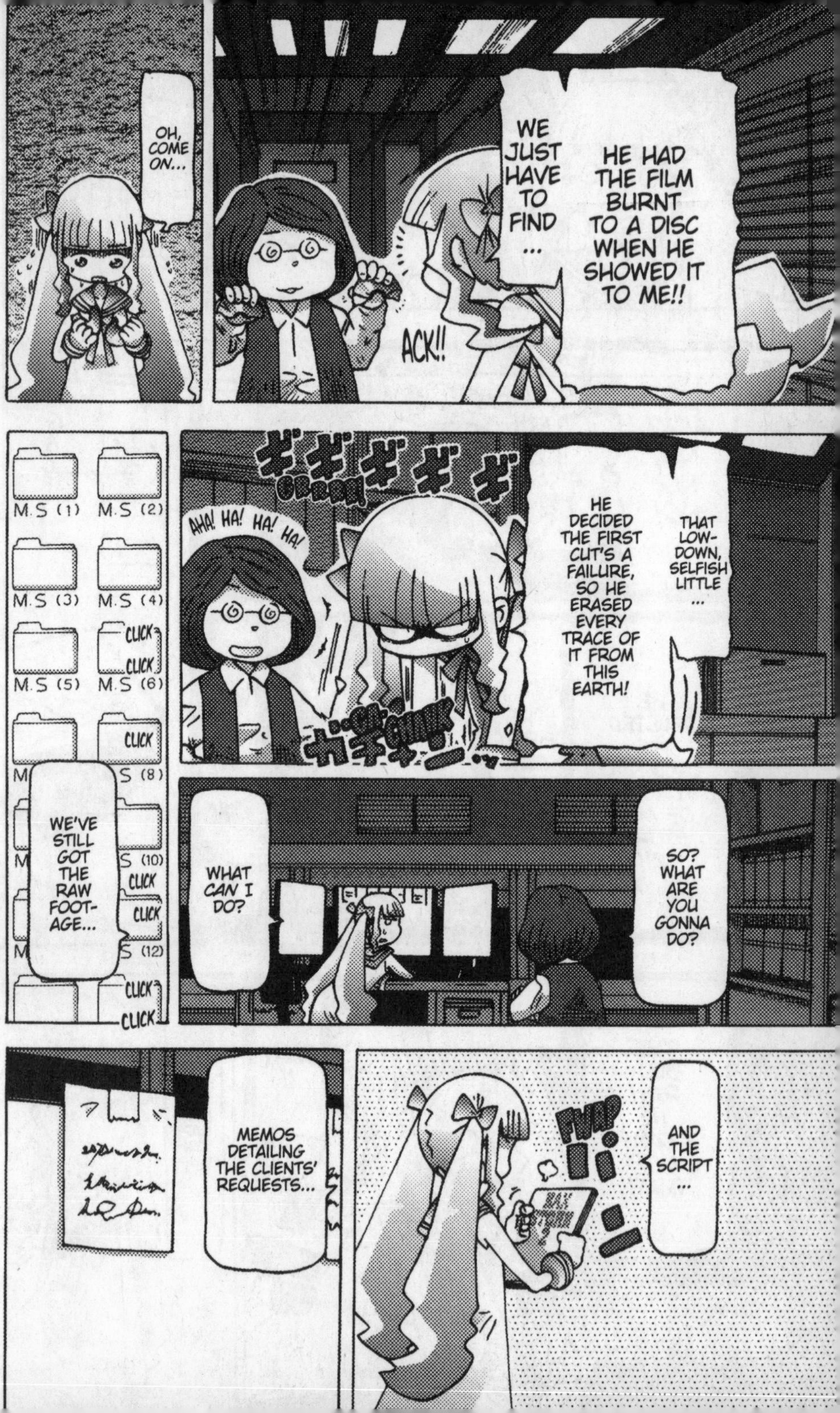
HE HAD THE FILM BURNT TO A DISC WHEN HE SHOWED IT TO ME!!
WE JUST HAVE TO FIND ...
ACK!!
OH, COME ON...
THAT LOW-DOWN, SELFISH LITTLE ...
HE DECIDED THE FIRST CUT'S A FAILURE, SO HE ERASED EVERY TRACE OF IT FROM THIS EARTH!
AHA! HA! HA! HA!
SO? WHAT ARE YOU GONNA DO?
WHAT CAN I DO?
M.S (1)
M.S (2)
M.S (3)
M.S (4)
M.S (5)
M.S (6)
CLICK
CLICK
CLICK
WE'VE STILL GOT THE RAW FOOT-AGE...
CLICK
CLICK
CLICK
CLICK
AND THE SCRIPT ...
FWAP
MEMOS DETAILING THE CLIENTS' REQUESTS...

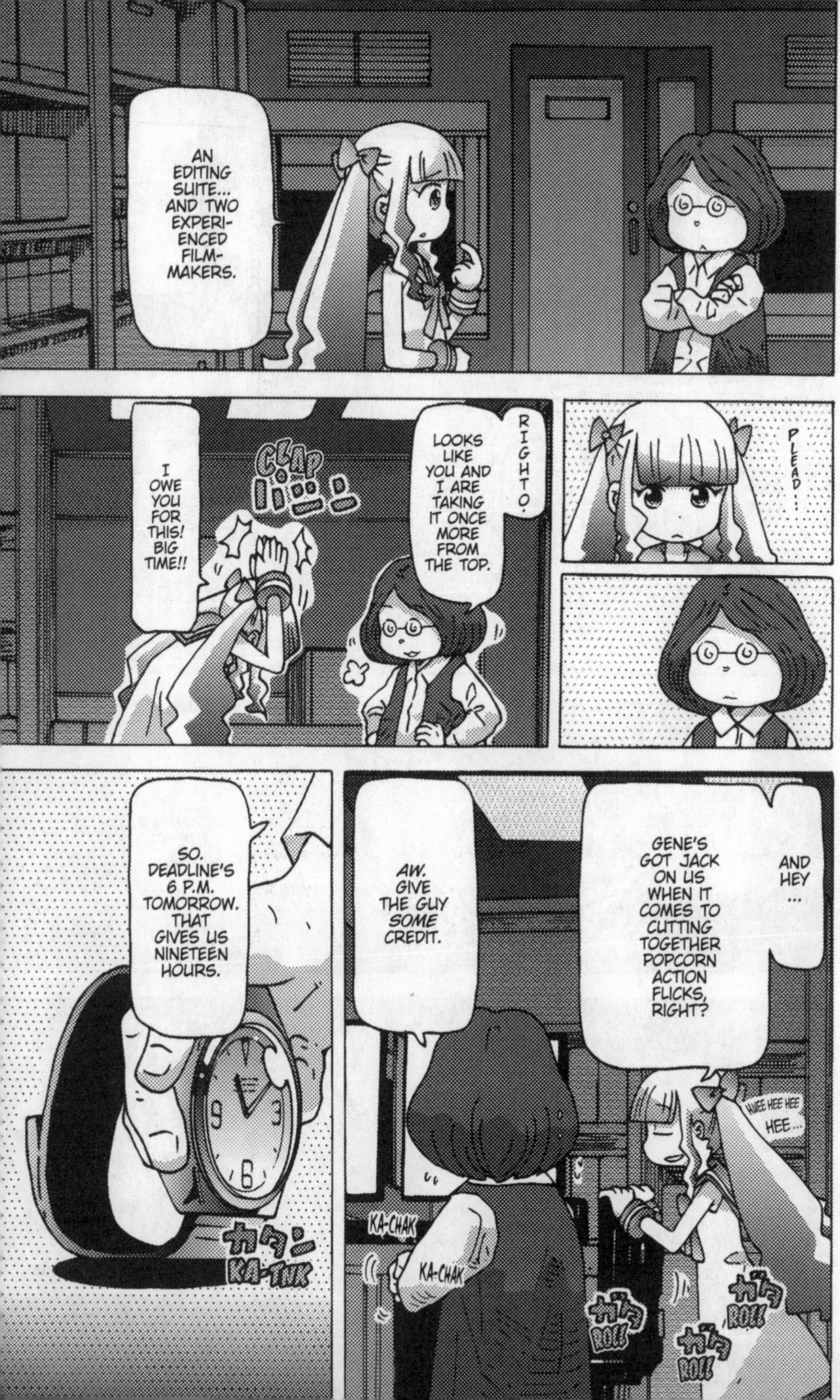
AN EDITING SUITE... AND TWO EXPERIENCED FILMMAKERS.
PLEAD...
RIGHTO.
LOOKS LIKE YOU AND I ARE TAKING IT ONCE MORE FROM THE TOP.
CLAP
I OWE YOU FOR THIS! BIG TIME!!
AND HEY ...
GENE'S GOT JACK ON US WHEN IT COMES TO CUTTING TOGETHER POPCORN ACTION FLICKS, RIGHT?
AW. GIVE THE GUY SOME CREDIT.
WHEE HEE HEE HEE...
KA-CHAK
KA-CHAK
ROLL
ROLL
ROLL
SO. DEADLINE'S 6 P.M. TOMORROW. THAT GIVES US NINETEEN HOURS.
KA-TNK

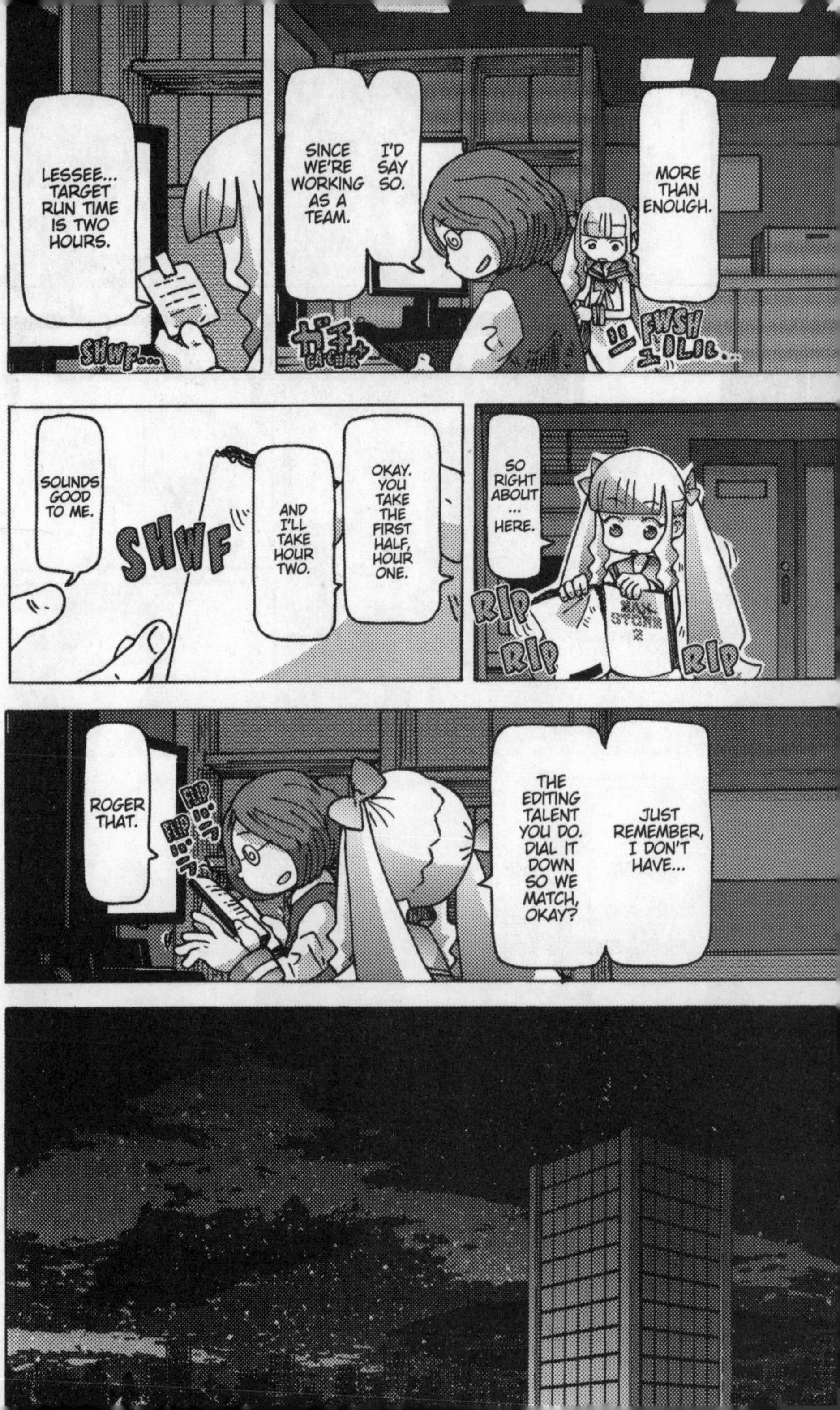
MORE THAN ENOUGH.
FWSH
I'D SAY SO.
SINCE WE'RE WORKING AS A TEAM.
LESSEE... TARGET RUN TIME IS TWO HOURS.
SHWF...
SO RIGHT ABOUT ... HERE.
RIP
RIP
RIP
OKAY. YOU TAKE THE FIRST HALF, HOUR ONE.
AND I'LL TAKE HOUR TWO.
SHWF
SOUNDS GOOD TO ME.
JUST REMEMBER, I DON'T HAVE...
THE EDITING TALENT YOU DO. DIAL IT DOWN SO WE MATCH, OKAY?
FLIP
FLIP
ROGER THAT.

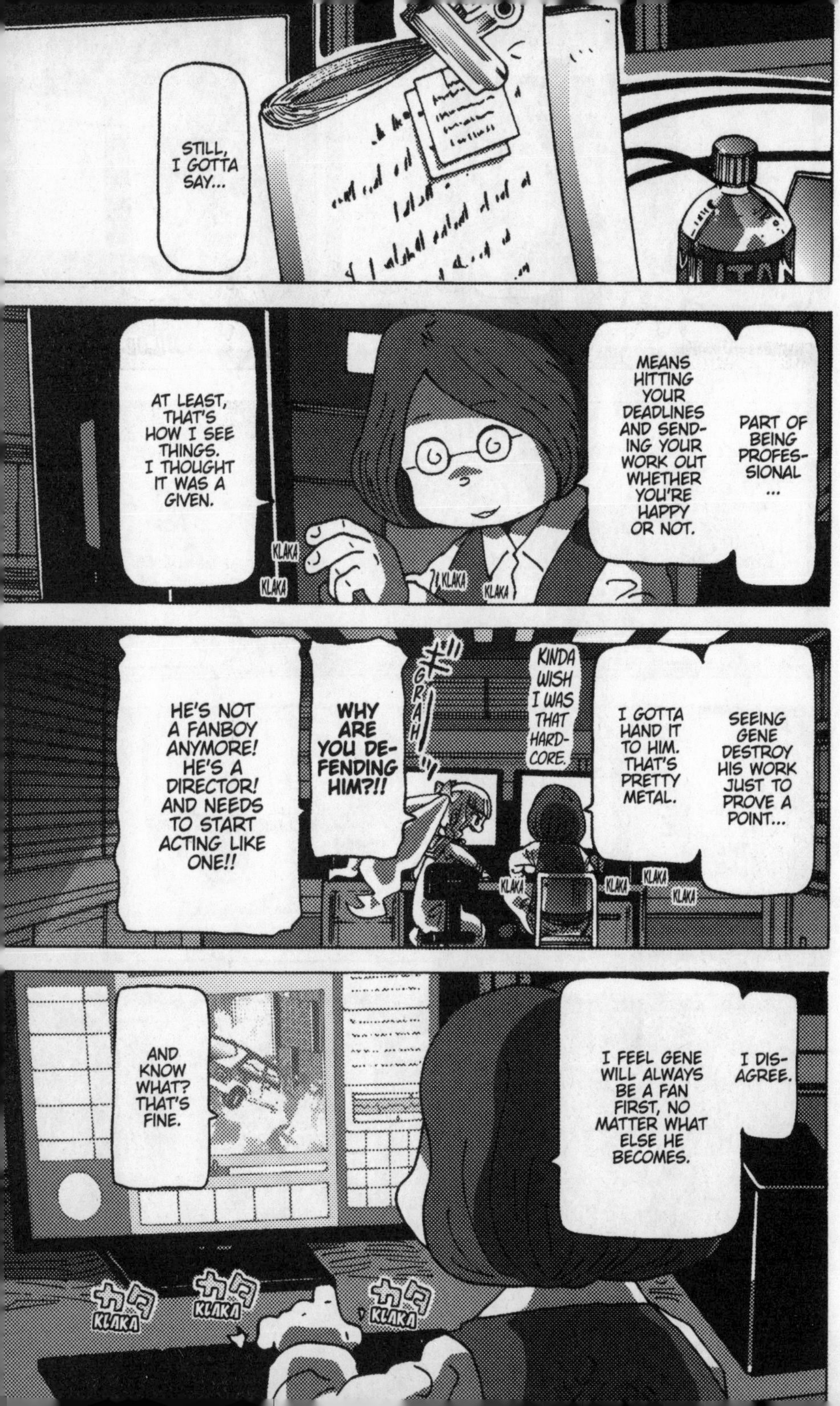
STILL, I GOTTA SAY...
PART OF BEING PROFES-SIONAL ...
MEANS HITTING YOUR DEADLINES AND SEND-ING YOUR WORK OUT WHETHER YOU'RE HAPPY OR NOT.
AT LEAST, THAT'S HOW I SEE THINGS. I THOUGHT IT WAS A GIVEN.
KLAKA
KLAKA
KLAKA
KLAKA
SEEING GENE DESTROY HIS WORK JUST TO PROVE A POINT...
I GOTTA HAND IT TO HIM. THAT'S PRETTY METAL.
KINDA WISH I WAS THAT HARD-CORE.
KLAKA
KLAKA
KLAKA
KLAKA
GRAH
WHY ARE YOU DE-FENDING HIM?!!
HE'S NOT A FANBOY ANYMORE! HE'S A DIRECTOR! AND NEEDS TO START ACTING LIKE ONE!!
I DIS-AGREE.
I FEEL GENE WILL ALWAYS BE A FAN FIRST, NO MATTER WHAT ELSE HE BECOMES.
AND KNOW WHAT? THAT'S FINE.
KLAKA
KLAKA
KLAKA

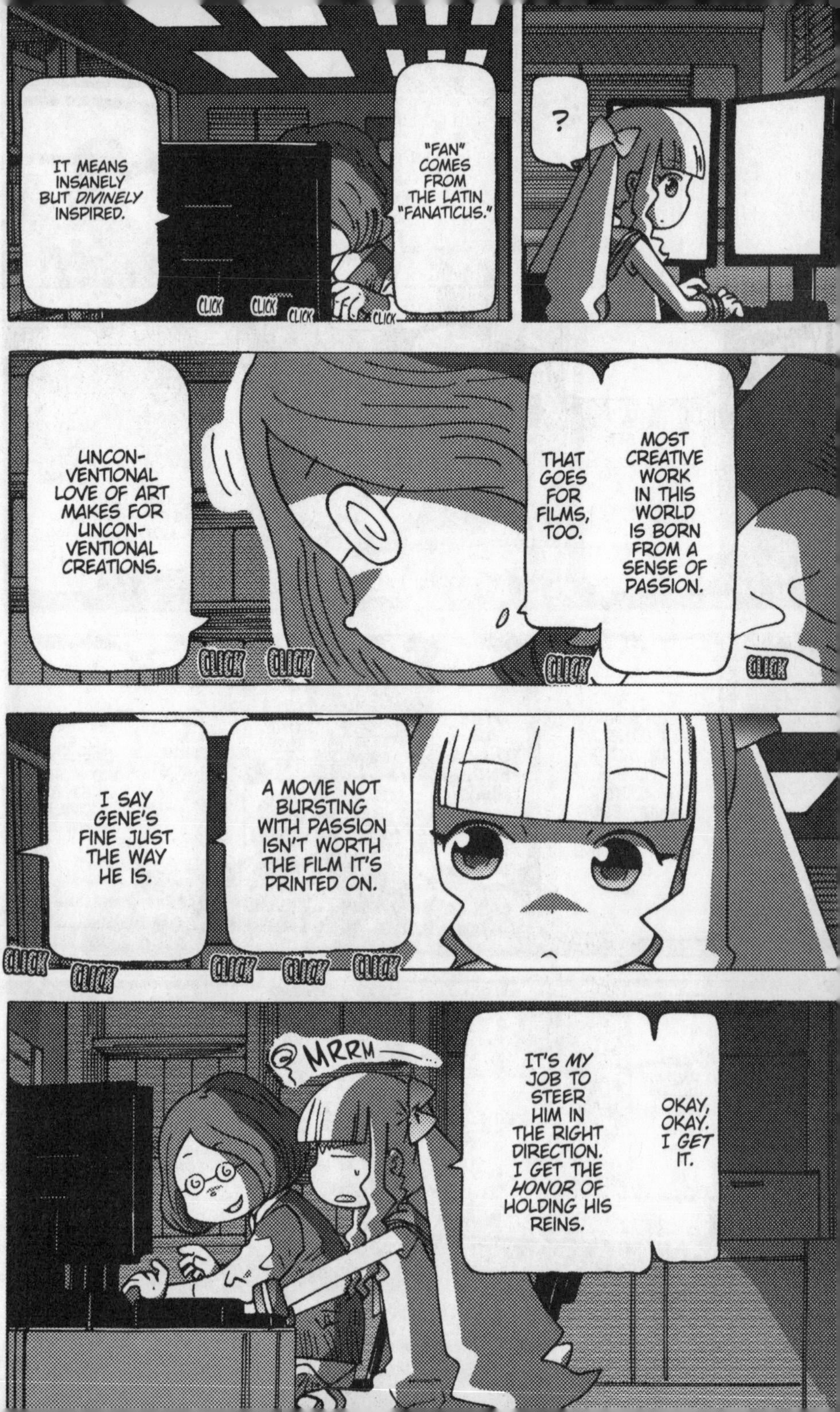
?
"FAN" COMES FROM THE LATIN "FANATICUS."
IT MEANS INSANELY BUT *DIVINELY* INSPIRED.
CLICK
CLICK
CLICK
CLICK
MOST CREATIVE WORK IN THIS WORLD IS BORN FROM A SENSE OF PASSION.
THAT GOES FOR FILMS, TOO.
UNCON-VENTIONAL LOVE OF ART MAKES FOR UNCON-VENTIONAL CREATIONS.
CLICK
CLICK
CLICK
CLICK
A MOVIE NOT BURSTING WITH PASSION ISN'T WORTH THE FILM IT'S PRINTED ON.
I SAY GENE'S FINE JUST THE WAY HE IS.
CLICK
CLICK
CLICK
CLICK
CLICK
OKAY, OKAY. I *GET* IT.
IT'S *MY* JOB TO STEER HIM IN THE RIGHT DIRECTION. I GET THE *HONOR* OF HOLDING HIS REINS.
MRRM

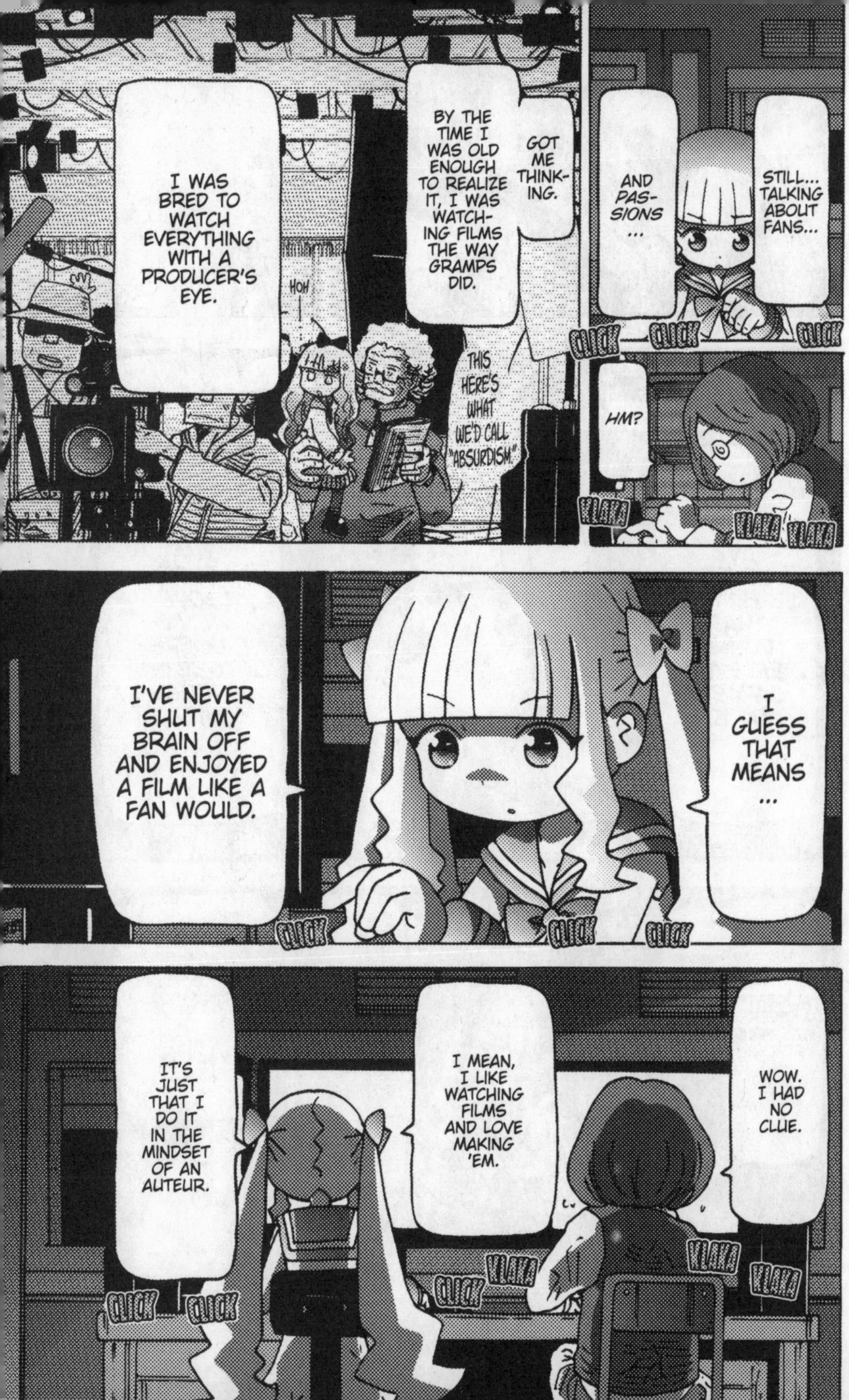
STILL... TALKING ABOUT FANS...
AND PASSIONS...
CLICK
CLICK
CLICK
HM?
KLAKA
KLAKA
KLAKA
GOT ME THINKING.
BY THE TIME I WAS OLD ENOUGH TO REALIZE IT, I WAS WATCHING FILMS THE WAY GRAMPS DID.
I WAS BRED TO WATCH EVERYTHING WITH A PRODUCER'S EYE.
THIS HERE'S WHAT WE'D CALL "ABSURDISM."
HOH
I GUESS THAT MEANS...
I'VE NEVER SHUT MY BRAIN OFF AND ENJOYED A FILM LIKE A FAN WOULD.
CLICK
CLICK
CLICK
WOW. I HAD NO CLUE.
I MEAN, I LIKE WATCHING FILMS AND LOVE MAKING 'EM.
IT'S JUST THAT I DO IT IN THE MINDSET OF AN AUTEUR.
KLAKA
KLAKA
KLAKA
CLICK
CLICK
CLICK

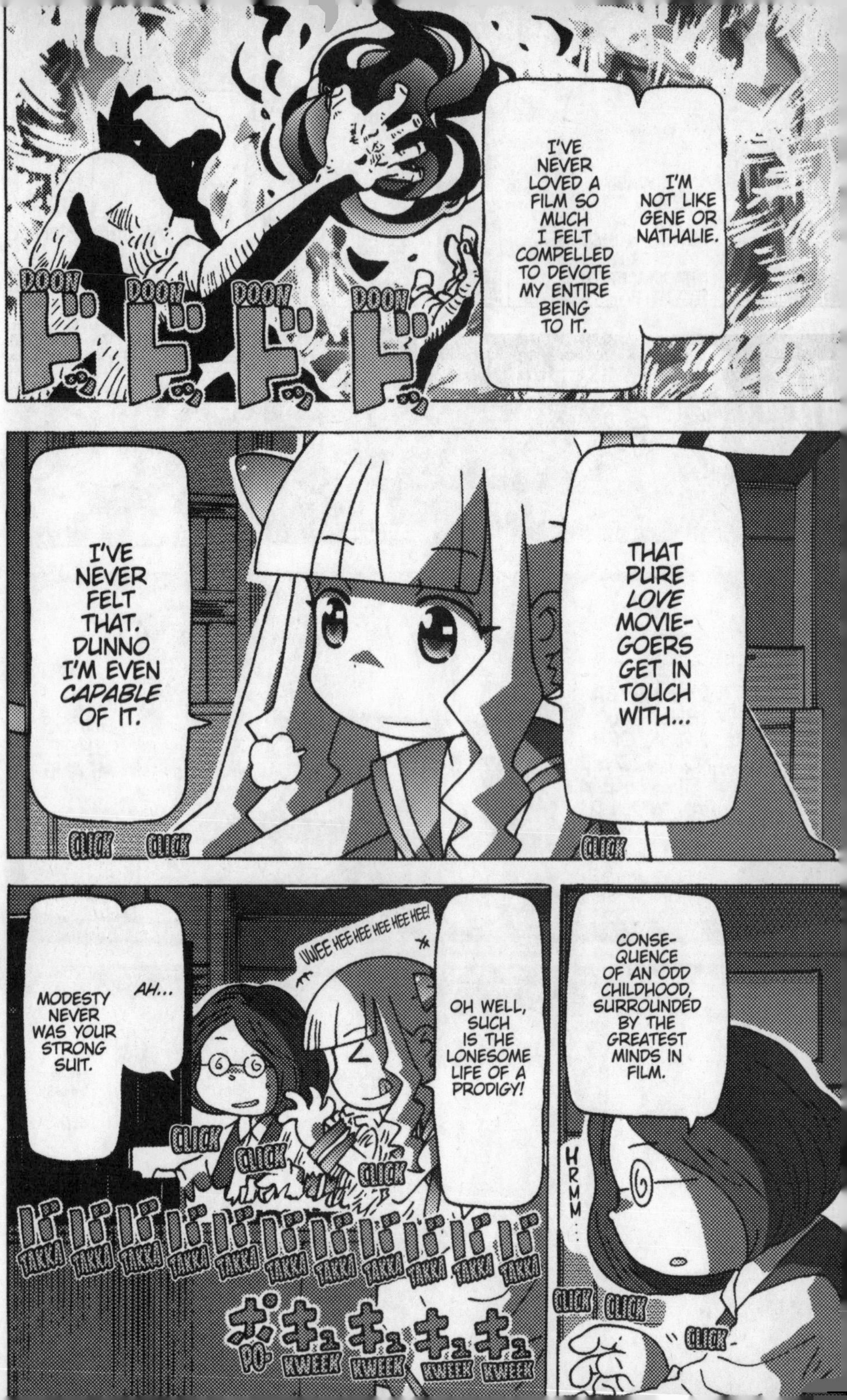
I'M NOT LIKE GENE OR NATHALIE.
I'VE NEVER LOVED A FILM SO MUCH I FELT COMPELLED TO DEVOTE MY ENTIRE BEING TO IT.
DOON DOON DOON DOON
THAT PURE *LOVE* MOVIEGOERS GET IN TOUCH WITH...
I'VE NEVER FELT THAT. DUNNO I'M EVEN *CAPABLE* OF IT.
CLICK CLICK CLICK
CONSEQUENCE OF AN ODD CHILDHOOD, SURROUNDED BY THE GREATEST MINDS IN FILM.
HRMM...
CLICK CLICK CLICK
OH WELL, SUCH IS THE LONESOME LIFE OF A PRODIGY!
UWEE HEE HEE HEE HEE HEE!
AH...
MODESTY NEVER WAS YOUR STRONG SUIT.
CLICK CLICK CLICK
TAKKA TAKKA TAKKA TAKKA TAKKA TAKKA TAKKA TAKKA TAKKA TAKKA TAKKA
PO- KWEEK KWEEK KWEEK KWEEK

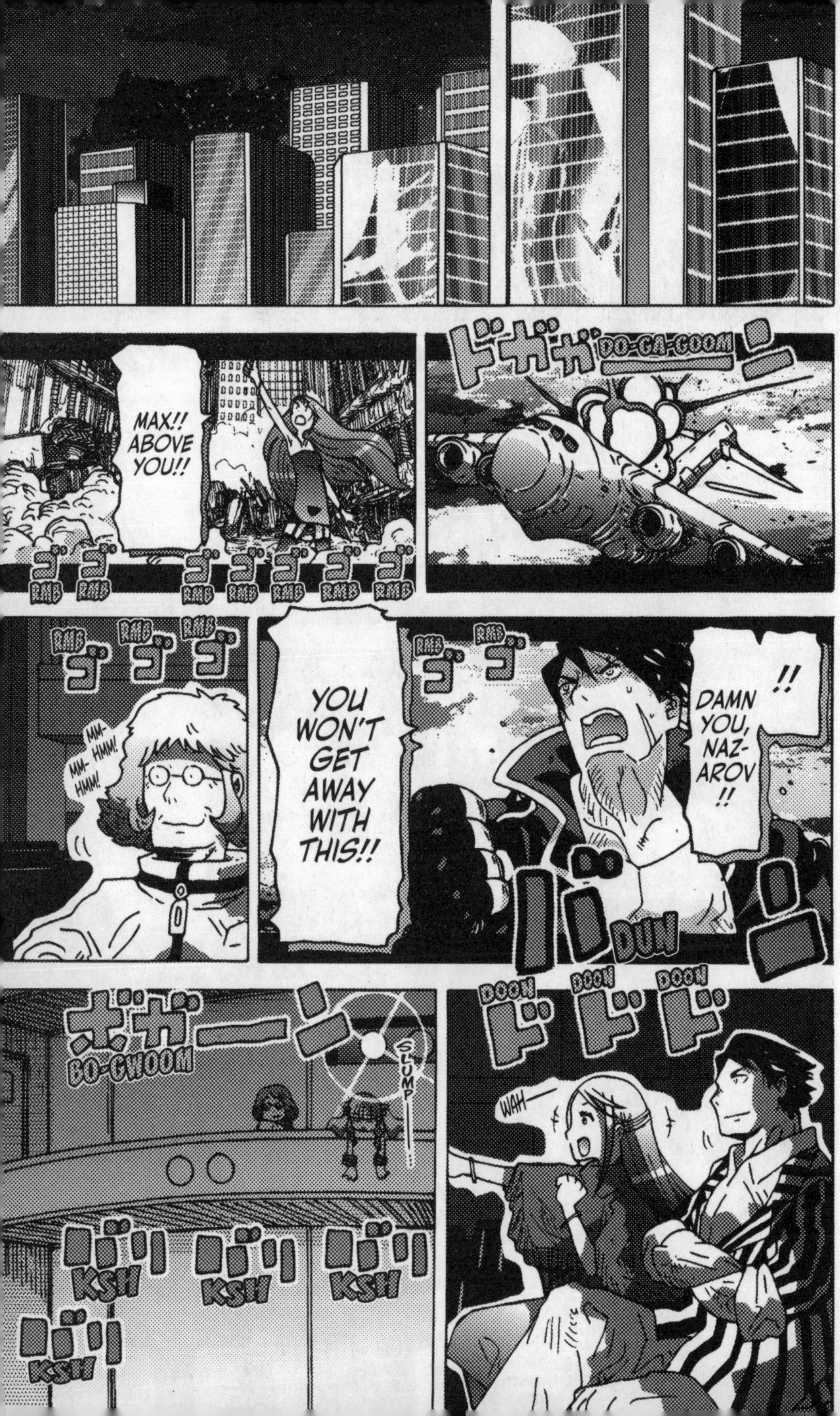

ドガガ DO-GA-GOOM ン
MAX!! ABOVE YOU!!
ゴゴ RMB RMB
ゴゴゴゴゴ RMB RMB RMB RMB RMB
ゴゴ RMB RMB
!!
DAMN YOU, NAZAROV!!
ド DO DUN ン
YOU WON'T GET AWAY WITH THIS!!
ゴゴゴ RMB RMB RMB
MM-HMM! MM-HMM!
ドドド DOON DOON DOON
WAH—
ボガーン BO-GWOOM
SLUMP
バリ KSH
バリ KSH
バリ KSH
バリ KSH

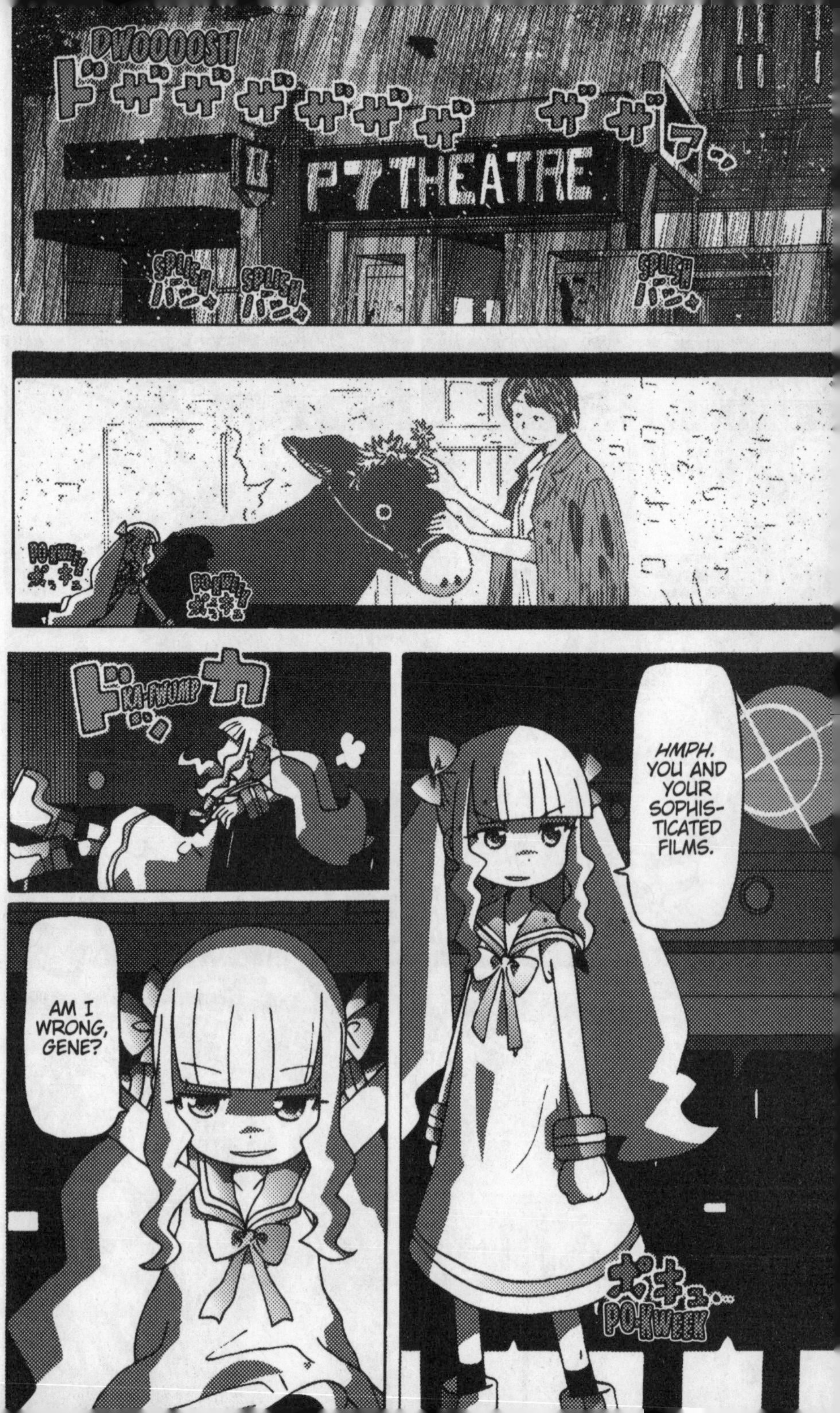

DWOOOOOSH
P7 THEATRE
SPLISH
SPLISH
SPLISH
PO-KWEEK
PO-KWEEK
HMPH. YOU AND YOUR SOPHISTICATED FILMS.
PO-KWEEK
KA-FWOMP
AM I WRONG, GENE?

HEH ...
HEH HEH HEH ...
SKRCH SKRCH...
WH...
WHAT HAP-PENED WITH MAX STORM?
CORVETTE MANAGED TO PULL A MIRACLE OFF.
I DON'T THINK I'LL EVER BE ABLE TO THANK HIM ENOUGH.
TH... THAT'S GOOD.
......
LOOK ...
I CAN ACCEPT THAT A TINY PART OF THIS IS MY BAD, PUSHING YOU INTO A PROJECT BEYOND YOUR COMFORT ZONE.

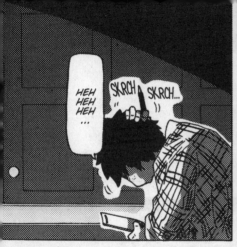

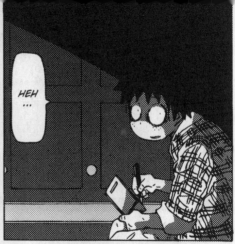

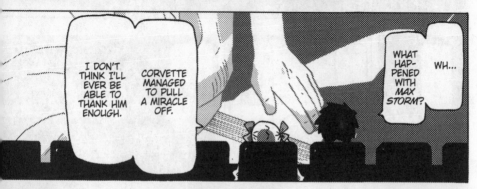

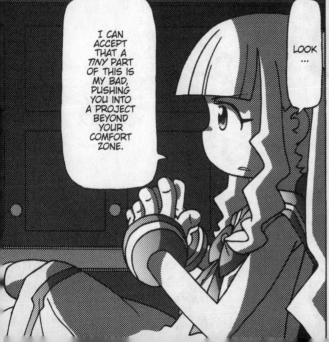

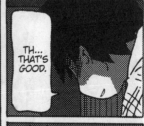

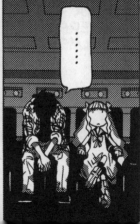

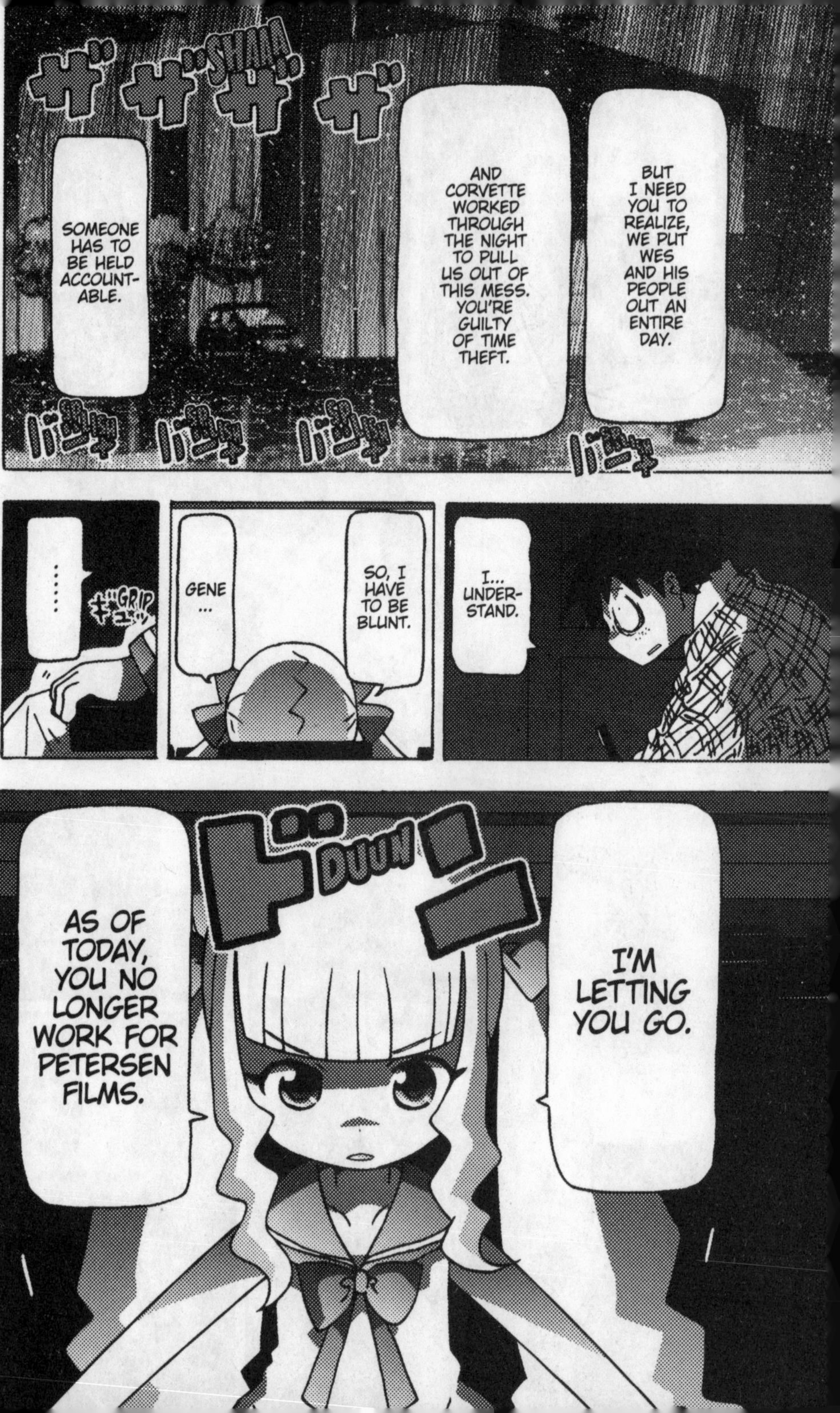
SHAA
BUT I NEED YOU TO REALIZE, WE PUT WES AND HIS PEOPLE OUT AN ENTIRE DAY.
AND CORVETTE WORKED THROUGH THE NIGHT TO PULL US OUT OF THIS MESS. YOU'RE GUILTY OF TIME THEFT.
SOMEONE HAS TO BE HELD ACCOUNTABLE.
I... UNDERSTAND.
SO, I HAVE TO BE BLUNT.
GENE...
GRIP
......
I'M LETTING YOU GO.
DUUN
AS OF TODAY, YOU NO LONGER WORK FOR PETERSEN FILMS.

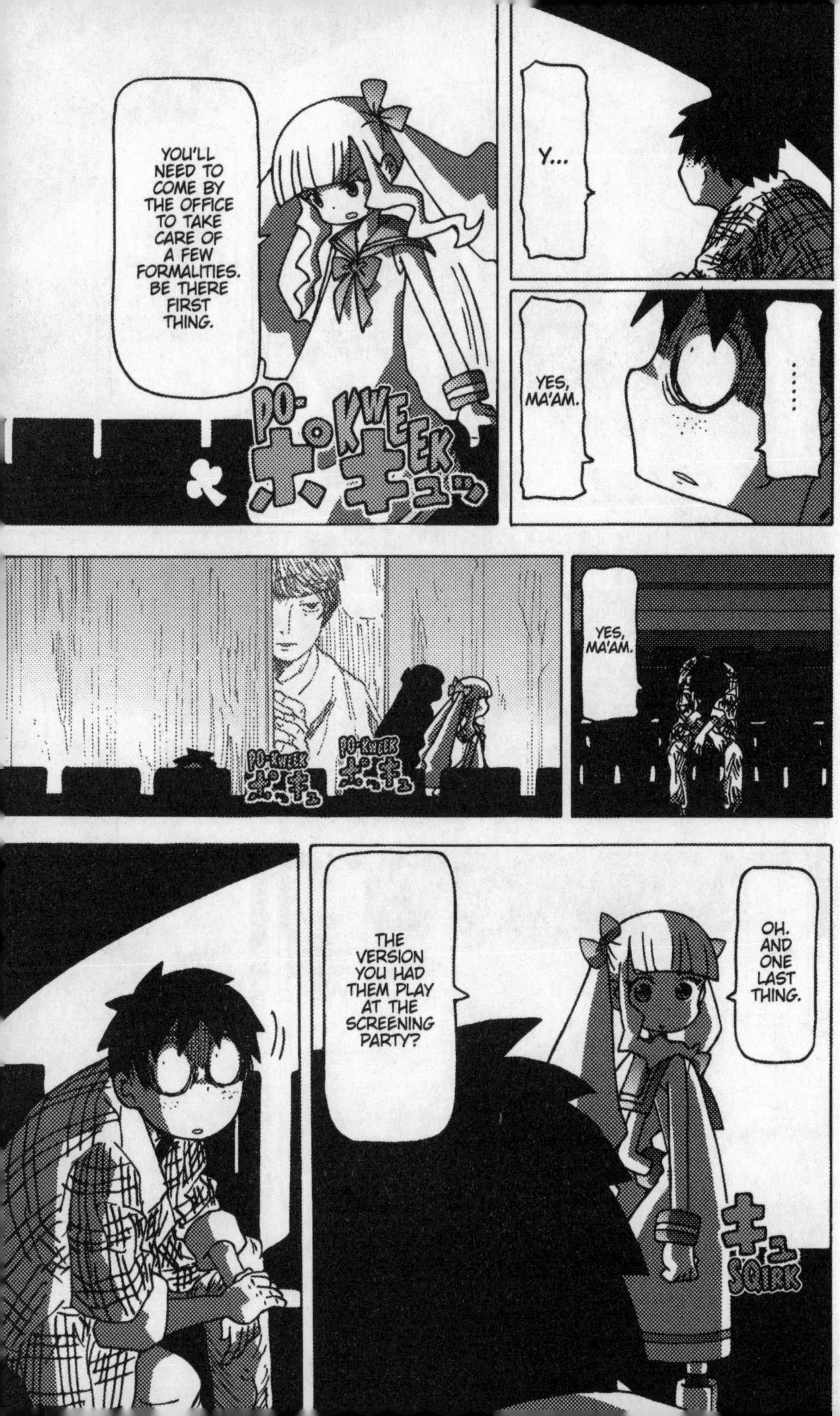
Y...
YES, MA'AM.
......
YOU'LL NEED TO COME BY THE OFFICE TO TAKE CARE OF A FEW FORMALITIES. BE THERE FIRST THING.
PO-KWEEK
YES, MA'AM.
PO-KWEEK
PO-KWEEK
OH. AND ONE LAST THING.
THE VERSION YOU HAD THEM PLAY AT THE SCREENING PARTY?
SQIRK

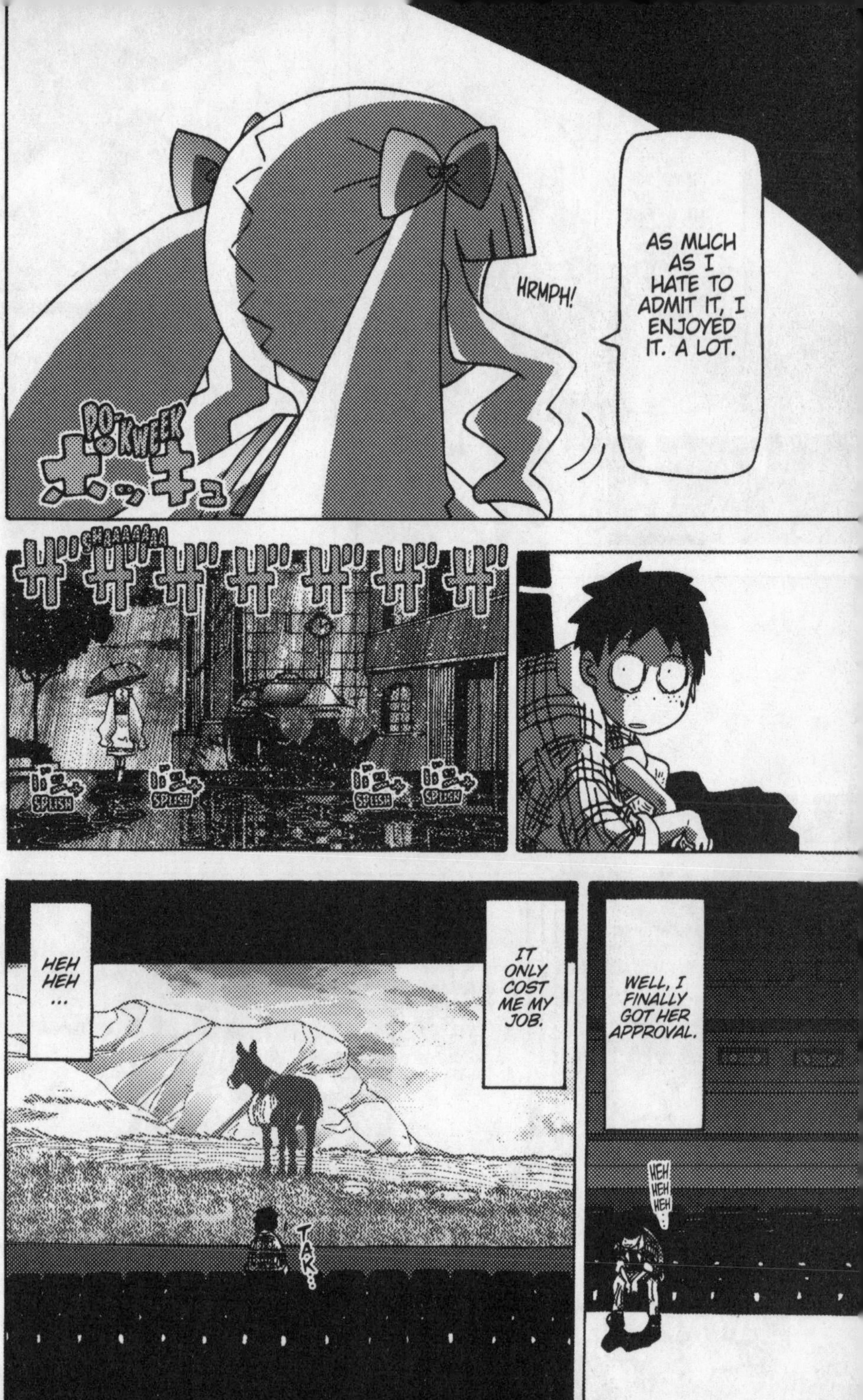
AS MUCH AS I HATE TO ADMIT IT, I ENJOYED IT. A LOT.
HRMPH!
PO-KWEEK
SHAAAAAAA
SPLISH
SPLISH
SPLISH
SPLISH
WELL, I FINALLY GOT HER APPROVAL.
HEH HEH HEH...
IT ONLY COST ME MY JOB.
HEH HEH ...
TAK..

POMPO
THE CINÉPHILE

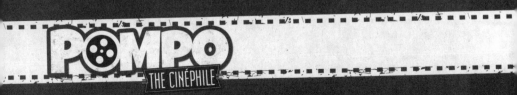

POMPO
THE CINÉPHILE

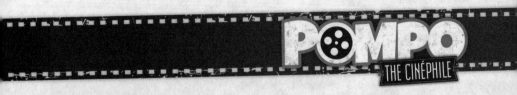

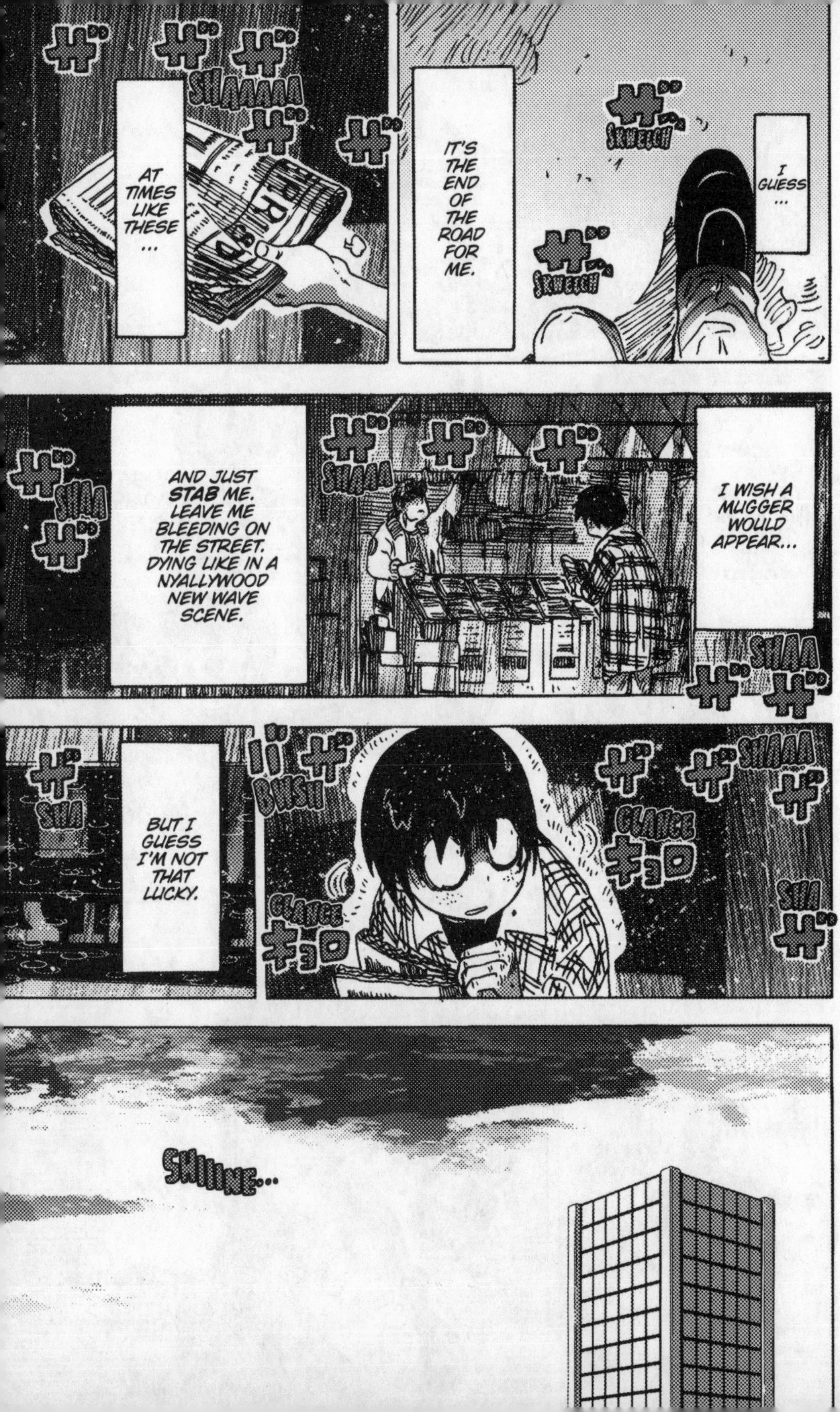

SKWETCH
SKWETCH
I GUESS ...
IT'S THE END OF THE ROAD FOR ME.
SHAAAAA
AT TIMES LIKE THESE ...
SHAA
I WISH A MUGGER WOULD APPEAR...
SHAAA
AND JUST STAB ME. LEAVE ME BLEEDING ON THE STREET. DYING LIKE IN A NYALLYWOOD NEW WAVE SCENE.
SHAA
SHAAA
SHA
GLANCE
BWSH
GLANCE
SHA
BUT I GUESS I'M NOT THAT LUCKY.
SHIINE...

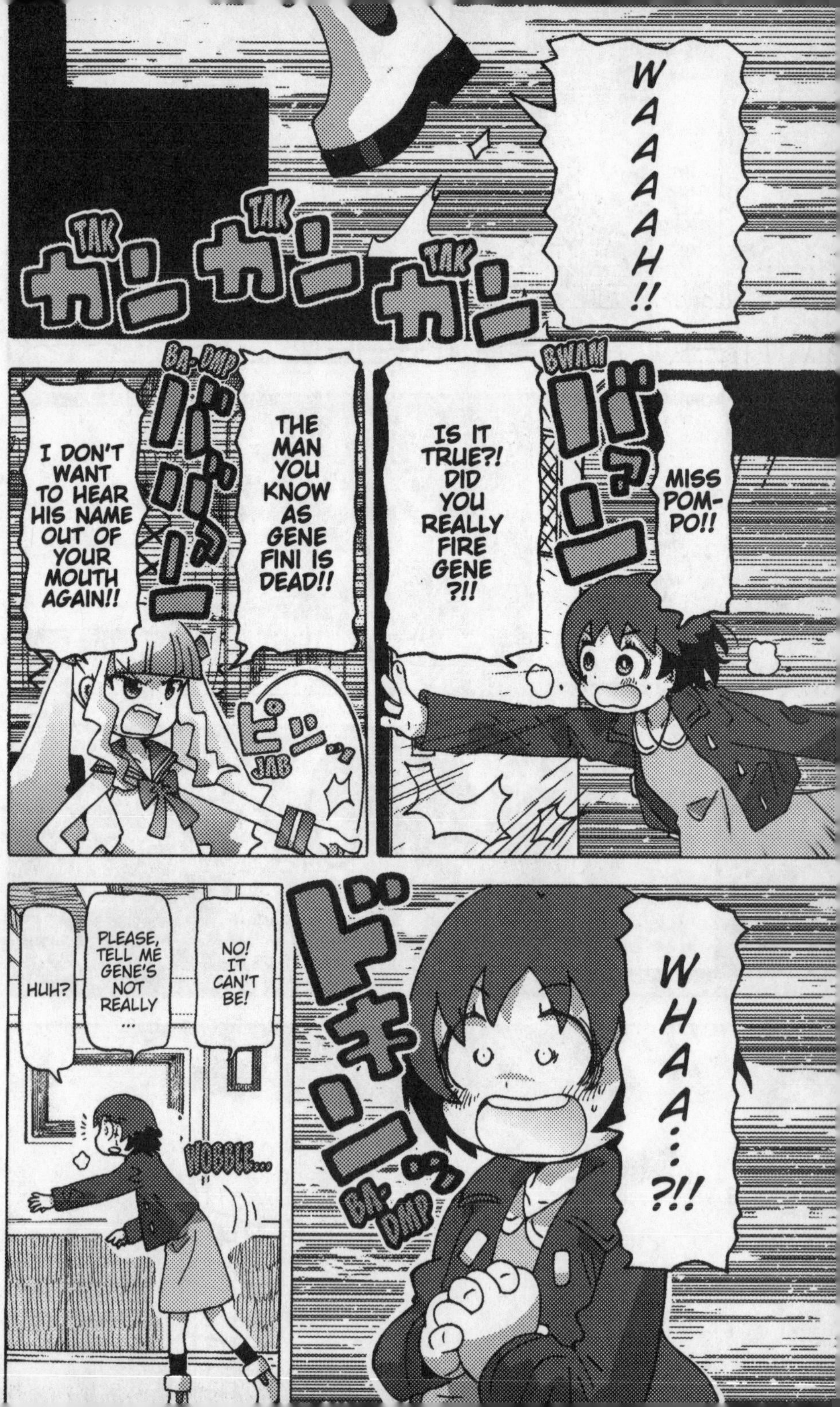
WAAAAAH!!
TAK
TAK
TAK
BWAM
MISS POM-PO!!
IS IT TRUE?! DID YOU REALLY FIRE GENE?!!
BA-DMP
THE MAN YOU KNOW AS GENE FINI IS DEAD!!
I DON'T WANT TO HEAR HIS NAME OUT OF YOUR MOUTH AGAIN!!
JAB
WHAA...?!!
BA-DMP
NO! IT CAN'T BE!
PLEASE, TELL ME GENE'S NOT REALLY ...
HUH?
WOBBLE...

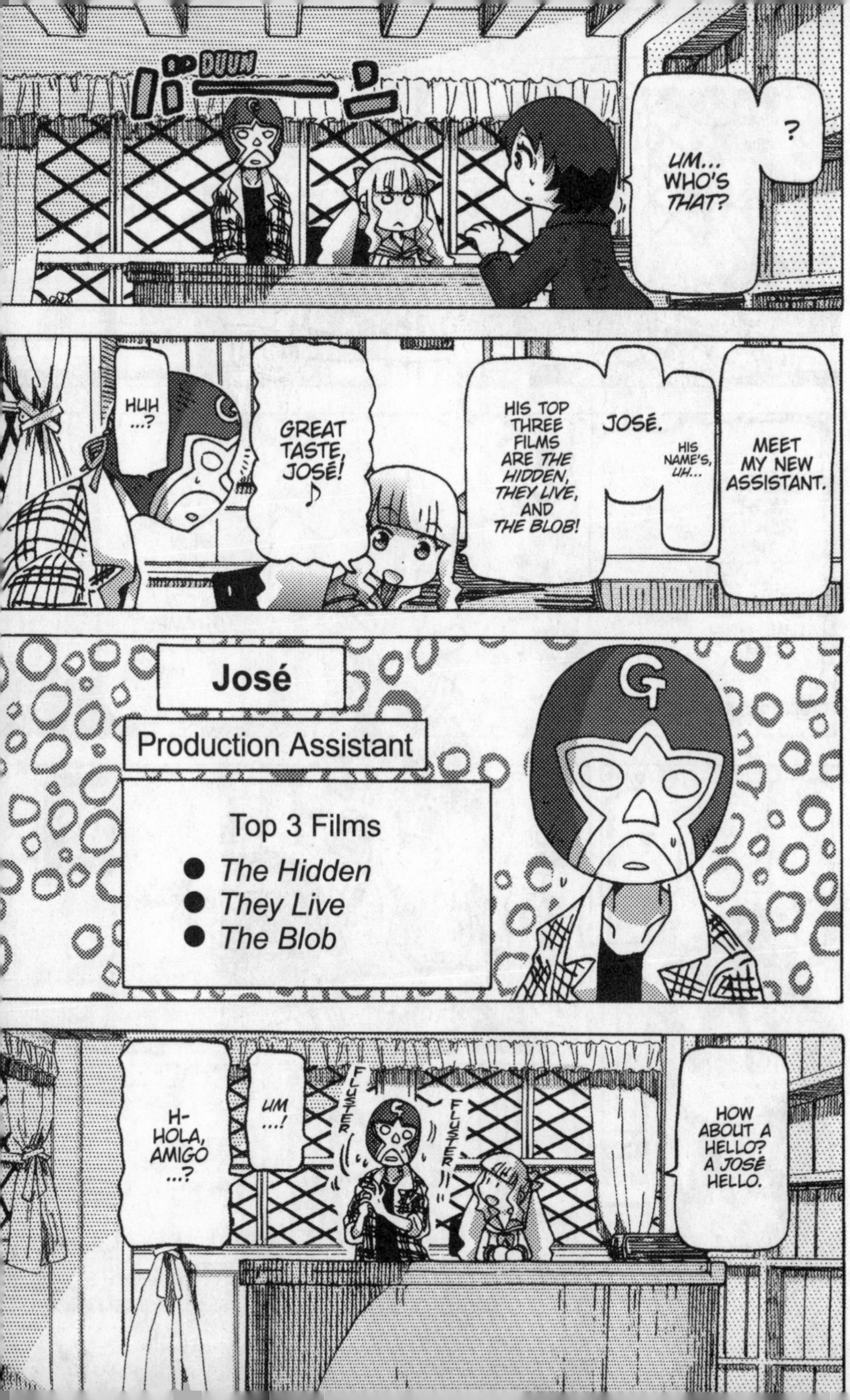
?
UM... WHO'S THAT?
BA DUUN
MEET MY NEW ASSISTANT.
HIS NAME'S, UH...
JOSÉ.
HIS TOP THREE FILMS ARE *THE HIDDEN*, *THEY LIVE*, AND *THE BLOB*!
GREAT TASTE, JOSÉ! ♪
HUH ...?
José
Production Assistant
Top 3 Films
● *The Hidden*
● *They Live*
● *The Blob*
HOW ABOUT A HELLO? A *JOSÉ* HELLO.
FLUSTER
FLUSTER
UM ...!
H-HOLA, AMIGO ...?

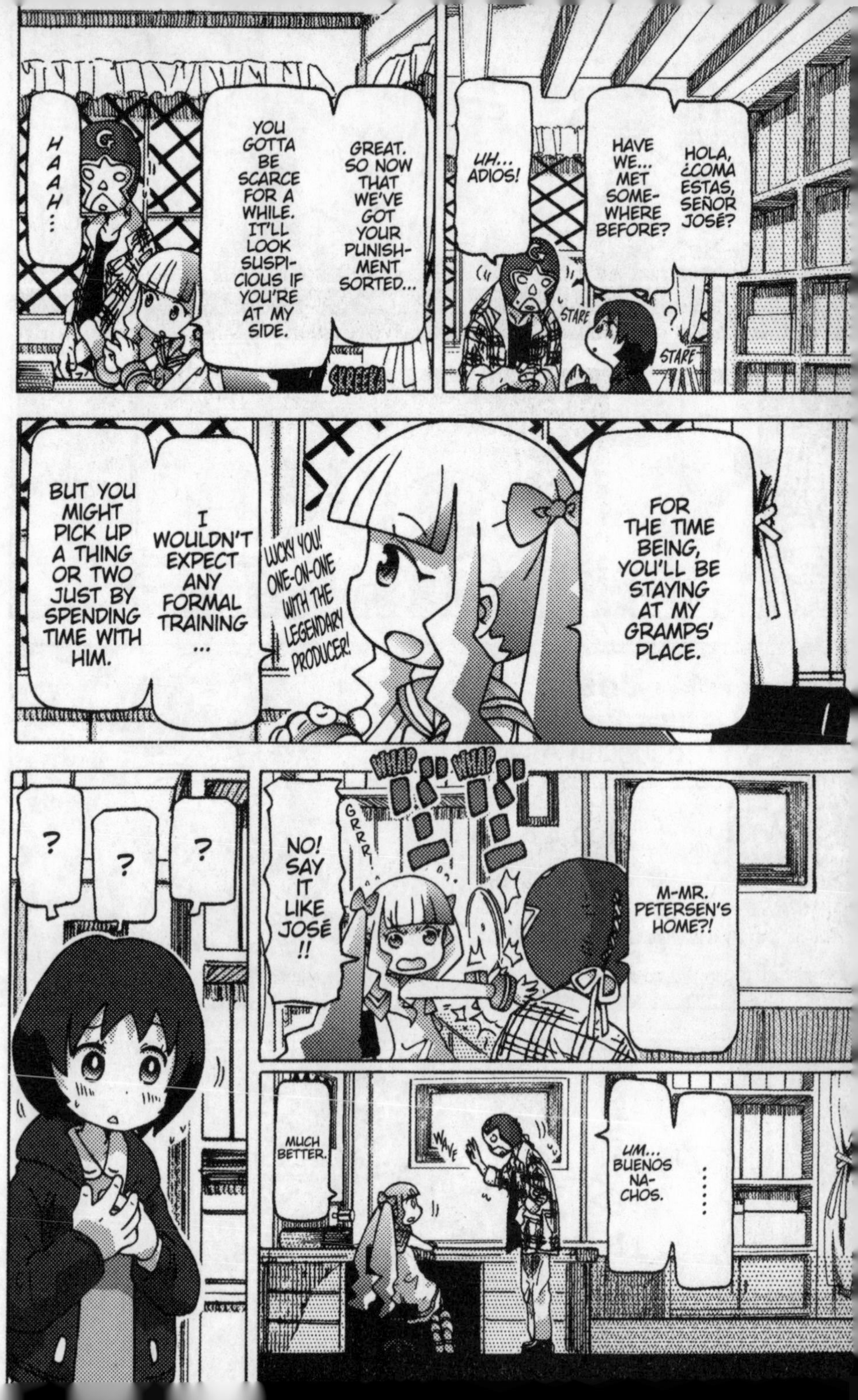
HOLA, ¿COMA ESTAS, SEÑOR JOSÉ?
HAVE WE... MET SOME-WHERE BEFORE?
STARE
STARE
UH... ADIOS!
GREAT. SO NOW THAT WE'VE GOT YOUR PUNISH-MENT SORTED...
YOU GOTTA BE SCARCE FOR A WHILE. IT'LL LOOK SUSPI-CIOUS IF YOU'RE AT MY SIDE.
HAAH...
FOR THE TIME BEING, YOU'LL BE STAYING AT MY GRAMPS' PLACE.
LUCKY YOU! ONE-ON-ONE WITH THE LEGENDARY PRODUCER!
I WOULDN'T EXPECT ANY FORMAL TRAINING ...
BUT YOU MIGHT PICK UP A THING OR TWO JUST BY SPENDING TIME WITH HIM.
M-MR. PETERSEN'S HOME?!
WHAP WHAP
GRRR!
NO! SAY IT LIKE JOSÉ !!
UM... BUENOS NA-CHOS.
......
MUCH BETTER.
?
?
?

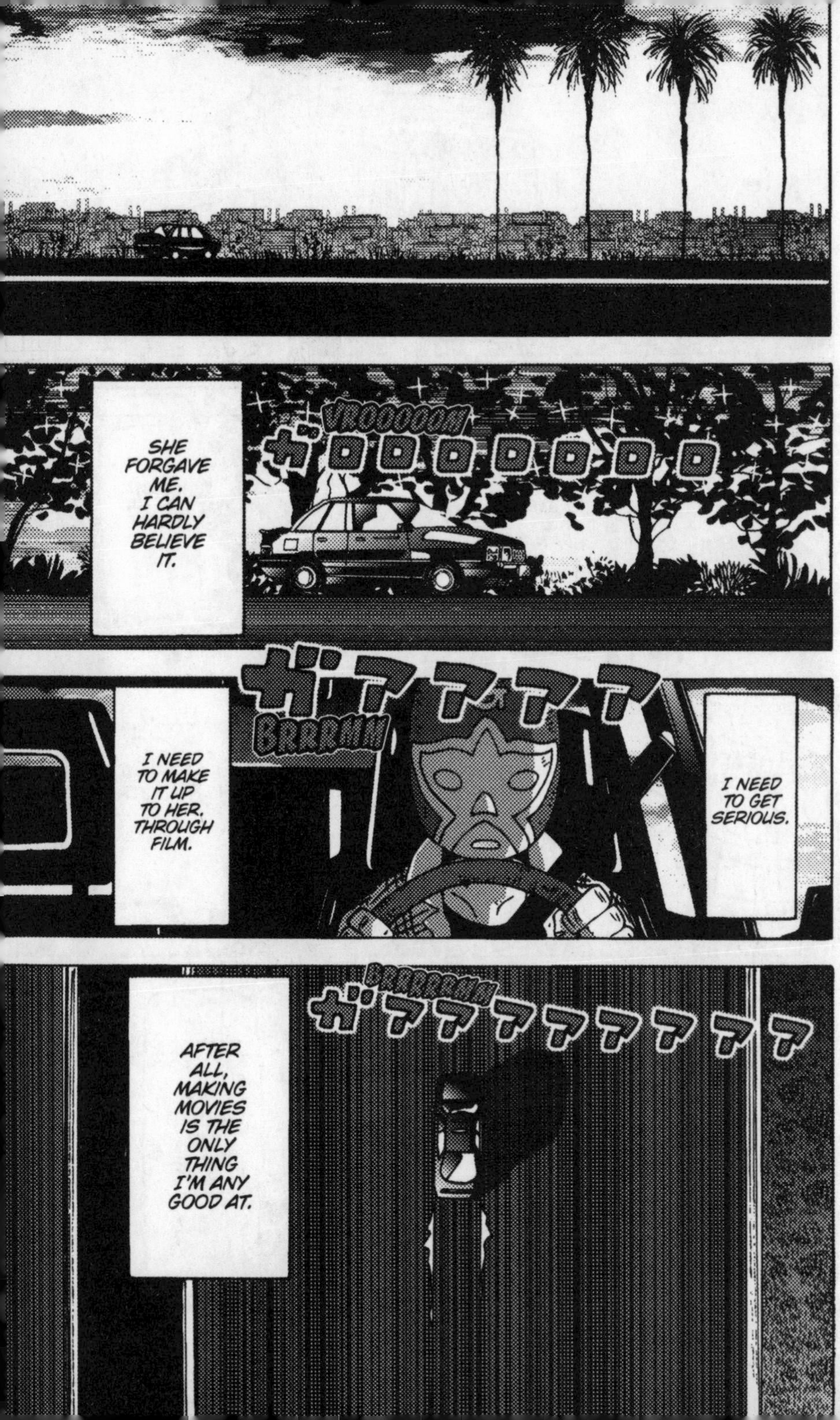
VROOOOOM
SHE FORGAVE ME. I CAN HARDLY BELIEVE IT.
I NEED TO GET SERIOUS.
BRRRMM
I NEED TO MAKE IT UP TO HER. THROUGH FILM.
BRRRRRMM
AFTER ALL, MAKING MOVIES IS THE ONLY THING I'M ANY GOOD AT.

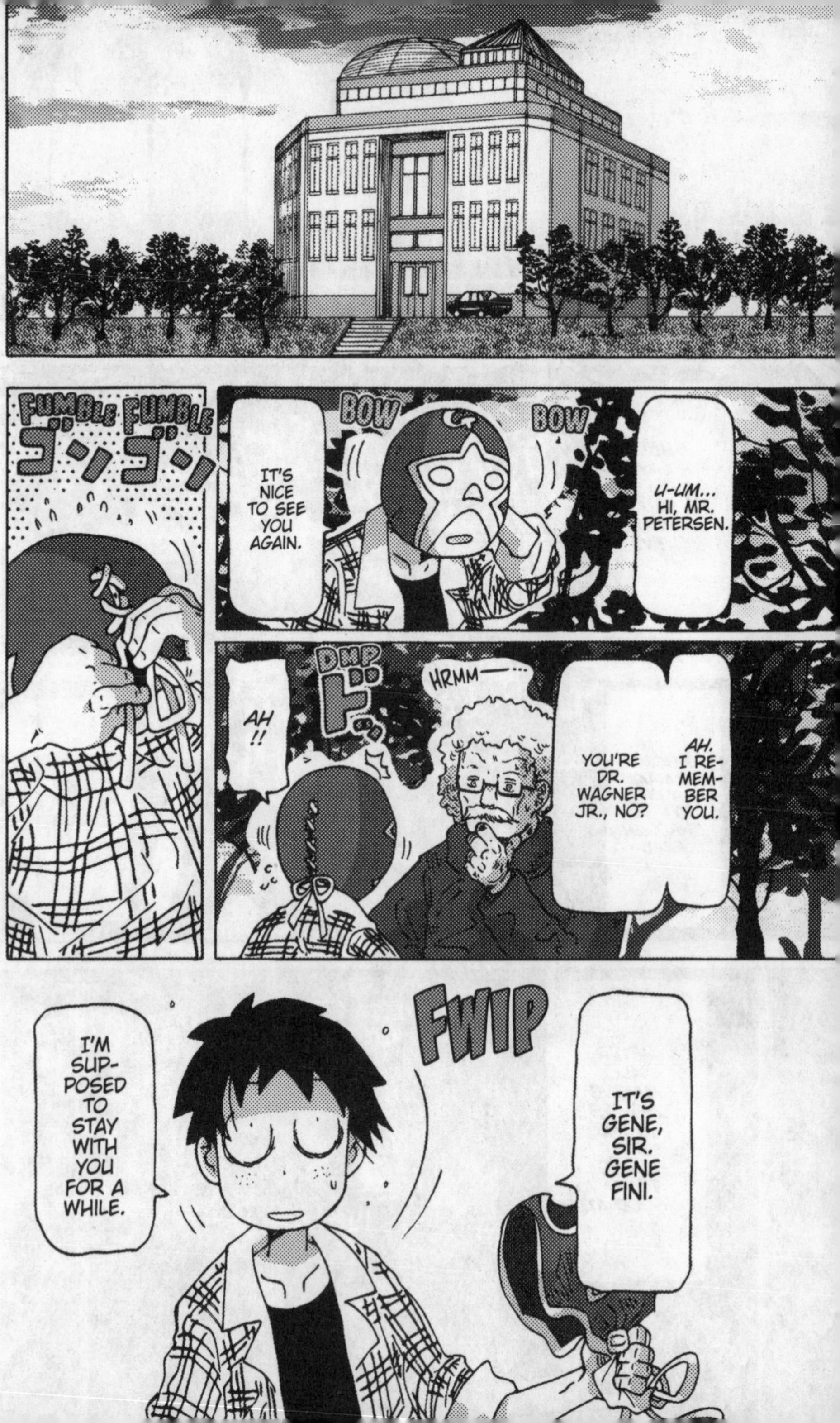
BOW
BOW
U-UM... HI, MR. PETERSEN.
IT'S NICE TO SEE YOU AGAIN.
HRMM——
AH. I RE-MEMBER YOU.
YOU'RE DR. WAGNER JR., NO?
DHP
AH!!
FUMBLE FUMBLE
IT'S GENE, SIR. GENE FINI.
FWIP
I'M SUP-POSED TO STAY WITH YOU FOR A WHILE.

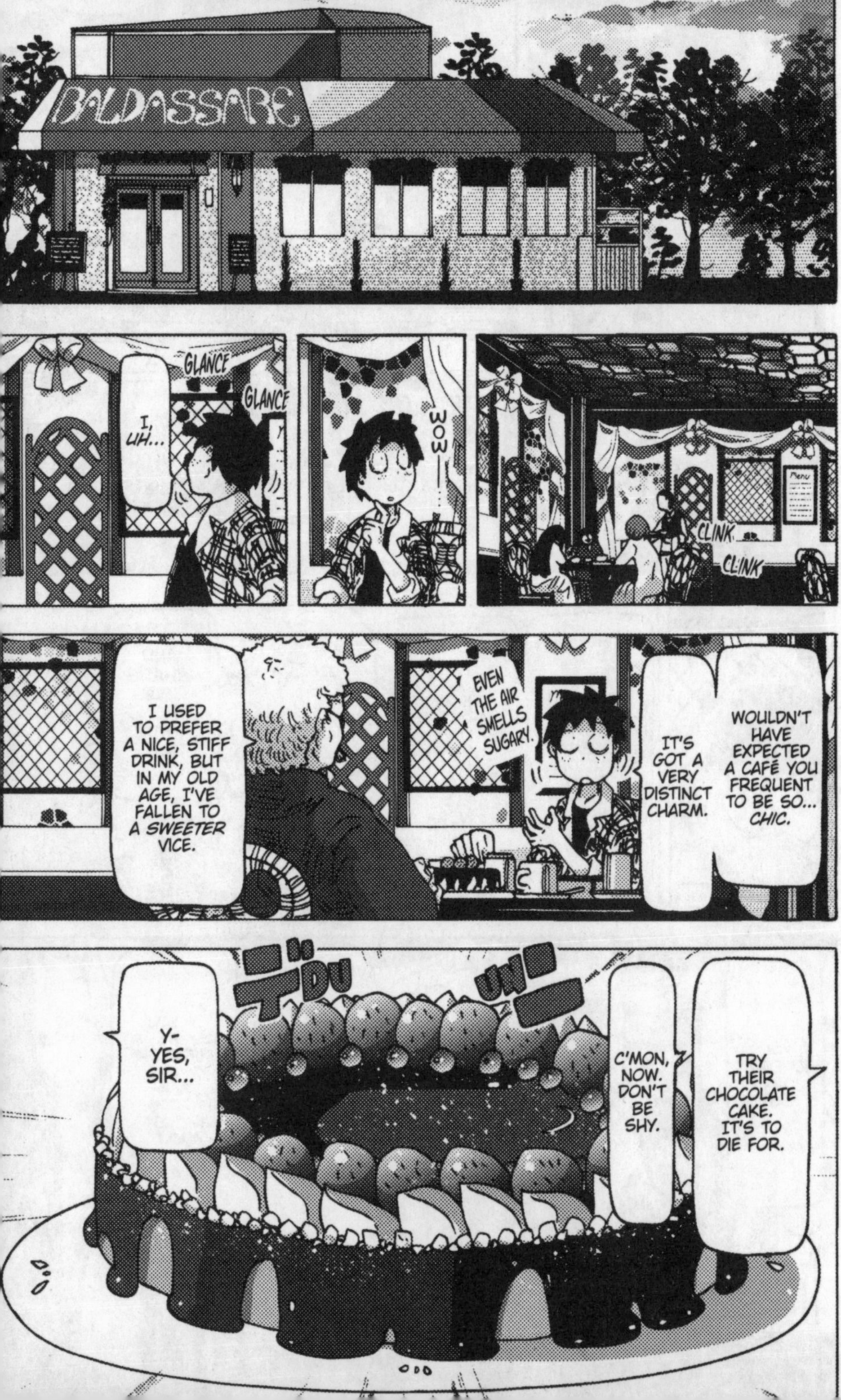
BALDASSARE
CLINK
CLINK
WOW...
GLANCE
GLANCE
I, UH...
WOULDN'T HAVE EXPECTED A CAFÉ YOU FREQUENT TO BE SO... *CHIC.*
IT'S GOT A VERY DISTINCT CHARM.
EVEN THE AIR SMELLS SUGARY.
I USED TO PREFER A NICE, STIFF DRINK, BUT IN MY OLD AGE, I'VE FALLEN TO A *SWEETER* VICE.
TRY THEIR CHOCOLATE CAKE. IT'S TO DIE FOR.
C'MON, NOW. DON'T BE SHY.
DU
UN
Y-YES, SIR...

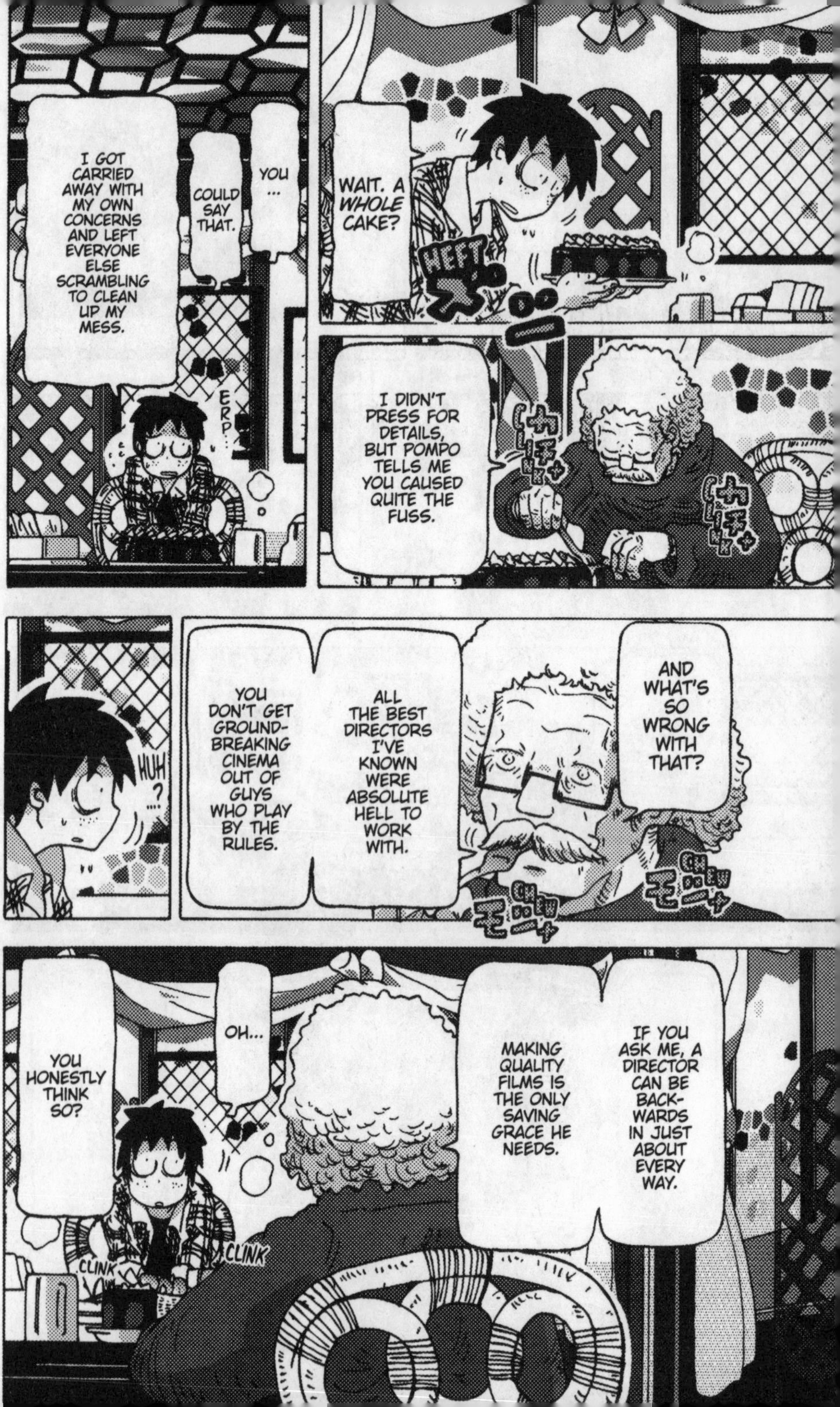
WAIT. A *WHOLE* CAKE?
HEFT
I DIDN'T PRESS FOR DETAILS, BUT POMPO TELLS ME YOU CAUSED QUITE THE FUSS.
YOU ...
COULD SAY THAT.
I GOT CARRIED AWAY WITH MY OWN CONCERNS AND LEFT EVERYONE ELSE SCRAMBLING TO CLEAN UP MY MESS.
ERP...
AND WHAT'S SO WRONG WITH THAT?
CHEW
ALL THE BEST DIRECTORS I'VE KNOWN WERE ABSOLUTE HELL TO WORK WITH.
YOU DON'T GET GROUND-BREAKING CINEMA OUT OF GUYS WHO PLAY BY THE RULES.
CHEW
HUH?
IF YOU ASK ME, A DIRECTOR CAN BE BACK-WARDS IN JUST ABOUT EVERY WAY.
MAKING QUALITY FILMS IS THE ONLY SAVING GRACE HE NEEDS.
OH...
YOU HONESTLY THINK SO?
CLINK
CLINK

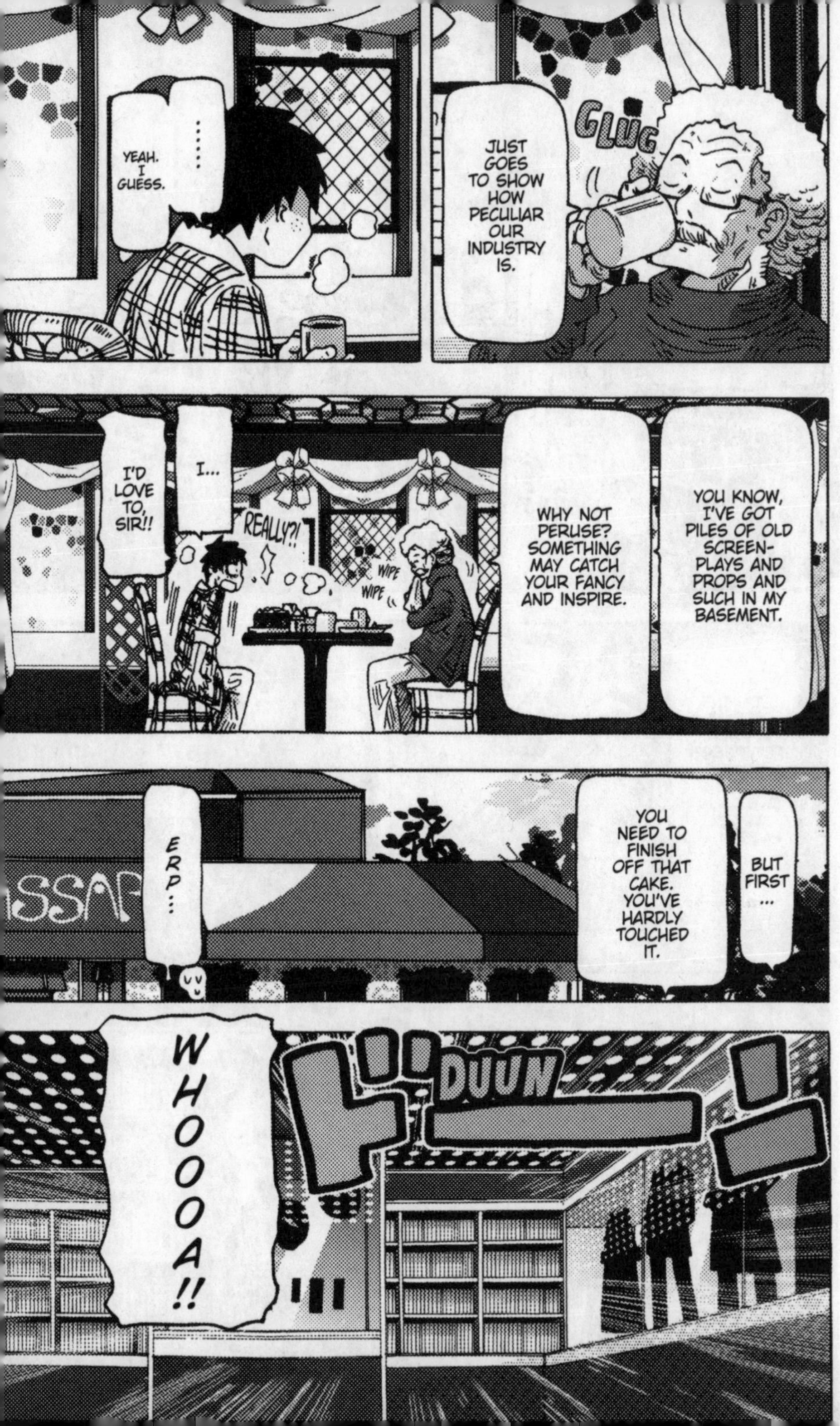
GLUG
JUST GOES TO SHOW HOW PECULIAR OUR INDUSTRY IS.
......
YEAH. I GUESS.
YOU KNOW, I'VE GOT PILES OF OLD SCREEN-PLAYS AND PROPS AND SUCH IN MY BASEMENT.
WHY NOT PERUSE? SOMETHING MAY CATCH YOUR FANCY AND INSPIRE.
WIPE WIPE
REALLY?!
I...
I'D LOVE TO, SIR!!
BUT FIRST ...
YOU NEED TO FINISH OFF THAT CAKE. YOU'VE HARDLY TOUCHED IT.
ERP...
DUUN
WHOOOA!!

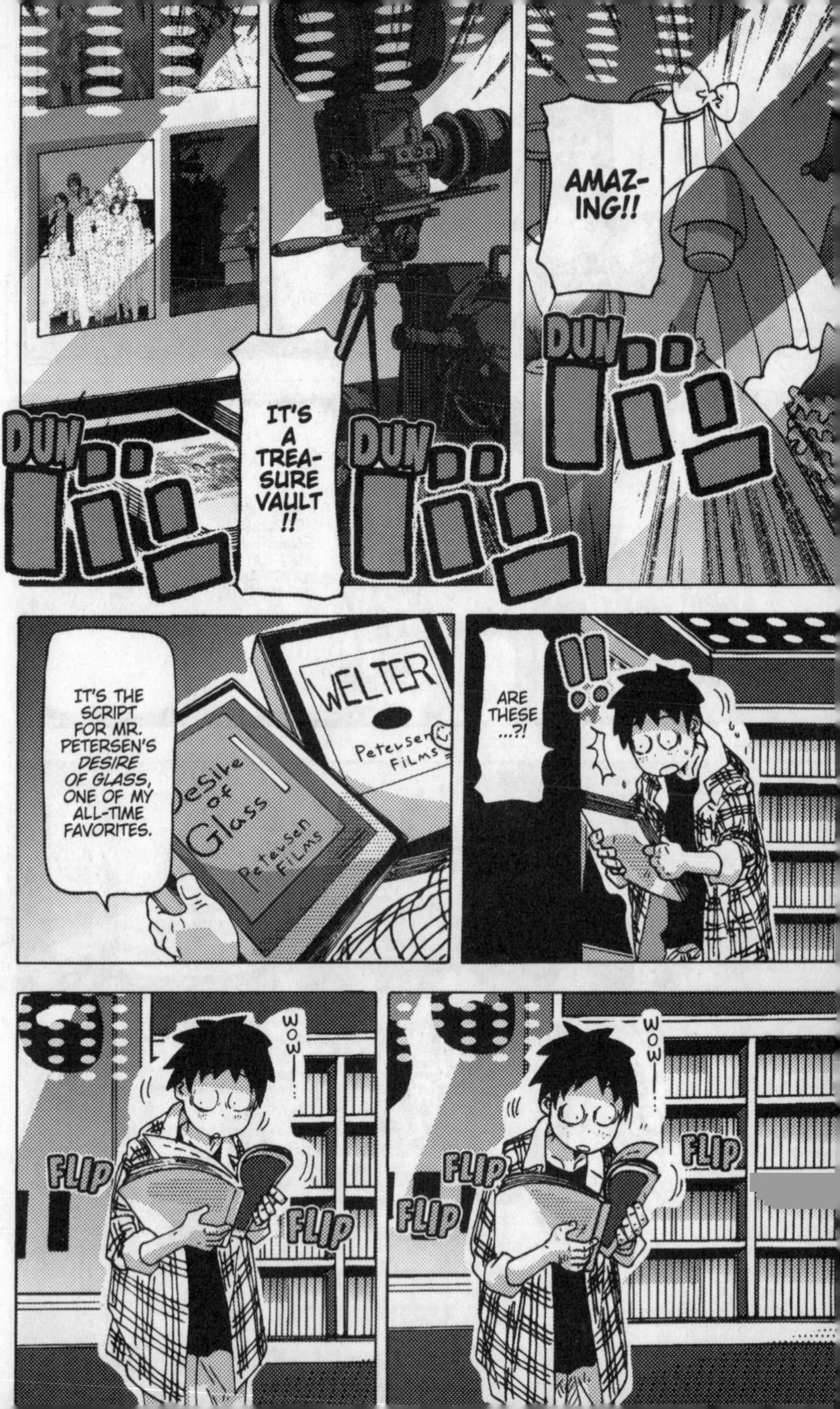
AMAZ-ING!!
DUN
DUN
IT'S A TREASURE VAULT!!
DUN
!!
ARE THESE ...?!
WELTER
Petersen Films
IT'S THE SCRIPT FOR MR. PETERSEN'S *DESIRE OF GLASS*, ONE OF MY ALL-TIME FAVORITES.
Desire of Glass
Petersen Films
WOW—...
FLIP
FLIP
FLIP
WOW—...
FLIP
FLIP

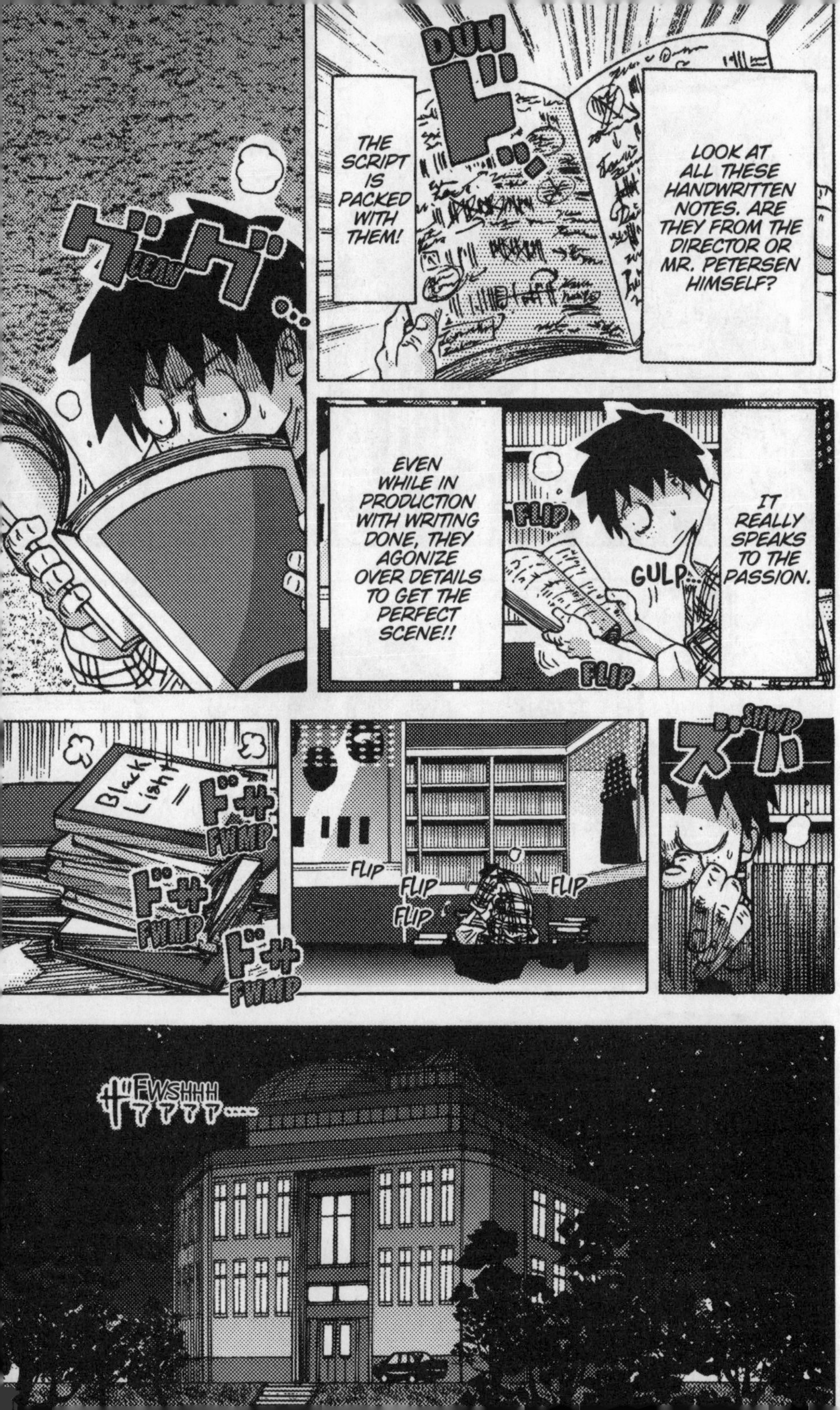

LOOK AT ALL THESE HANDWRITTEN NOTES. ARE THEY FROM THE DIRECTOR OR MR. PETERSEN HIMSELF?
DUN
THE SCRIPT IS PACKED WITH THEM!
IT REALLY SPEAKS TO THE PASSION.
GULP...
FLIP
FLIP
EVEN WHILE IN PRODUCTION WITH WRITING DONE, THEY AGONIZE OVER DETAILS TO GET THE PERFECT SCENE!!
FLIP
FLIP
FLIP
FLIP
Black Light
FWMP
FWMP
FWMP
FWSHHH...

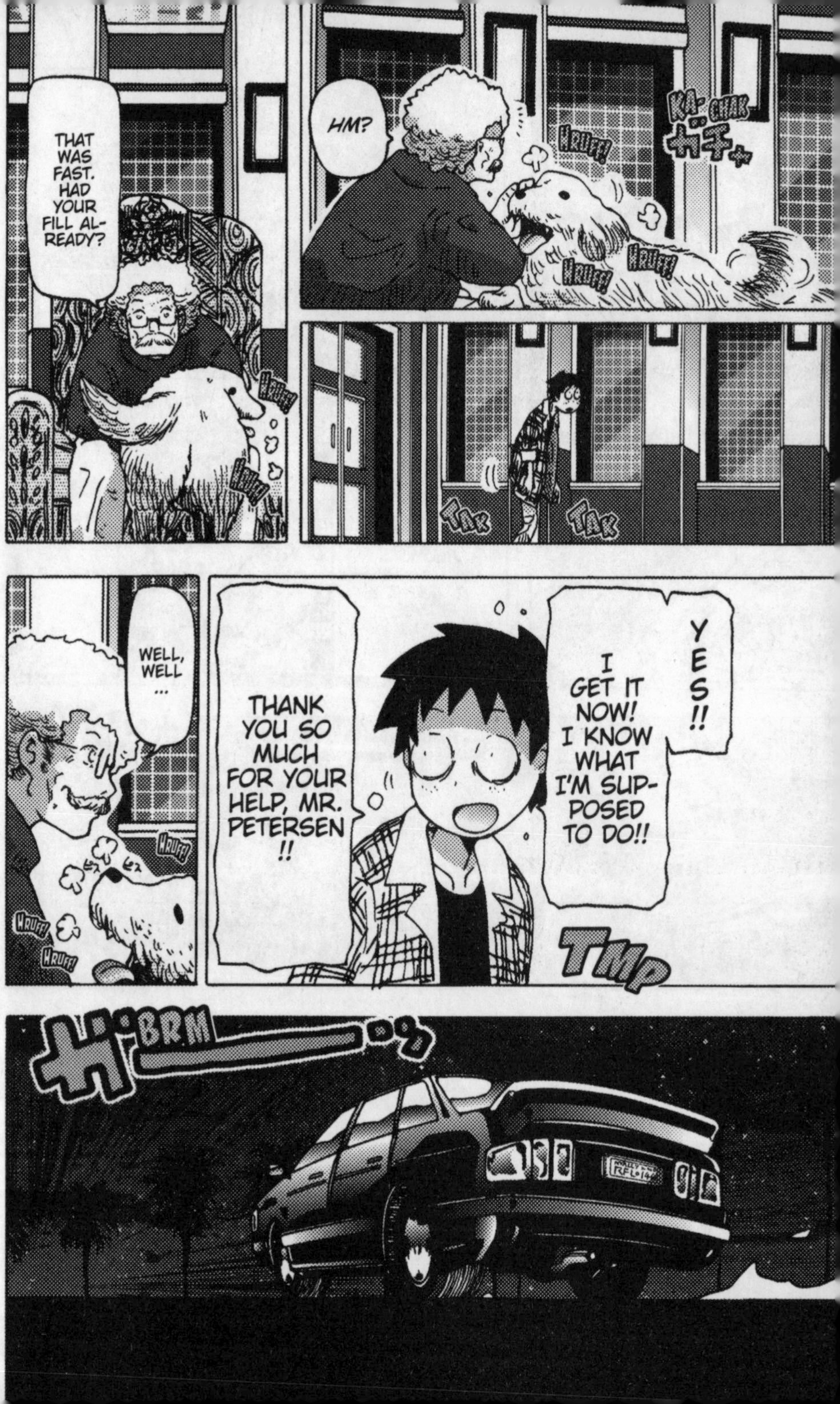
KA-CHAK
ガチャ
HM?
HRUFF!
HRUFF!
HRUFF!
TAK
TAK
THAT WAS FAST. HAD YOUR FILL AL-READY?
HRUFF
HRUFF
YES!!
I GET IT NOW! I KNOW WHAT I'M SUP-POSED TO DO!!
THANK YOU SO MUCH FOR YOUR HELP, MR. PETERSEN!!
TMP
WELL, WELL ...
HRUFF!
HRUFF!
HRUFF!
BRM

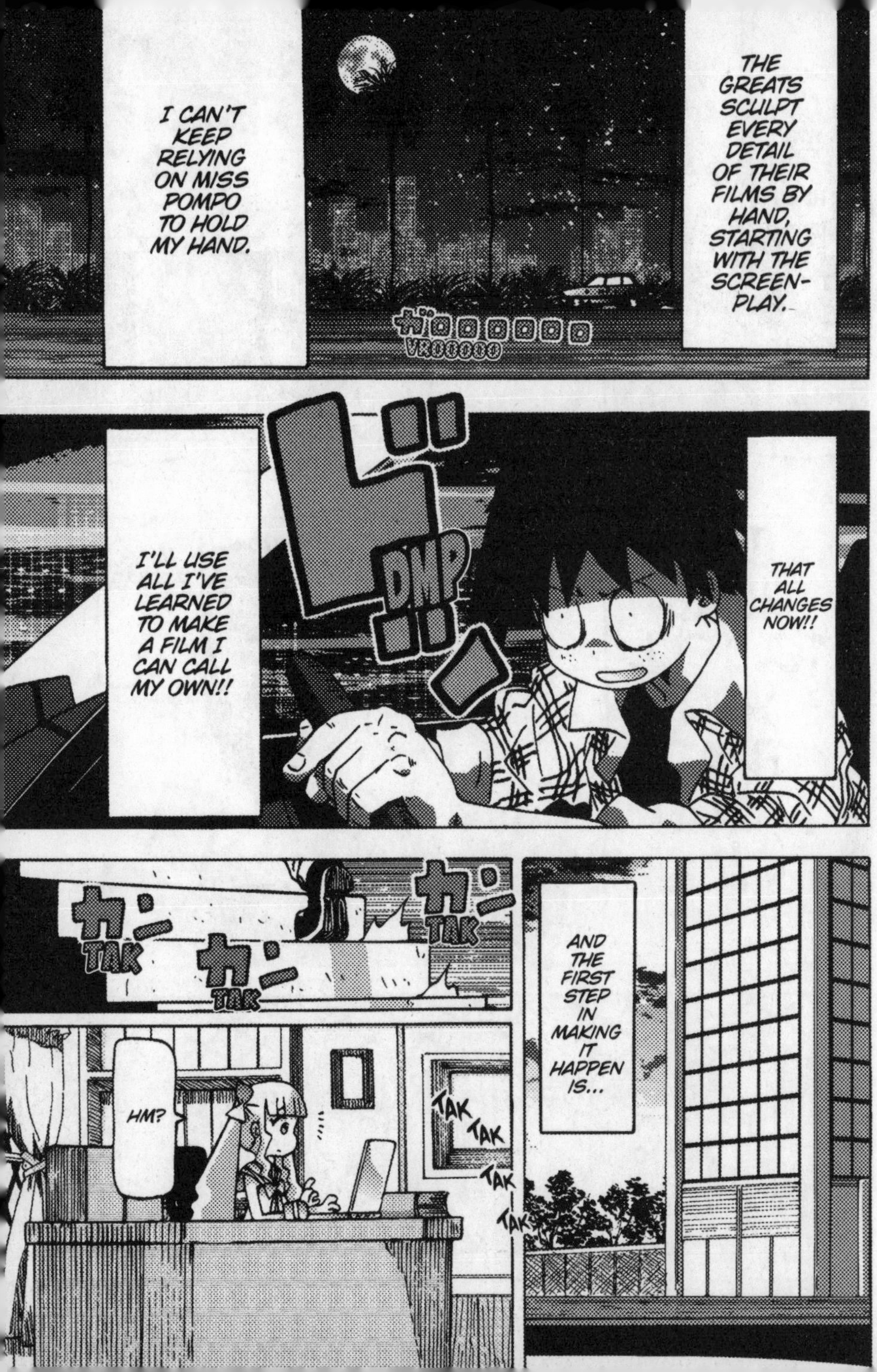
THE GREATS SCULPT EVERY DETAIL OF THEIR FILMS BY HAND, STARTING WITH THE SCREEN-PLAY.
I CAN'T KEEP RELYING ON MISS POMPO TO HOLD MY HAND.
THAT ALL CHANGES NOW!!
DMP
I'LL USE ALL I'VE LEARNED TO MAKE A FILM I CAN CALL MY OWN!!
AND THE FIRST STEP IN MAKING IT HAPPEN IS...
TAK
TAK
TAK
TAK
TAK
TAK
TAK
HM?

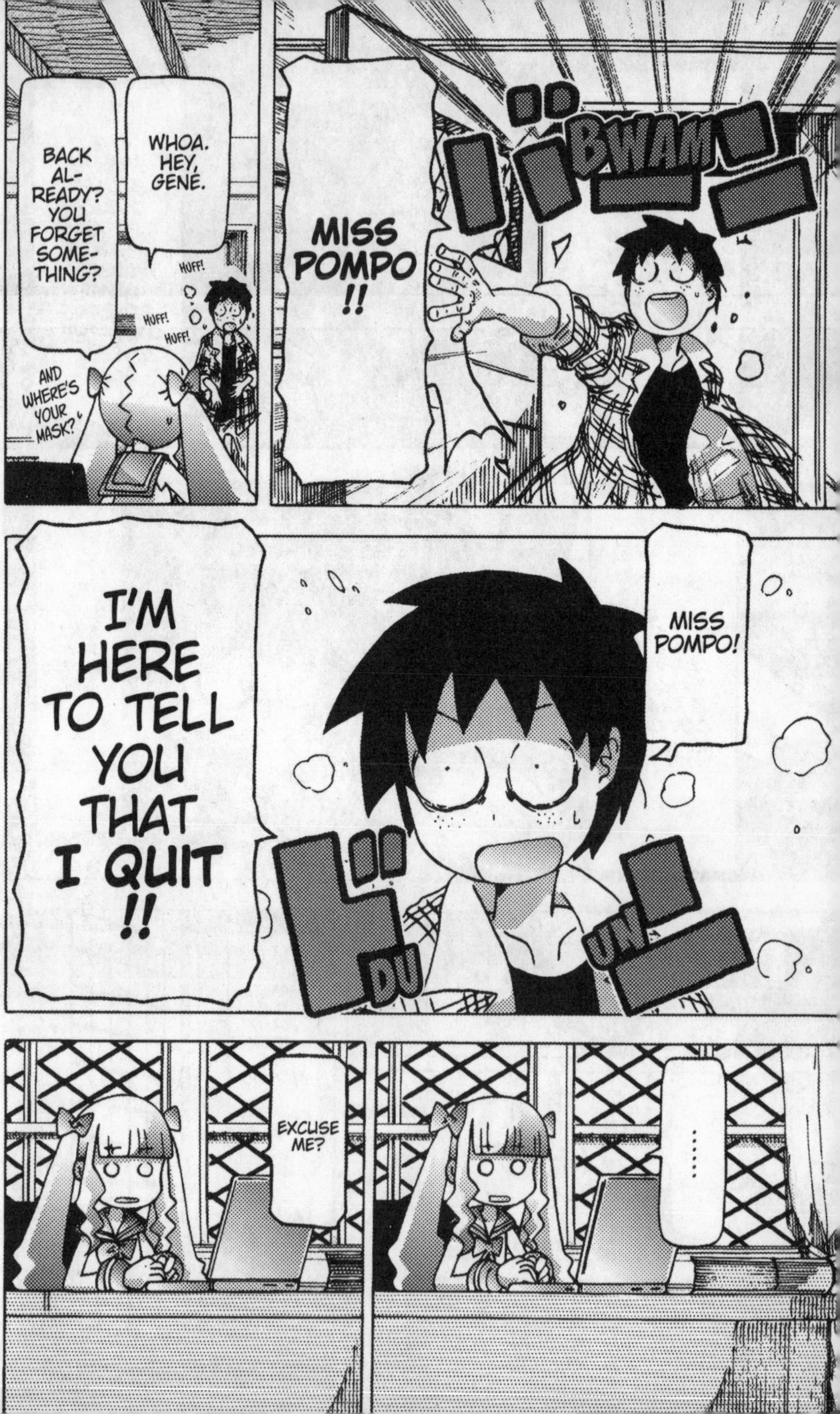
BWAM
MISS POMPO!!
WHOA. HEY, GENE.
BACK AL-READY? YOU FORGET SOME-THING?
HUFF!
HUFF!
HUFF!
AND WHERE'S YOUR MASK?
MISS POMPO!
DUN
I'M HERE TO TELL YOU THAT I QUIT!!
......
EXCUSE ME?

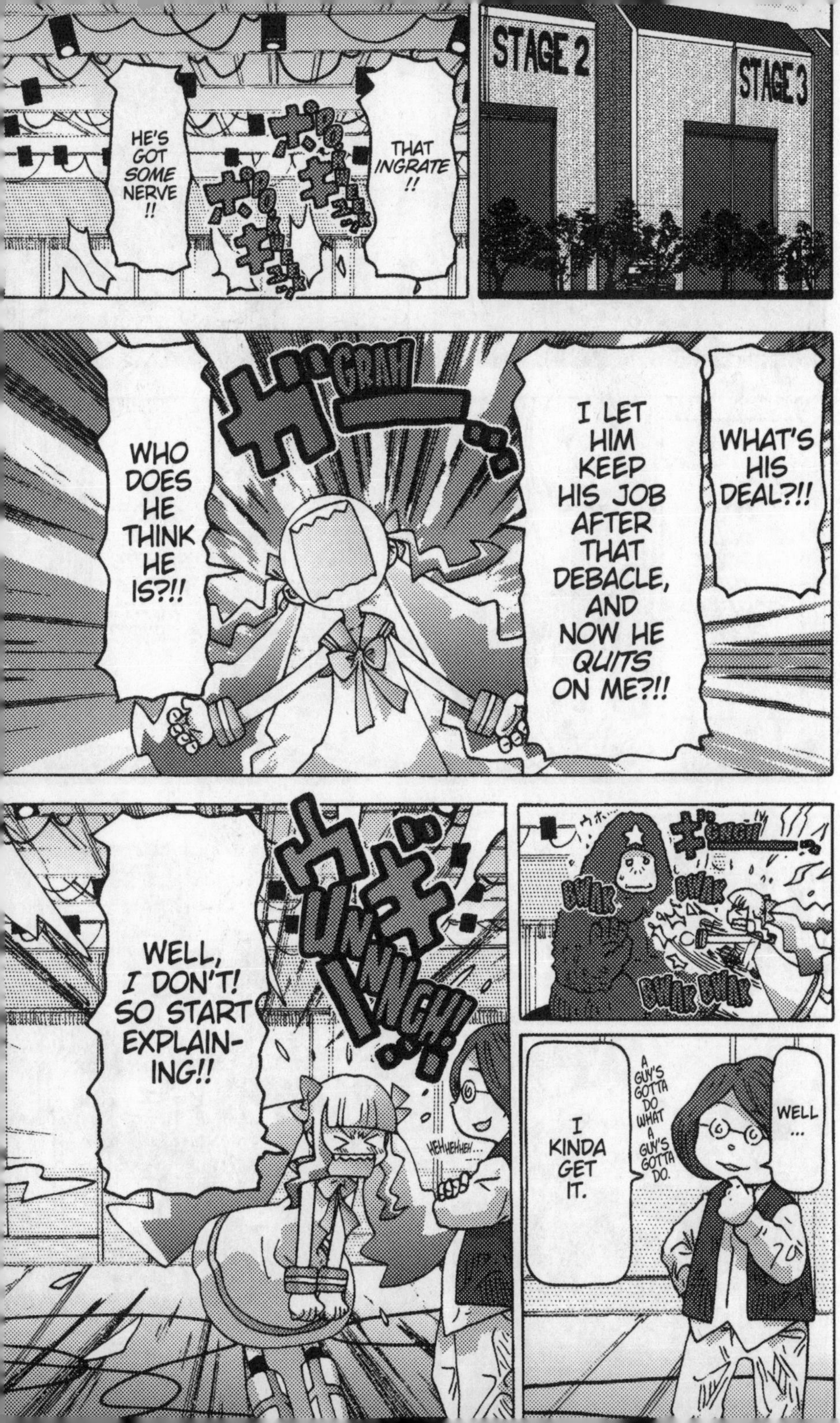
STAGE 2
STAGE 3
THAT INGRATE!!
HE'S GOT SOME NERVE!!
WHAT'S HIS DEAL?!!
I LET HIM KEEP HIS JOB AFTER THAT DEBACLE, AND NOW HE QUITS ON ME?!!
GRAW
WHO DOES HE THINK HE IS?!!
BWAK
BWAK
BWAK BWAK
WELL...
A GUY'S GOTTA DO WHAT A GUY'S GOTTA DO.
I KINDA GET IT.
HEHHEHHEH...
WELL, I DON'T! SO START EXPLAINING!!

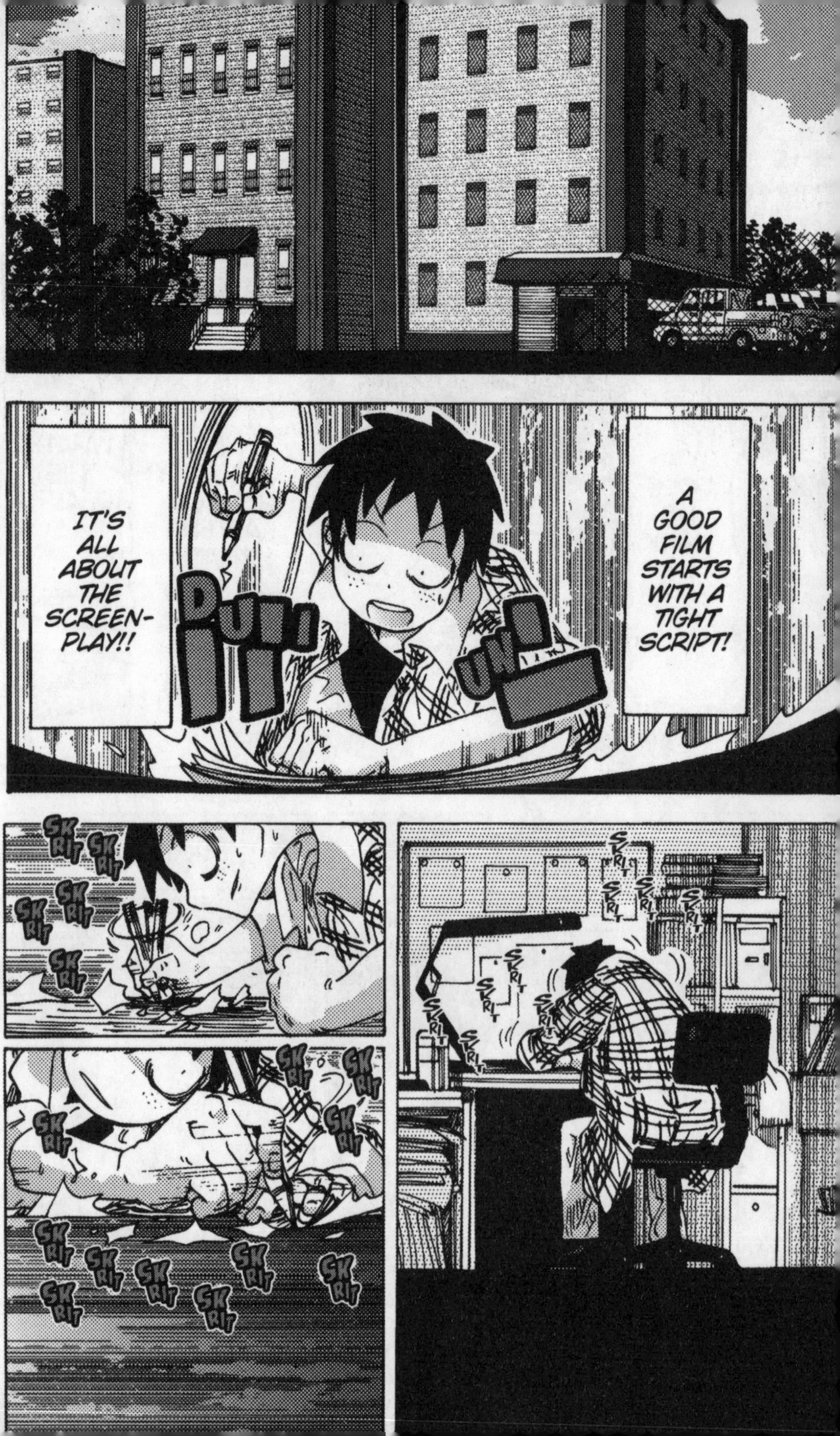
A GOOD FILM STARTS WITH A TIGHT SCRIPT!
IT'S ALL ABOUT THE SCREEN-PLAY!!
SKRIT
SKRIT
SKRIT
SKRIT
SKRIT
SKRIT

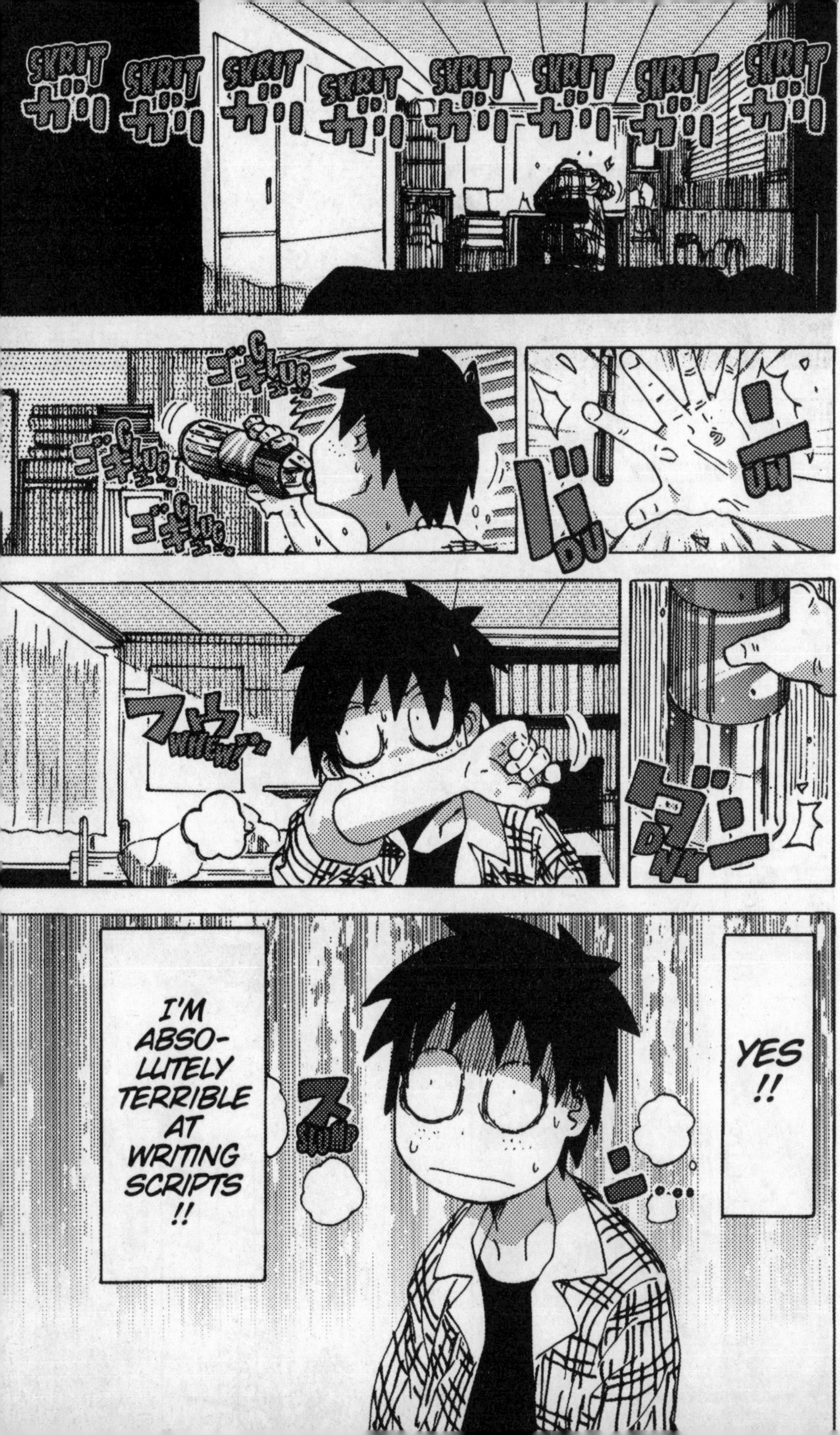
SKRIT
SKRIT
SKRIT
SKRIT
SKRIT
SKRIT
SKRIT
SKRIT
DU
UN
GLUG
GLUG
GLUG
DUNK
WHEW!
YES !!
...
SLUMP
I'M ABSO-LUTELY TERRIBLE AT WRITING SCRIPTS !!

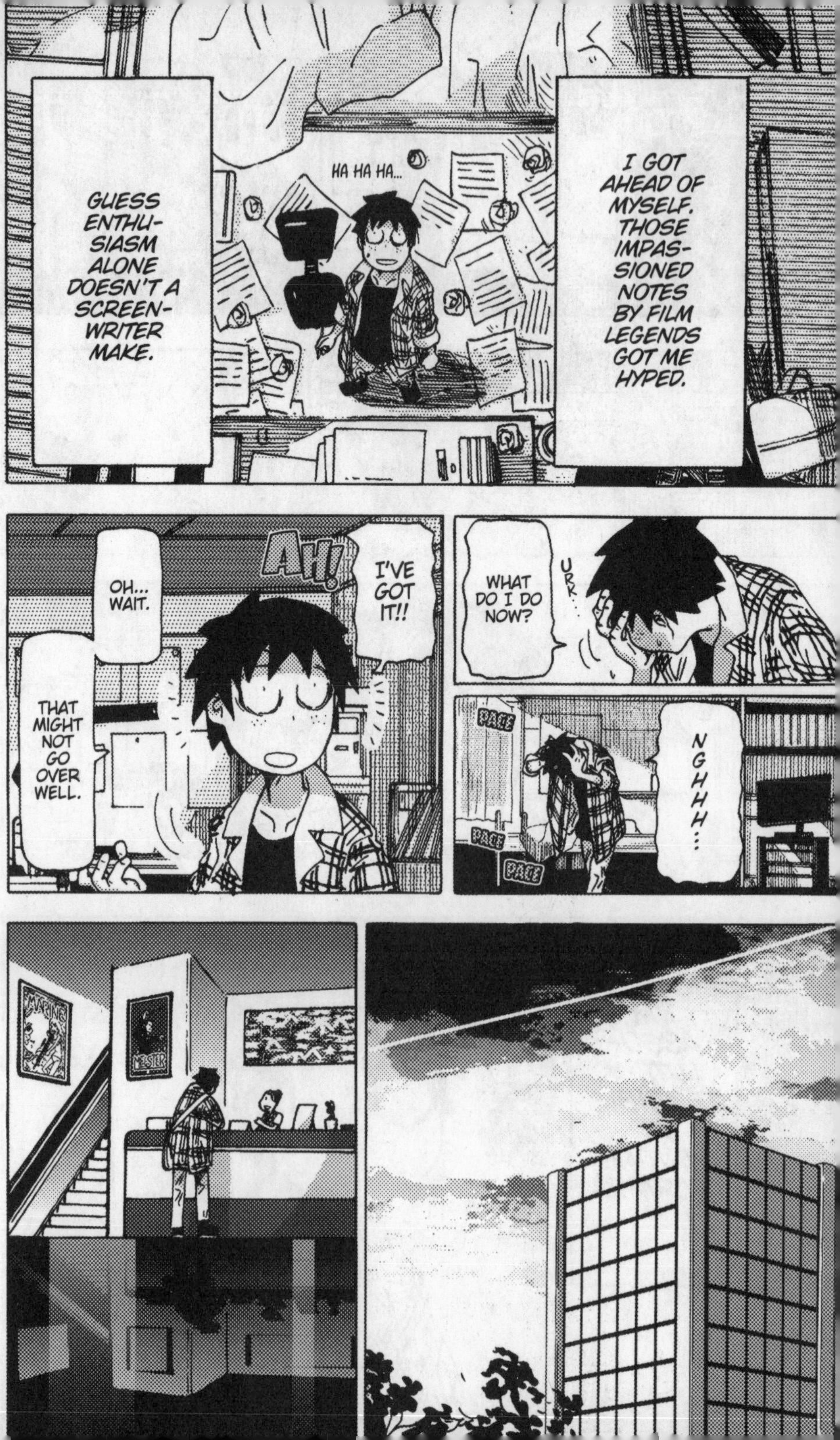
I GOT AHEAD OF MYSELF. THOSE IMPASSIONED NOTES BY FILM LEGENDS GOT ME HYPED.
HA HA HA...
GUESS ENTHUSIASM ALONE DOESN'T A SCREENWRITER MAKE.
WHAT DO I DO NOW?
URK...
NGHHH...
PACE
PACE
PACE
I'VE GOT IT!!
AH!
OH... WAIT.
THAT MIGHT NOT GO OVER WELL.

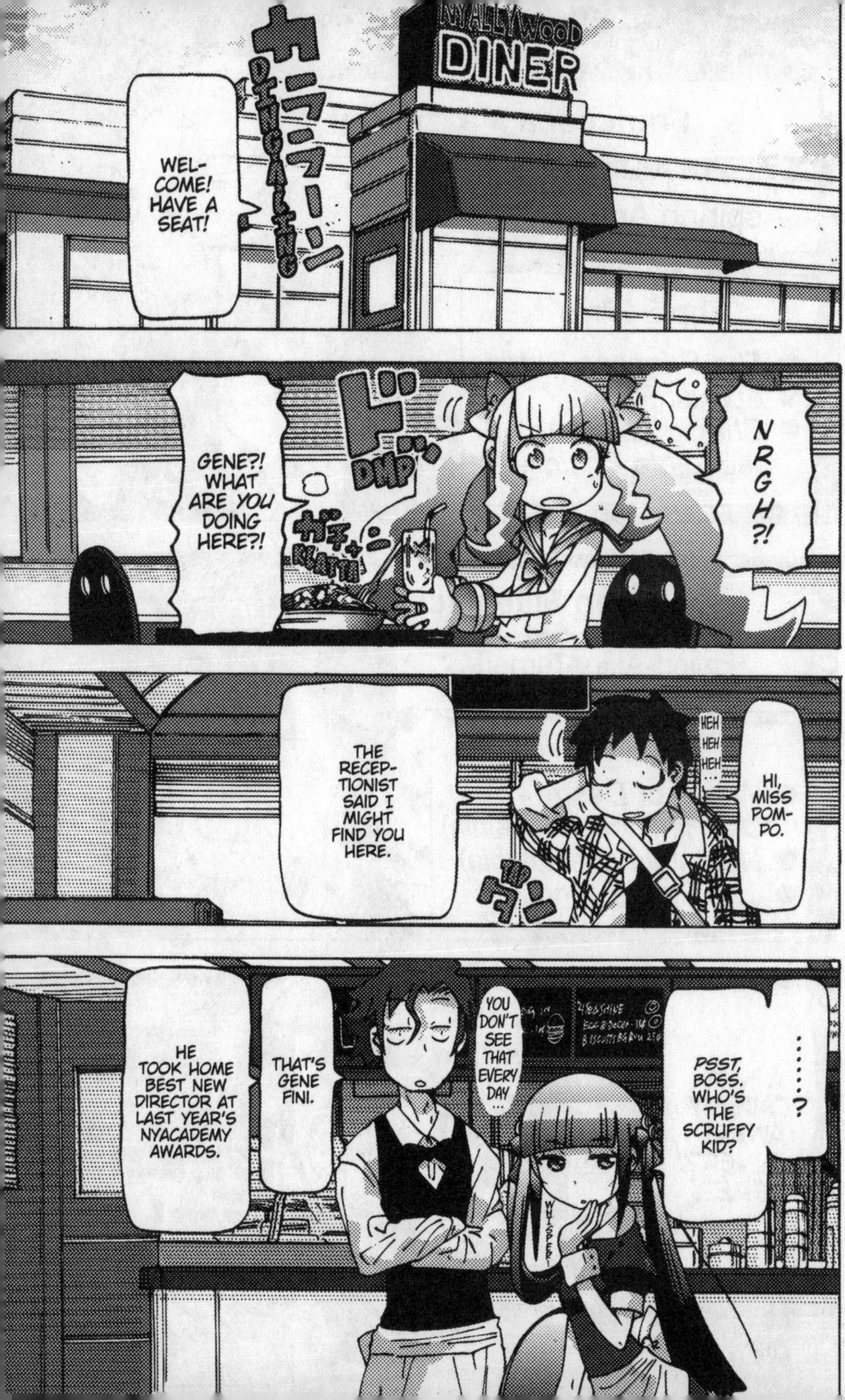
NYALLYWOOD
DINER
DING-A-LING
WEL-COME! HAVE A SEAT!
NRGH?!
DMP
RLATTR
GENE?! WHAT ARE YOU DOING HERE?!
HI, MISS POM-PO.
HEH HEH HEH...
TAP
THE RECEP-TIONIST SAID I MIGHT FIND YOU HERE.
......?
PSST, BOSS. WHO'S THE SCRUFFY KID?
WHISPER
YOU DON'T SEE THAT EVERY DAY...
THAT'S GENE FINI.
HE TOOK HOME BEST NEW DIRECTOR AT LAST YEAR'S NYACADEMY AWARDS.

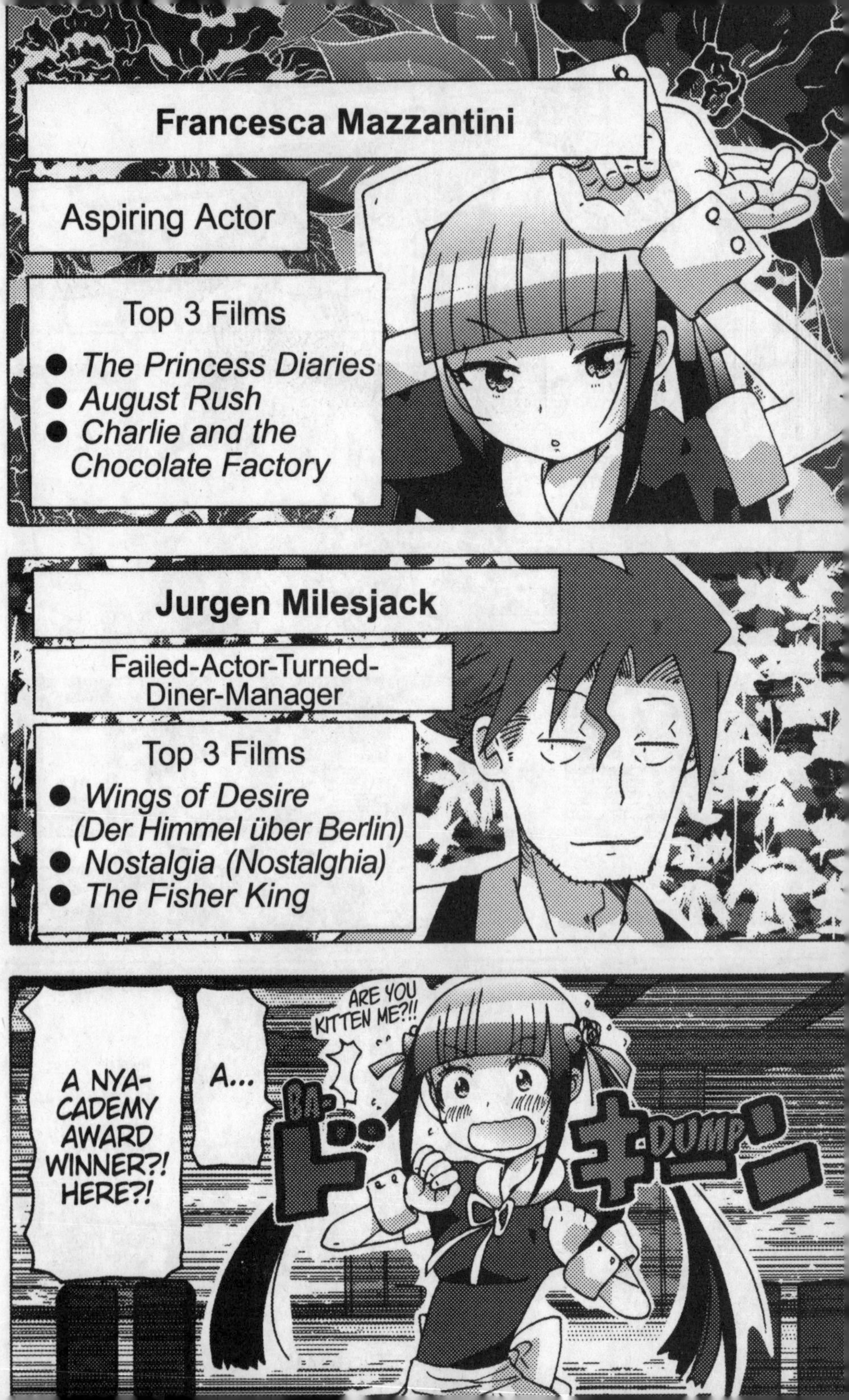
Francesca Mazzantini
Aspiring Actor
Top 3 Films
● The Princess Diaries
● August Rush
● Charlie and the Chocolate Factory
Jurgen Milesjack
Failed-Actor-Turned-Diner-Manager
Top 3 Films
● Wings of Desire (Der Himmel über Berlin)
● Nostalgia (Nostalghia)
● The Fisher King
BA-DO-DUMP
ARE YOU KITTEN ME?!!
A...
A NYA-CADEMY AWARD WINNER?! HERE?!

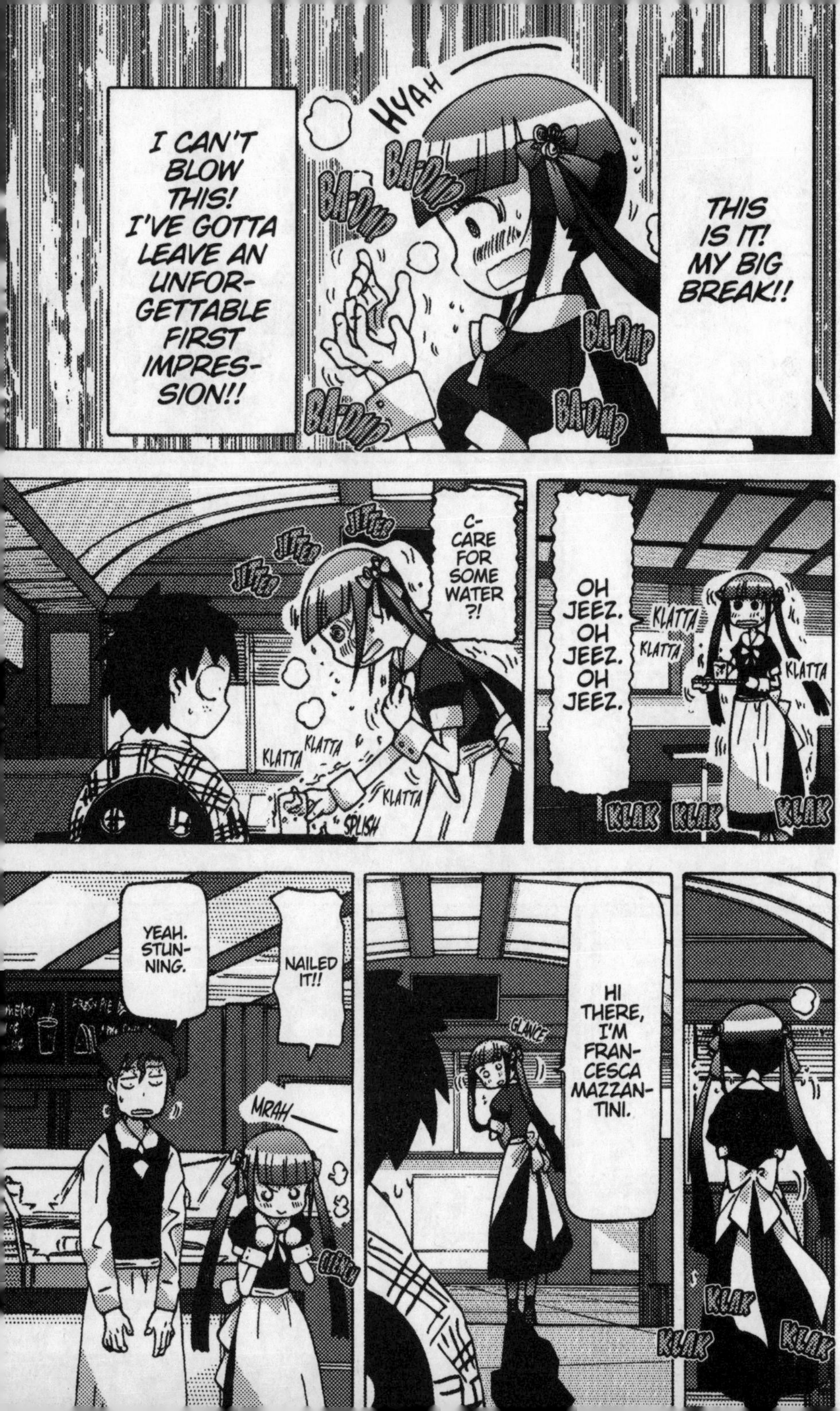
THIS IS IT! MY BIG BREAK!!
HYAH
BA-DUMP
BA-DUMP
BA-DUMP
BA-DUMP
BA-DUMP
BA-DUMP
I CAN'T BLOW THIS! I'VE GOTTA LEAVE AN UNFOR-GETTABLE FIRST IMPRES-SION!!
OH JEEZ. OH JEEZ. OH JEEZ.
KLATTA
KLATTA
KLATTA
KLAK
KLAK
KLAK
C-CARE FOR SOME WATER?!
JITTER
JITTER
JITTER
KLATTA
KLATTA
KLATTA
SPLISH
KLAK
KLAK
KLAK
KLAK
HI THERE, I'M FRAN-CESCA MAZZAN-TINI.
GLANCE
NAILED IT!!
YEAH. STUN-NING.
MRAH

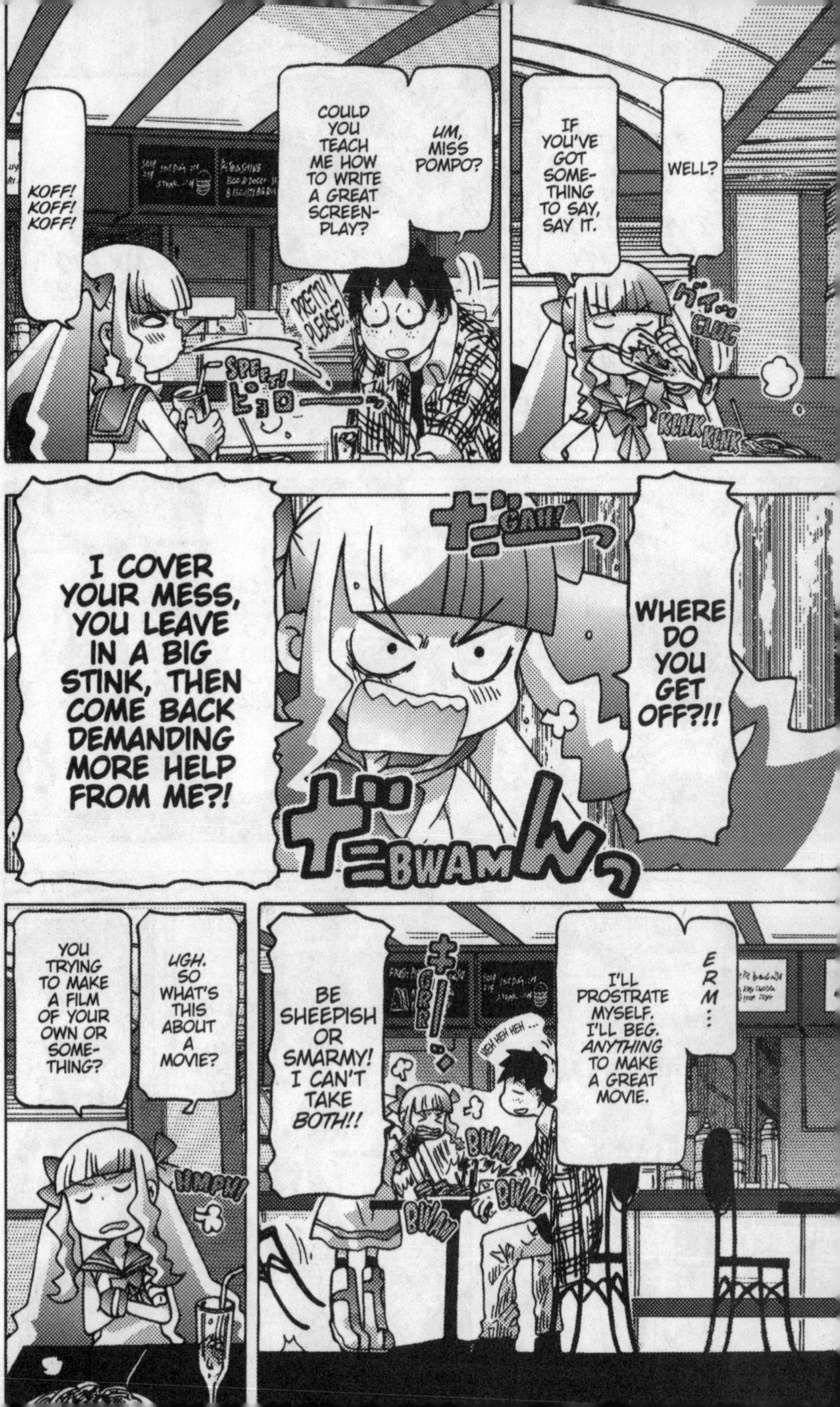
WELL?
IF YOU'VE GOT SOME-THING TO SAY, SAY IT.
CLUG
KLINK KLINK
UM, MISS POMPO?
COULD YOU TEACH ME HOW TO WRITE A GREAT SCREEN-PLAY?
PRETTY PLEASE!
SPFFT!
KOFF! KOFF! KOFF!
WHERE DO YOU GET OFF?!!
GAW
I COVER YOUR MESS, YOU LEAVE IN A BIG STINK, THEN COME BACK DEMANDING MORE HELP FROM ME?!
BWAM
ERM...
I'LL PROSTRATE MYSELF. I'LL BEG. *ANYTHING* TO MAKE A GREAT MOVIE.
HEH HEH HEH...
BE SHEEPISH OR SMARMY! I CAN'T TAKE *BOTH*!!
BWAM
BWAM
BWAM
UGH. SO WHAT'S THIS ABOUT A MOVIE?
YOU TRYING TO MAKE A FILM OF YOUR OWN OR SOME-THING?
HMPH!

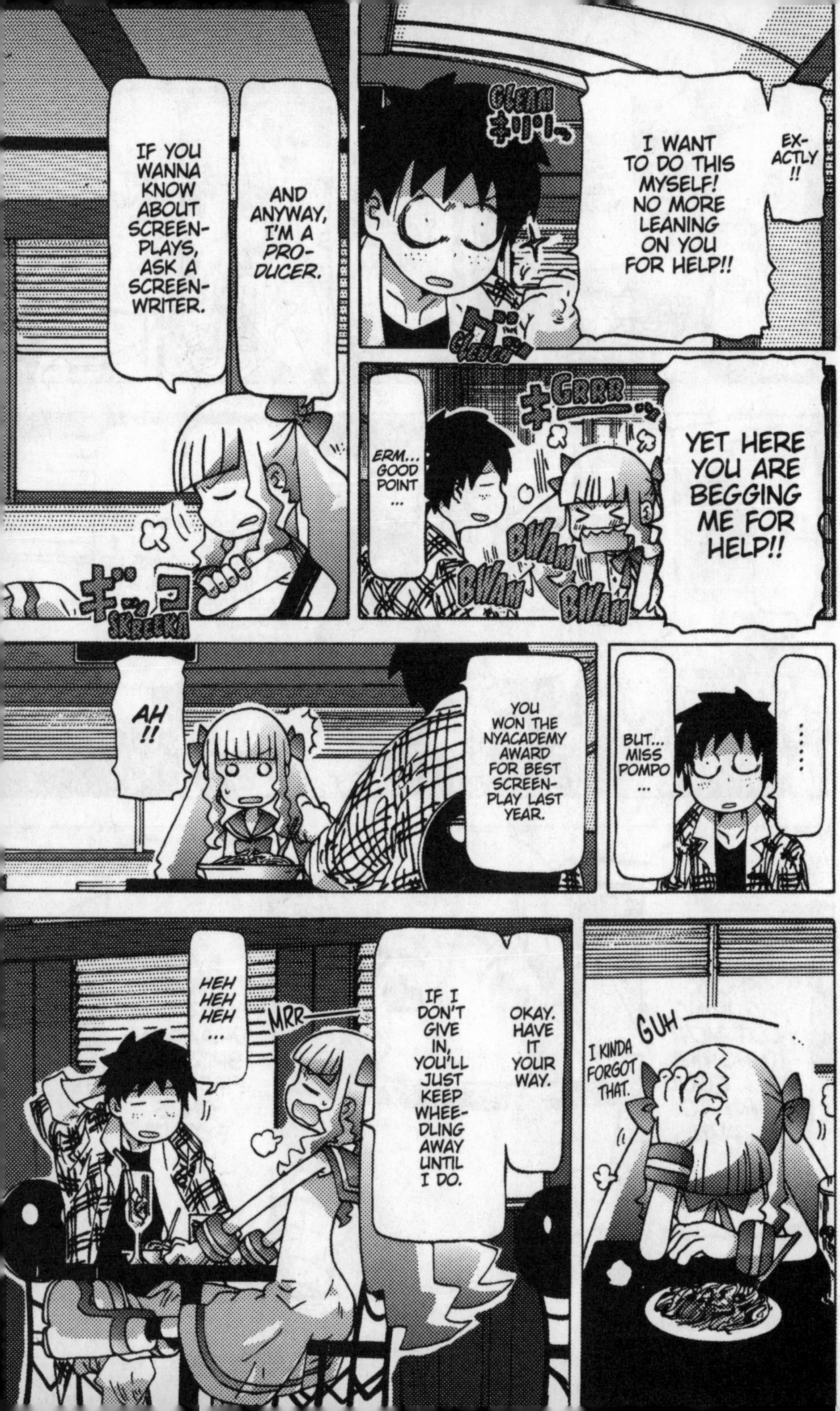
GLEAM
EX-ACTLY!!
I WANT TO DO THIS MYSELF! NO MORE LEANING ON YOU FOR HELP!!
GRRR
YET HERE YOU ARE BEGGING ME FOR HELP!!
ERM... GOOD POINT...
BWAM
BWAM
BWAM
AND ANYWAY, I'M A PRODUCER.
IF YOU WANNA KNOW ABOUT SCREENPLAYS, ASK A SCREENWRITER.
......
BUT... MISS POMPO...
YOU WON THE NYACADEMY AWARD FOR BEST SCREENPLAY LAST YEAR.
AH!!
GUH—
I KINDA FORGOT THAT.
OKAY. HAVE IT YOUR WAY.
IF I DON'T GIVE IN, YOU'LL JUST KEEP WHEEDLING AWAY UNTIL I DO.
MRR
HEH HEH HEH...

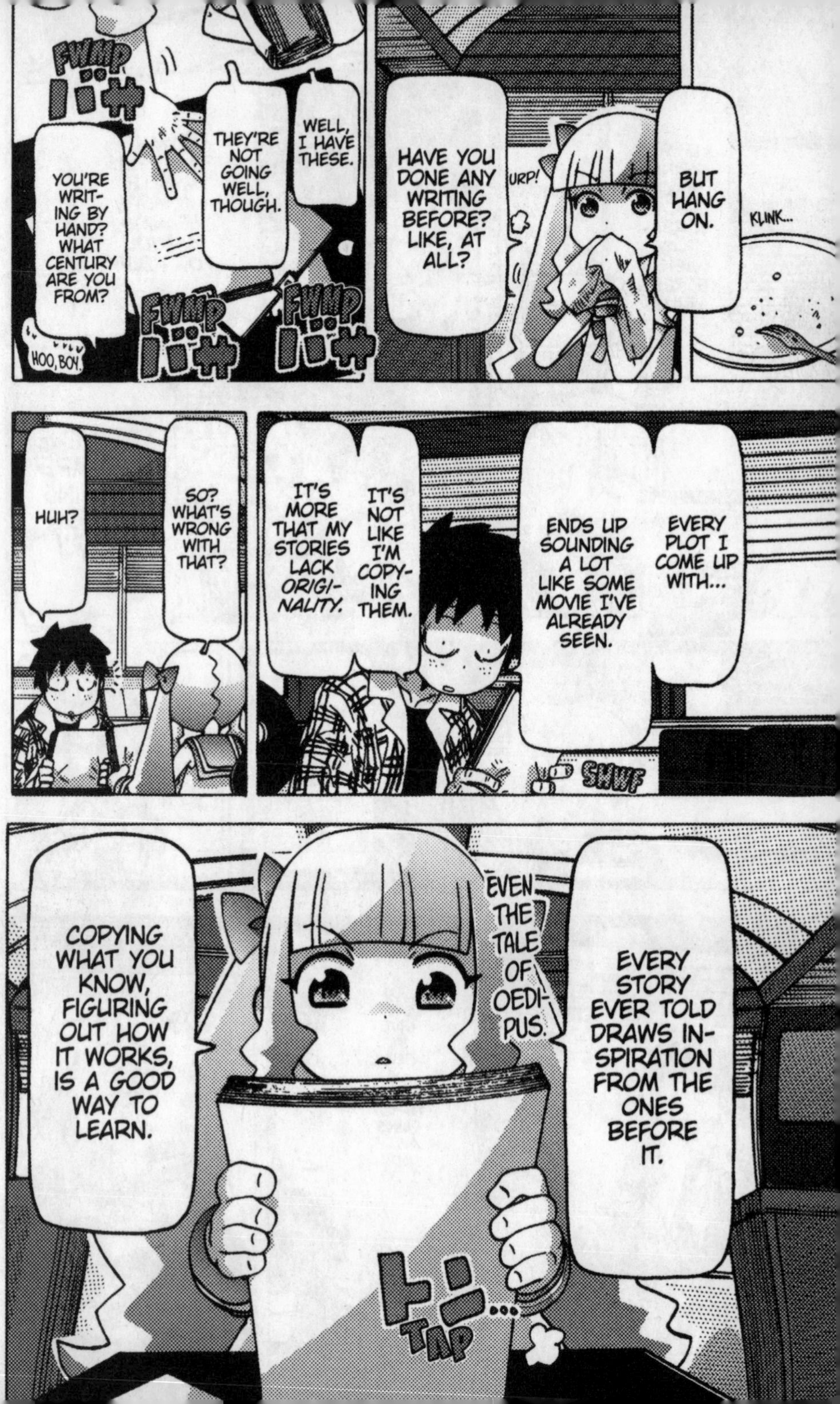

KLINK...
BUT HANG ON.
URP!
HAVE YOU DONE ANY WRITING BEFORE? LIKE, AT ALL?
WELL, I HAVE THESE.
THEY'RE NOT GOING WELL, THOUGH.
FWMP
FWMP
FWMP
YOU'RE WRITING BY HAND? WHAT CENTURY ARE YOU FROM?
HOO, BOY.
EVERY PLOT I COME UP WITH...
ENDS UP SOUNDING A LOT LIKE SOME MOVIE I'VE ALREADY SEEN.
IT'S NOT LIKE I'M COPYING THEM.
IT'S MORE THAT MY STORIES LACK ORIGINALITY.
SHUF
SO? WHAT'S WRONG WITH THAT?
HUH?
EVERY STORY EVER TOLD DRAWS INSPIRATION FROM THE ONES BEFORE IT.
EVEN THE TALE OF OEDIPUS.
COPYING WHAT YOU KNOW, FIGURING OUT HOW IT WORKS, IS A GOOD WAY TO LEARN.
TAP...

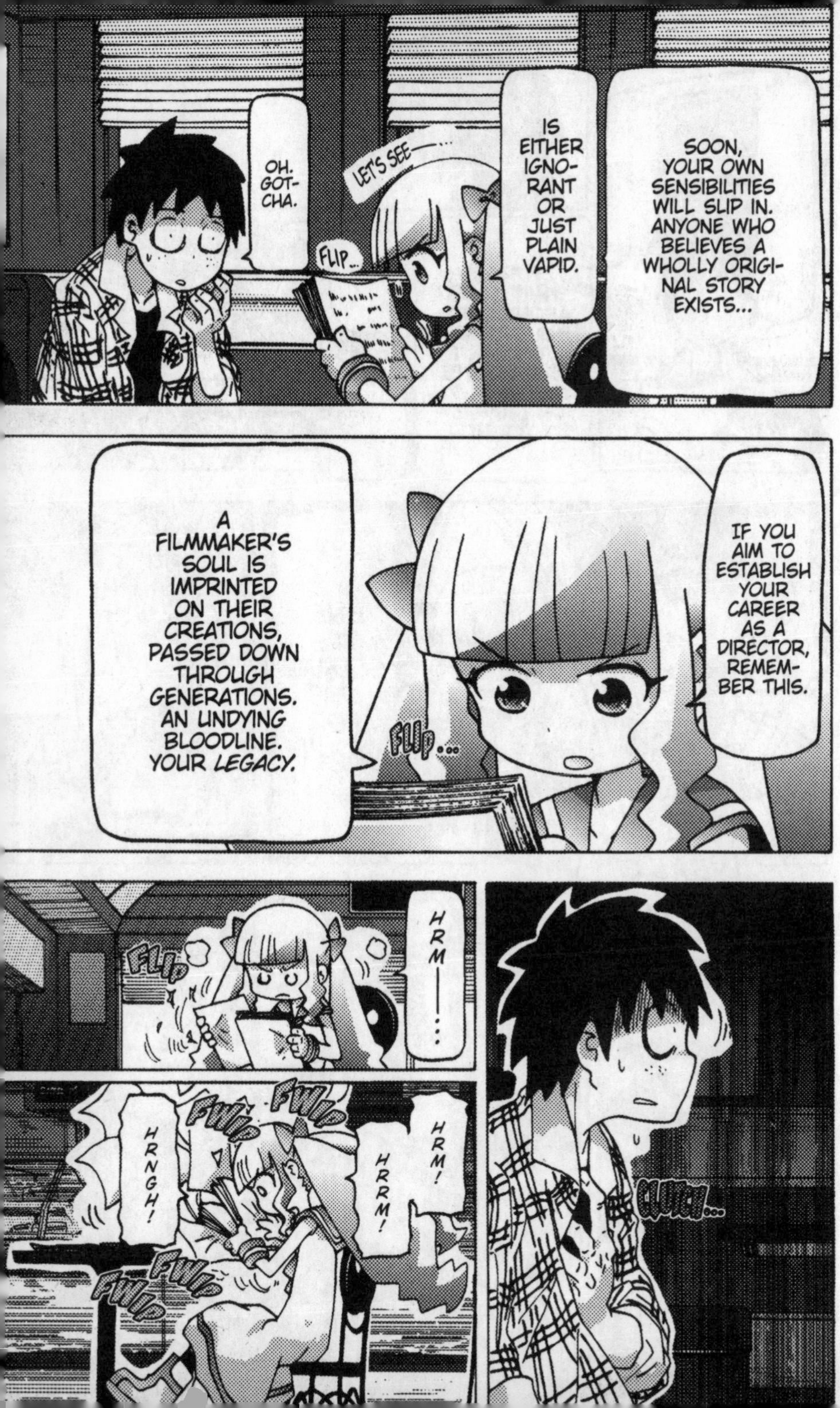
SOON, YOUR OWN SENSIBILITIES WILL SLIP IN. ANYONE WHO BELIEVES A WHOLLY ORIGINAL STORY EXISTS...
IS EITHER IGNORANT OR JUST PLAIN VAPID.
LET'S SEE—...
FLIP...
OH. GOTCHA.
IF YOU AIM TO ESTABLISH YOUR CAREER AS A DIRECTOR, REMEMBER THIS.
FLIP...
A FILMMAKER'S SOUL IS IMPRINTED ON THEIR CREATIONS, PASSED DOWN THROUGH GENERATIONS. AN UNDYING BLOODLINE. YOUR *LEGACY.*
CLUTCH...
HRM—...
FLIP
HRM!
HRRM!
HRNGH!
FWIP
FWIP
FWIP
FWIP

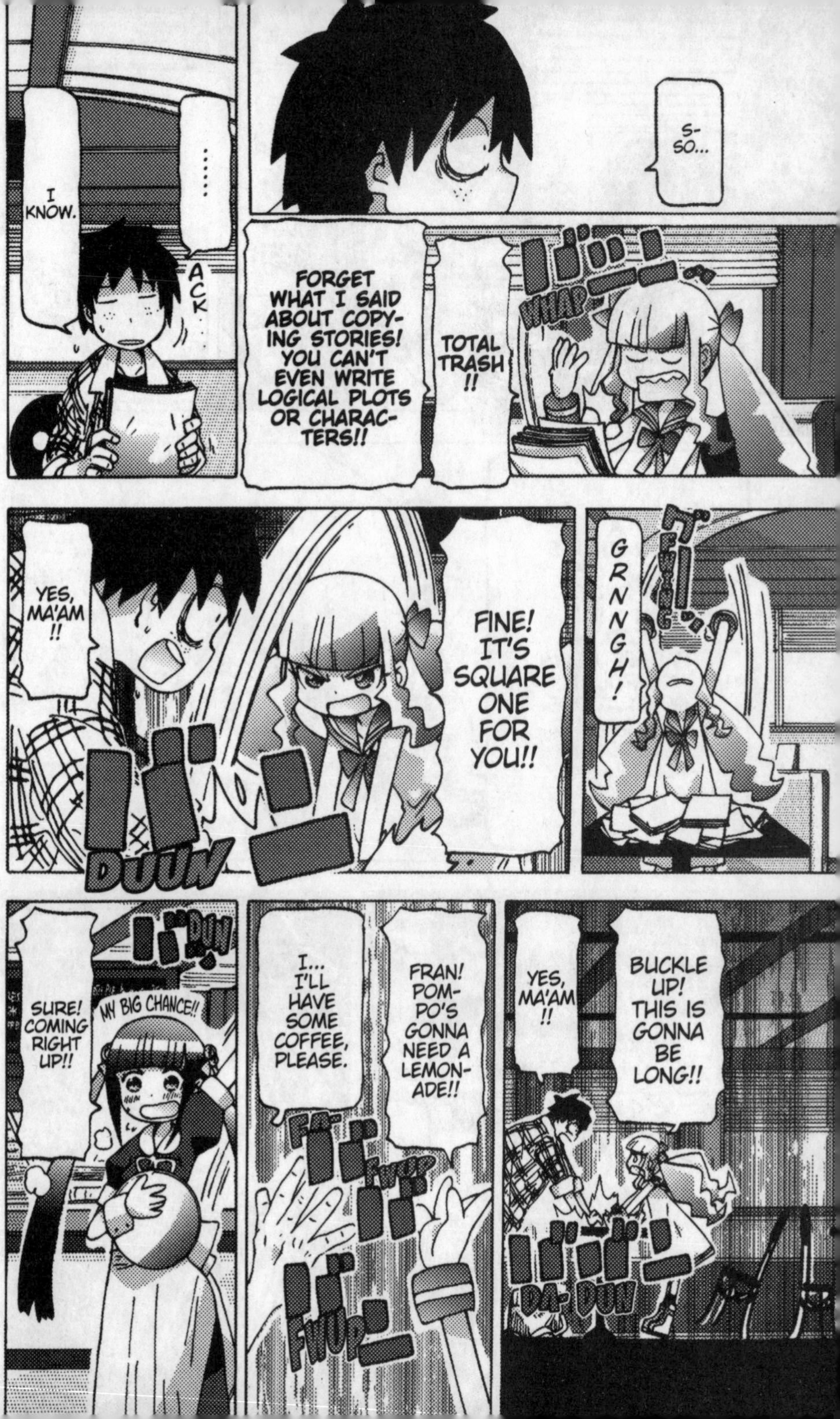
S-
SO...
WHAP
TOTAL TRASH!!
FORGET WHAT I SAID ABOUT COPYING STORIES! YOU CAN'T EVEN WRITE LOGICAL PLOTS OR CHARACTERS!!
......
ACK
I KNOW.
GRNNGH!
FINE! IT'S SQUARE ONE FOR YOU!!
YES, MA'AM!!
DUUN
BUCKLE UP! THIS IS GONNA BE LONG!!
YES, MA'AM!!
DA-DUN
FRAN! POMPO'S GONNA NEED A LEMONADE!!
I... I'LL HAVE SOME COFFEE, PLEASE.
FWUP
FWUP
DUN
SURE! COMING RIGHT UP!!
MY BIG CHANCE!!

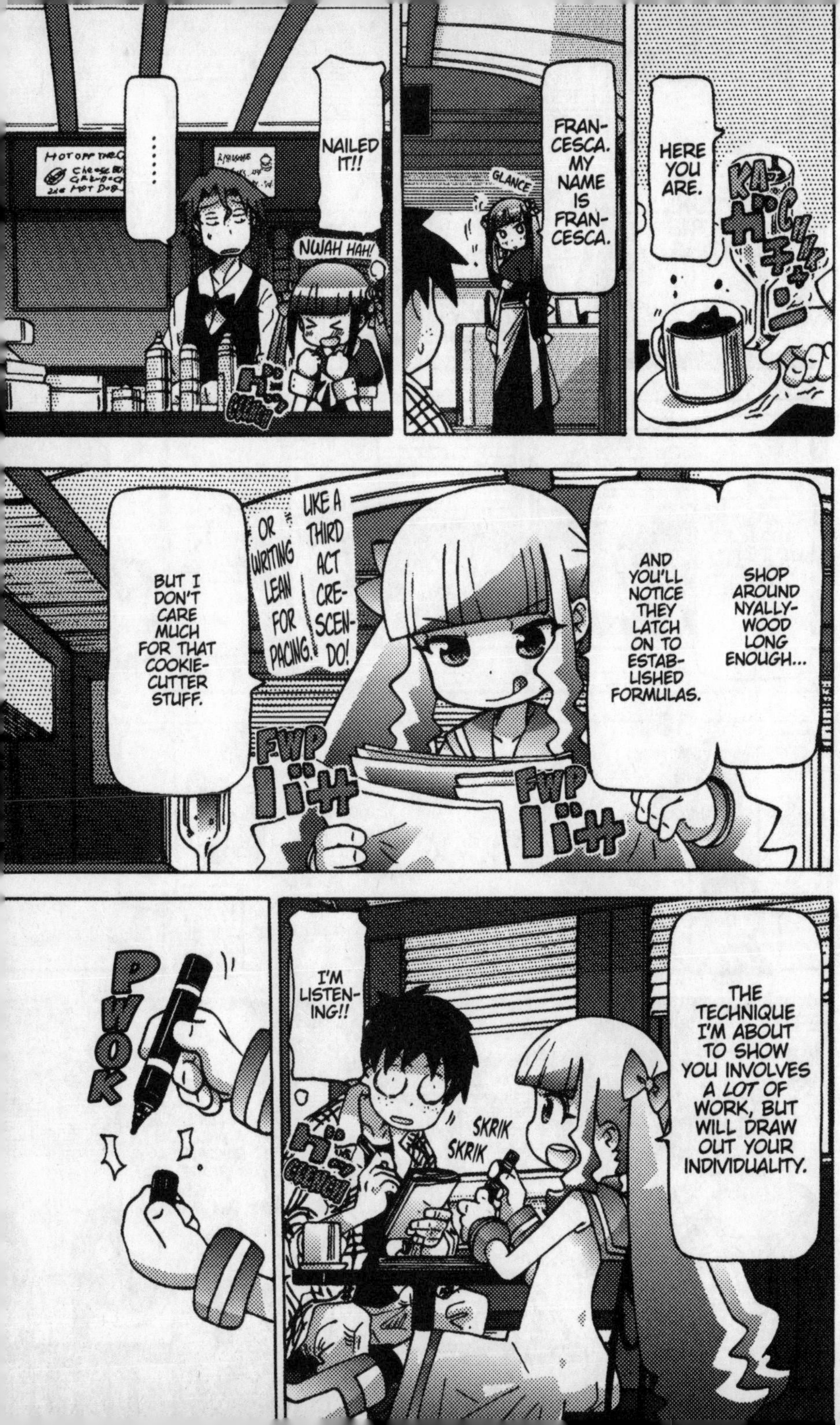
HERE YOU ARE.
FRAN-CESCA. MY NAME IS FRAN-CESCA.
GLANCE
NAILED IT!!
NWAH HAH!
......
SHOP AROUND NYALLY-WOOD LONG ENOUGH...
AND YOU'LL NOTICE THEY LATCH ON TO ESTAB-LISHED FORMULAS.
LIKE A THIRD ACT CRE-SCEN-DO!
OR WRITING LEAN FOR PACING.
BUT I DON'T CARE MUCH FOR THAT COOKIE-CUTTER STUFF.
FWP
FWP
THE TECHNIQUE I'M ABOUT TO SHOW YOU INVOLVES A *LOT* OF WORK, BUT WILL DRAW OUT YOUR INDIVIDUALITY.
SKRIK SKRIK
I'M LISTEN-ING!!
PWOK

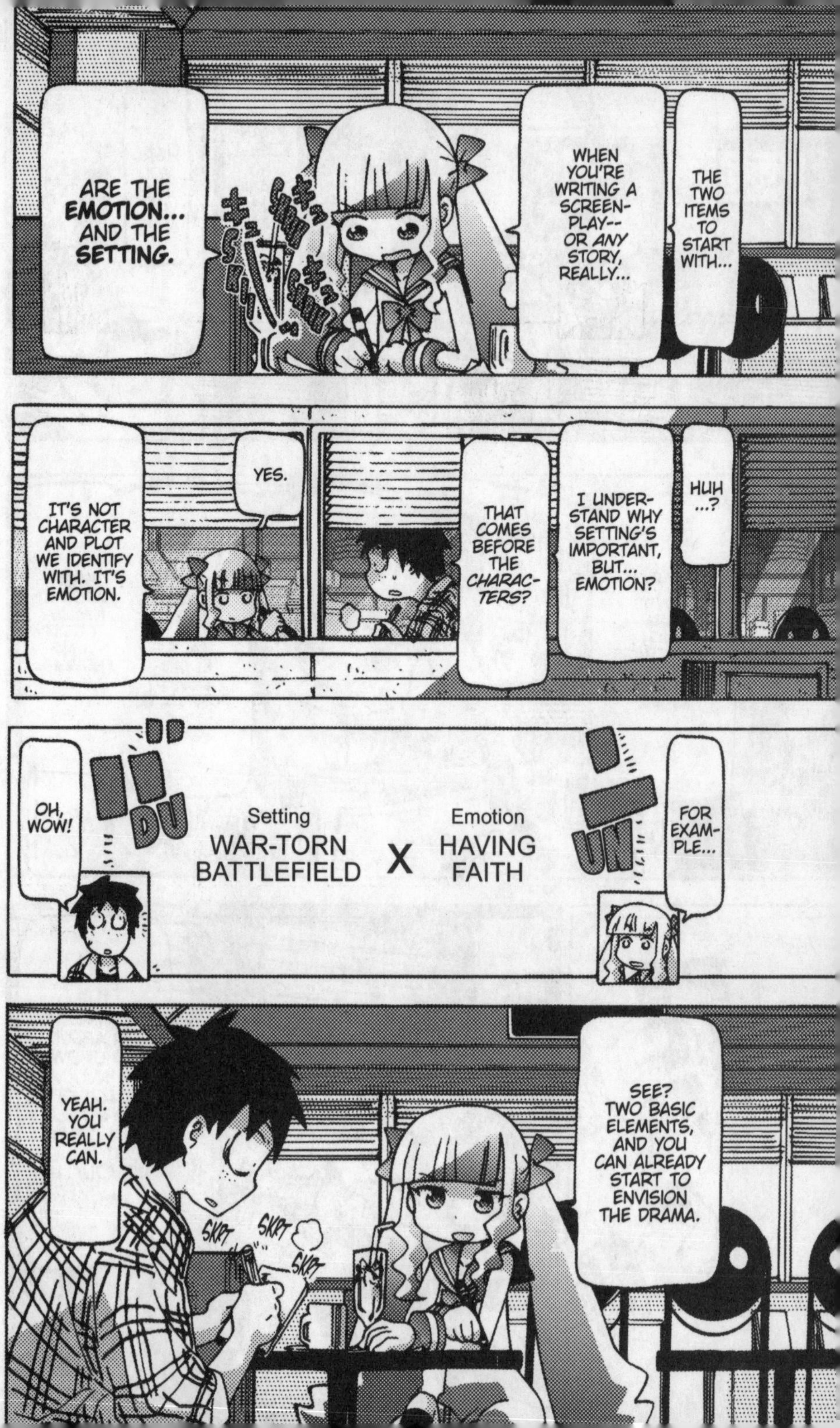
THE TWO ITEMS TO START WITH...
WHEN YOU'RE WRITING A SCREEN-PLAY-- OR ANY STORY, REALLY...
ARE THE EMOTION... AND THE SETTING.
HUH ...?
I UNDER-STAND WHY SETTING'S IMPORTANT, BUT... EMOTION?
THAT COMES BEFORE THE CHARAC-TERS?
YES.
IT'S NOT CHARACTER AND PLOT WE IDENTIFY WITH. IT'S EMOTION.
FOR EXAM-PLE...
UN
Setting
WAR-TORN BATTLEFIELD
X
Emotion
HAVING FAITH
DU
OH, WOW!
SEE? TWO BASIC ELEMENTS, AND YOU CAN ALREADY START TO ENVISION THE DRAMA.
SKRT SKRT SKRT
YEAH. YOU REALLY CAN.

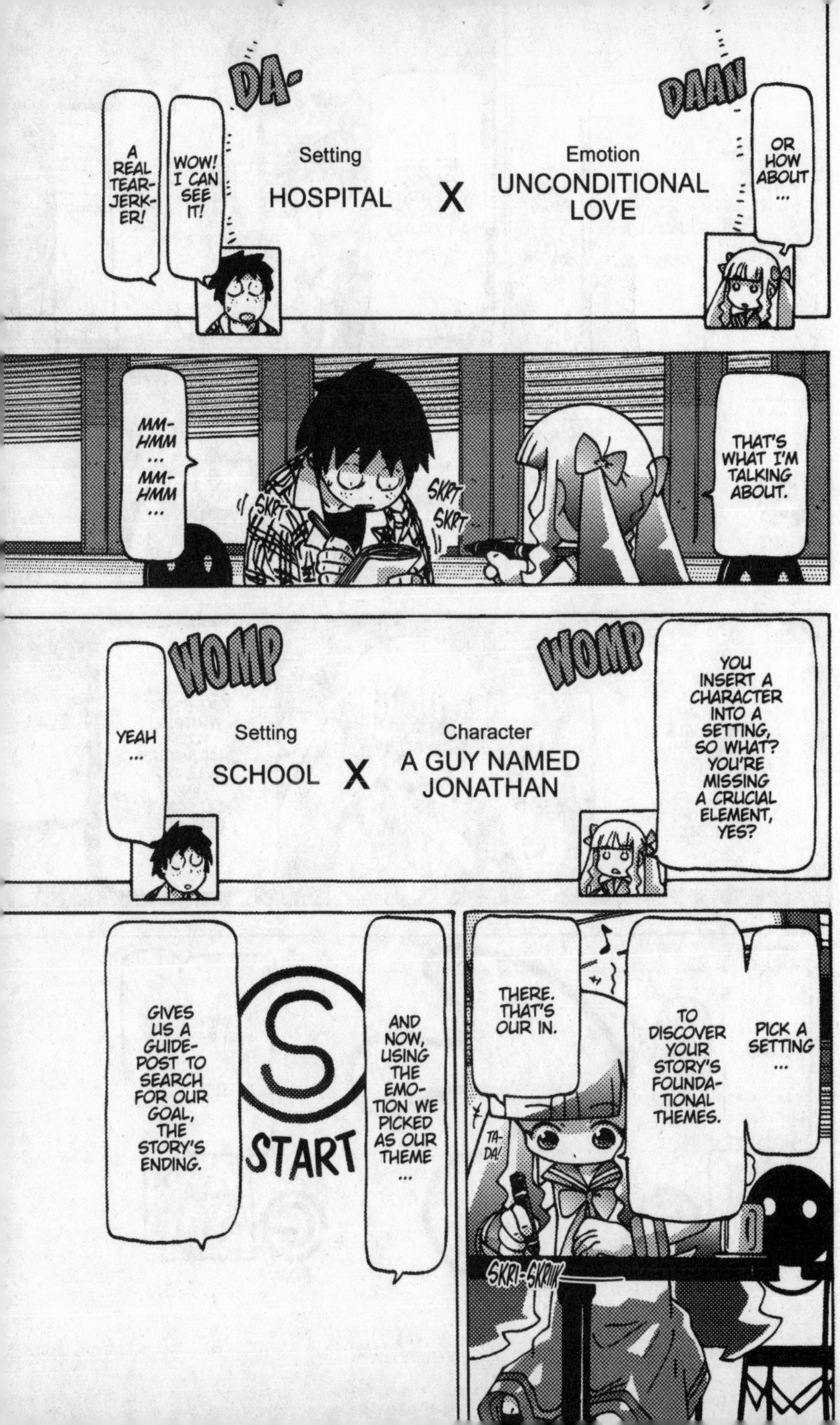
DAAN
OR HOW ABOUT ...
Emotion
UNCONDITIONAL LOVE
X
Setting
HOSPITAL
DA-
WOW! I CAN SEE IT!
A REAL TEARJERKER!
THAT'S WHAT I'M TALKING ABOUT.
SKRT SKRT
SKRT
MM-HMM ... MM-HMM ...
WOMP
YOU INSERT A CHARACTER INTO A SETTING, SO WHAT? YOU'RE MISSING A CRUCIAL ELEMENT, YES?
Character
A GUY NAMED JONATHAN
X
Setting
SCHOOL
WOMP
YEAH ...
PICK A SETTING ...
TO DISCOVER YOUR STORY'S FOUNDATIONAL THEMES.
THERE. THAT'S OUR IN.
TA-DA!
SKRI-SKRIIK
AND NOW, USING THE EMOTION WE PICKED AS OUR THEME ...
S
START
GIVES US A GUIDEPOST TO SEARCH FOR OUR GOAL, THE STORY'S ENDING.

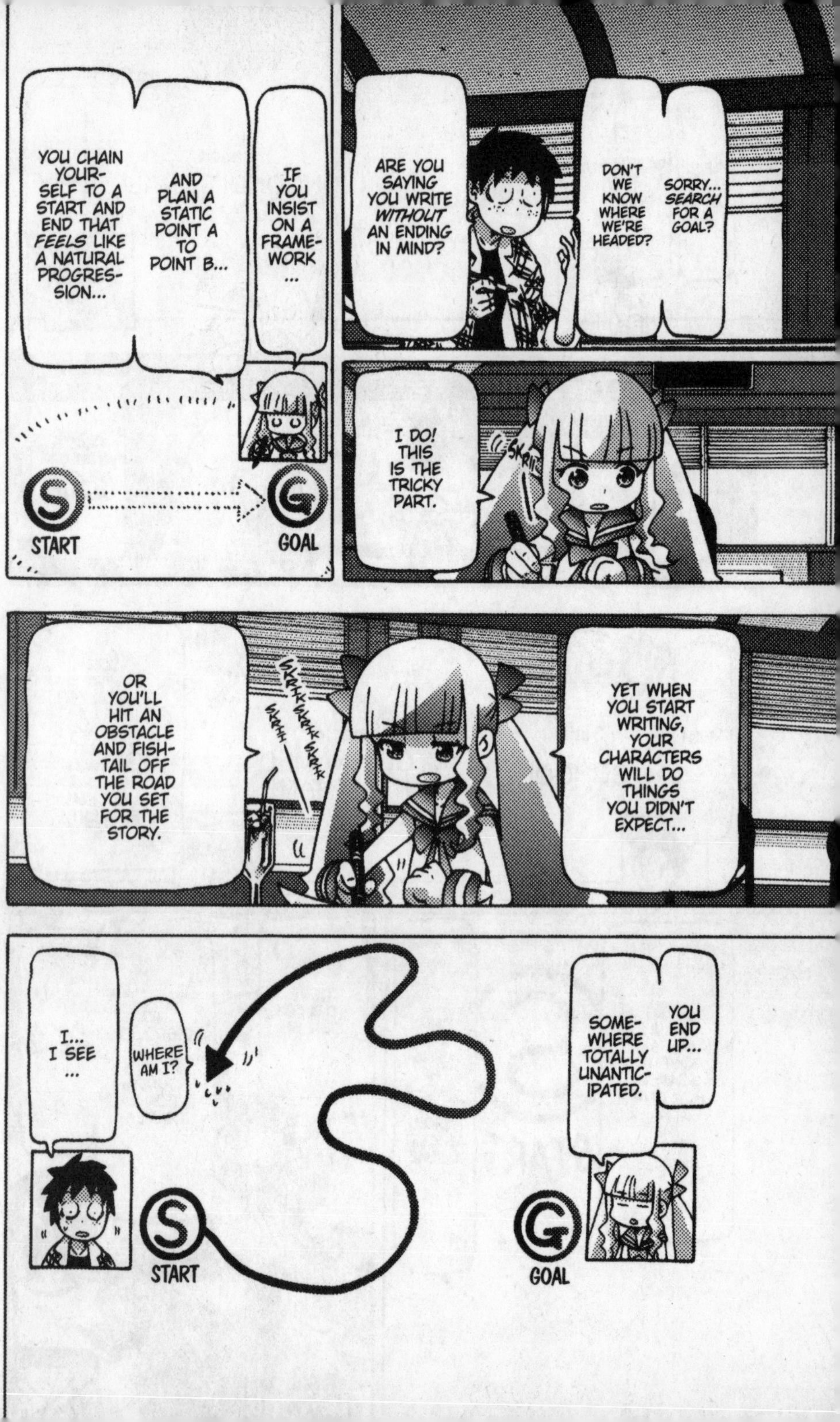
SORRY... *SEARCH* FOR A GOAL?
DON'T WE KNOW WHERE WE'RE HEADED?
ARE YOU SAYING YOU WRITE *WITHOUT* AN ENDING IN MIND?
SKRII
I DO! THIS IS THE TRICKY PART.
IF YOU INSIST ON A FRAMEWORK...
AND PLAN A STATIC POINT A TO POINT B...
YOU CHAIN YOURSELF TO A START AND END THAT *FEELS* LIKE A NATURAL PROGRESSION...
START
GOAL
YET WHEN YOU START WRITING, YOUR CHARACTERS WILL DO THINGS YOU DIDN'T EXPECT...
SKRIK SKRIK SKRIK
SKRII
OR YOU'LL HIT AN OBSTACLE AND FISHTAIL OFF THE ROAD YOU SET FOR THE STORY.
YOU END UP...
SOMEWHERE TOTALLY UNANTICIPATED.
GOAL
START
WHERE AM I?
I... I SEE...

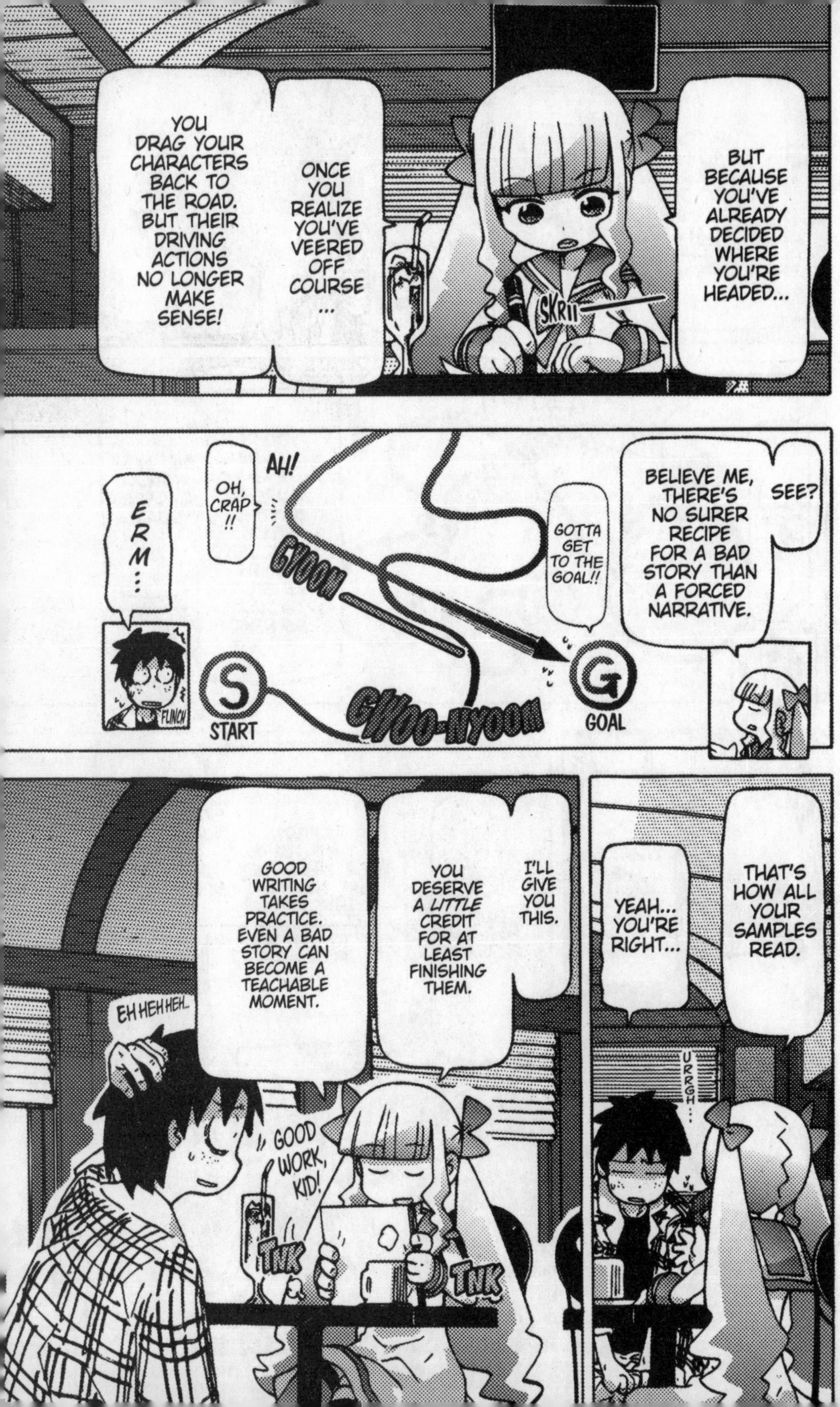
BUT BECAUSE YOU'VE ALREADY DECIDED WHERE YOU'RE HEADED...
SKRII
ONCE YOU REALIZE YOU'VE VEERED OFF COURSE ...
YOU DRAG YOUR CHARACTERS BACK TO THE ROAD. BUT THEIR DRIVING ACTIONS NO LONGER MAKE SENSE!
SEE?
BELIEVE ME, THERE'S NO SURER RECIPE FOR A BAD STORY THAN A FORCED NARRATIVE.
GOTTA GET TO THE GOAL!!
GOAL
GYOON
AH!
OH, CRAP!!
GWOO-NYOOM
START
ERM...
FLINCH
THAT'S HOW ALL YOUR SAMPLES READ.
YEAH... YOU'RE RIGHT...
URRGH...
I'LL GIVE YOU THIS.
YOU DESERVE A *LITTLE* CREDIT FOR AT LEAST FINISHING THEM.
GOOD WRITING TAKES PRACTICE. EVEN A BAD STORY CAN BECOME A TEACHABLE MOMENT.
GOOD WORK, KID!
TNK
TNK
EH HEH HEH...

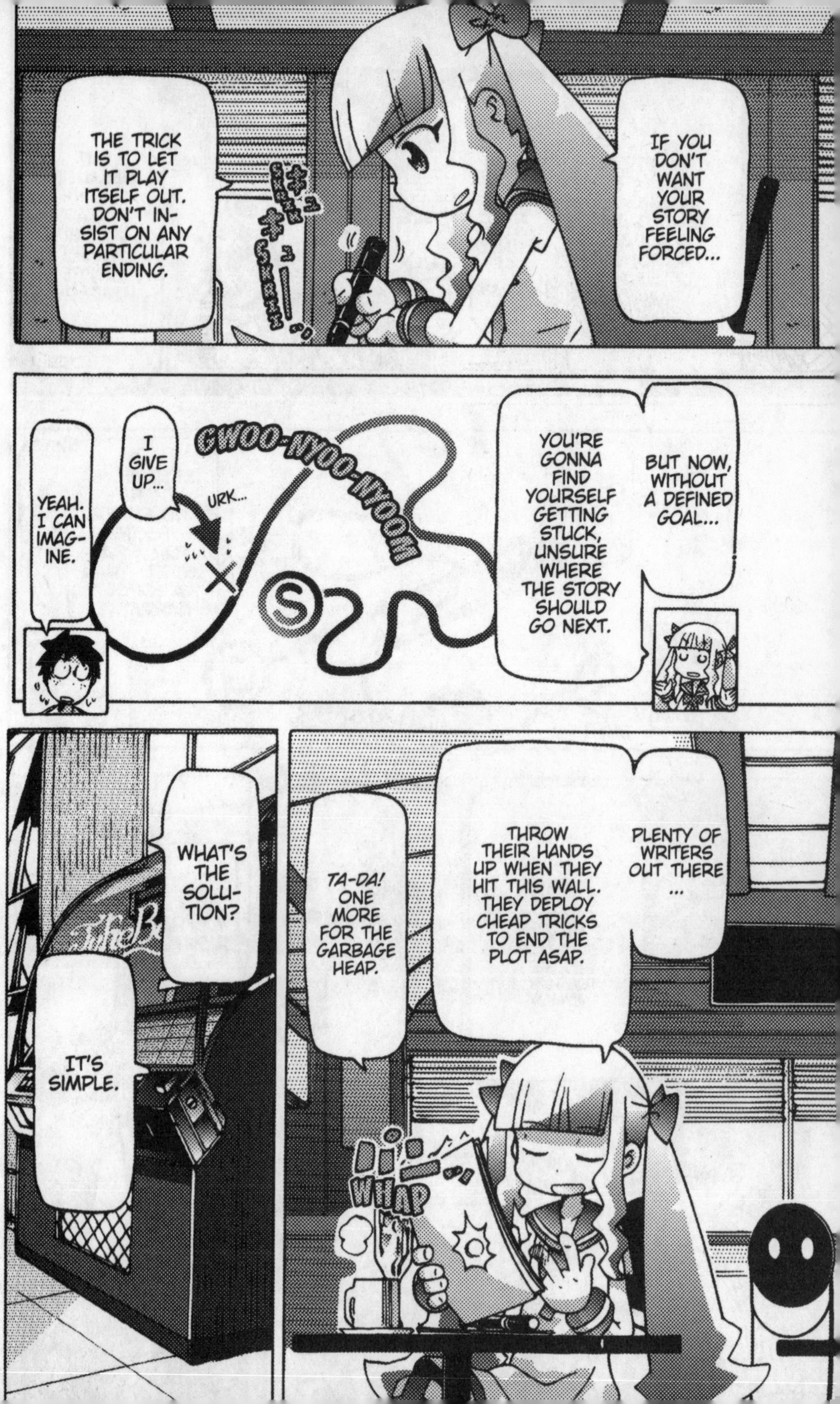
IF YOU DON'T WANT YOUR STORY FEELING FORCED...
THE TRICK IS TO LET IT PLAY ITSELF OUT. DON'T IN-SIST ON ANY PARTICULAR ENDING.
BUT NOW, WITHOUT A DEFINED GOAL...
YOU'RE GONNA FIND YOURSELF GETTING STUCK, UNSURE WHERE THE STORY SHOULD GO NEXT.
GWOO-NYOO-NYOOM
URK...
I GIVE UP...
YEAH. I CAN IMAG-INE.
PLENTY OF WRITERS OUT THERE ...
THROW THEIR HANDS UP WHEN THEY HIT THIS WALL. THEY DEPLOY CHEAP TRICKS TO END THE PLOT ASAP.
TA-DA! ONE MORE FOR THE GARBAGE HEAP.
WHAP
WHAT'S THE SOLU-TION?
IT'S SIMPLE.

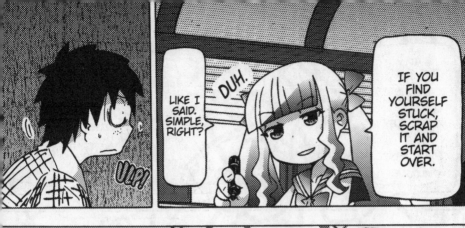

IF YOU FIND YOURSELF STUCK, SCRAP IT AND START OVER.
DUH.
LIKE I SAID. SIMPLE, RIGHT?
ULP!
PLAY WITH A CHARACTERS' PERSONALITY AND GOALS.
PAIR THEM IN INTERESTING WAYS. MERGE THEM.
FWP
FWP
FWP
FWP
FWP
TRY IT OVER AND OVER...
AND OVER AND OVER AGAIN.
WRITE TEN, A *HUNDRED* DRAFTS, IF THAT'S WHAT IT TAKES.
FWP
FWP
FWP
FWP
FWP
KEEP SEARCHING FOR THE ROUTE THAT BREATHES LIFE...
INTO THAT EMOTIONAL CORE YOU CHOSE.
FWP
FWP
FWP
KEEP CRAWLING THROUGH THAT TUNNEL.
EVENTUALLY, YOU'LL SEE A FAINT LIGHT.
JUST A GLIMMER.
AS SOON AS YOU DO, GRAB HOLD. THAT LIGHT IS YOUR *TRUE* STORY.
GLEAM

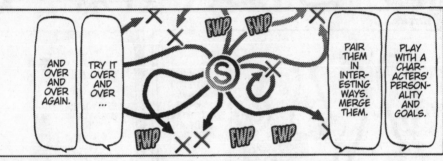

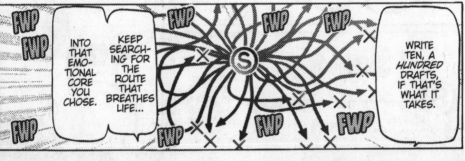

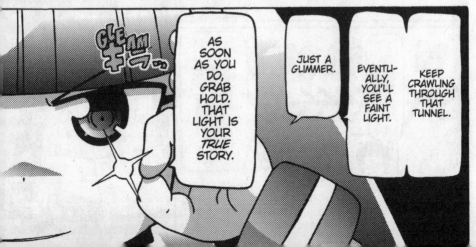

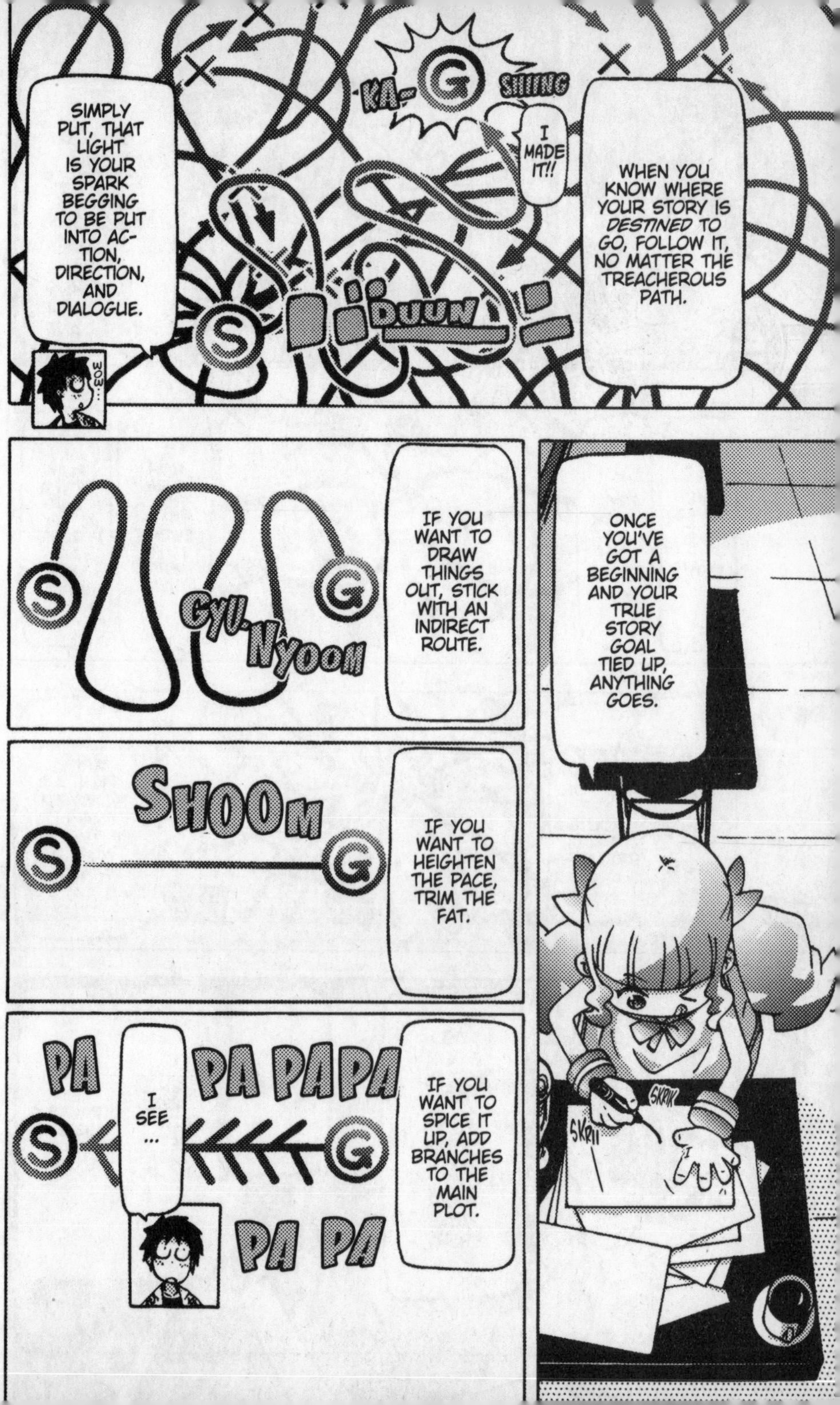
WHEN YOU KNOW WHERE YOUR STORY IS *DESTINED* TO GO, FOLLOW IT, NO MATTER THE TREACHEROUS PATH.
I MADE IT!!
KA-
SHIING
DUUN
SIMPLY PUT, THAT LIGHT IS YOUR SPARK BEGGING TO BE PUT INTO ACTION, DIRECTION, AND DIALOGUE.
WOW...
ONCE YOU'VE GOT A BEGINNING AND YOUR TRUE STORY GOAL TIED UP, ANYTHING GOES.
SKRIK
SKRII
IF YOU WANT TO DRAW THINGS OUT, STICK WITH AN INDIRECT ROUTE.
GYU-NYOOM
IF YOU WANT TO HEIGHTEN THE PACE, TRIM THE FAT.
SHOOM
IF YOU WANT TO SPICE IT UP, ADD BRANCHES TO THE MAIN PLOT.
PA PA PAPA
I SEE...
PA
PA PA

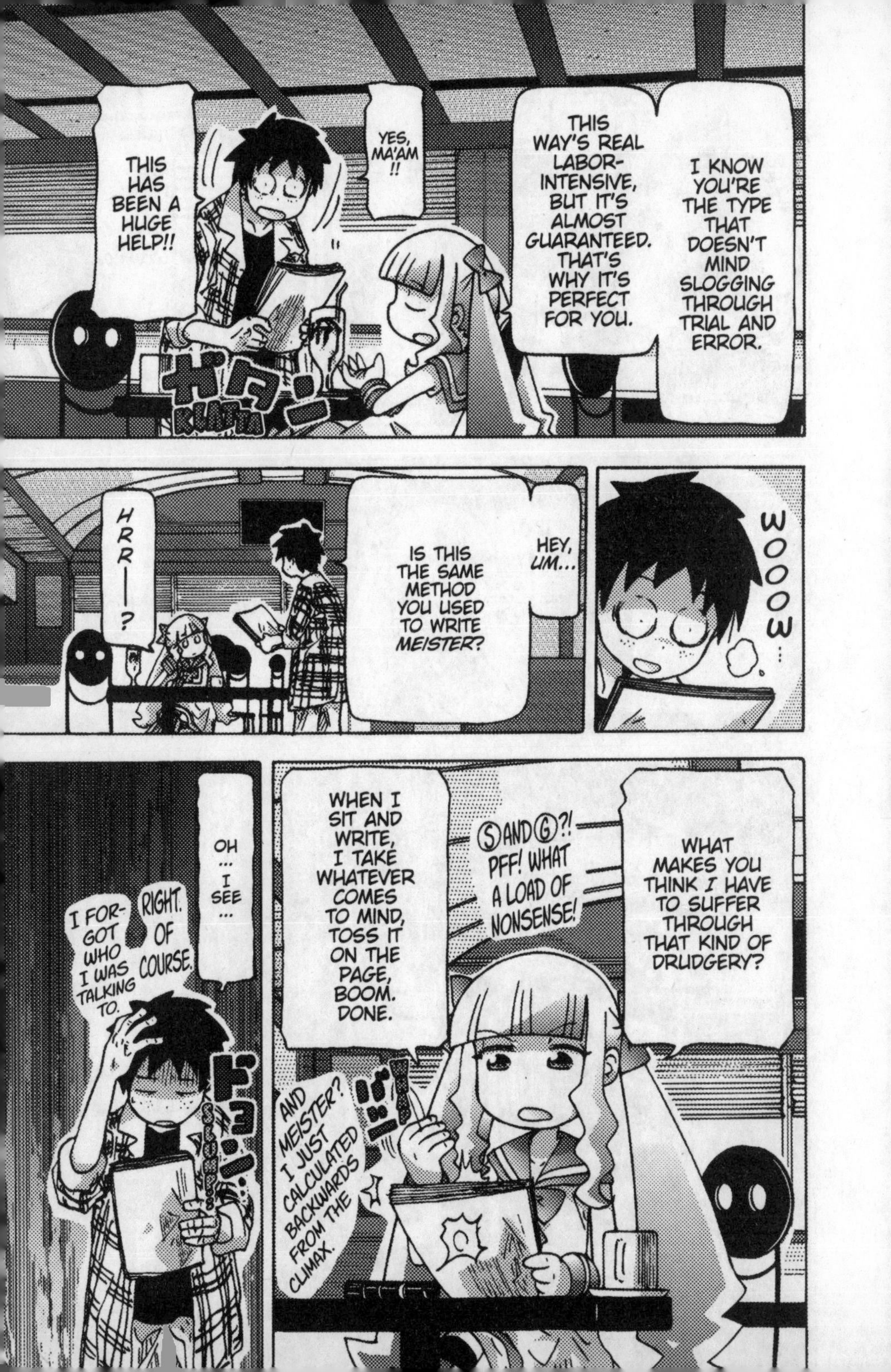
I KNOW YOU'RE THE TYPE THAT DOESN'T MIND SLOGGING THROUGH TRIAL AND ERROR.
THIS WAY'S REAL LABOR-INTENSIVE, BUT IT'S ALMOST GUARANTEED. THAT'S WHY IT'S PERFECT FOR YOU.
YES, MA'AM!!
THIS HAS BEEN A HUGE HELP!!
KLATTA
WOOOOW...
HEY, UM...
IS THIS THE SAME METHOD YOU USED TO WRITE MEISTER?
HRR—?
WHAT MAKES YOU THINK I HAVE TO SUFFER THROUGH THAT KIND OF DRUDGERY?
Ⓢ AND Ⓖ?! PFF! WHAT A LOAD OF NONSENSE!
WHEN I SIT AND WRITE, I TAKE WHATEVER COMES TO MIND, TOSS IT ON THE PAGE, BOOM. DONE.
AND MEISTER? I JUST CALCULATED BACKWARDS FROM THE CLIMAX.
OH... I SEE...
RIGHT. OF COURSE.
I FORGOT WHO I WAS TALKING TO.

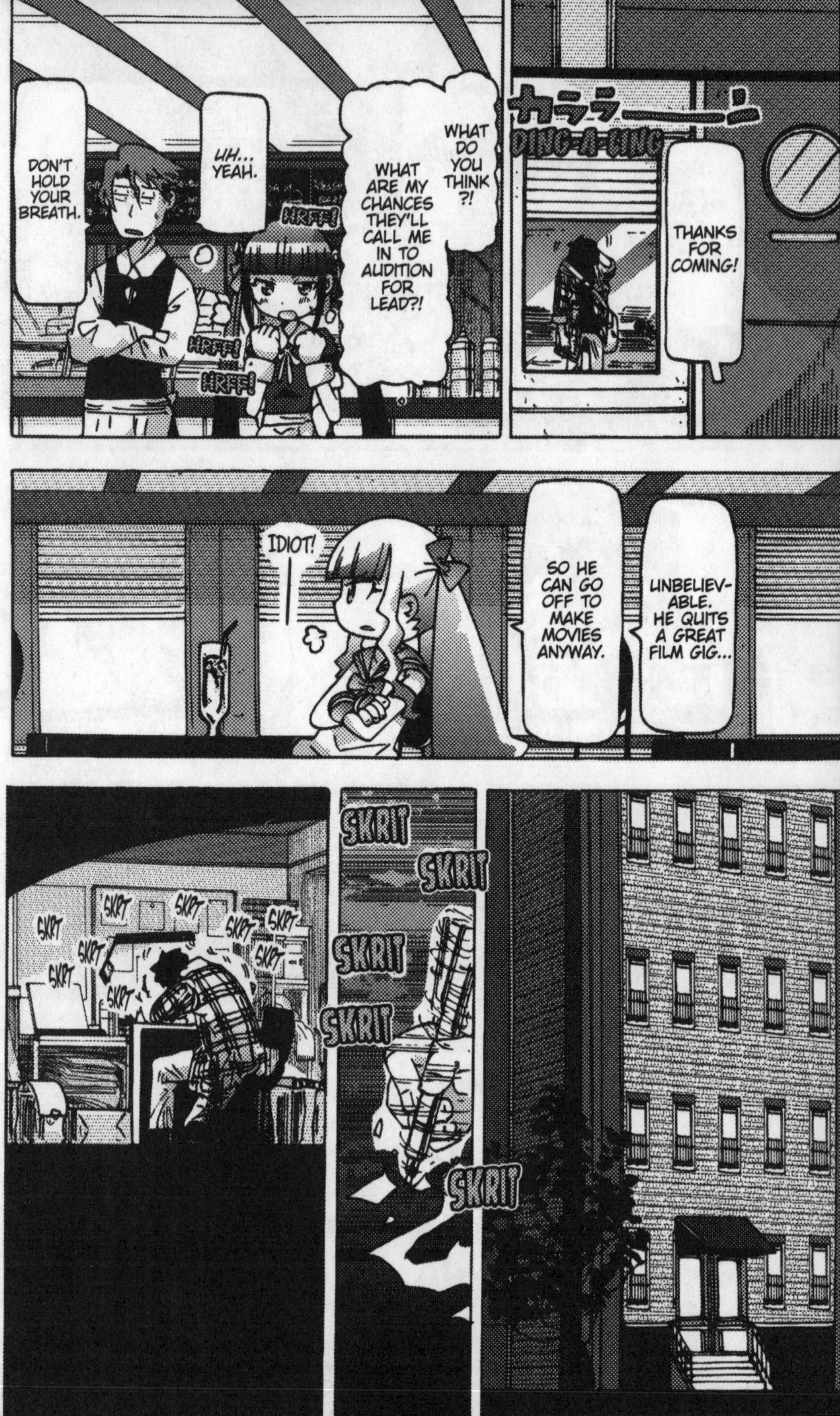
カララーン
DING-A-LING
THANKS FOR COMING!
WHAT DO YOU THINK?!
WHAT ARE MY CHANCES THEY'LL CALL ME IN TO AUDITION FOR LEAD?!
HRFF!
UH... YEAH.
DON'T HOLD YOUR BREATH.
HRFF!
HRFF!
UNBELIEV-ABLE. HE QUITS A GREAT FILM GIG...
SO HE CAN GO OFF TO MAKE MOVIES ANYWAY.
IDIOT!
SKRIT
SKRIT
SKRIT
SKRIT
SKRIT
SKRT
SKRT
SKRT
SKRT
SKRT
SKRT
SKRT
SKRT
SKRT

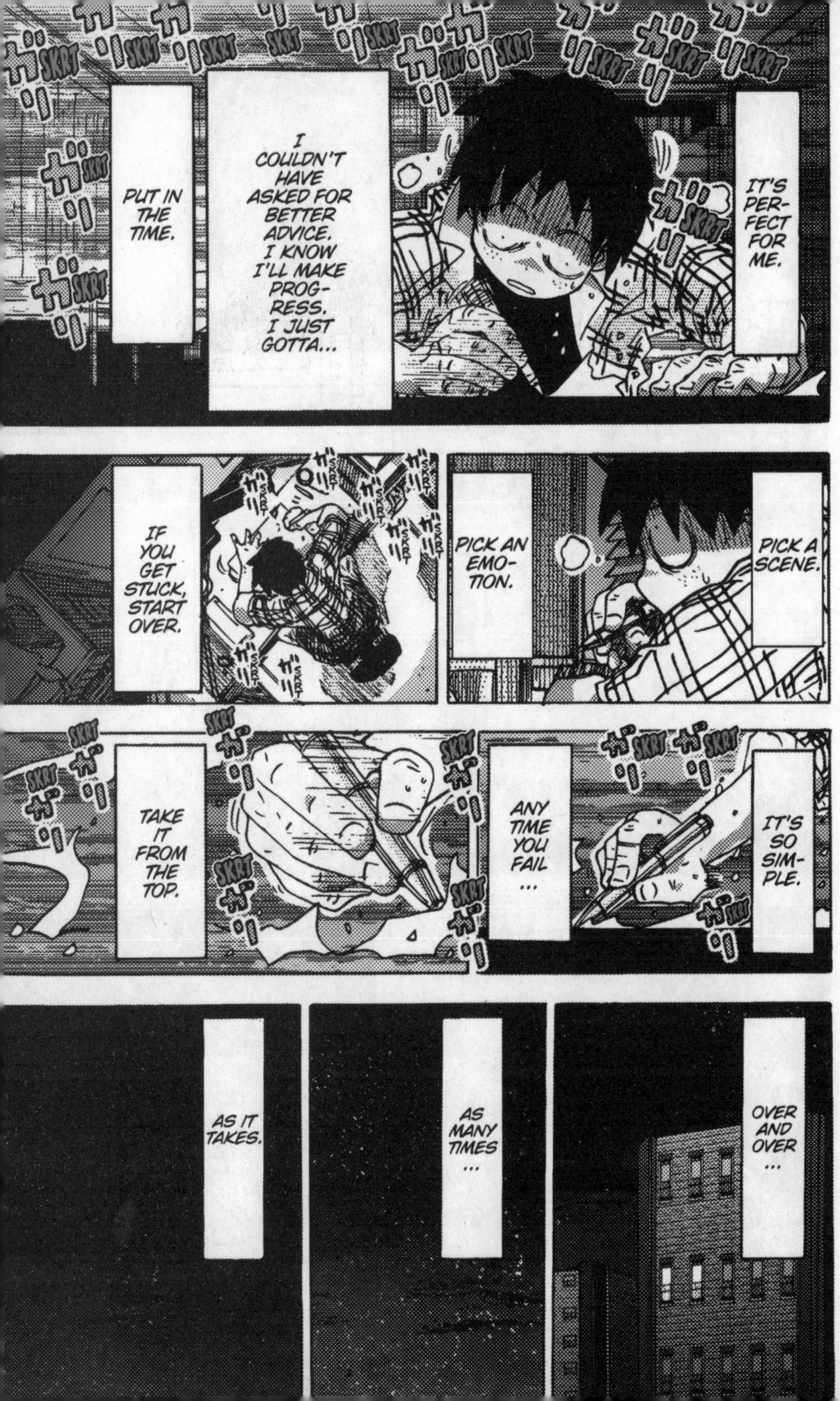
SKRT
IT'S PERFECT FOR ME.
I COULDN'T HAVE ASKED FOR BETTER ADVICE. I KNOW I'LL MAKE PROGRESS. I JUST GOTTA...
PUT IN THE TIME.
PICK A SCENE.
PICK AN EMOTION.
SKRT
IF YOU GET STUCK, START OVER.
SKRT
IT'S SO SIMPLE.
ANY TIME YOU FAIL...
SKRT
TAKE IT FROM THE TOP.
OVER AND OVER...
AS MANY TIMES...
AS IT TAKES.

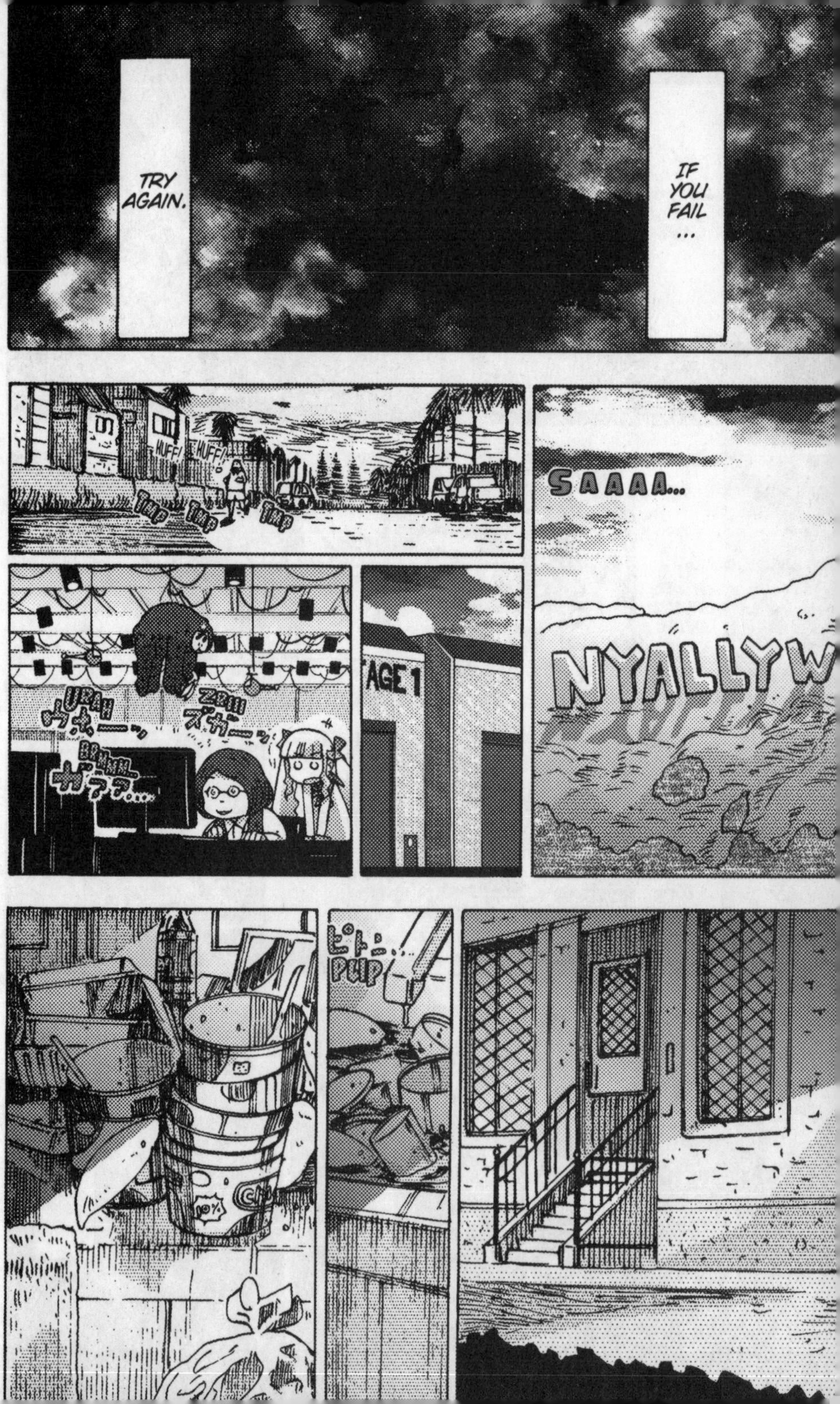
IF YOU FAIL ...
TRY AGAIN.
SAAAA...
NYALLYW
HUFF! HUFF!
TMP TMP TMP
AGE 1
ZRIII ズガーッ
URAH ウホーッ
BRMML ガアア...
ピト...
PLIP

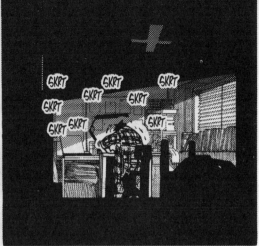

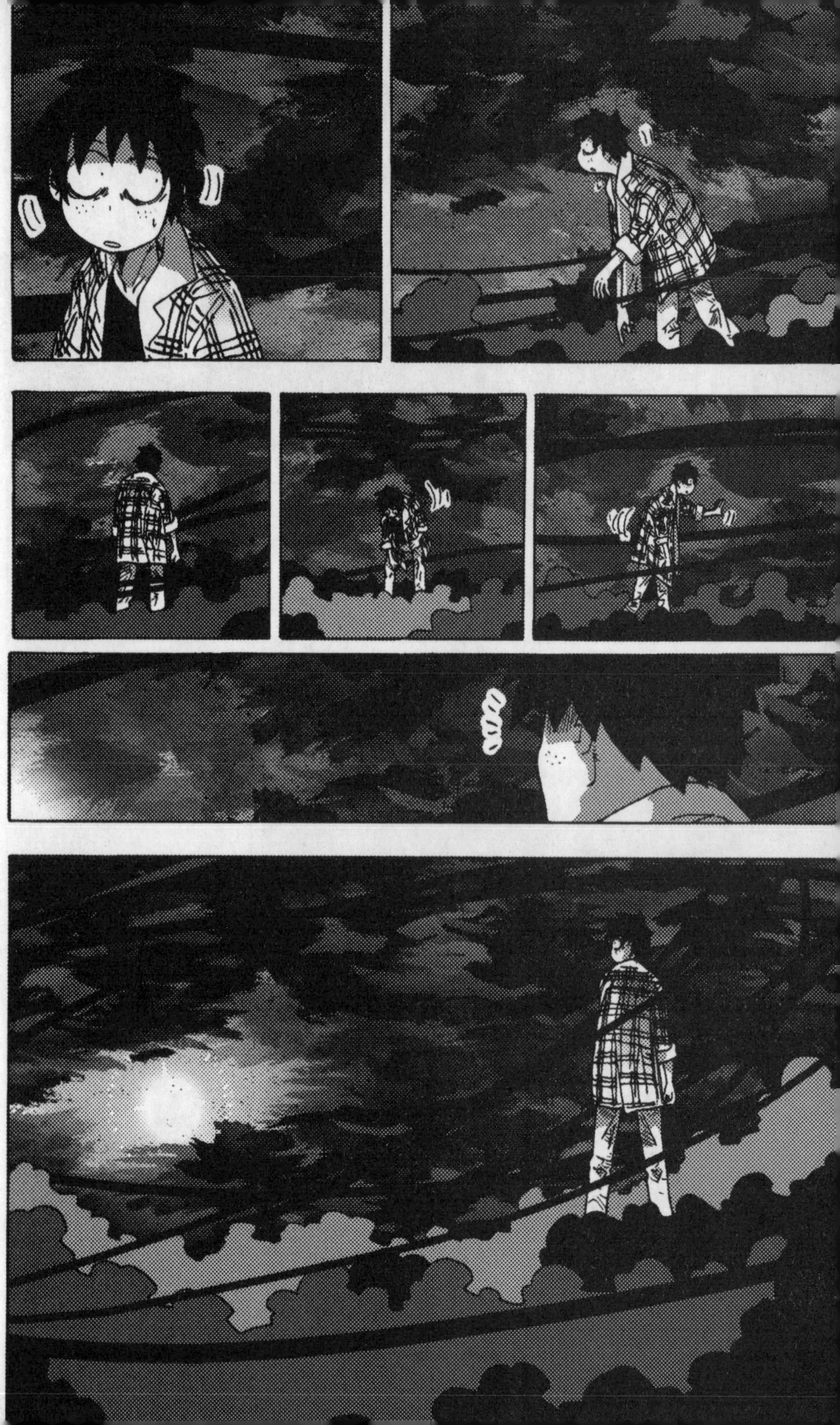

POMPO

THE CINÉPHILE

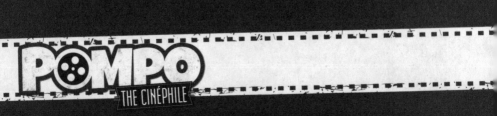

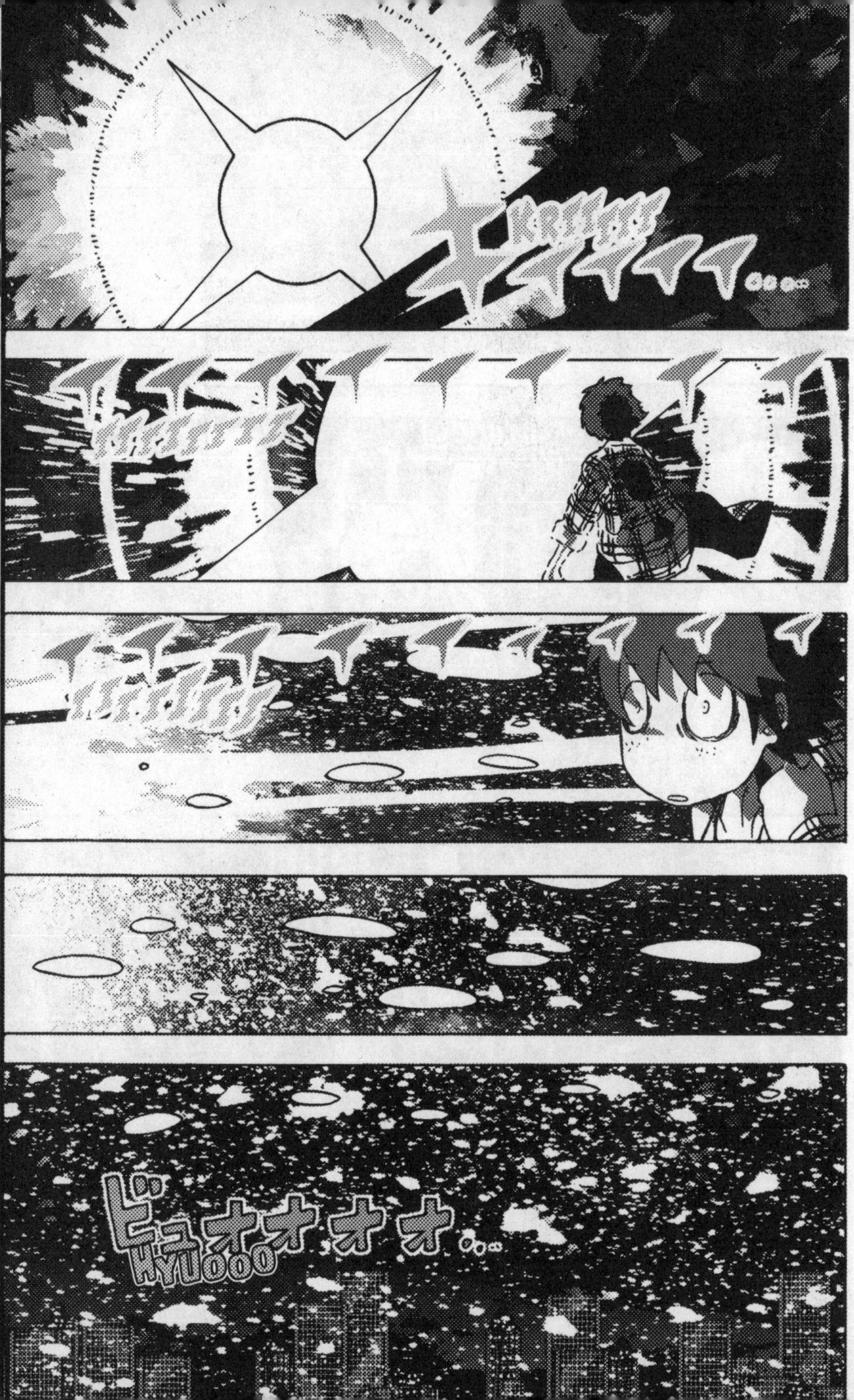
キイイイイ…
ビュオオオオオ…
WYUOOO

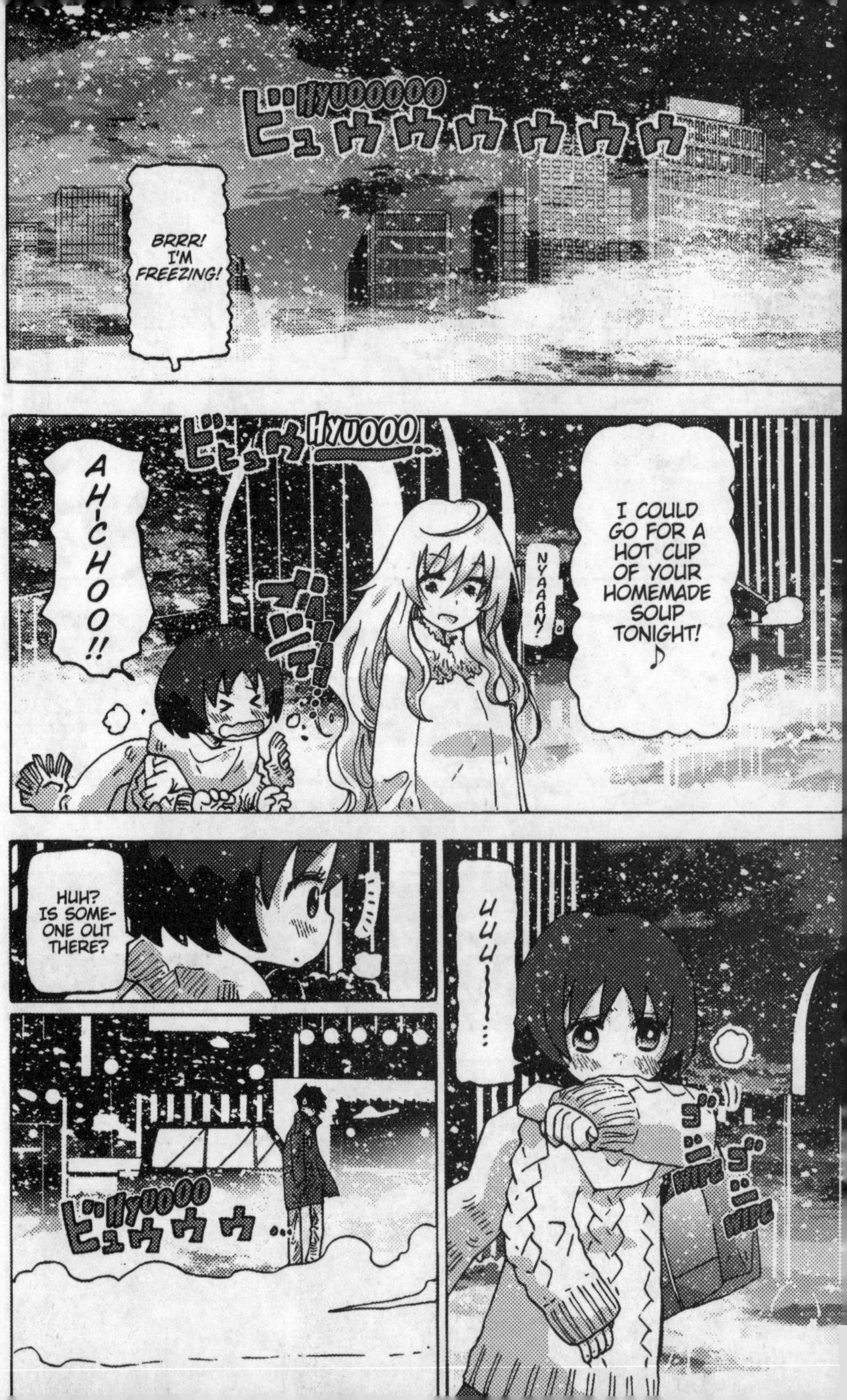
ビュウウウウウウウ HYUOOOOOO
BRRR! I'M FREEZING!
I COULD GO FOR A HOT CUP OF YOUR HOMEMADE SOUP TONIGHT! ♪
ビュウ— HYUOOO
NYAAAN!
AHICHOOO!!
UUU——...
WIPE WIPE
HUH? IS SOME-ONE OUT THERE?
ビュウウウ... HYUOOO

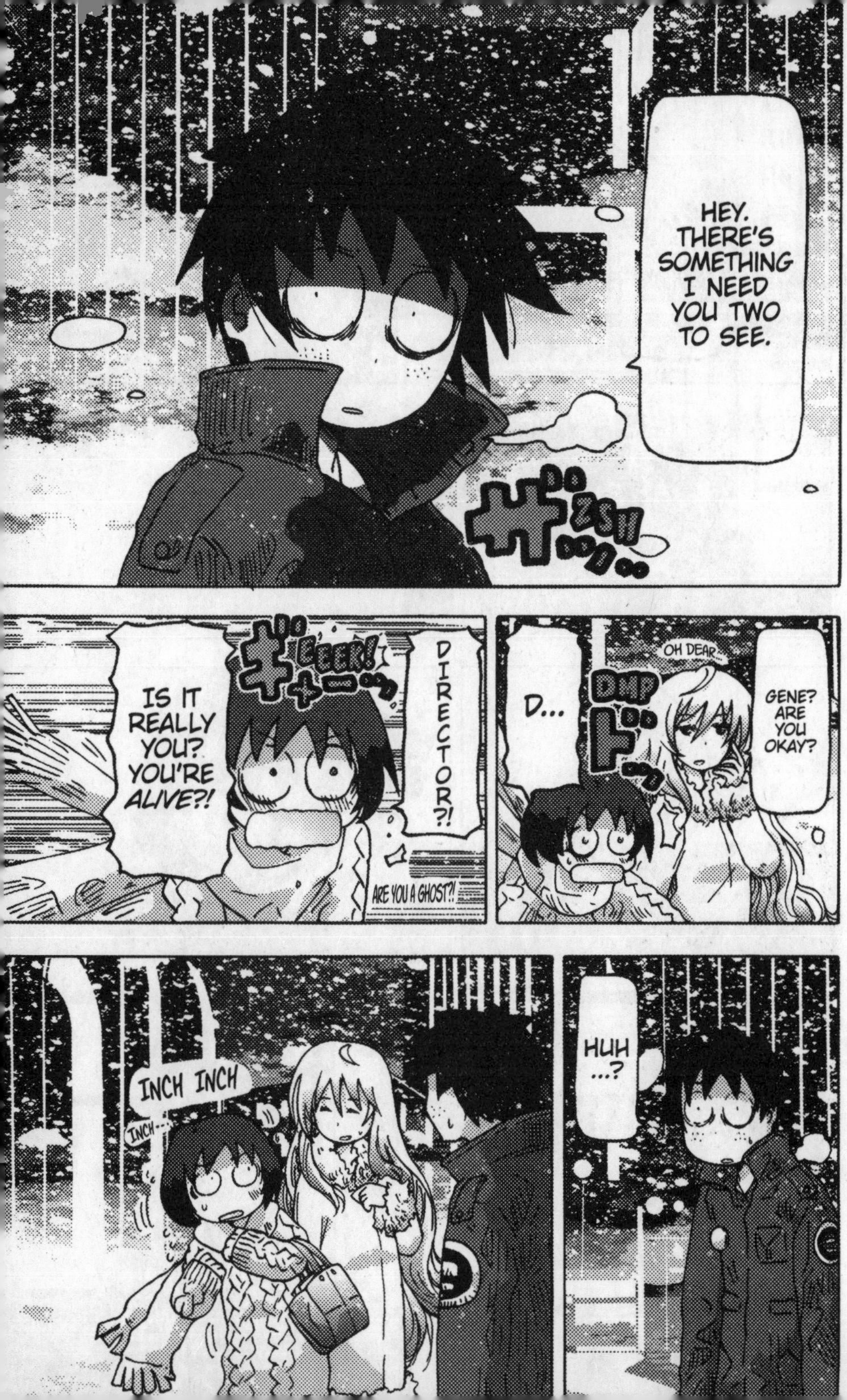
HEY. THERE'S SOMETHING I NEED YOU TWO TO SEE.
ZSH
OH DEAR...
GENE? ARE YOU OKAY?
DMP
D...
DIRECTOR?!
EEEK!
IS IT REALLY YOU? YOU'RE ALIVE?!
ARE YOU A GHOST?!
HUH ...?
INCH INCH
INCH...

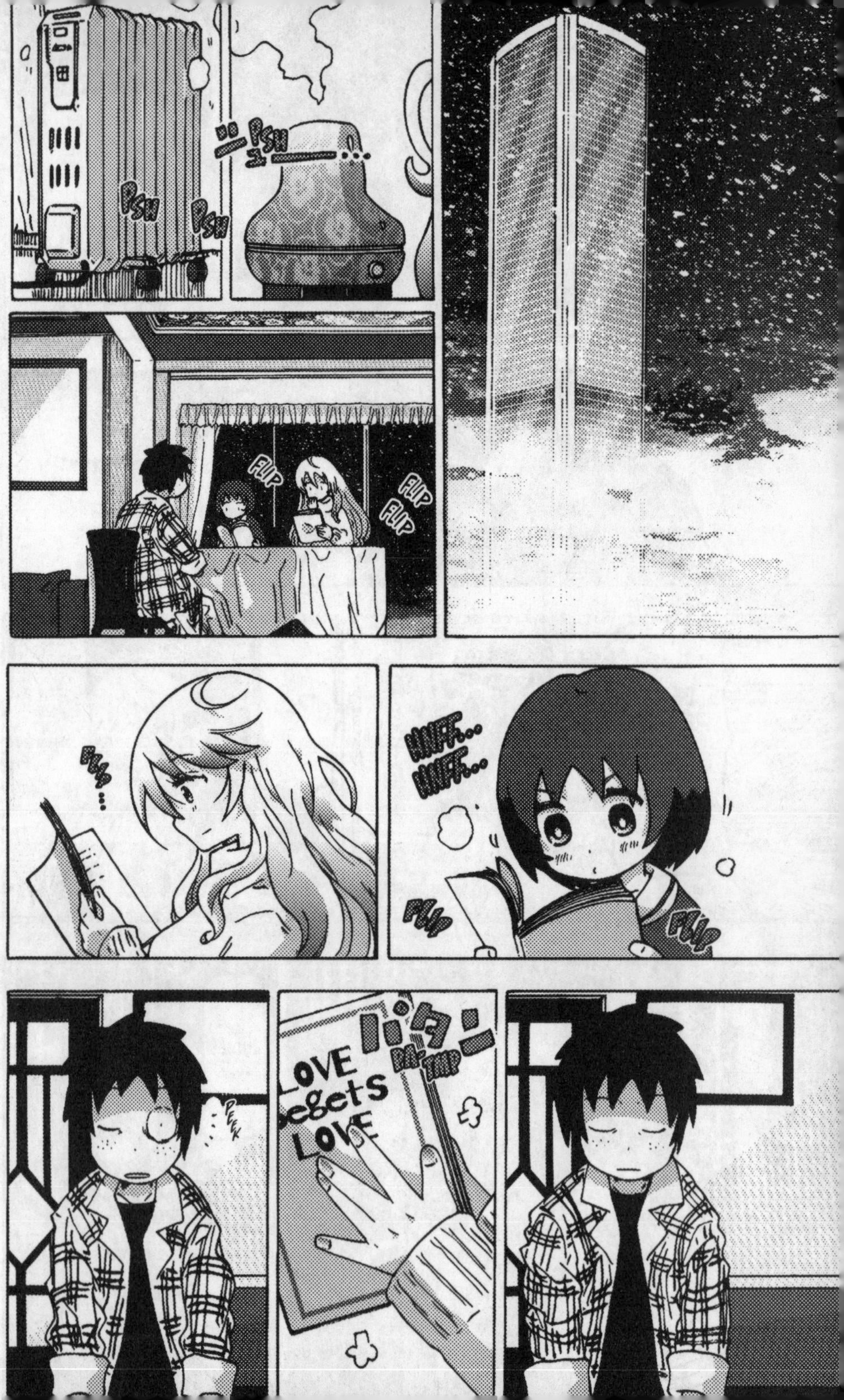

シュー
PSH———...
PSH
PSH
FLIP
FLIP
FLIP
HNFF...
HNFF...
FLIP
FLIP
FLIP...
パタン
PA-TMP
LOVE begets LOVE
PEEK

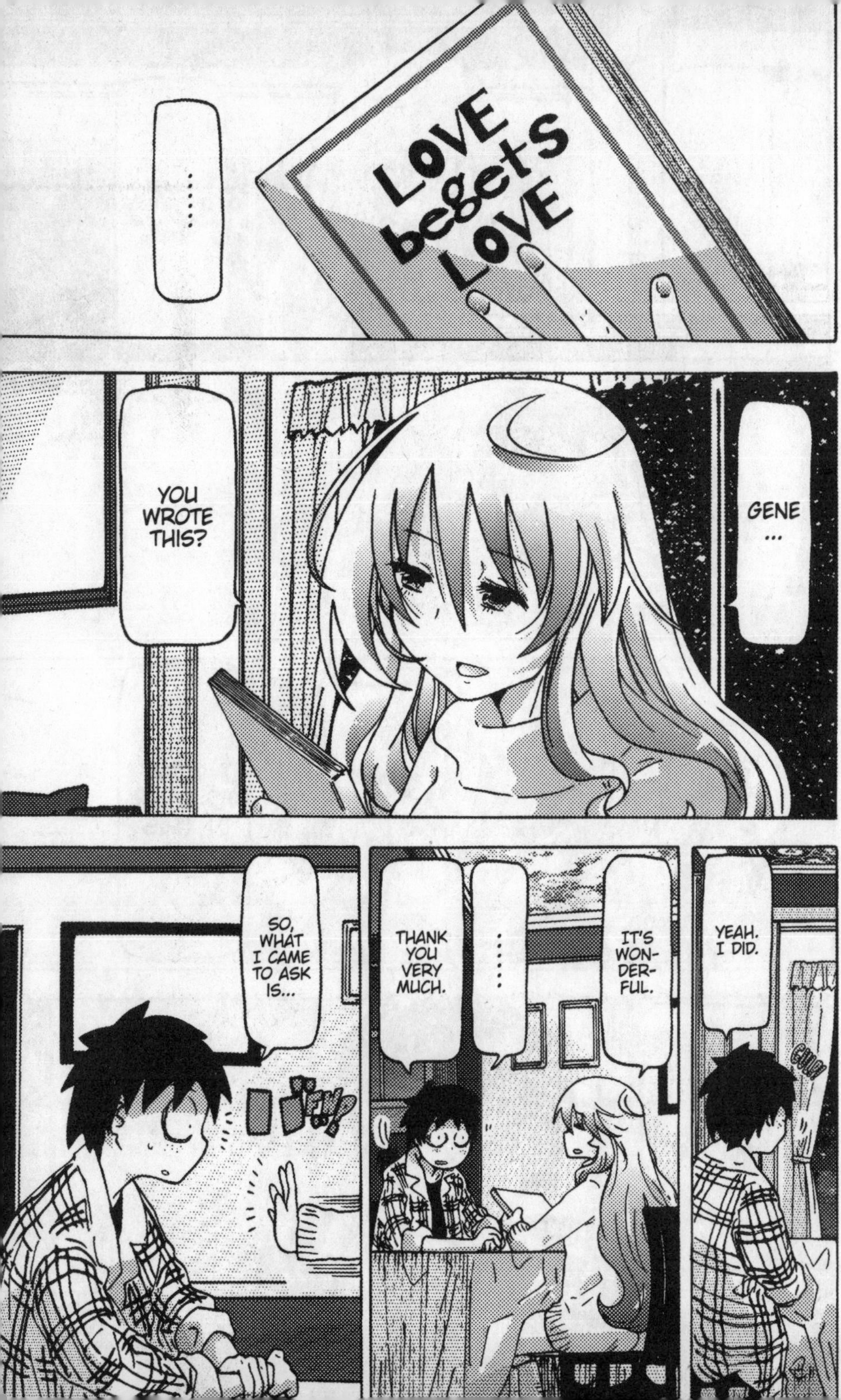
LOVE begets LOVE
......
GENE ...
YOU WROTE THIS?
YEAH. I DID.
IT'S WONDER-FUL.
......
THANK YOU VERY MUCH.
SO, WHAT I CAME TO ASK IS...

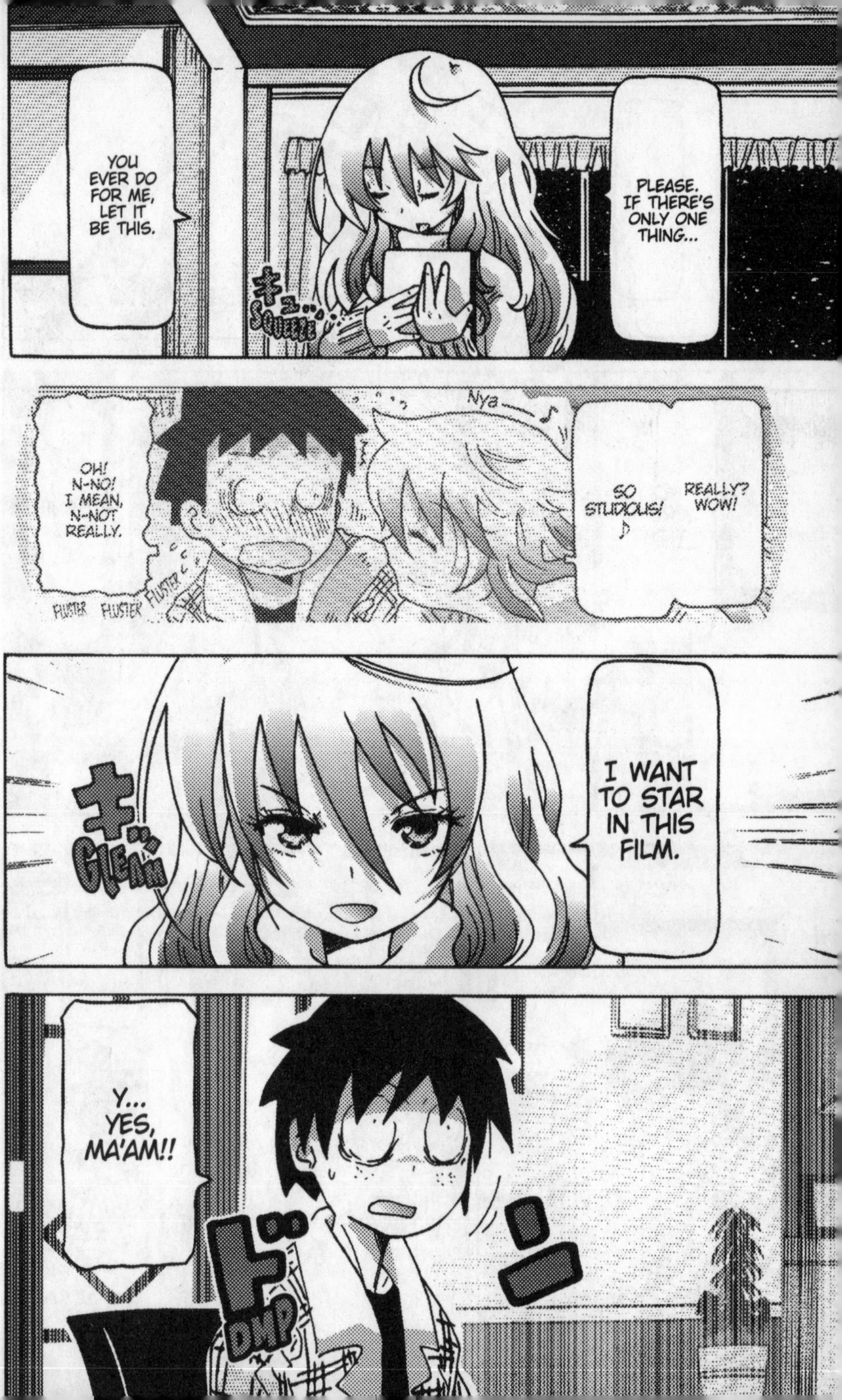
PLEASE. IF THERE'S ONLY ONE THING...
YOU EVER DO FOR ME, LET IT BE THIS.
SQUEEZE
REALLY? WOW!
SO STUDIOUS! ♪
Nya ♪
OH! N-NO! I MEAN, N-NOT REALLY.
FLUSTER FLUSTER FLUSTER
I WANT TO STAR IN THIS FILM.
GLEAM
Y... YES, MA'AM!!
DMP

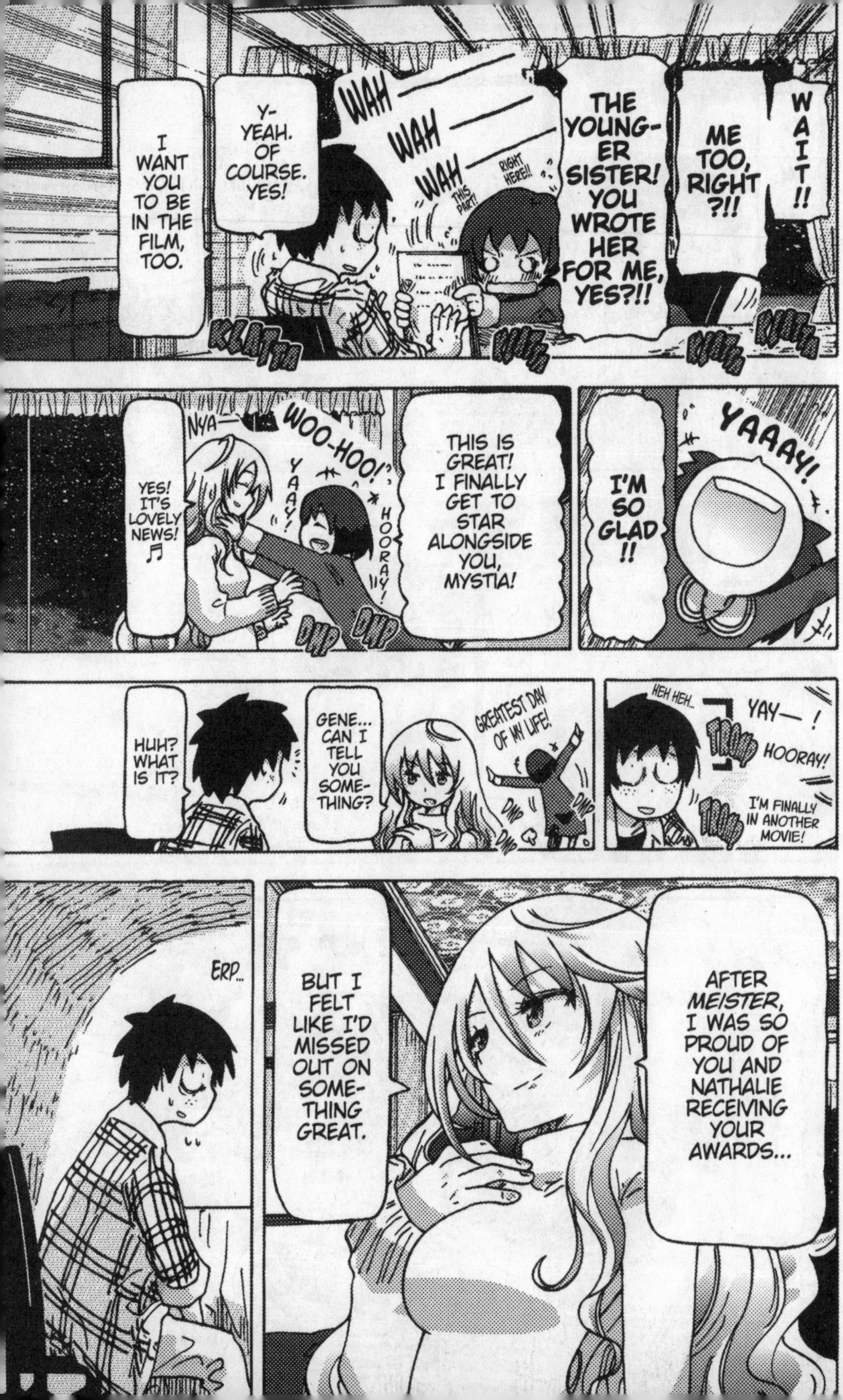
WAIT!!
ME TOO, RIGHT?!!
THE YOUNGER-SISTER! YOU WROTE HER FOR ME, YES?!!
RIGHT HERE!!
THIS PART!
WAH — WAH — WAH —
Y-YEAH. OF COURSE. YES!
I WANT YOU TO BE IN THE FILM, TOO.
YAAAY!
I'M SO GLAD!!
THIS IS GREAT! I FINALLY GET TO STAR ALONGSIDE YOU, MYSTIA!
HOORAY!
YAAAY!
WOO-HOO!
NYA—
YES! IT'S LOVELY NEWS! ♬
HEH HEH...
YAY— !
HOORAY!
I'M FINALLY IN ANOTHER MOVIE!
GREATEST DAY OF MY LIFE!
GENE... CAN I TELL YOU SOMETHING?
HUH? WHAT IS IT?
AFTER MEISTER, I WAS SO PROUD OF YOU AND NATHALIE RECEIVING YOUR AWARDS...
BUT I FELT LIKE I'D MISSED OUT ON SOMETHING GREAT.
ERP...

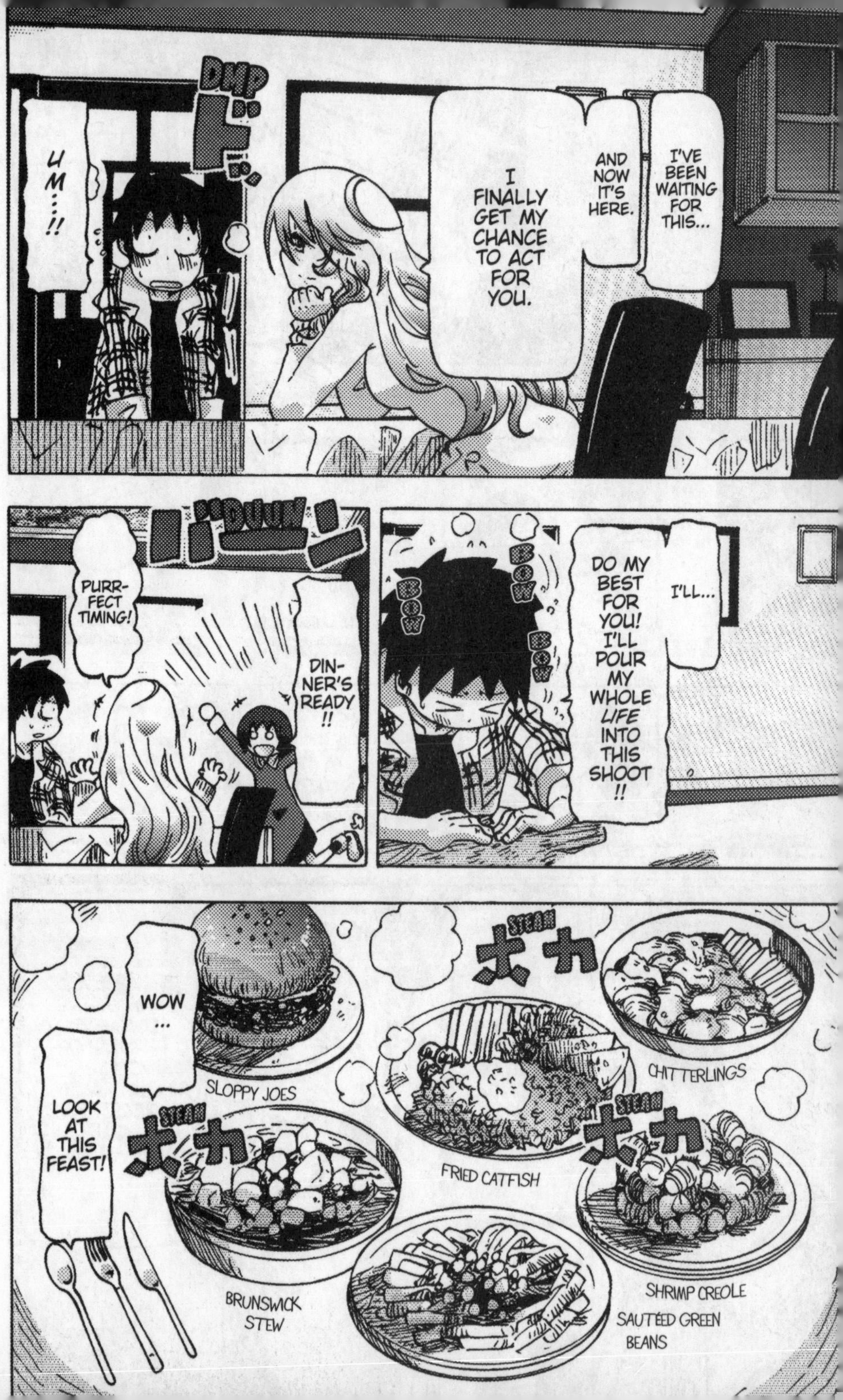
I'VE BEEN WAITING FOR THIS...
AND NOW IT'S HERE.
I FINALLY GET MY CHANCE TO ACT FOR YOU.
DMP
UM...!!
I'LL...
DO MY BEST FOR YOU! I'LL POUR MY WHOLE *LIFE* INTO THIS SHOOT!!
BOW BOW
DIN-NER'S READY!!
PURR-FECT TIMING!
STEAM
CHITTERLINGS
WOW...
SLOPPY JOES
FRIED CATFISH
STEAM
SHRIMP CREOLE
SAUTÉED GREEN BEANS
STEAM
LOOK AT THIS FEAST!
BRUNSWICK STEW

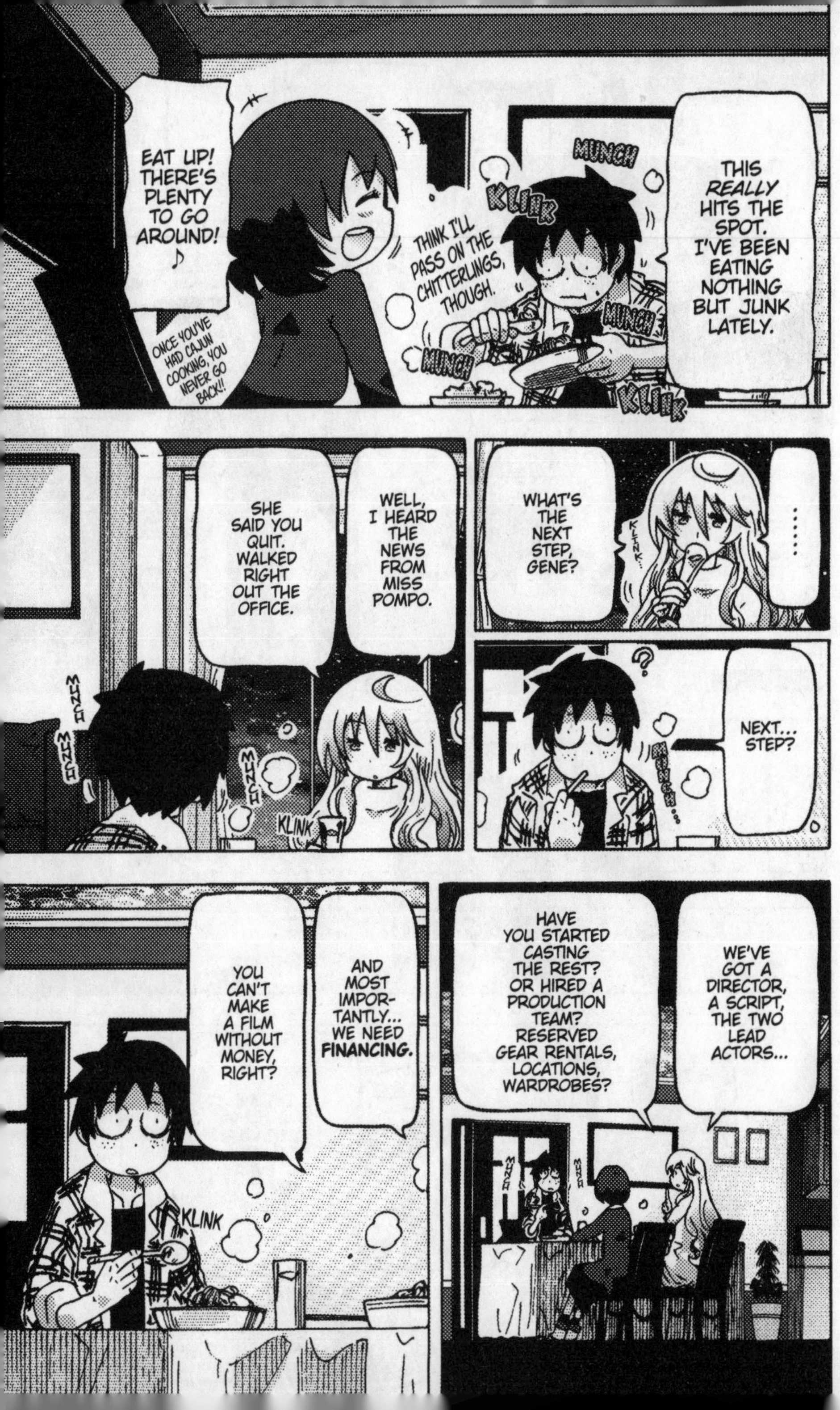
THIS REALLY HITS THE SPOT. I'VE BEEN EATING NOTHING BUT JUNK LATELY.
MUNCH
KLINK
MUNCH
KLINK
THINK I'LL PASS ON THE CHITTERLINGS, THOUGH.
MUNCH
EAT UP! THERE'S PLENTY TO GO AROUND! ♪
ONCE YOU'VE HAD CAJUN COOKING, YOU NEVER GO BACK!!
......
WHAT'S THE NEXT STEP, GENE?
KLINK...
NEXT... STEP?
MUNCH...
WELL, I HEARD THE NEWS FROM MISS POMPO.
SHE SAID YOU QUIT. WALKED RIGHT OUT THE OFFICE.
MUNCH
MUNCH
MUNCH
KLINK
WE'VE GOT A DIRECTOR, A SCRIPT, THE TWO LEAD ACTORS...
HAVE YOU STARTED CASTING THE REST? OR HIRED A PRODUCTION TEAM? RESERVED GEAR RENTALS, LOCATIONS, WARDROBES?
MUNCH
MUNCH
AND MOST IMPORTANTLY... WE NEED FINANCING.
YOU CAN'T MAKE A FILM WITHOUT MONEY, RIGHT?
KLINK

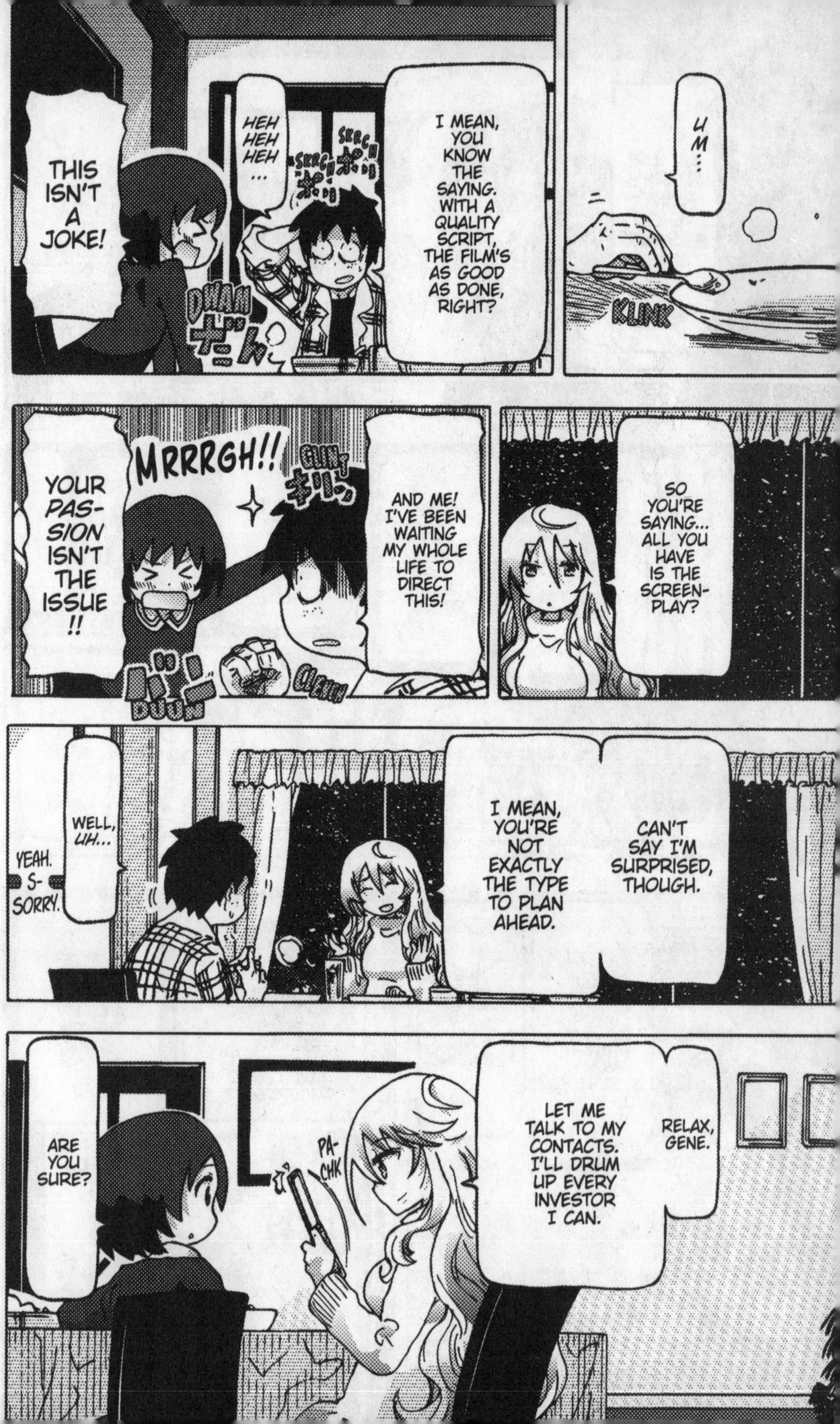
UM...
KLINK
I MEAN, YOU KNOW THE SAYING. WITH A QUALITY SCRIPT, THE FILM'S AS GOOD AS DONE, RIGHT?
SKRCH
SKRCH
HEH HEH HEH...
DHAM
THIS ISN'T A JOKE!
SO YOU'RE SAYING... ALL YOU HAVE IS THE SCREENPLAY?
AND ME! I'VE BEEN WAITING MY WHOLE LIFE TO DIRECT THIS!
CLINK
MRRRGH!!
YOUR PASSION ISN'T THE ISSUE!!
CLENCH
DUUN
CAN'T SAY I'M SURPRISED, THOUGH.
I MEAN, YOU'RE NOT EXACTLY THE TYPE TO PLAN AHEAD.
WELL, UH...
YEAH. S-SORRY.
RELAX, GENE.
LET ME TALK TO MY CONTACTS. I'LL DRUM UP EVERY INVESTOR I CAN.
PA-CHK
ARE YOU SURE?

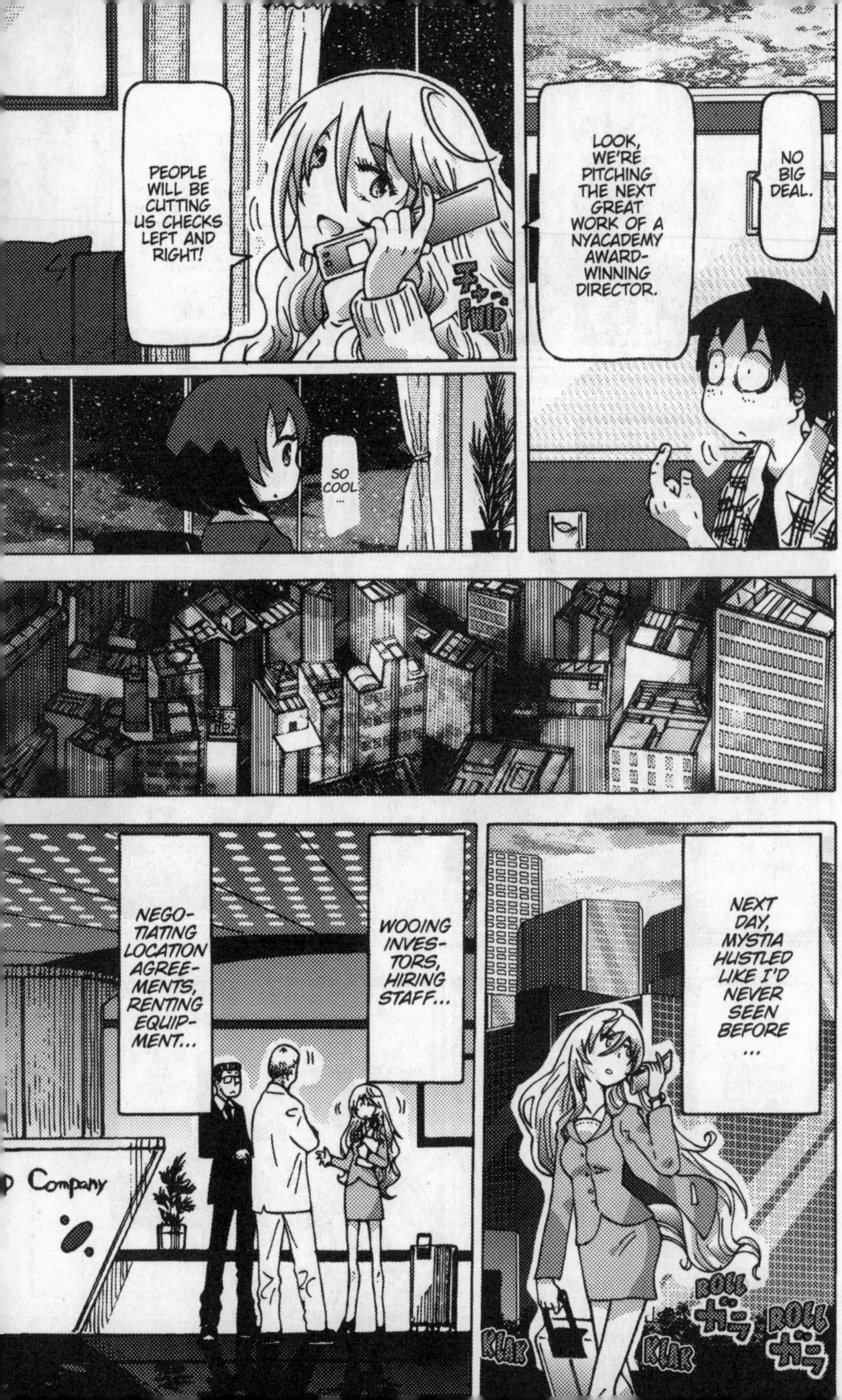

NO BIG DEAL.
LOOK, WE'RE PITCHING THE NEXT GREAT WORK OF A NYACADEMY AWARD-WINNING DIRECTOR.
PEOPLE WILL BE CUTTING US CHECKS LEFT AND RIGHT!
HUP
SO COOL...
NEXT DAY, MYSTIA HUSTLED LIKE I'D NEVER SEEN BEFORE...
ROLL
ROLL
KLAK
KLAK
WOOING INVESTORS, HIRING STAFF...
NEGOTIATING LOCATION AGREEMENTS, RENTING EQUIPMENT...
Company

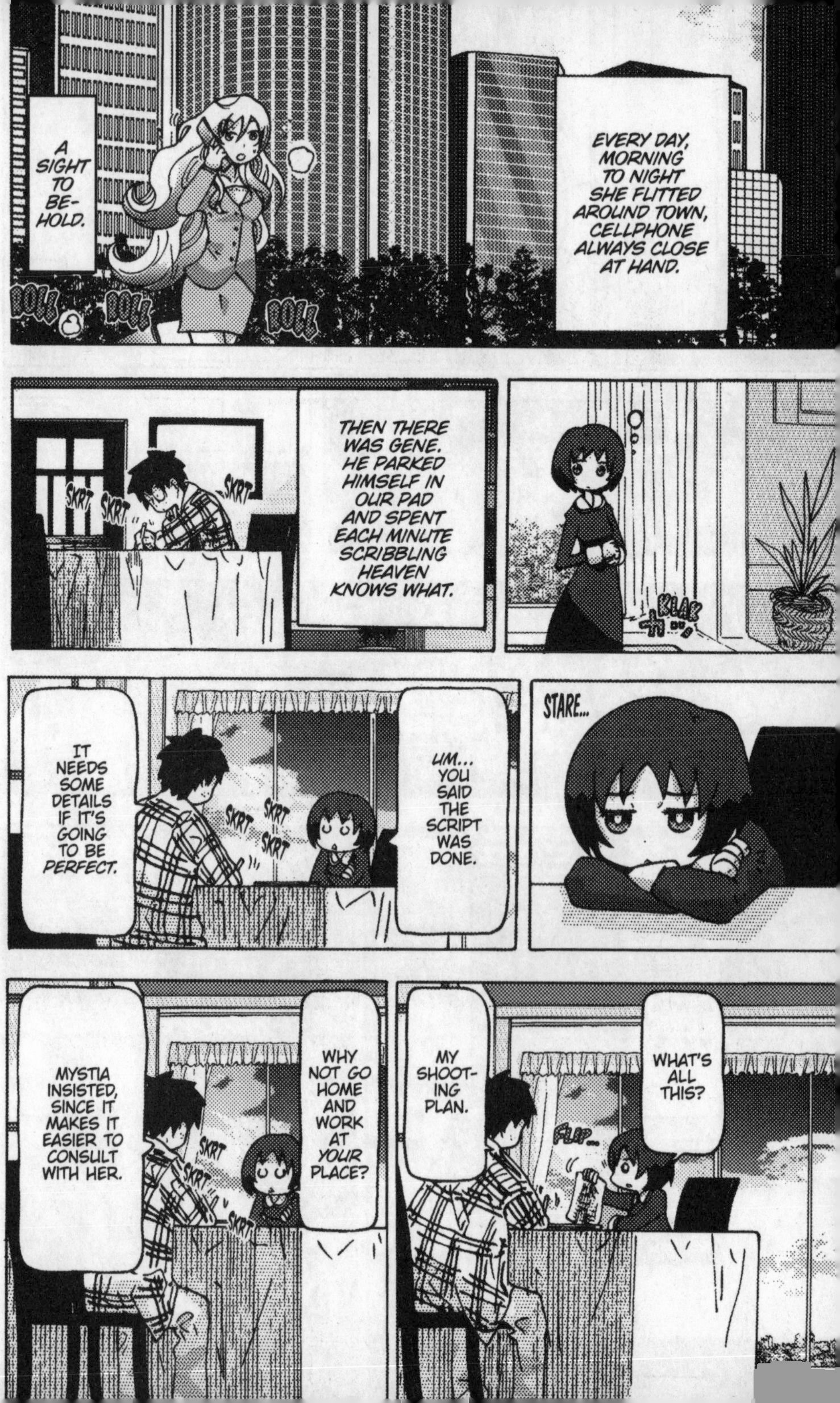
EVERY DAY, MORNING TO NIGHT SHE FLITTED AROUND TOWN, CELLPHONE ALWAYS CLOSE AT HAND.
A SIGHT TO BE-HOLD.
ROLL
ROLL
ROLL
KLAK
THEN THERE WAS GENE. HE PARKED HIMSELF IN OUR PAD AND SPENT EACH MINUTE SCRIBBLING HEAVEN KNOWS WHAT.
SKRT
SKRT
SKRT
STARE...
UM... YOU SAID THE SCRIPT WAS DONE.
SKRT
SKRT
SKRT
IT NEEDS SOME DETAILS IF IT'S GOING TO BE PERFECT.
WHAT'S ALL THIS?
FLIP...
MY SHOOT-ING PLAN.
WHY NOT GO HOME AND WORK AT YOUR PLACE?
SKRT
SKRT
SKRT
MYSTIA INSISTED, SINCE IT MAKES IT EASIER TO CONSULT WITH HER.

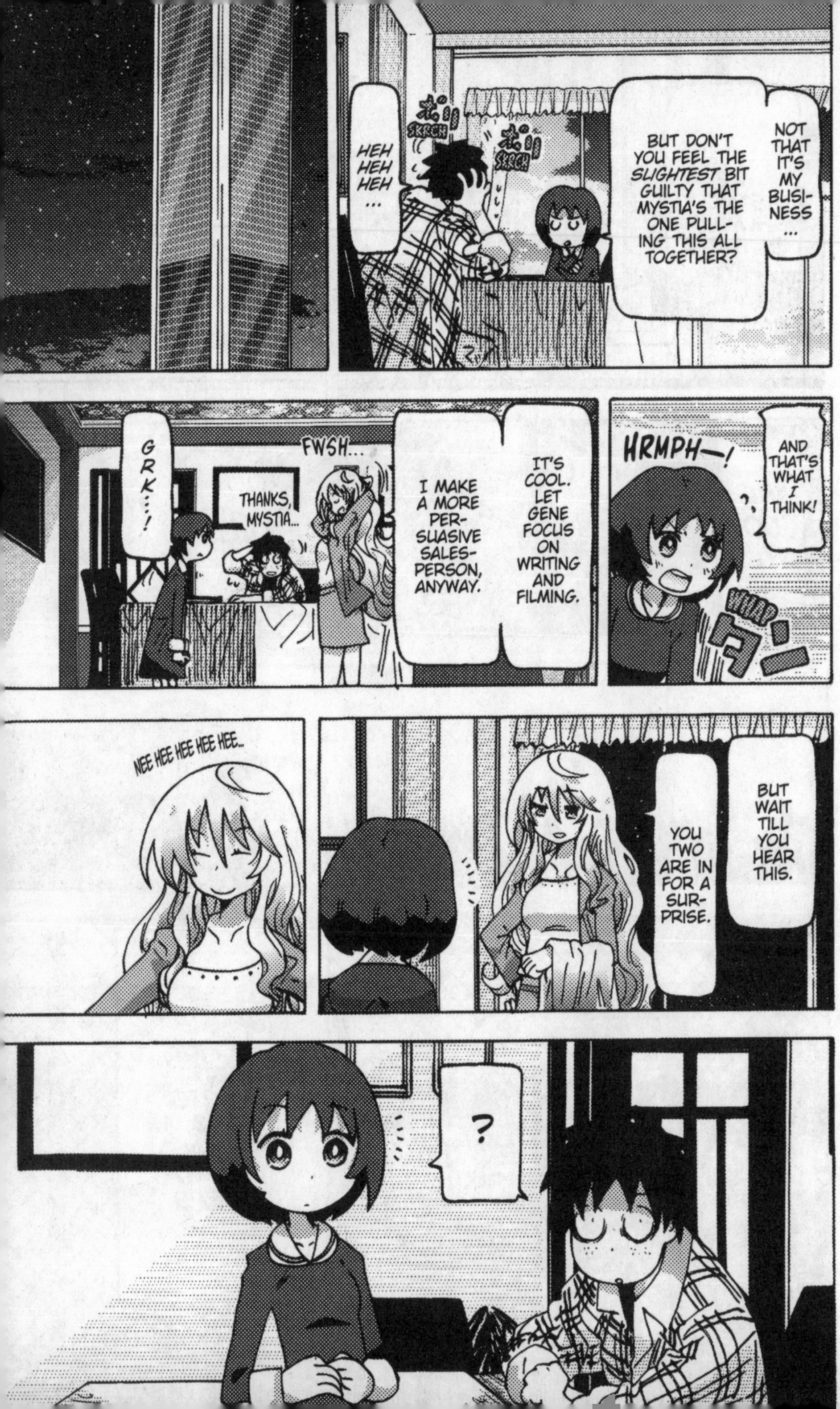
NOT THAT IT'S MY BUSINESS...
BUT DON'T YOU FEEL THE SLIGHTEST BIT GUILTY THAT MYSTIA'S THE ONE PULLING THIS ALL TOGETHER?
SKRCH
SKRCH
HEH HEH HEH...
AND THAT'S WHAT I THINK!
HRMPH—!
WHAP
IT'S COOL. LET GENE FOCUS ON WRITING AND FILMING.
I MAKE A MORE PERSUASIVE SALESPERSON, ANYWAY.
FWSH...
THANKS, MYSTIA...
GRK...!
BUT WAIT TILL YOU HEAR THIS.
YOU TWO ARE IN FOR A SURPRISE.
NEE HEE HEE HEE HEE...
?

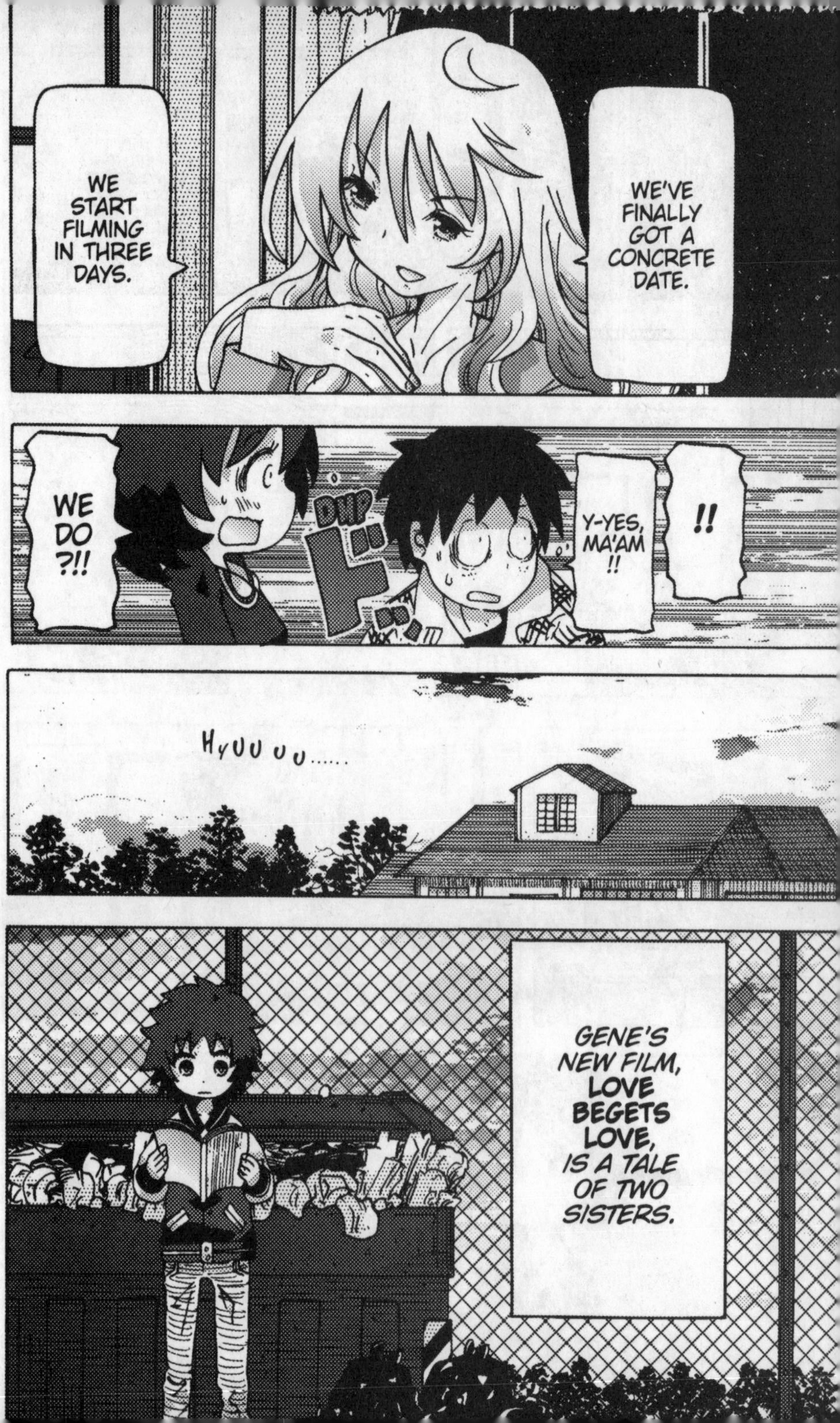
WE'VE FINALLY GOT A CONCRETE DATE.
WE START FILMING IN THREE DAYS.
!!
Y-YES, MA'AM!!
DWP
WE DO?!!
HYUUUU......
GENE'S NEW FILM, LOVE BEGETS LOVE, IS A TALE OF TWO SISTERS.

LOVE•Begets•LOVE

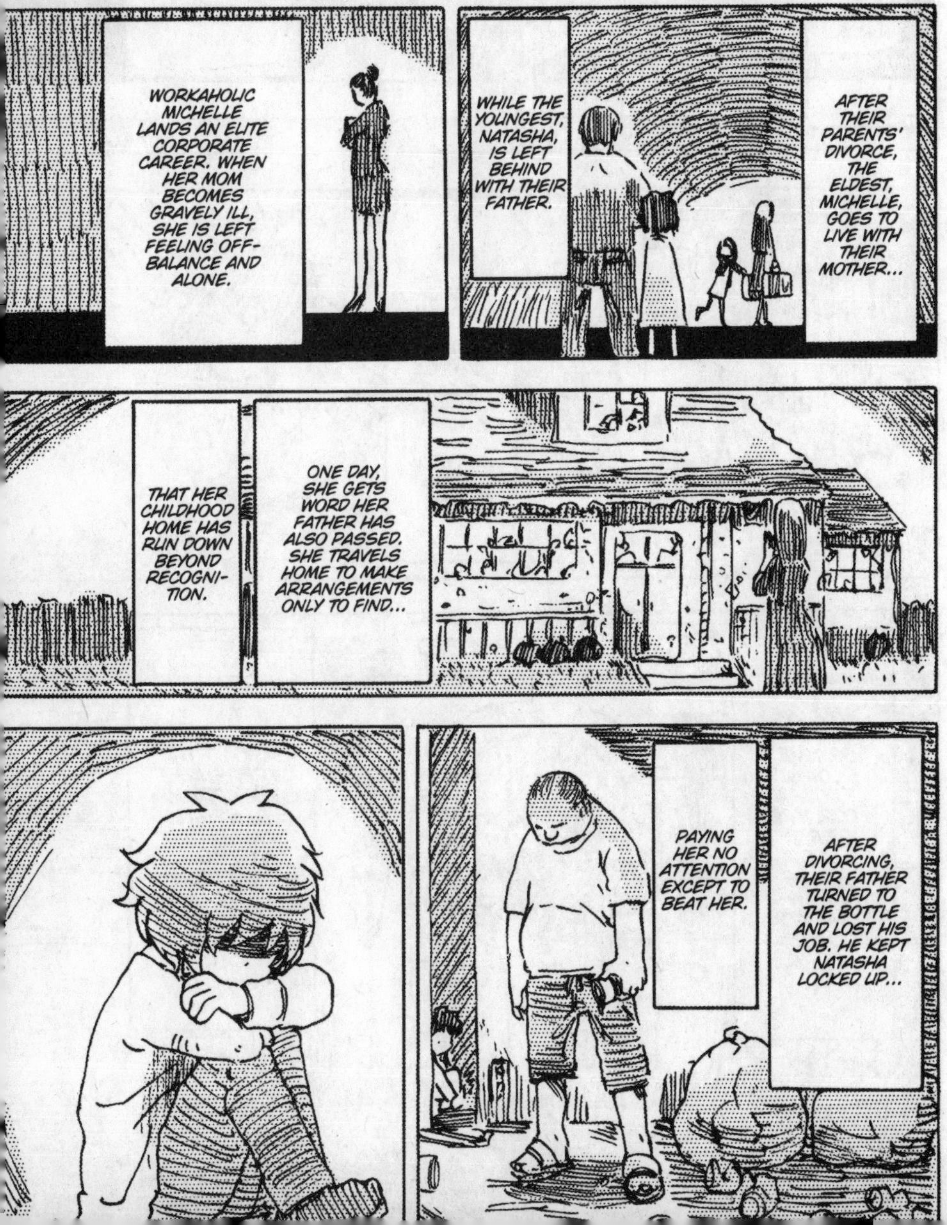
AFTER THEIR PARENTS' DIVORCE, THE ELDEST, MICHELLE, GOES TO LIVE WITH THEIR MOTHER...
WHILE THE YOUNGEST, NATASHA, IS LEFT BEHIND WITH THEIR FATHER.
WORKAHOLIC MICHELLE LANDS AN ELITE CORPORATE CAREER. WHEN HER MOM BECOMES GRAVELY ILL, SHE IS LEFT FEELING OFF-BALANCE AND ALONE.
ONE DAY, SHE GETS WORD HER FATHER HAS ALSO PASSED. SHE TRAVELS HOME TO MAKE ARRANGEMENTS ONLY TO FIND...
THAT HER CHILDHOOD HOME HAS RUN DOWN BEYOND RECOGNITION.
AFTER DIVORCING, THEIR FATHER TURNED TO THE BOTTLE AND LOST HIS JOB. HE KEPT NATASHA LOCKED UP...
PAYING HER NO ATTENTION EXCEPT TO BEAT HER.

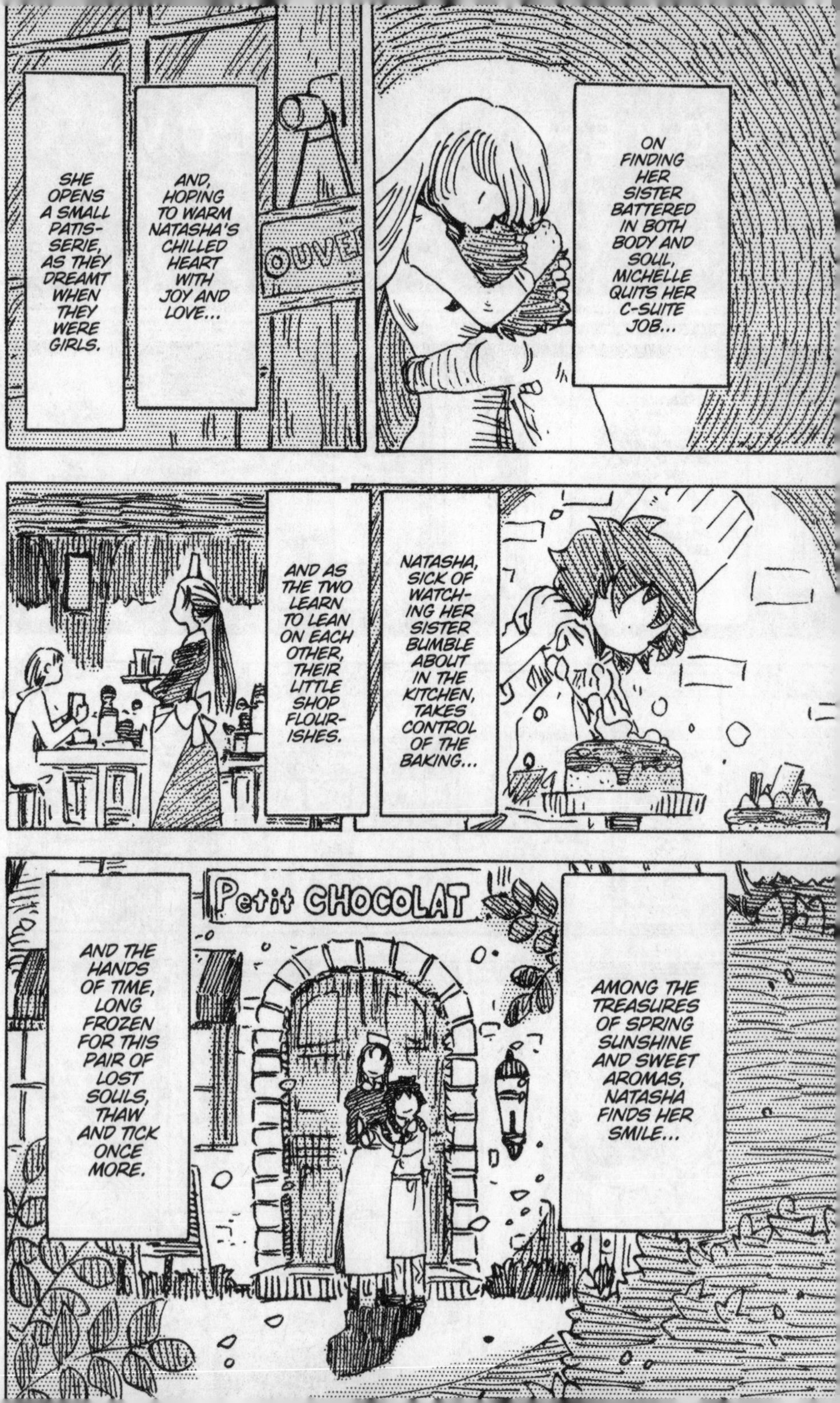
ON FINDING HER SISTER BATTERED IN BOTH BODY AND SOUL, MICHELLE QUITS HER C-SUITE JOB...
AND, HOPING TO WARM NATASHA'S CHILLED HEART WITH JOY AND LOVE...
SHE OPENS A SMALL PATIS-SERIE, AS THEY DREAMT WHEN THEY WERE GIRLS.
NATASHA, SICK OF WATCH-ING HER SISTER BUMBLE ABOUT IN THE KITCHEN, TAKES CONTROL OF THE BAKING...
AND AS THE TWO LEARN TO LEAN ON EACH OTHER, THEIR LITTLE SHOP FLOUR-ISHES.
Petit CHOCOLAT
AMONG THE TREASURES OF SPRING SUNSHINE AND SWEET AROMAS, NATASHA FINDS HER SMILE...
AND THE HANDS OF TIME, LONG FROZEN FOR THIS PAIR OF LOST SOULS, THAW AND TICK ONCE MORE.

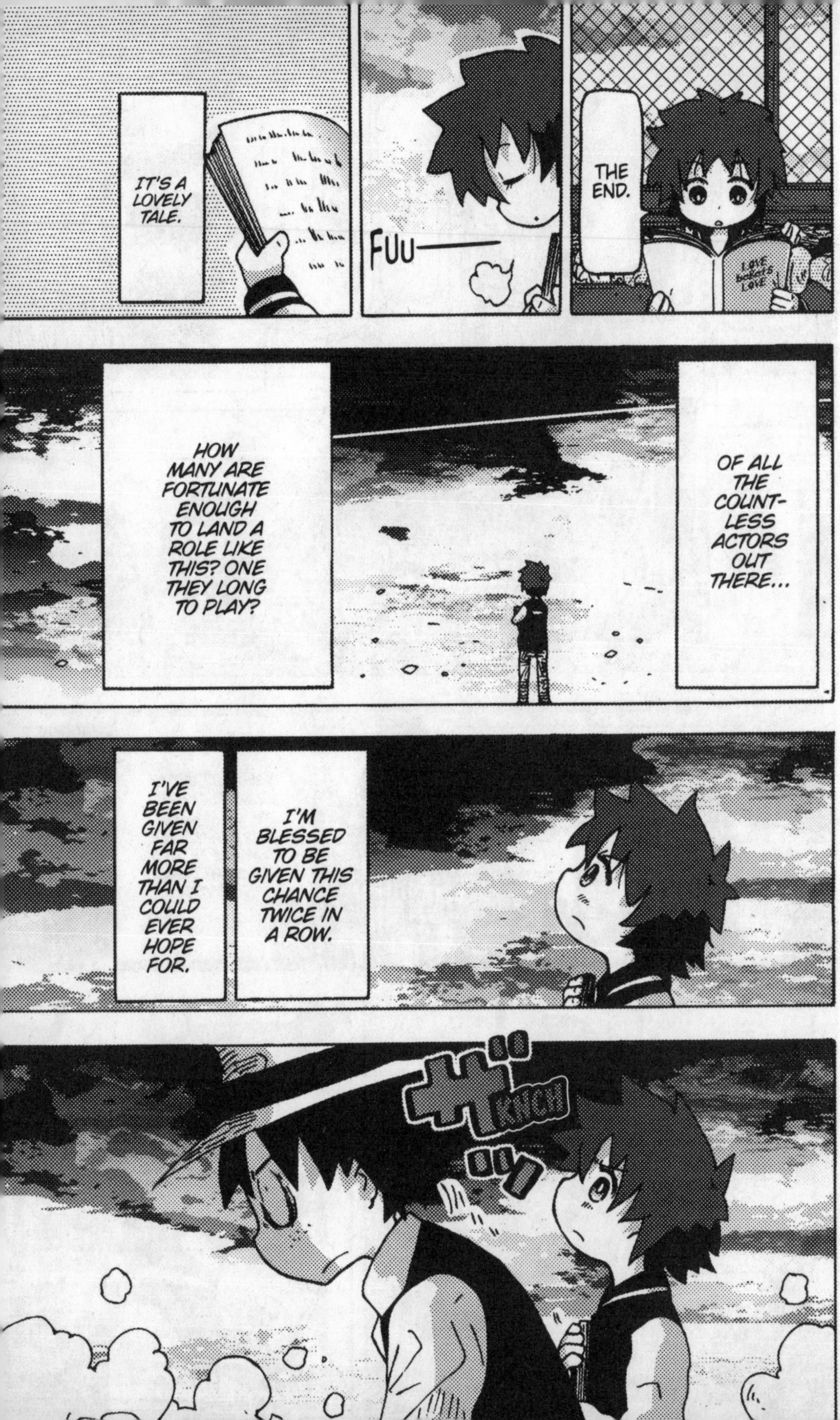
THE END.
FUU—
IT'S A LOVELY TALE.
OF ALL THE COUNT-LESS ACTORS OUT THERE...
HOW MANY ARE FORTUNATE ENOUGH TO LAND A ROLE LIKE THIS? ONE THEY LONG TO PLAY?
I'M BLESSED TO BE GIVEN THIS CHANCE TWICE IN A ROW.
I'VE BEEN GIVEN FAR MORE THAN I COULD EVER HOPE FOR.
KNCH

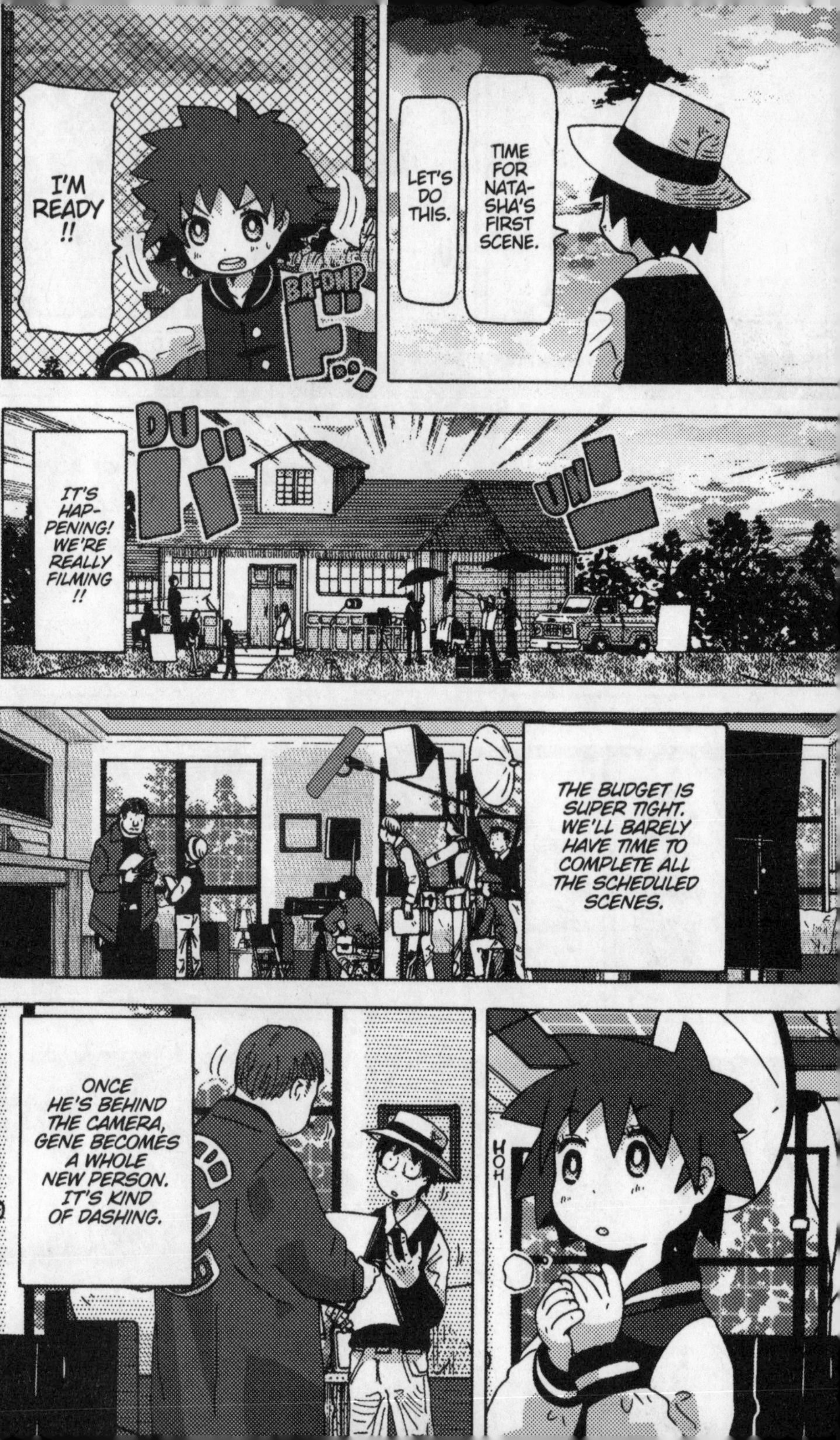
TIME FOR NATA-SHA'S FIRST SCENE.
LET'S DO THIS.
I'M READY!!
BA-DMP
DU
UN
IT'S HAP-PENING! WE'RE REALLY FILMING!!
THE BUDGET IS SUPER TIGHT. WE'LL BARELY HAVE TIME TO COMPLETE ALL THE SCHEDULED SCENES.
HOH—
ONCE HE'S BEHIND THE CAMERA, GENE BECOMES A WHOLE NEW PERSON. IT'S KIND OF DASHING.

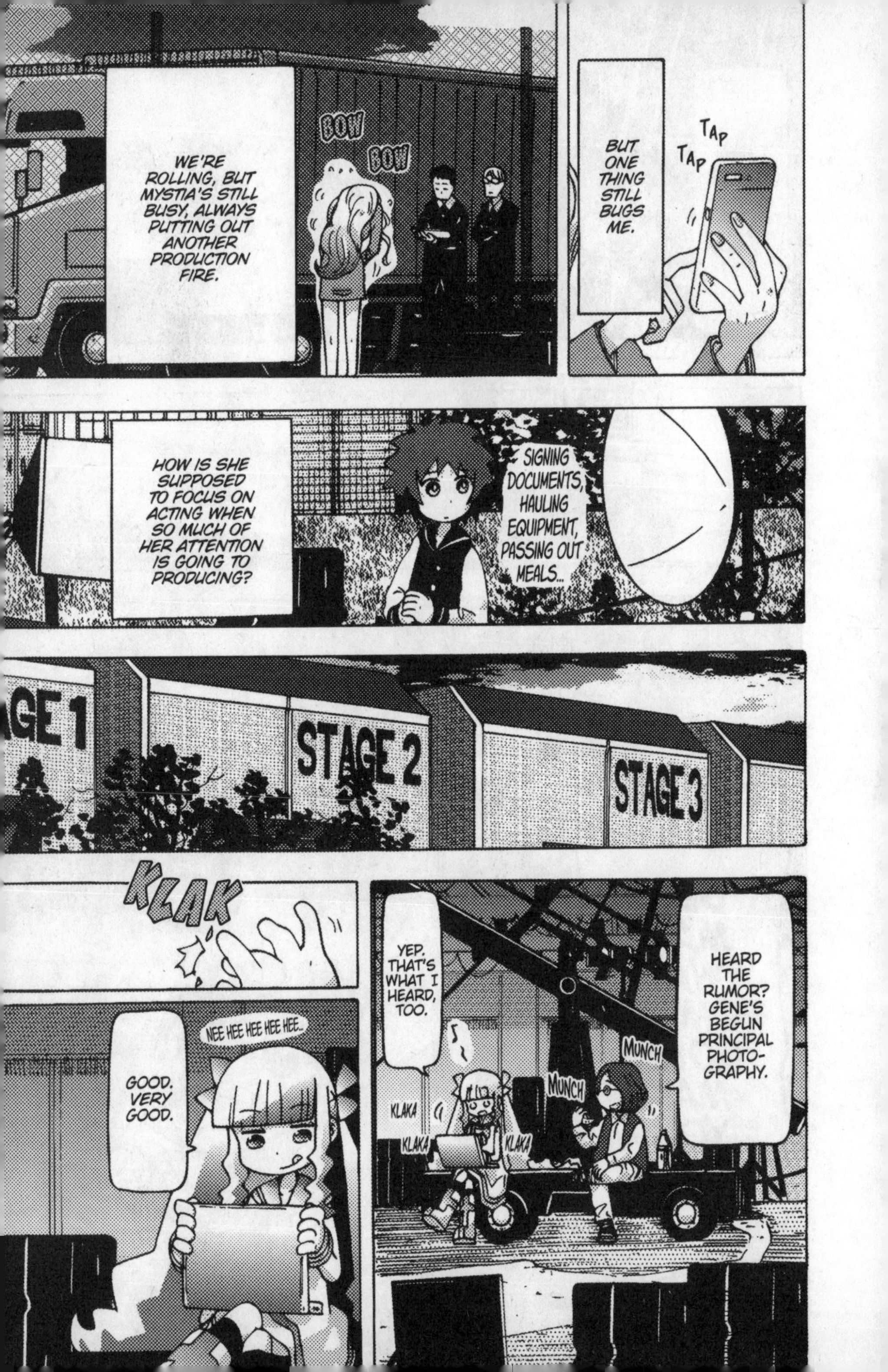
BUT ONE THING STILL BUGS ME.
TAP
TAP
WE'RE ROLLING, BUT MYSTIA'S STILL BUSY, ALWAYS PUTTING OUT ANOTHER PRODUCTION FIRE.
BOW
BOW
SIGNING DOCUMENTS, HAULING EQUIPMENT, PASSING OUT MEALS...
HOW IS SHE SUPPOSED TO FOCUS ON ACTING WHEN SO MUCH OF HER ATTENTION IS GOING TO PRODUCING?
STAGE 3
STAGE 2
AGE 1
HEARD THE RUMOR? GENE'S BEGUN PRINCIPAL PHOTO-GRAPHY.
MUNCH
MUNCH
YEP. THAT'S WHAT I HEARD, TOO.
KLAKA
KLAKA
KLAKA
KLAK
NEE HEE HEE HEE HEE...
GOOD. VERY GOOD.

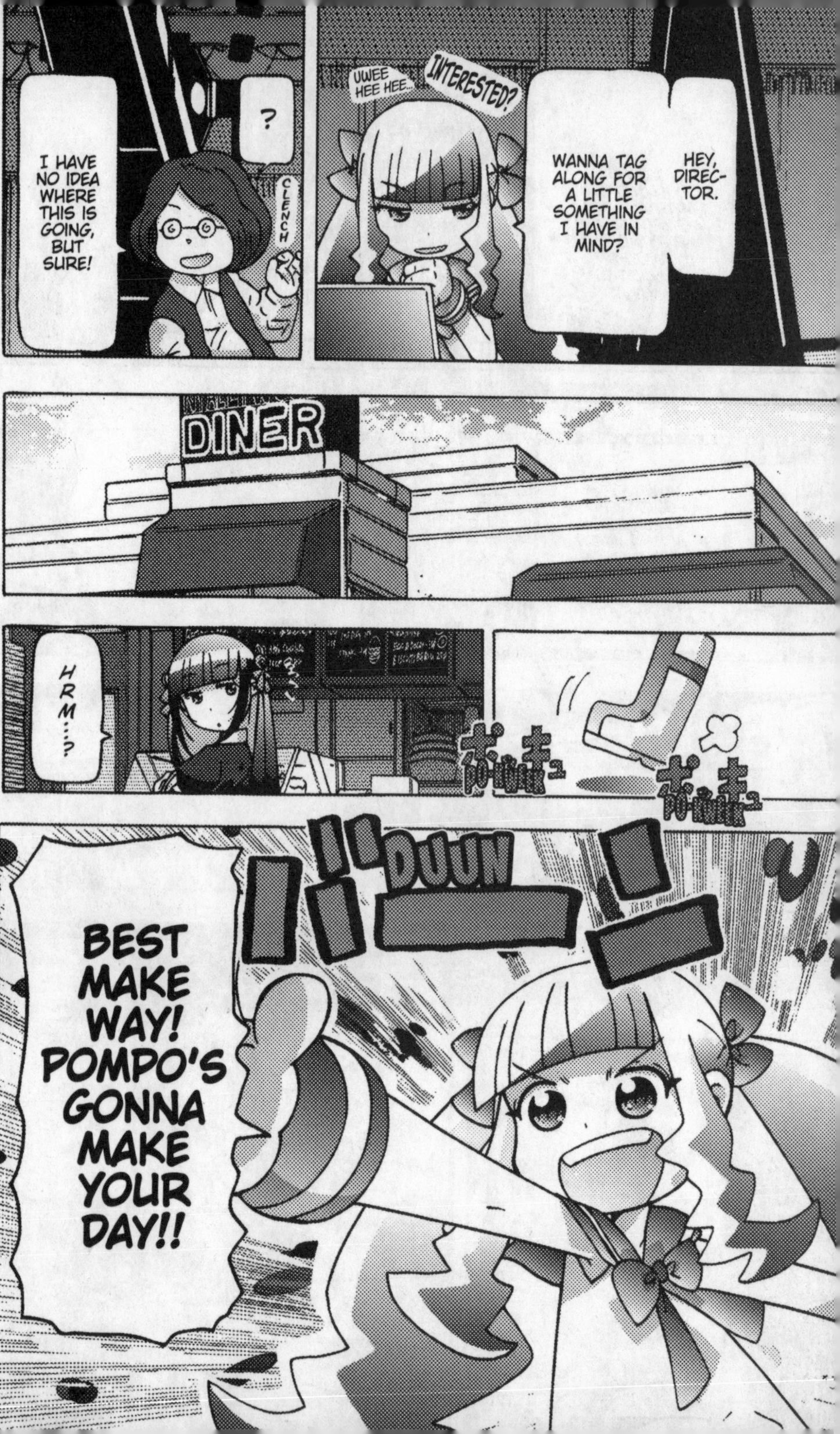

HEY, DIRECTOR.
WANNA TAG ALONG FOR A LITTLE SOMETHING I HAVE IN MIND?
UWEE HEE HEE...
INTERESTED?
?
CLENCH
I HAVE NO IDEA WHERE THIS IS GOING, BUT SURE!
DINER
HRM...?
DUUN
BEST MAKE WAY! POMPO'S GONNA MAKE YOUR DAY!!

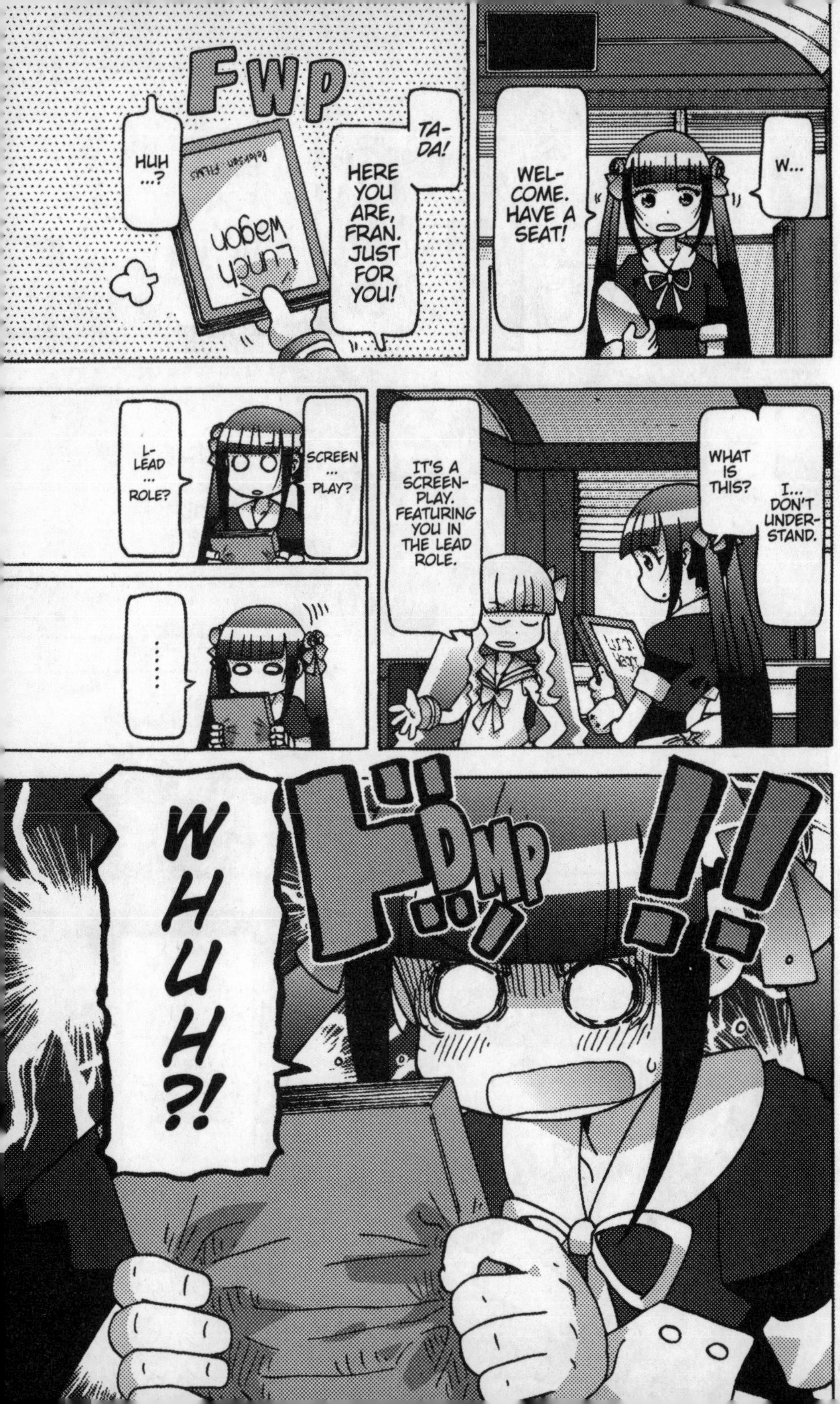
W...
WEL-COME. HAVE A SEAT!
TA-DA!
HERE YOU ARE, FRAN. JUST FOR YOU!
FWP
Lunch Wagon
HUH...?
WHAT IS THIS?
I... DON'T UNDER-STAND.
IT'S A SCREEN-PLAY. FEATURING YOU IN THE LEAD ROLE.
SCREEN... PLAY?
L-LEAD... ROLE?
......
DMP!!
WHUH?!

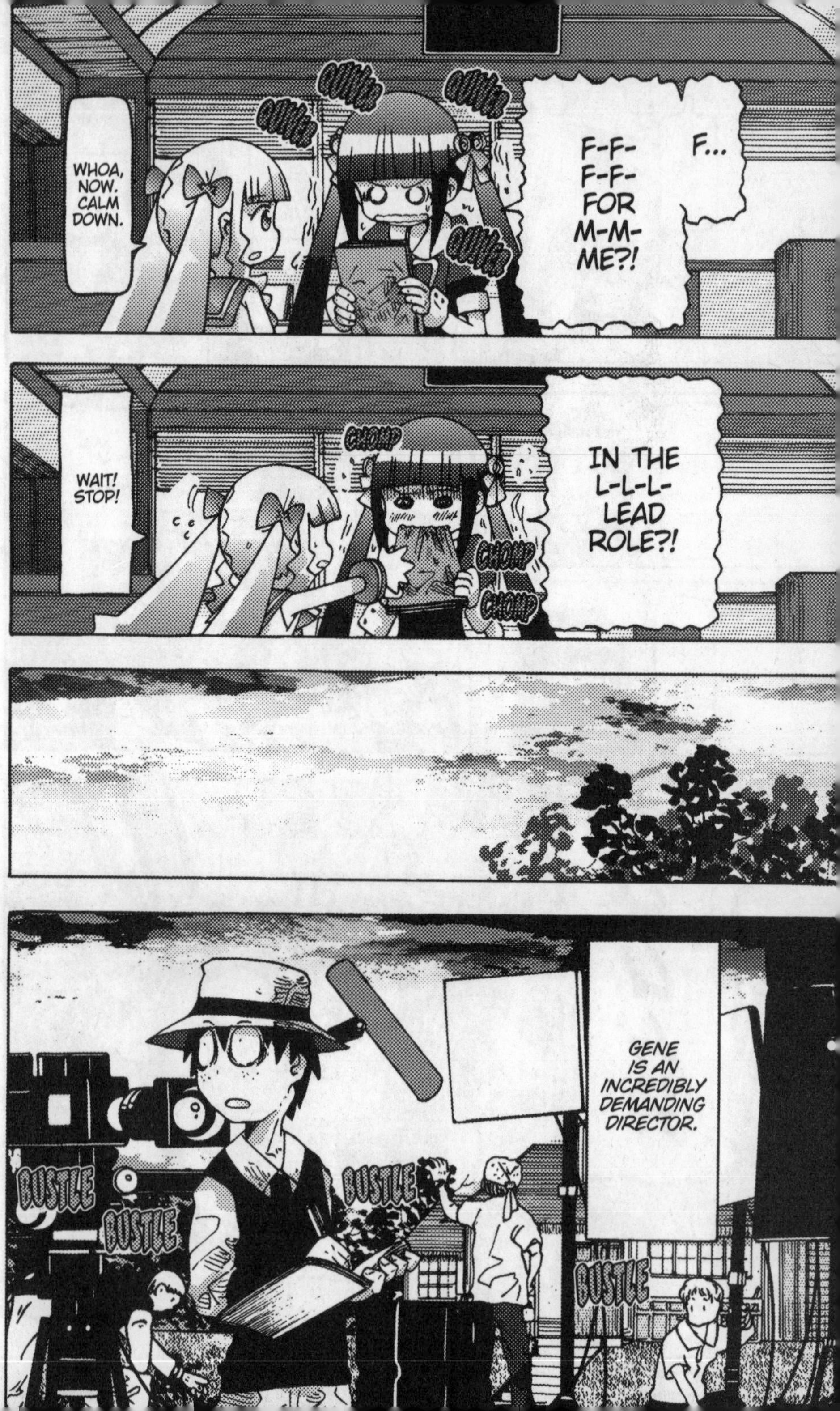
F...
F-F-F-F-FOR M-M-ME?!
WHOA, NOW. CALM DOWN.
IN THE L-L-L-LEAD ROLE?!
CHOMP
CHOMP
CHOMP
WAIT! STOP!
GENE IS AN INCREDIBLY DEMANDING DIRECTOR.
BUSTLE
BUSTLE
BUSTLE
BUSTLE

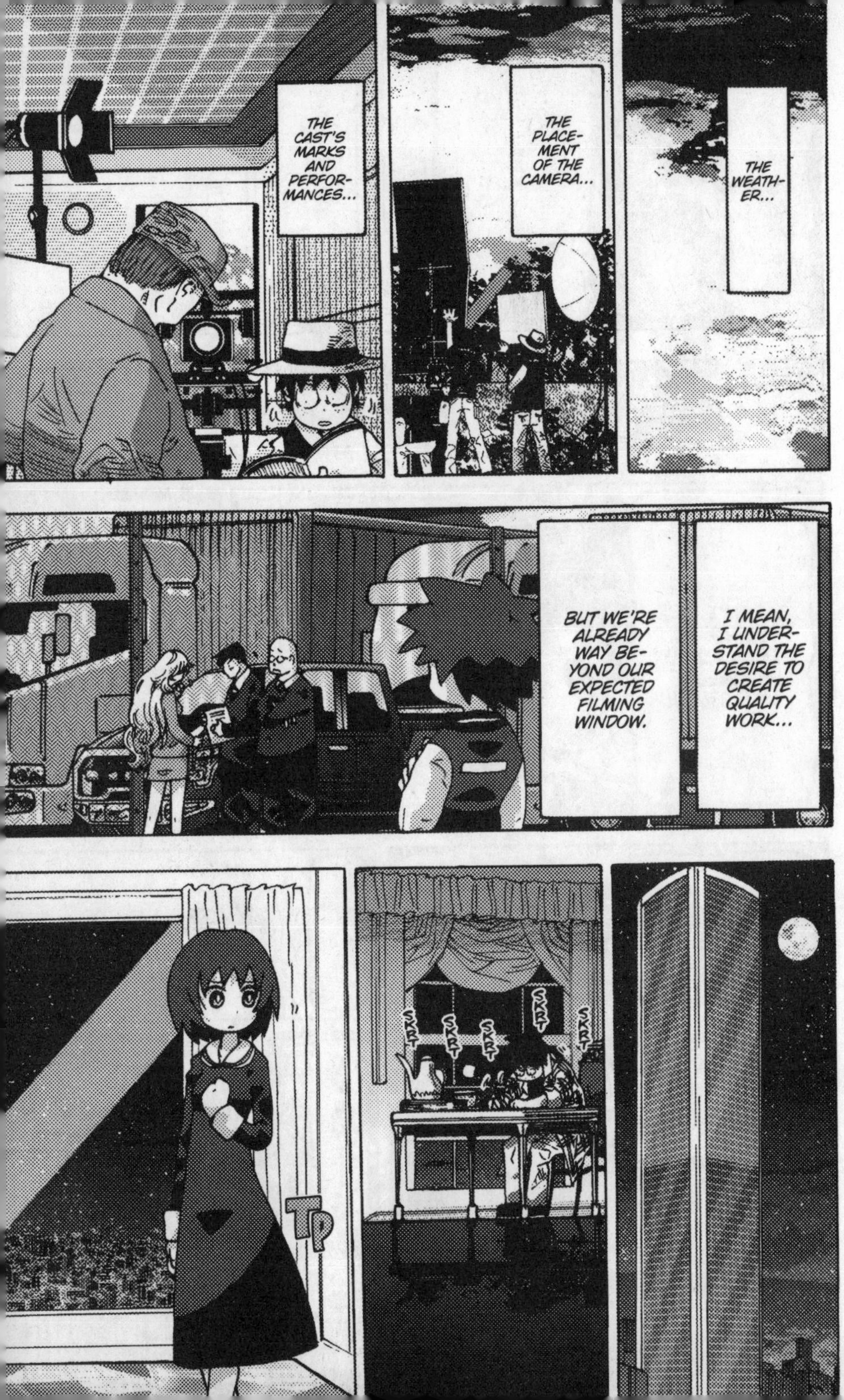
THE WEATHER...
THE PLACEMENT OF THE CAMERA...
THE CAST'S MARKS AND PERFORMANCES...
I MEAN, I UNDERSTAND THE DESIRE TO CREATE QUALITY WORK...
BUT WE'RE ALREADY WAY BEYOND OUR EXPECTED FILMING WINDOW.
SKRT
SKRT
SKRT
SKRT
SKRT
TP

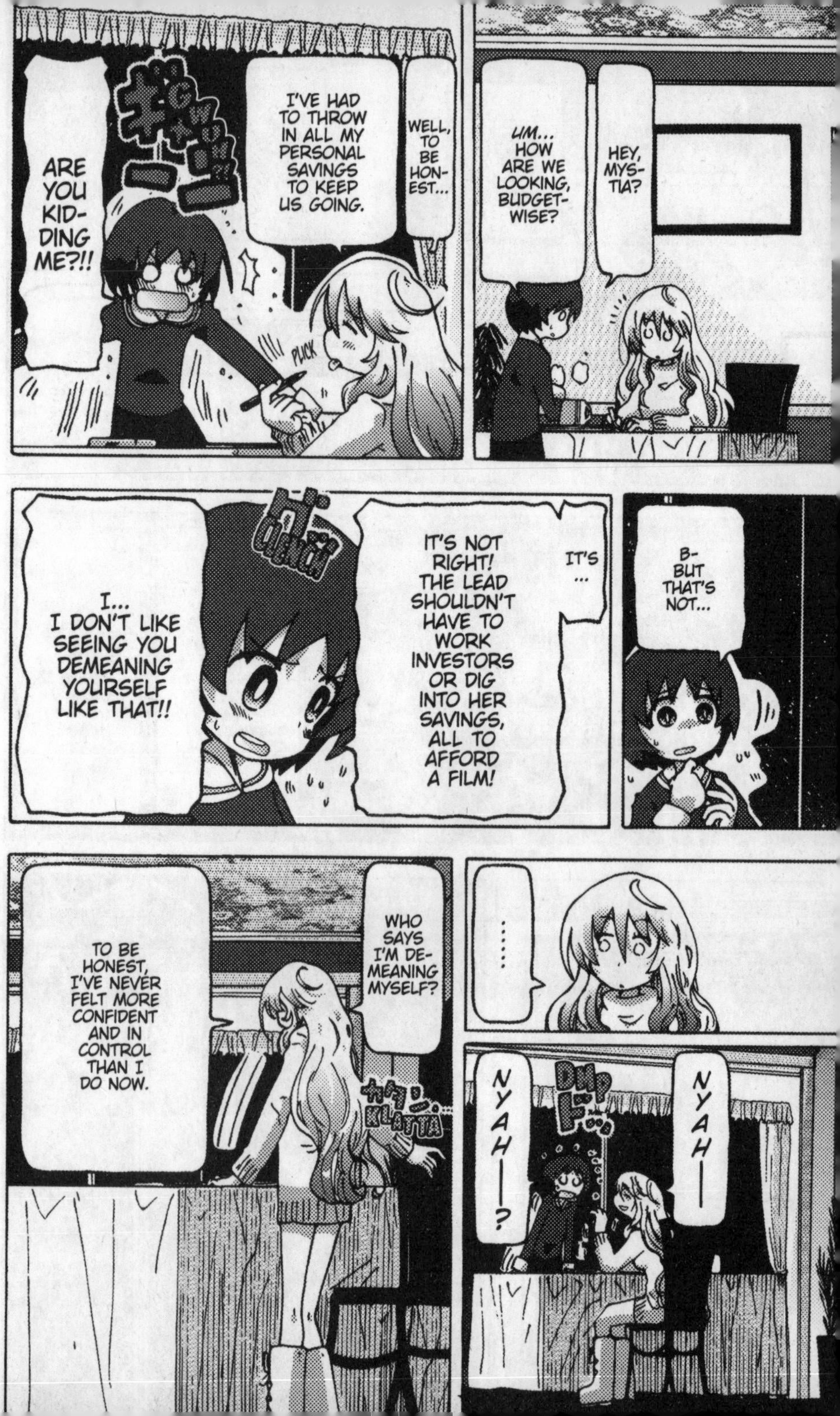

HEY, MYSTIA?
UM... HOW ARE WE LOOKING, BUDGET-WISE?
WELL, TO BE HONEST...
I'VE HAD TO THROW IN ALL MY PERSONAL SAVINGS TO KEEP US GOING.
PLUCK
ARE YOU KIDDING ME?!!
B-BUT THAT'S NOT...
IT'S...
IT'S NOT RIGHT! THE LEAD SHOULDN'T HAVE TO WORK INVESTORS OR DIG INTO HER SAVINGS, ALL TO AFFORD A FILM!
I... I DON'T LIKE SEEING YOU DEMEANING YOURSELF LIKE THAT!!
......
NYAH—
NYAH—?
WHO SAYS I'M DEMEANING MYSELF?
TO BE HONEST, I'VE NEVER FELT MORE CONFIDENT AND IN CONTROL THAN I DO NOW.
KLATTA

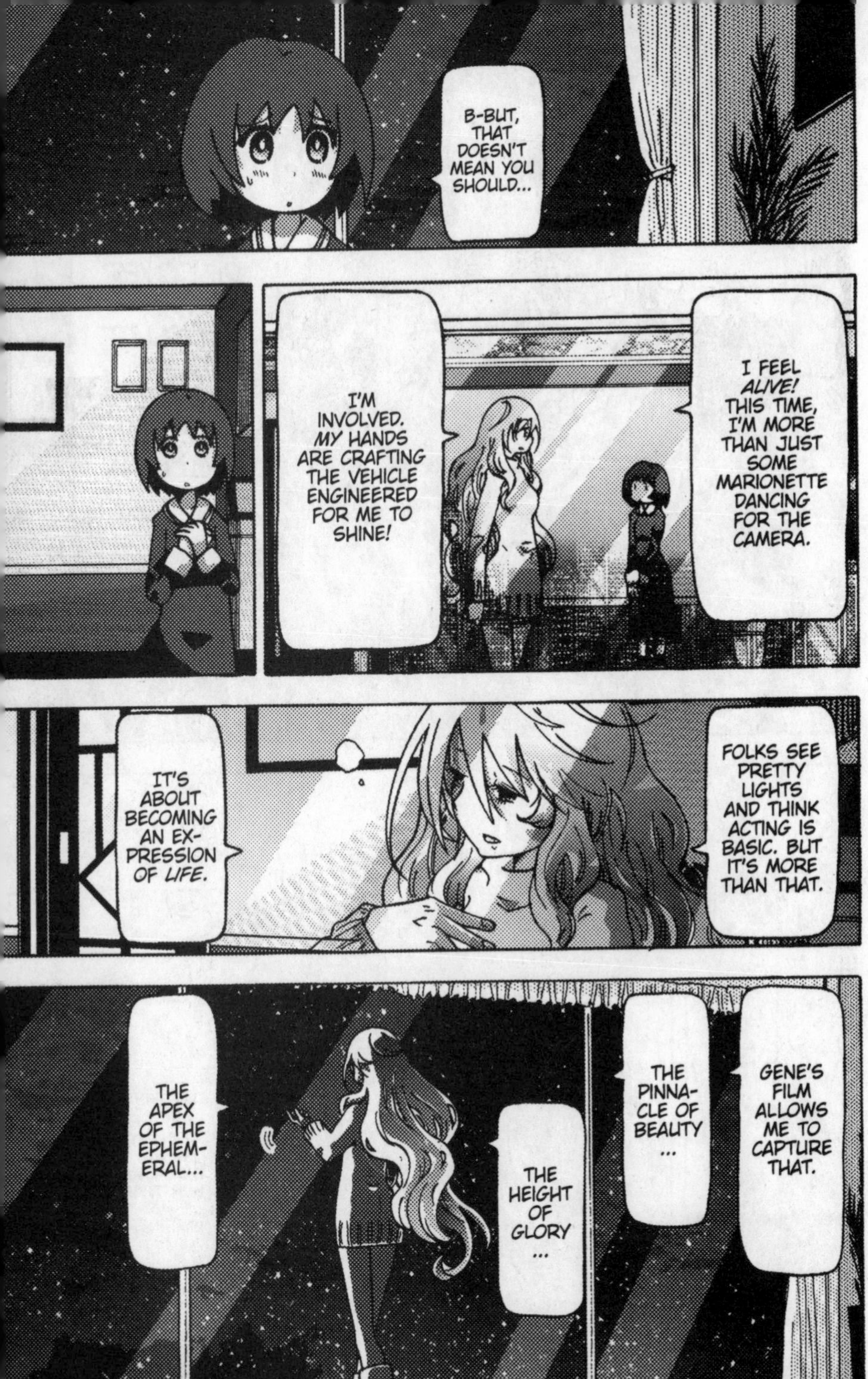
B-BUT, THAT DOESN'T MEAN YOU SHOULD...
I FEEL *ALIVE!* THIS TIME, I'M MORE THAN JUST SOME MARIONETTE DANCING FOR THE CAMERA.
I'M INVOLVED. *MY HANDS* ARE CRAFTING THE VEHICLE ENGINEERED FOR ME TO SHINE!
FOLKS SEE PRETTY LIGHTS AND THINK ACTING IS BASIC. BUT IT'S MORE THAN THAT.
IT'S ABOUT BECOMING AN EX-PRESSION OF *LIFE.*
GENE'S FILM ALLOWS ME TO CAPTURE THAT.
THE PINNA-CLE OF BEAUTY ...
THE HEIGHT OF GLORY ...
THE APEX OF THE EPHEM-ERAL...

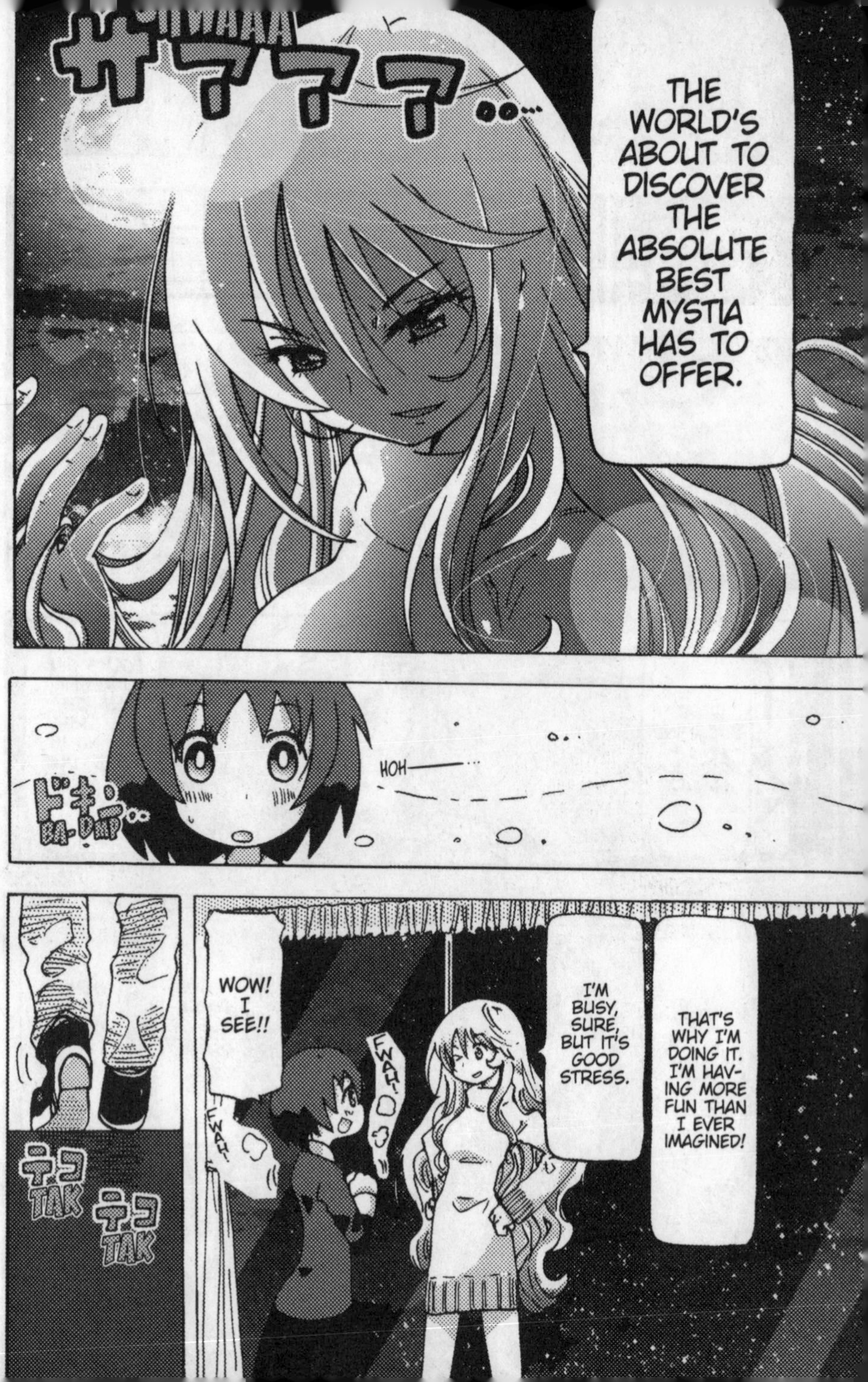
THE WORLD'S ABOUT TO DISCOVER THE ABSOLUTE BEST MYSTIA HAS TO OFFER.
サアアア…
HOH——…
ドキッ
BA-DMP
THAT'S WHY I'M DOING IT. I'M HAV-ING MORE FUN THAN I EVER IMAGINED!
I'M BUSY, SURE, BUT IT'S GOOD STRESS.
FWAH!
WOW! I SEE!!
FWAH!
テコ
TAK
テコ
TAK

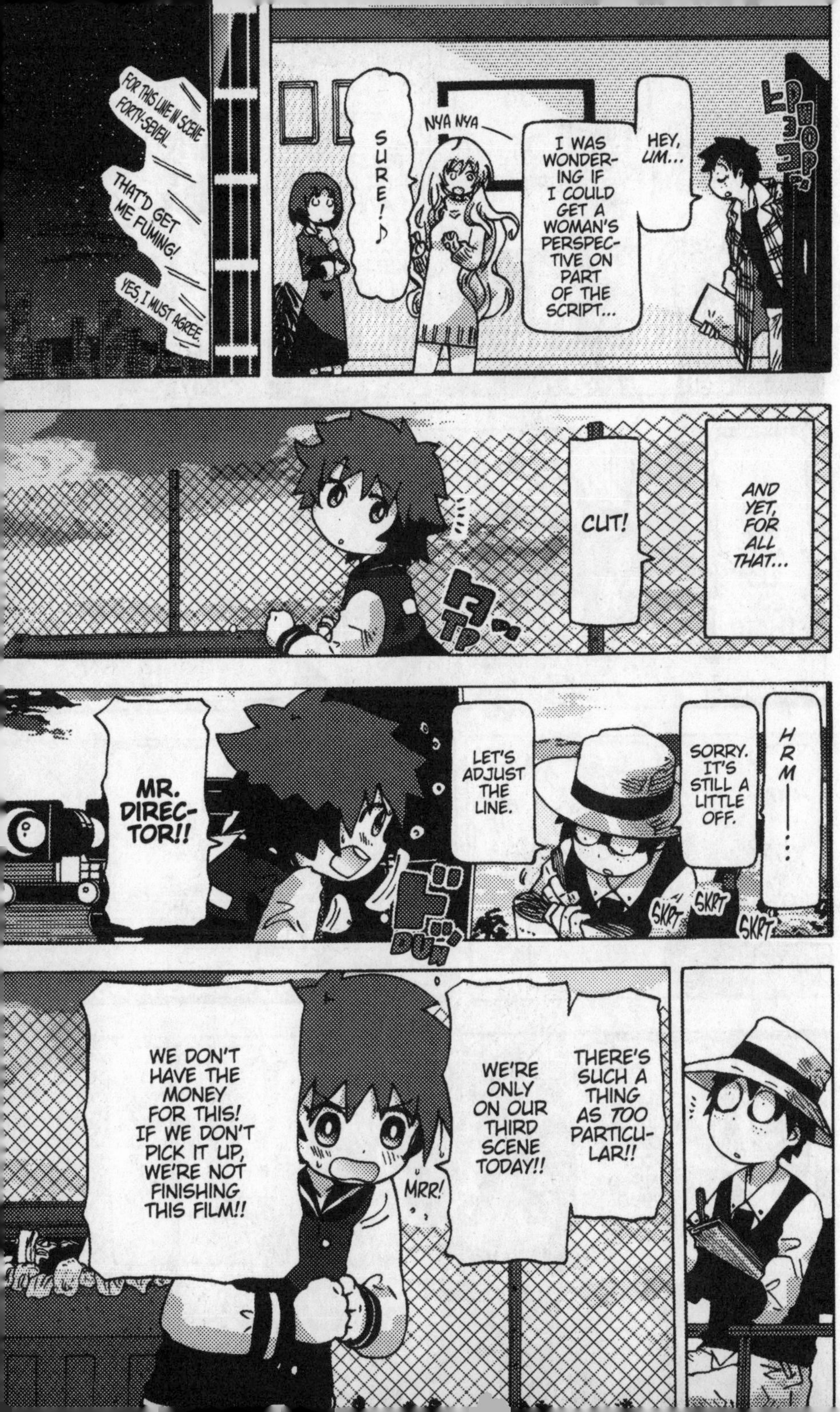
HEY, UM...
I WAS WONDERING IF I COULD GET A WOMAN'S PERSPECTIVE ON PART OF THE SCRIPT...
NYA NYA
SURE!♪
FOR THIS LINE IN SCENE FORTY-SEVEN...
THAT'D GET ME FUMING!
YES, I MUST AGREE.
AND YET, FOR ALL THAT...
CUT!
TP
HRM—...
SORRY. IT'S STILL A LITTLE OFF.
SKRT
SKRT
SKRT
LET'S ADJUST THE LINE.
MR. DIRECTOR!!
DUN
THERE'S SUCH A THING AS TOO PARTICULAR!!
WE'RE ONLY ON OUR THIRD SCENE TODAY!!
MRR!
WE DON'T HAVE THE MONEY FOR THIS! IF WE DON'T PICK IT UP, WE'RE NOT FINISHING THIS FILM!!

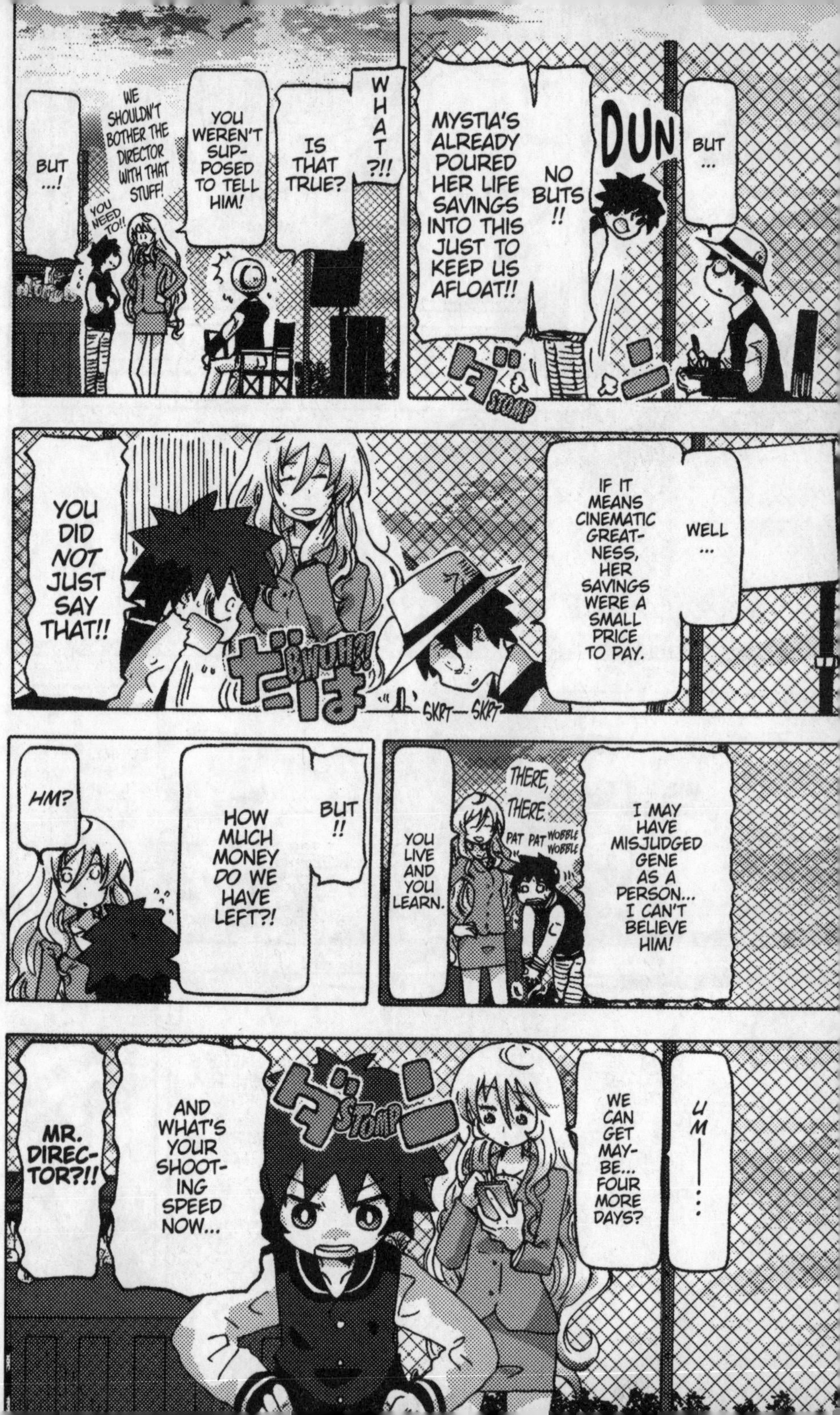
BUT ...
DUN
NO BUTS!!
MYSTIA'S ALREADY POURED HER LIFE SAVINGS INTO THIS JUST TO KEEP US AFLOAT!!
STOMP
WHAT?!!
IS THAT TRUE?
YOU WEREN'T SUP-POSED TO TELL HIM!
WE SHOULDN'T BOTHER THE DIRECTOR WITH THAT STUFF!
YOU NEED TO!!
BUT ...!
WELL ...
IF IT MEANS CINEMATIC GREAT-NESS, HER SAVINGS WERE A SMALL PRICE TO PAY.
SKRT— SKRT
BWOH!!
YOU DID NOT JUST SAY THAT!!
I MAY HAVE MISJUDGED GENE AS A PERSON... I CAN'T BELIEVE HIM!
THERE, THERE.
PAT PAT
WOBBLE WOBBLE
YOU LIVE AND YOU LEARN.
BUT !!
HOW MUCH MONEY DO WE HAVE LEFT?!
HM?
UM—...
WE CAN GET MAY-BE... FOUR MORE DAYS?
STOMP
AND WHAT'S YOUR SHOOT-ING SPEED NOW...
MR. DIREC-TOR?!!

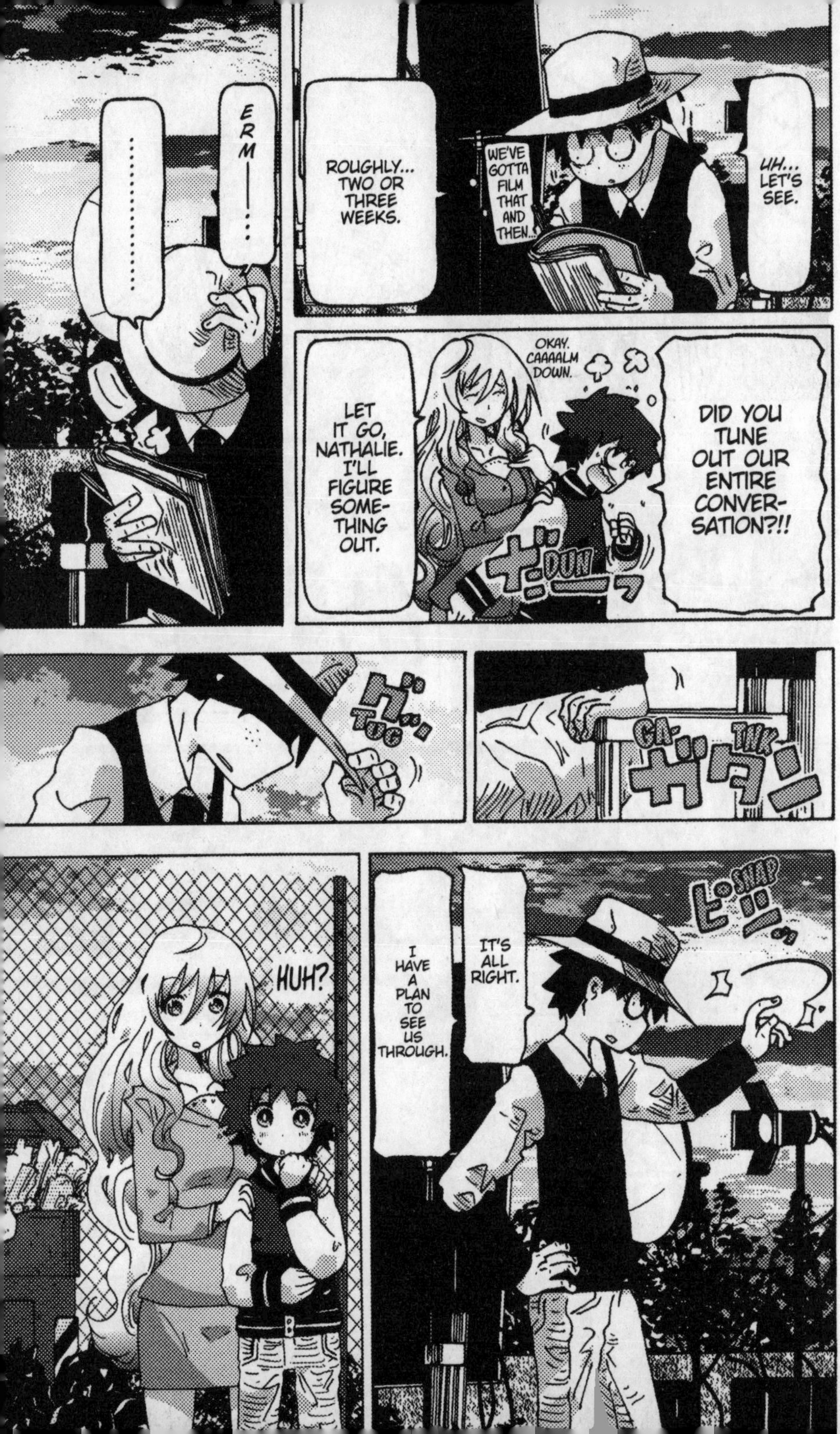
UH... LET'S SEE.
WE'VE GOTTA FILM THAT AND THEN...
ROUGHLY... TWO OR THREE WEEKS.
DID YOU TUNE OUT OUR ENTIRE CONVER-SATION?!!
OKAY. CAAAALM DOWN.
DUN
LET IT GO, NATHALIE. I'LL FIGURE SOME-THING OUT.
ERM——...
......
CA-THK
TUG
SNAP
IT'S ALL RIGHT.
I HAVE A PLAN TO SEE US THROUGH.
HUH?

DUUN
DOON
NGH—!!
TELL ME, GENE.
IS IT FAIR TO SAY...
YOU HAVE NO SENSE OF PRIDE? NOT A SHRED OF SELF-RESPECT?
YEAH. THAT'S PRETTY ACCURATE.

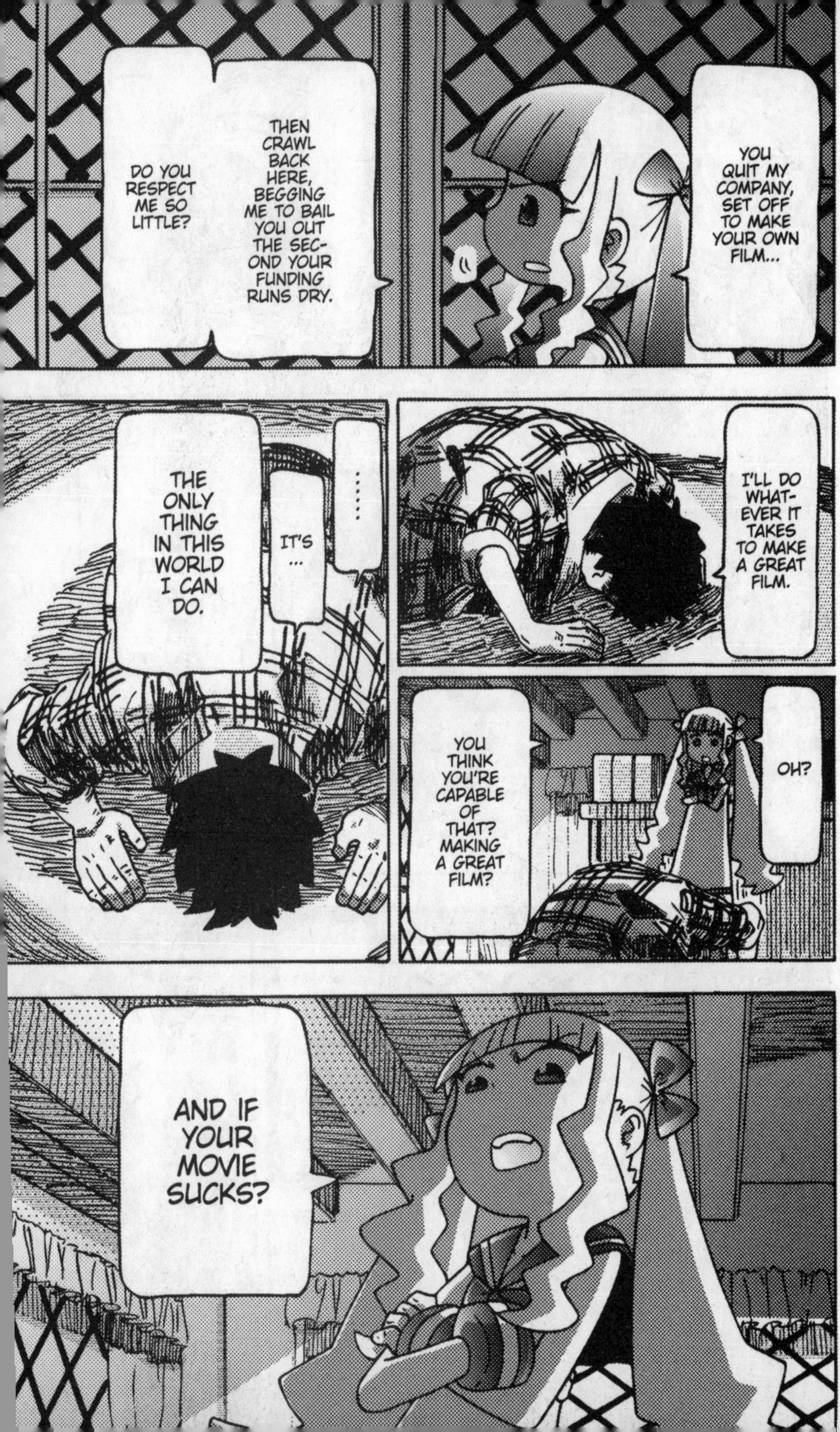
YOU QUIT MY COMPANY, SET OFF TO MAKE YOUR OWN FILM...
THEN CRAWL BACK HERE, BEGGING ME TO BAIL YOU OUT THE SEC-OND YOUR FUNDING RUNS DRY.
DO YOU RESPECT ME SO LITTLE?
I'LL DO WHAT-EVER IT TAKES TO MAKE A GREAT FILM.
OH?
YOU THINK YOU'RE CAPABLE OF THAT? MAKING A GREAT FILM?
......
IT'S ...
THE ONLY THING IN THIS WORLD I CAN DO.
AND IF YOUR MOVIE SUCKS?

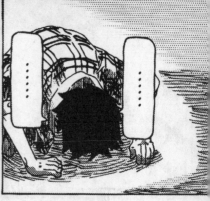

THAT WON'T HAPPEN. IT CAN'T.

SO BE IT!!

THWAP!

GRIN...

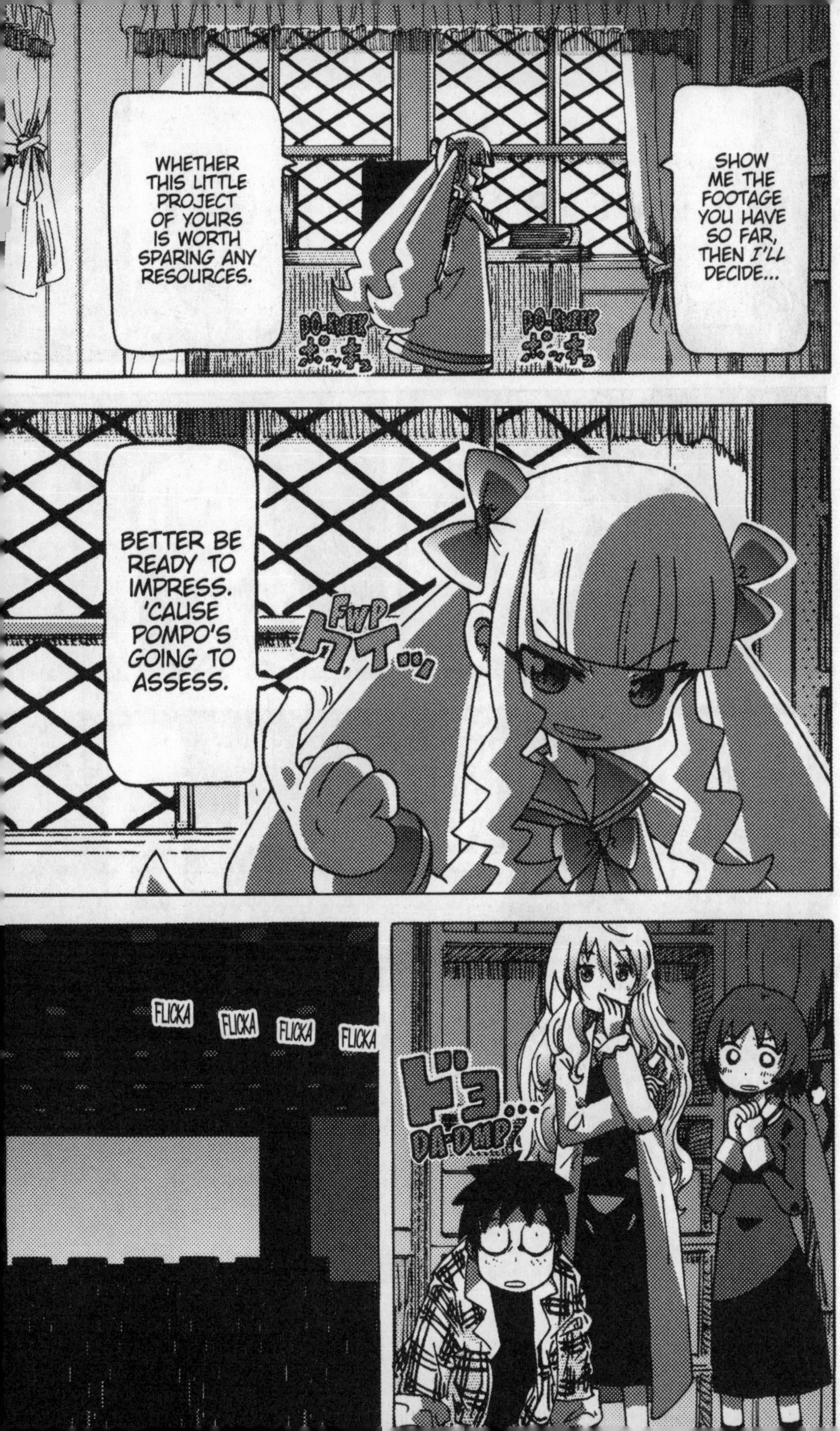
SHOW ME THE FOOTAGE YOU HAVE SO FAR, THEN I'LL DECIDE...
WHETHER THIS LITTLE PROJECT OF YOURS IS WORTH SPARING ANY RESOURCES.
PO-KEEK
PO-KEEK
BETTER BE READY TO IMPRESS. 'CAUSE POMPO'S GOING TO ASSESS.
FWP
DA-DMP
FLICKA
FLICKA
FLICKA
FLICKA

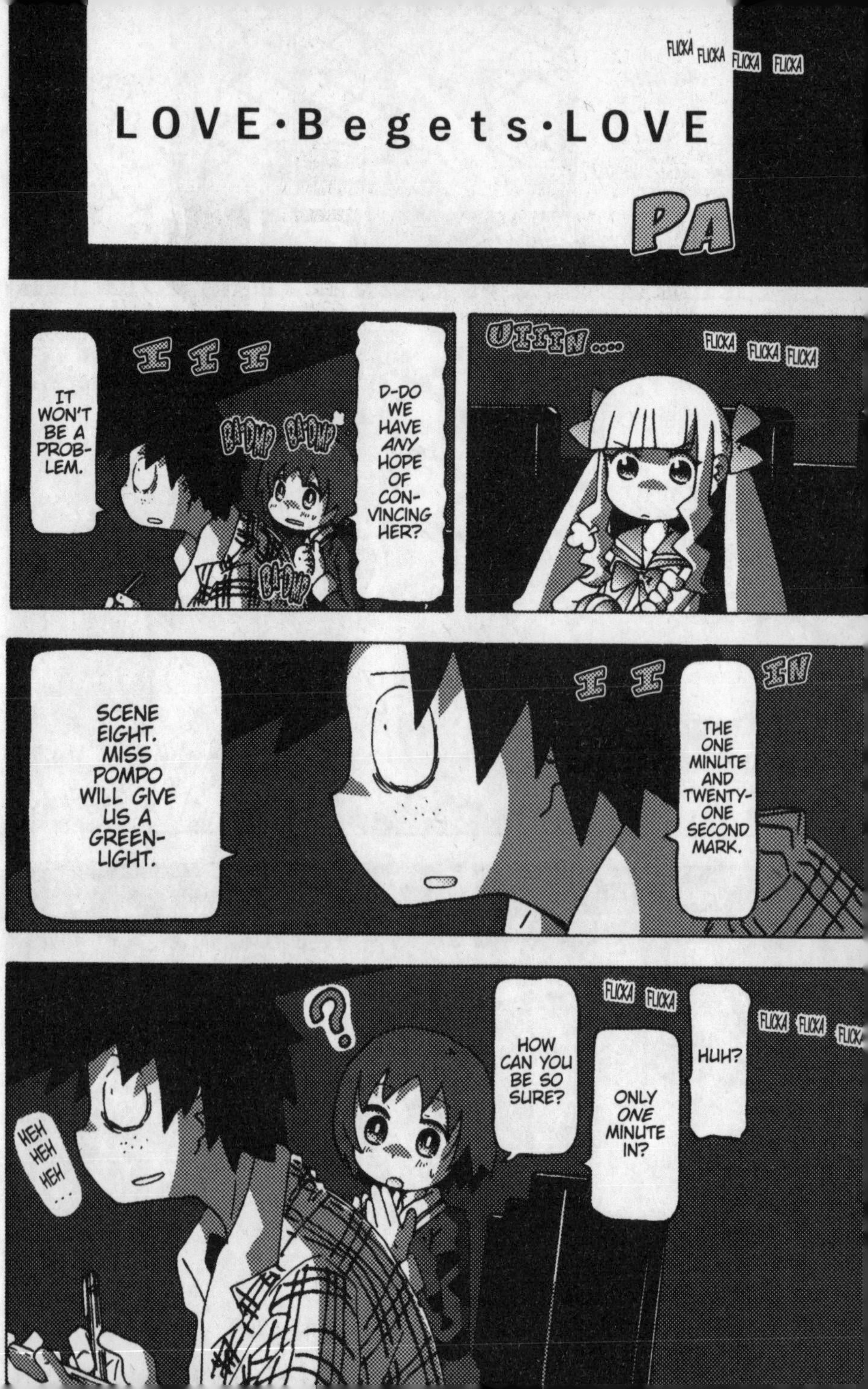

FLICKA FLICKA FLICKA FLICKA
LOVE•Begets•LOVE
PA
UIIIN....
FLICKA FLICKA FLICKA
D-DO WE HAVE ANY HOPE OF CONVINCING HER?
I I I
IT WON'T BE A PROBLEM.
THE ONE MINUTE AND TWENTY-ONE SECOND MARK.
I I IN
SCENE EIGHT. MISS POMPO WILL GIVE US A GREENLIGHT.
FLICKA FLICKA FLICKA
FLICKA FLICKA
HUH?
ONLY ONE MINUTE IN?
HOW CAN YOU BE SO SURE?
?
HEH HEH HEH...

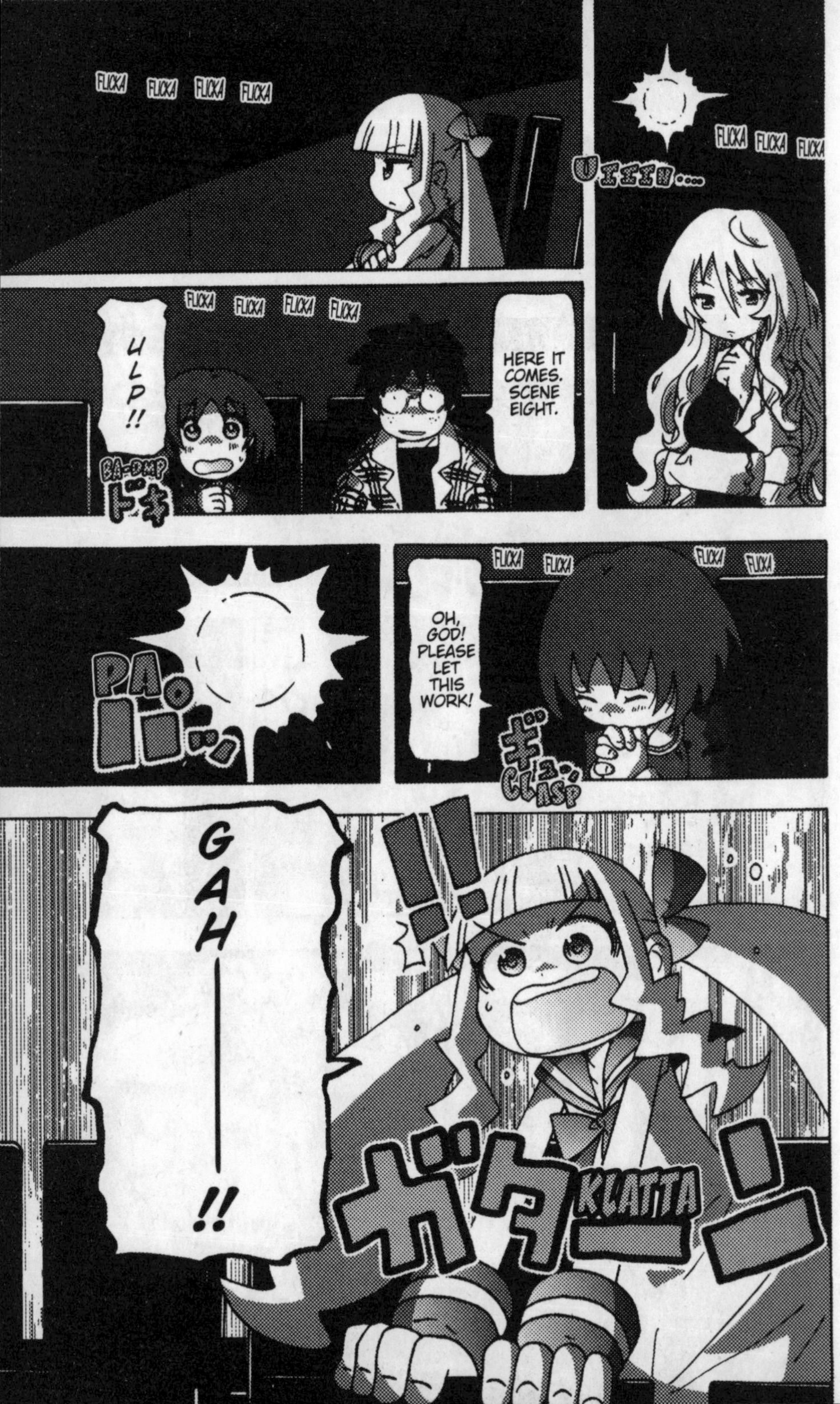
FLICKA FLICKA FLICKA
UIIIN...
FLICKA FLICKA FLICKA FLICKA
FLICKA FLICKA FLICKA FLICKA
HERE IT COMES. SCENE EIGHT.
ULP!!
BA-DMP
ドキ
FLICKA FLICKA FLICKA FLICKA
OH, GOD! PLEASE LET THIS WORK!
ギュッ
CLASP
PA
パッ
!!
GAH——!!
KLATTA
ガタン

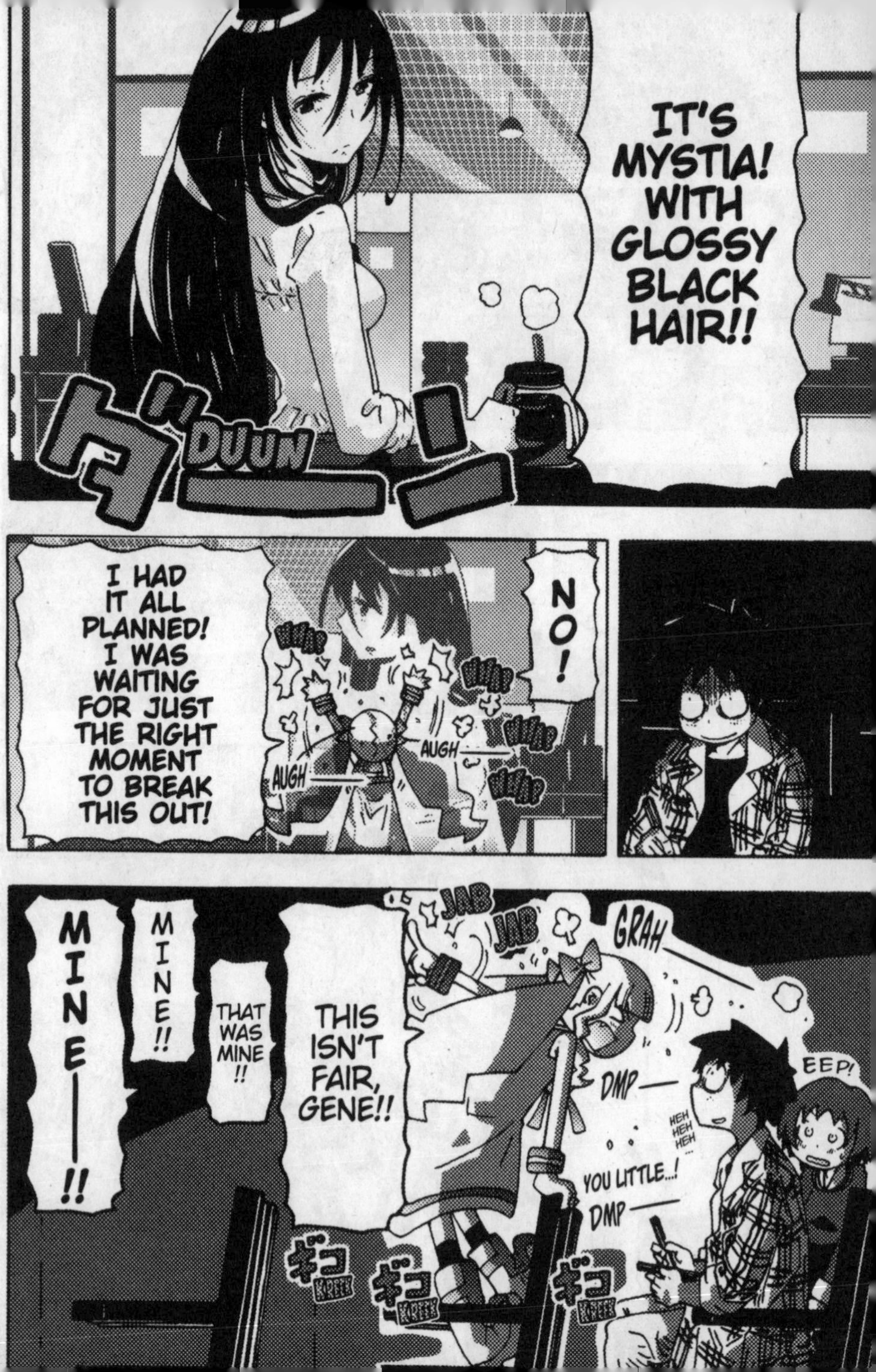
IT'S MYSTIA! WITH GLOSSY BLACK HAIR!!
DUUN
NO!
I HAD IT ALL PLANNED! I WAS WAITING FOR JUST THE RIGHT MOMENT TO BREAK THIS OUT!
AUGH
AUGH
GRAH
EEP!
DMP
HEH HEH HEH...
YOU LITTLE...!
DMP
JAB
JAB
KREEK
KREEK
KREEK
THIS ISN'T FAIR, GENE!!
THAT WAS MINE!!
MINE!!
MINE—!!

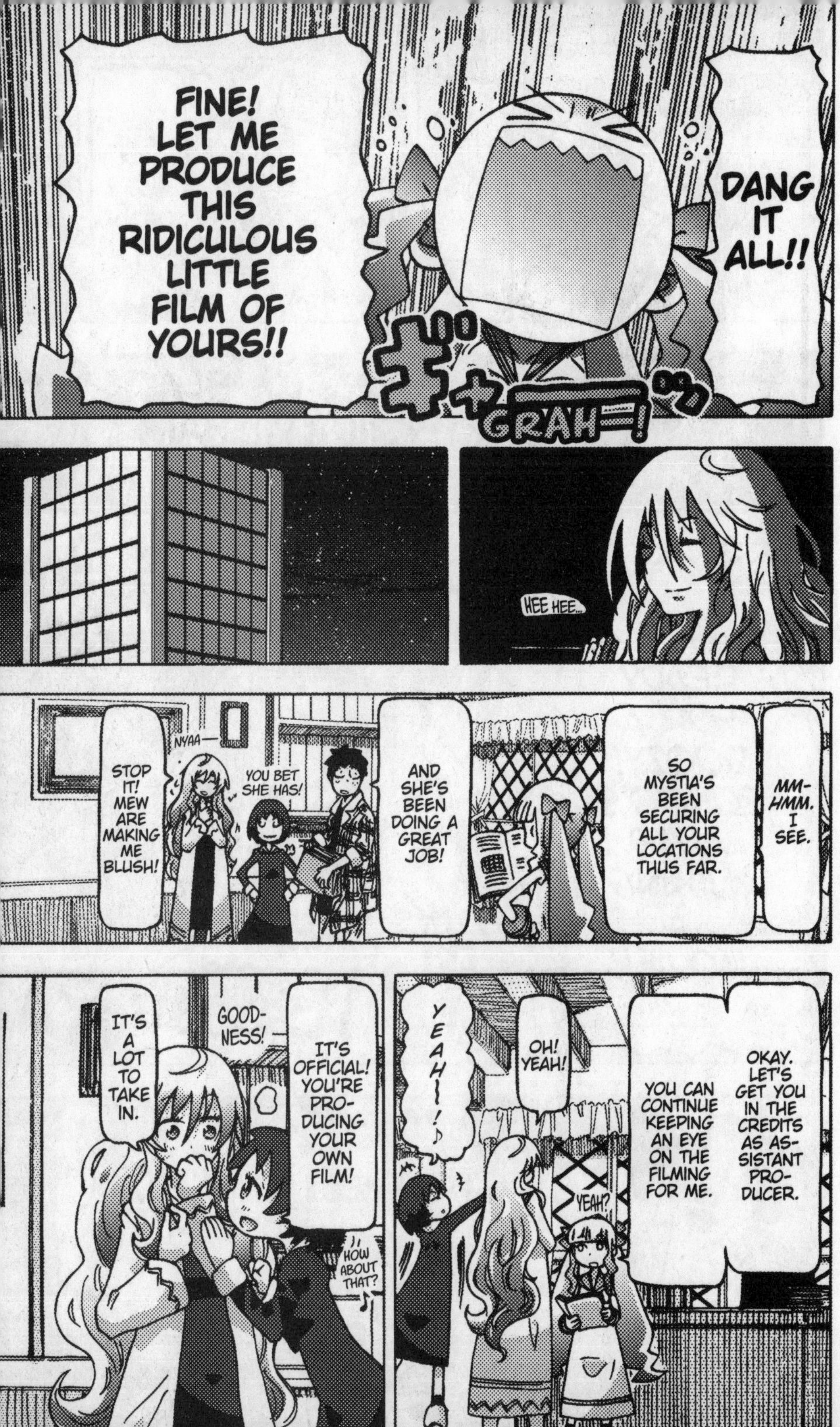
DANG IT ALL!!
FINE! LET ME PRODUCE THIS RIDICULOUS LITTLE FILM OF YOURS!!
GRAH—!
HEE HEE...
MM-HMM. I SEE.
SO MYSTIA'S BEEN SECURING ALL YOUR LOCATIONS THUS FAR.
AND SHE'S BEEN DOING A GREAT JOB!
YOU BET SHE HAS!
NYAA—
STOP IT! MEW ARE MAKING ME BLUSH!
OKAY. LET'S GET YOU IN THE CREDITS AS ASSISTANT PRODUCER.
YOU CAN CONTINUE KEEPING AN EYE ON THE FILMING FOR ME.
OH! YEAH!
YEAH~!♪
YEAH?
IT'S OFFICIAL! YOU'RE PRODUCING YOUR OWN FILM!
GOODNESS!—
IT'S A LOT TO TAKE IN.
HOW ABOUT THAT?♪

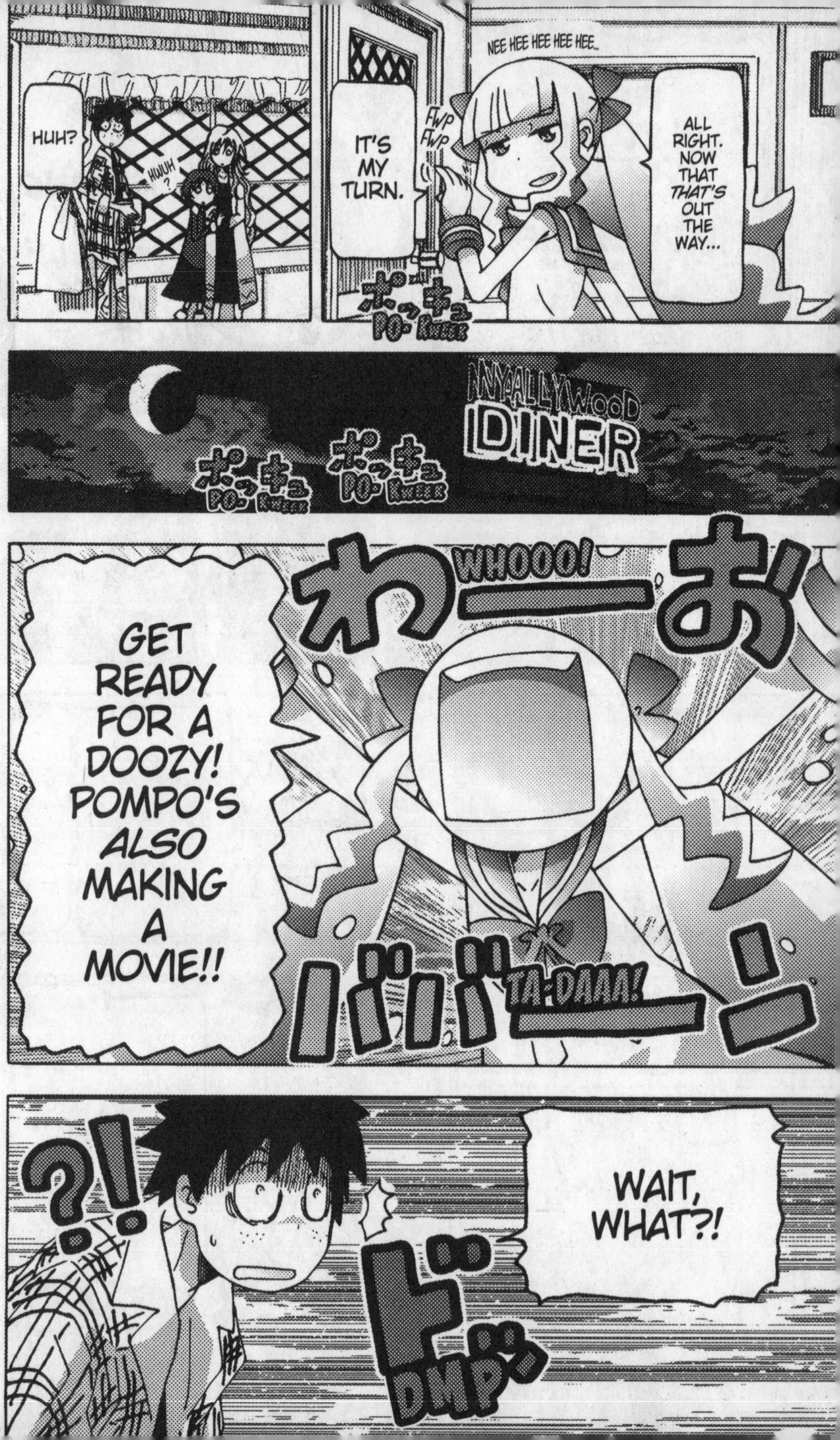
NEE HEE HEE HEE HEE...
ALL RIGHT. NOW THAT THAT'S OUT THE WAY...
FWP FWP
IT'S MY TURN.
PO-KWEEK
HUH?
HWUH?
NYALLYWOOD DINER
PO-KWEEK
PO-KWEEK
WHOOO!
GET READY FOR A DOOZY! POMPO'S ALSO MAKING A MOVIE!!
TA-DAAA!
WAIT, WHAT?!
?!
DMP

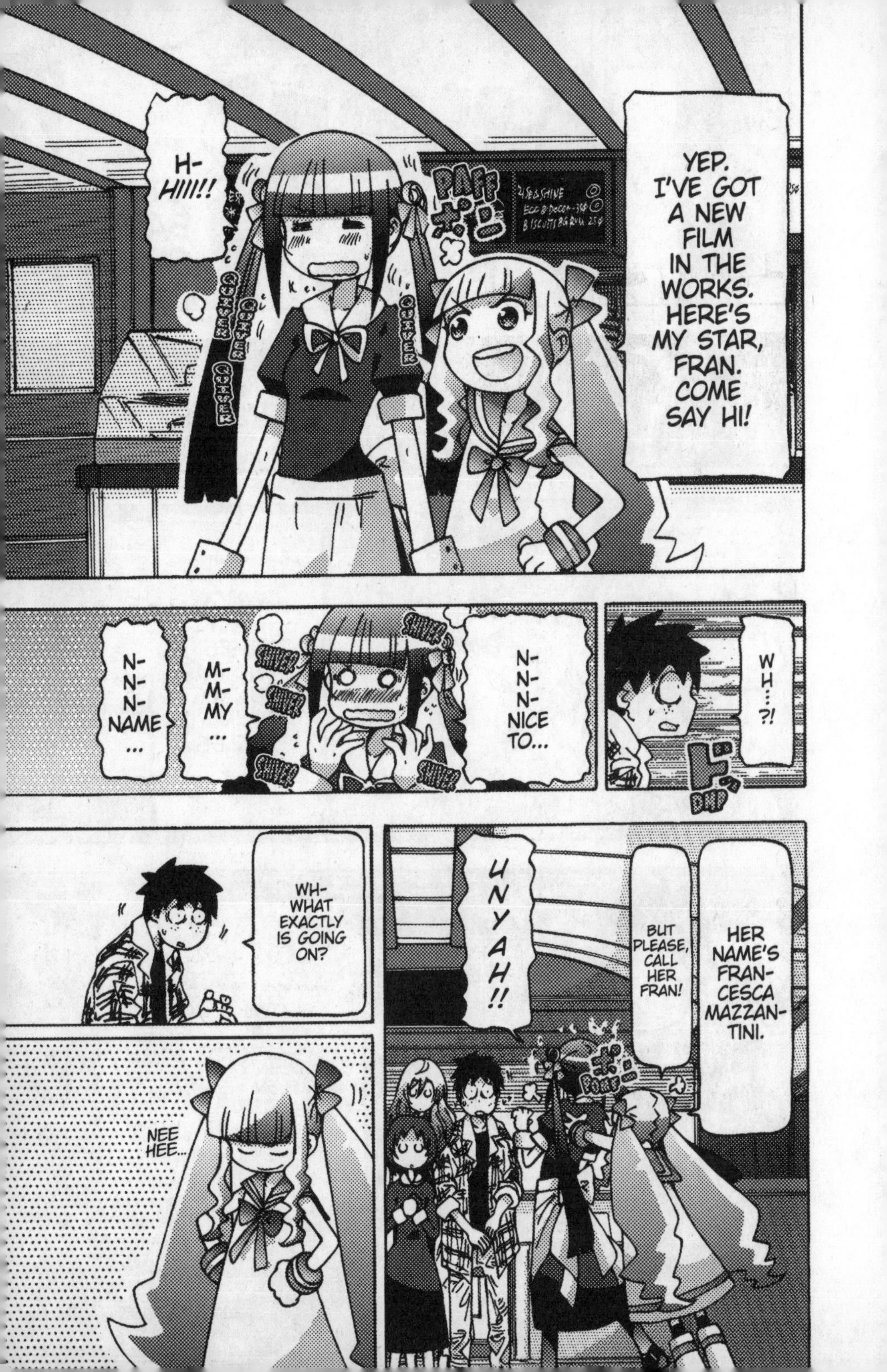
YEP. I'VE GOT A NEW FILM IN THE WORKS. HERE'S MY STAR, FRAN. COME SAY HI!
PAFF
H-HIII!!
QUIVER QUIVER QUIVER QUIVER
WH...?!
DMP
N-N-N-NICE TO...
SHIVER SHIVER SHIVER SHIVER SHIVER
M-M-MY...
N-N-N-NAME...
HER NAME'S FRAN-CESCA MAZZAN-TINI.
BUT PLEASE, CALL HER FRAN!
POMF
UNYAH!!
WH-WHAT EXACTLY IS GOING ON?
NEE HEE...

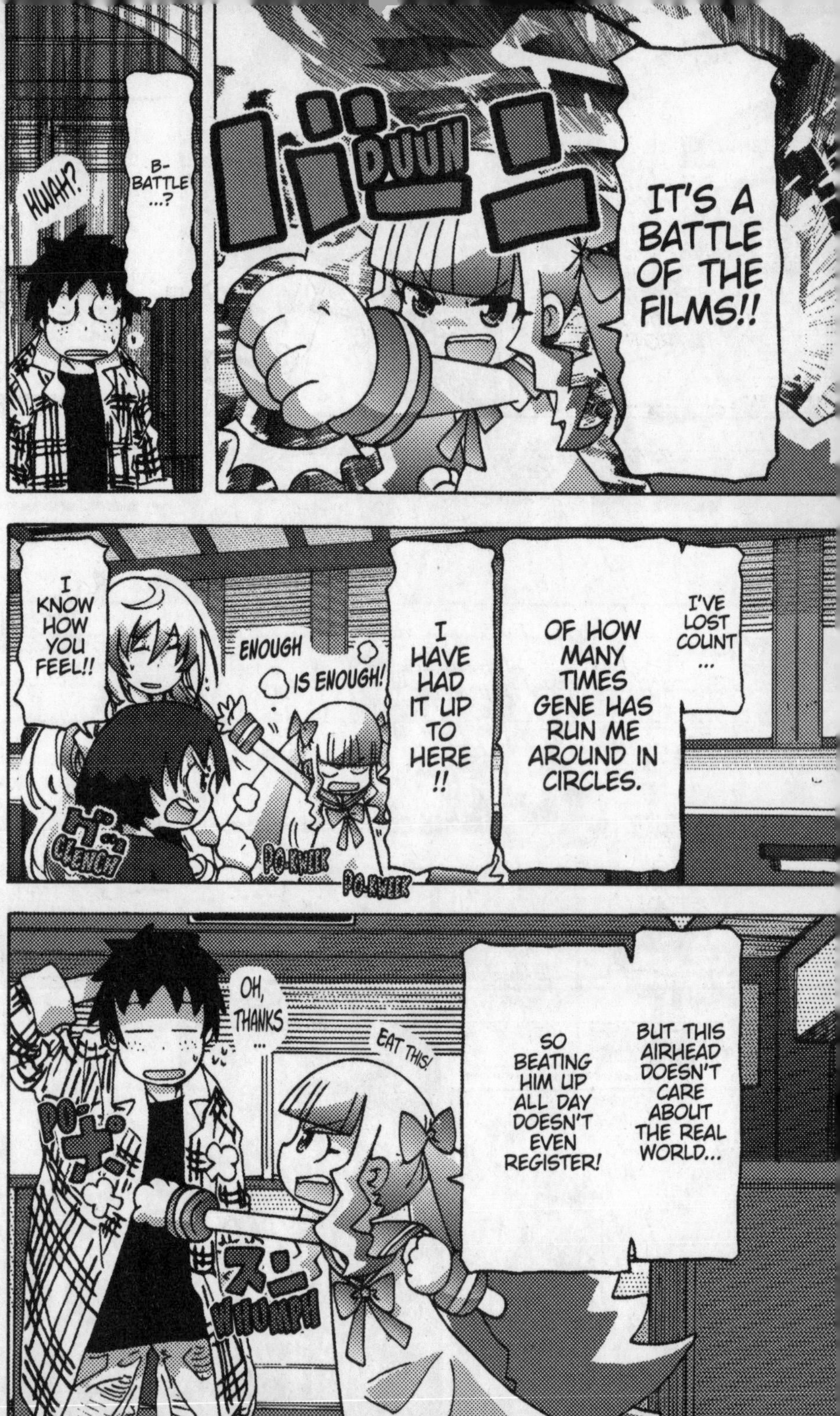
IT'S A BATTLE OF THE FILMS!!
DUUN
B-BATTLE ...?
HWAH?
I'VE LOST COUNT ...
OF HOW MANY TIMES GENE HAS RUN ME AROUND IN CIRCLES.
I HAVE HAD IT UP TO HERE !!
ENOUGH IS ENOUGH!
I KNOW HOW YOU FEEL!!
CLENCH
BUT THIS AIRHEAD DOESN'T CARE ABOUT THE REAL WORLD...
SO BEATING HIM UP ALL DAY DOESN'T EVEN REGISTER!
EAT THIS!
OH, THANKS ...
WHOMPH

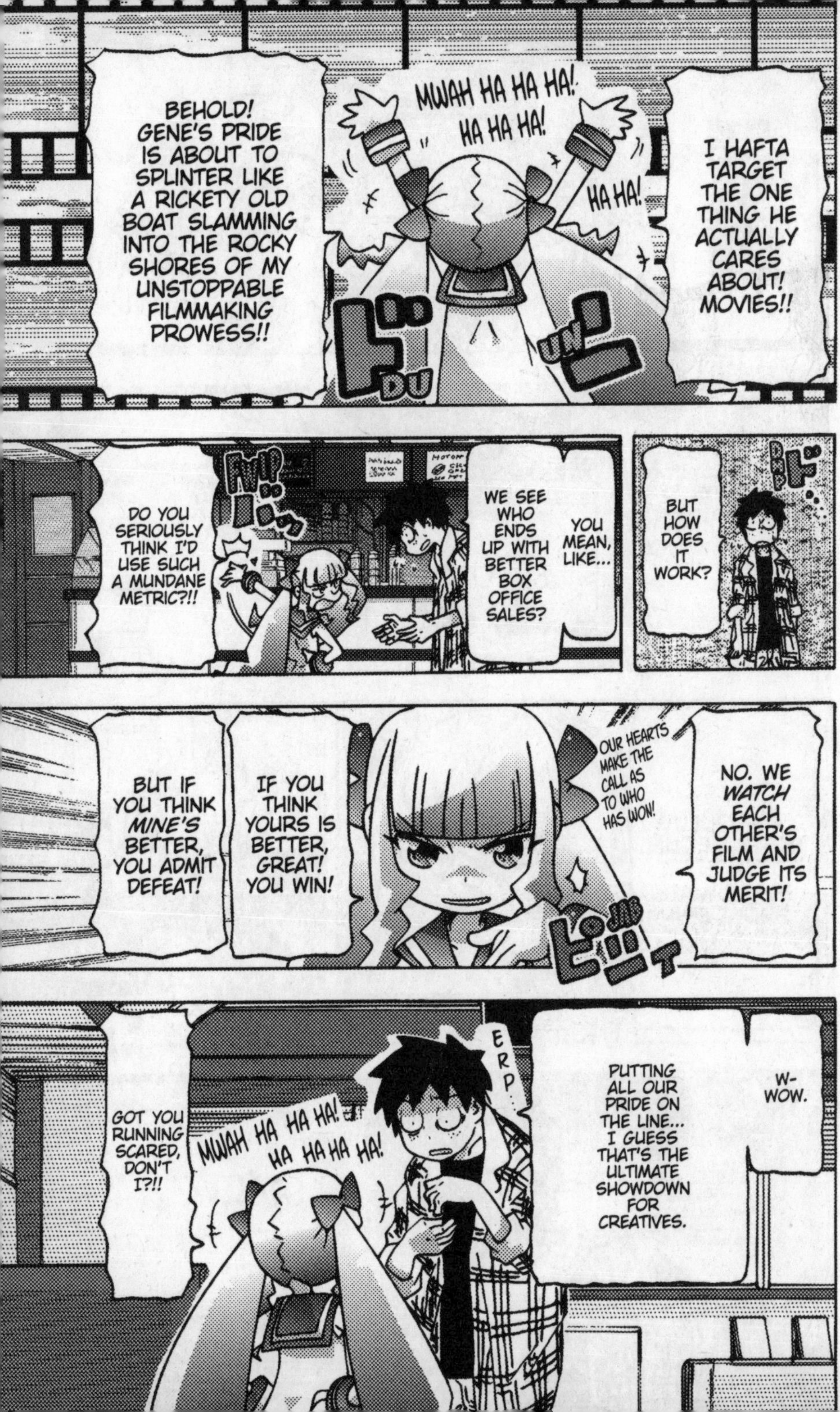
I HAFTA TARGET THE ONE THING HE ACTUALLY CARES ABOUT! MOVIES!!
MWAH HA HA HA! HA HA HA!
HA HA!
BEHOLD! GENE'S PRIDE IS ABOUT TO SPLINTER LIKE A RICKETY OLD BOAT SLAMMING INTO THE ROCKY SHORES OF MY UNSTOPPABLE FILMMAKING PROWESS!!
BUT HOW DOES IT WORK?
YOU MEAN, LIKE...
WE SEE WHO ENDS UP WITH BETTER BOX OFFICE SALES?
FWIP
DO YOU SERIOUSLY THINK I'D USE SUCH A MUNDANE METRIC?!!
NO. WE *WATCH* EACH OTHER'S FILM AND JUDGE ITS MERIT!
OUR HEARTS MAKE THE CALL AS TO WHO HAS WON!
IF YOU THINK YOURS IS BETTER, GREAT! YOU WIN!
BUT IF YOU THINK *MINE'S* BETTER, YOU ADMIT DEFEAT!
W-WOW.
PUTTING ALL OUR PRIDE ON THE LINE... I GUESS THAT'S THE ULTIMATE SHOWDOWN FOR CREATIVES.
ERP...
MWAH HA HA HA! HA HA HA HA!
GOT YOU RUNNING SCARED, DON'T I?!!

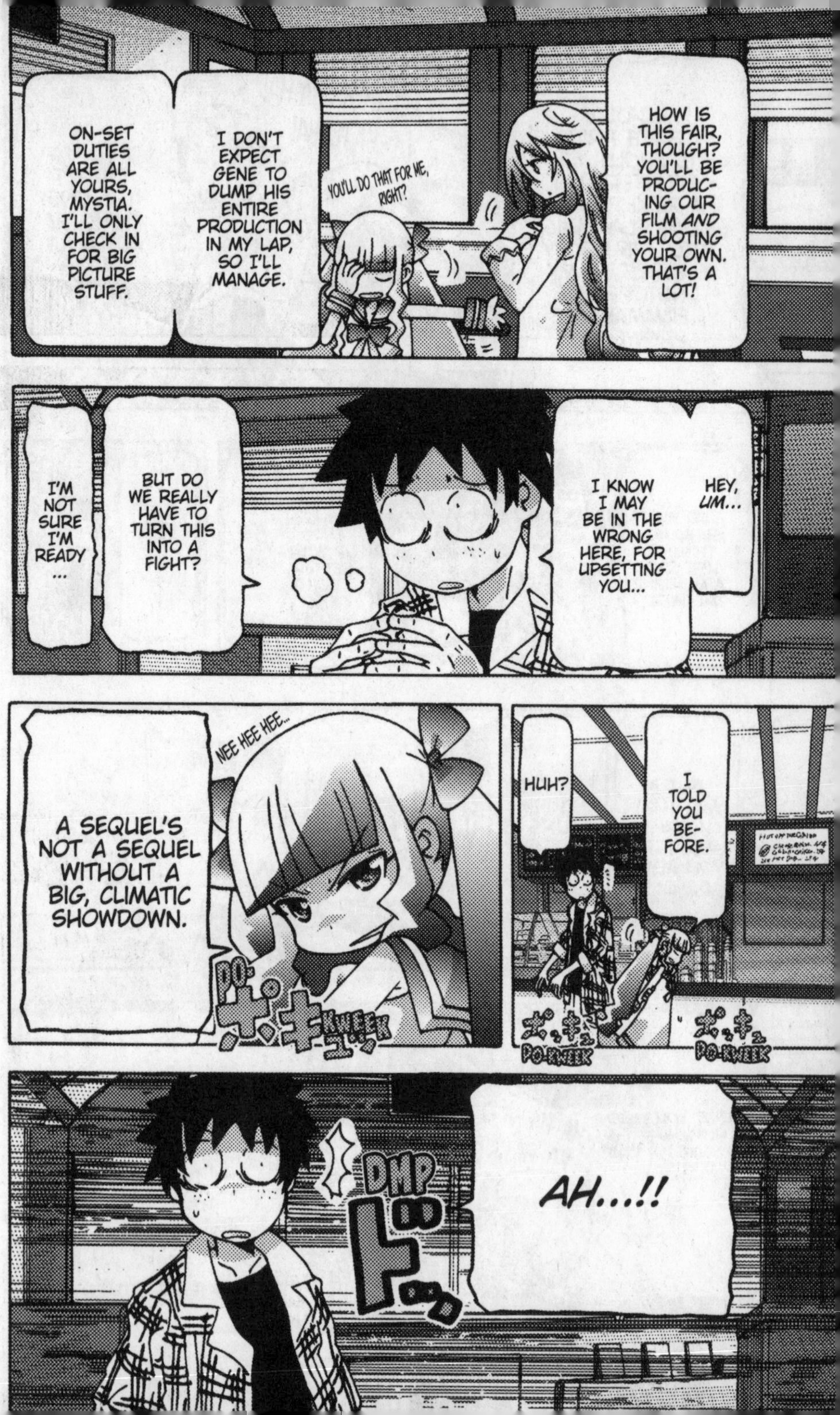
HOW IS THIS FAIR, THOUGH? YOU'LL BE PRODUCING OUR FILM AND SHOOTING YOUR OWN. THAT'S A LOT!
YOU'LL DO THAT FOR ME, RIGHT?
I DON'T EXPECT GENE TO DUMP HIS ENTIRE PRODUCTION IN MY LAP, SO I'LL MANAGE.
ON-SET DUTIES ARE ALL YOURS, MYSTIA. I'LL ONLY CHECK IN FOR BIG PICTURE STUFF.
HEY, UM...
I KNOW I MAY BE IN THE WRONG HERE, FOR UPSETTING YOU...
BUT DO WE REALLY HAVE TO TURN THIS INTO A FIGHT?
I'M NOT SURE I'M READY...
I TOLD YOU BEFORE.
HUH?
PO-KWEEK
PO-KWEEK
NEE HEE HEE...
A SEQUEL'S NOT A SEQUEL WITHOUT A BIG, CLIMATIC SHOWDOWN.
PO-KWEEK
AH...!!
DMP

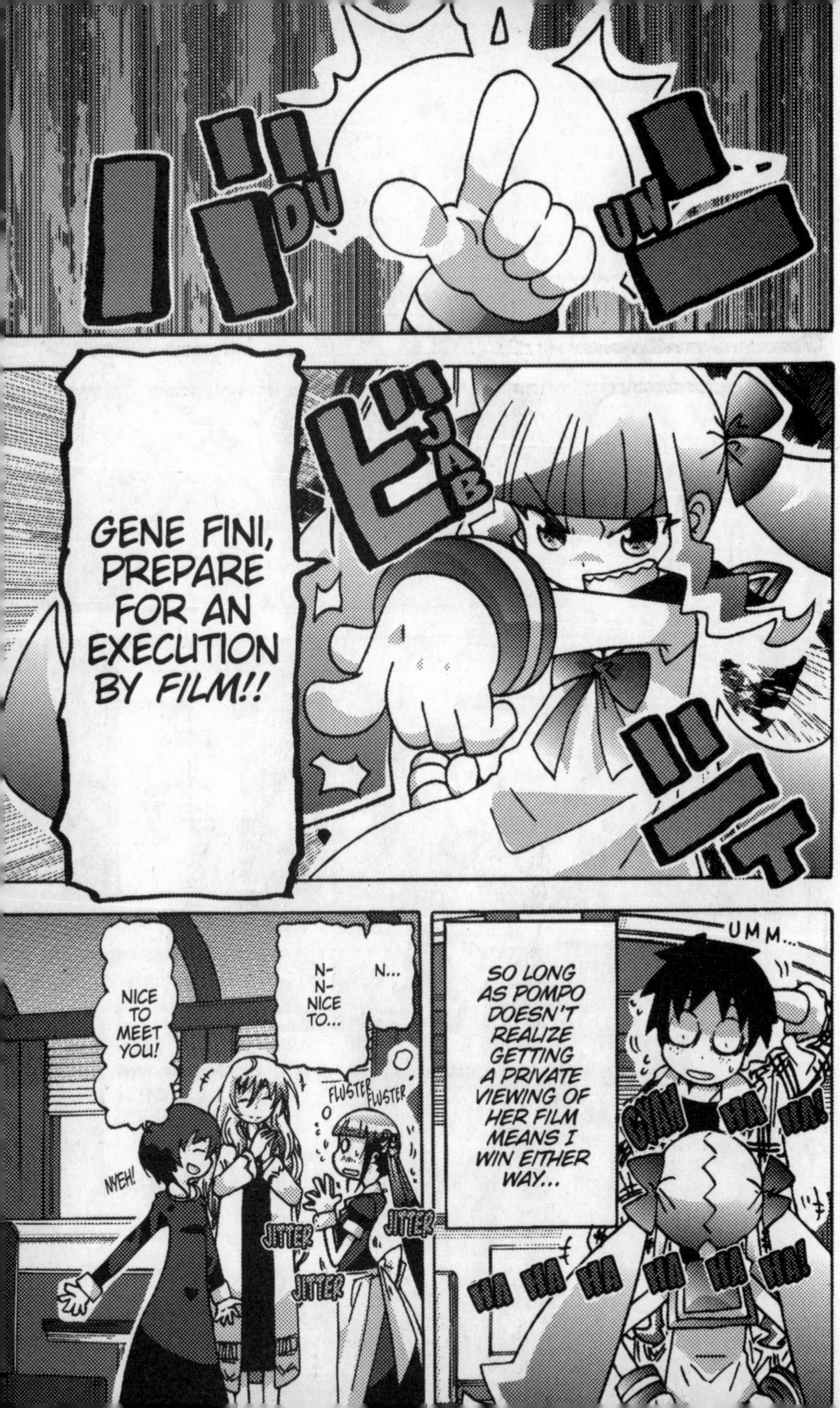
UN
DU
JAB
GENE FINI, PREPARE FOR AN EXECUTION BY FILM!!
UMM...
SO LONG AS POMPO DOESN'T REALIZE GETTING A PRIVATE VIEWING OF HER FILM MEANS I WIN EITHER WAY...
N...
N- N- NICE TO...
NICE TO MEET YOU!
FLUSTER FLUSTER
NYEH!
JITTER
JITTER
JITTER

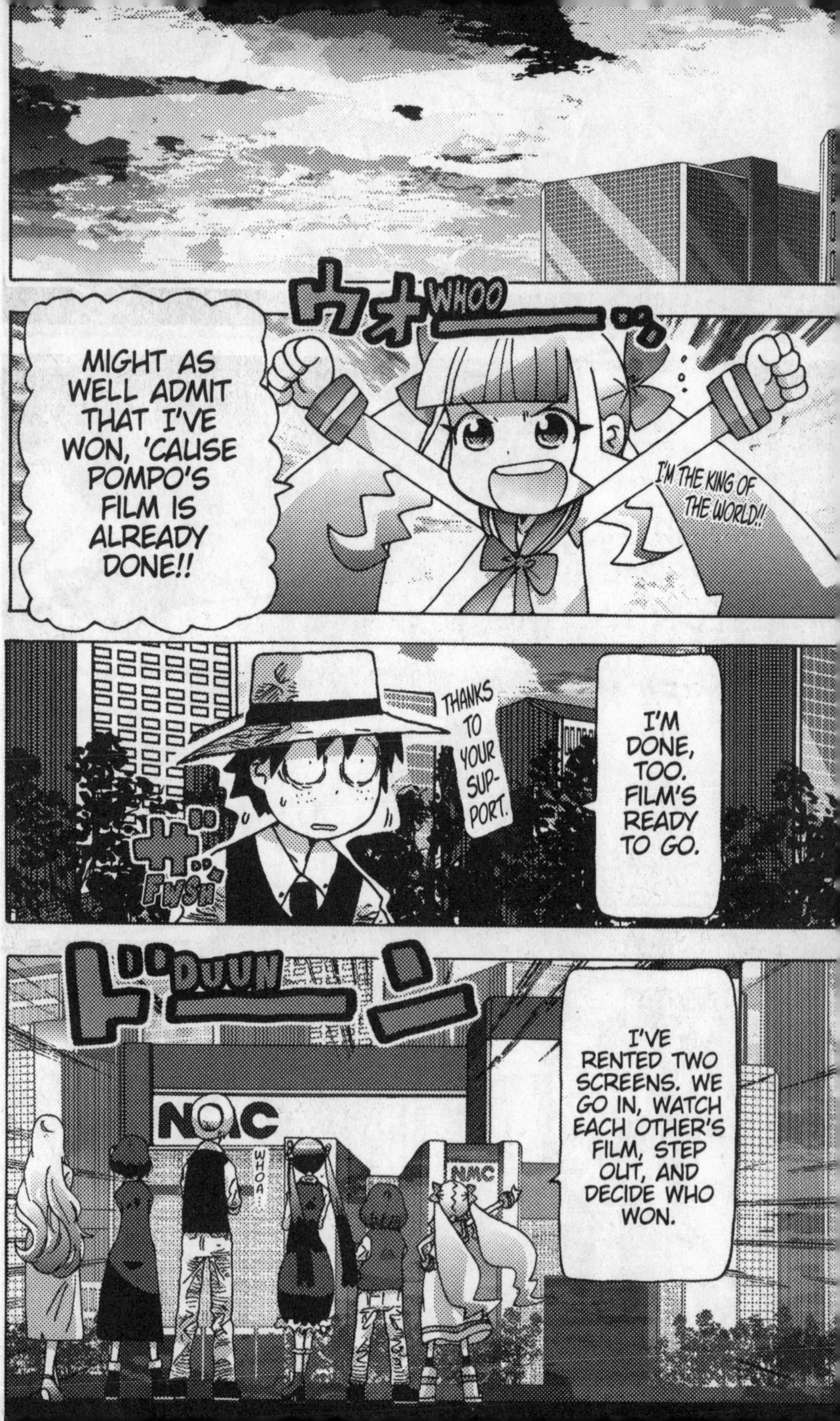
WHOO
MIGHT AS WELL ADMIT THAT I'VE WON, 'CAUSE POMPO'S FILM IS ALREADY DONE!!
I'M THE KING OF THE WORLD!!
I'M DONE, TOO. FILM'S READY TO GO.
THANKS TO YOUR SUP-PORT.
FWSH
DUUN
I'VE RENTED TWO SCREENS. WE GO IN, WATCH EACH OTHER'S FILM, STEP OUT, AND DECIDE WHO WON.
NAC
WHOA...

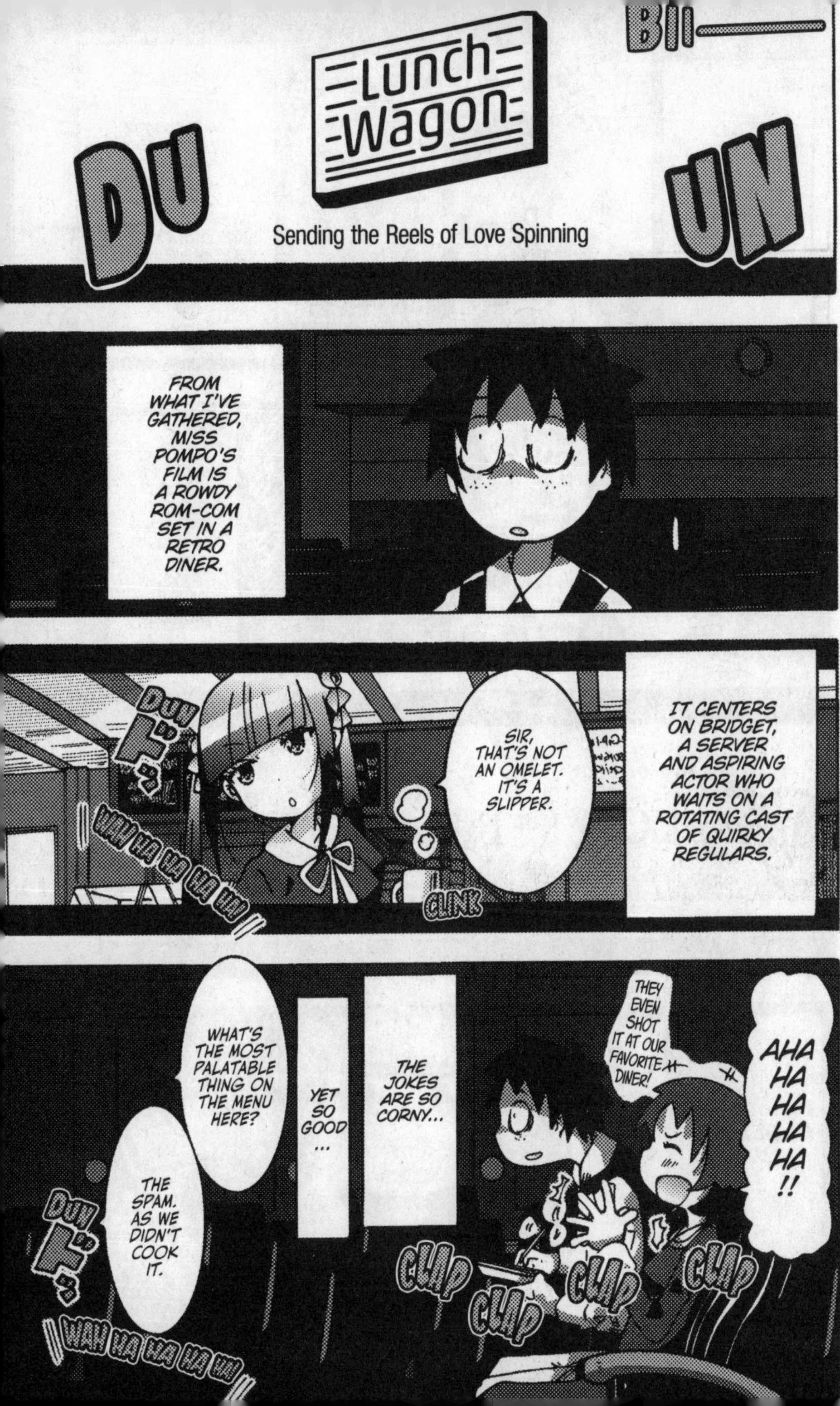
BII—
Lunch Wagon
DU
UN
Sending the Reels of Love Spinning
FROM WHAT I'VE GATHERED, MISS POMPO'S FILM IS A ROWDY ROM-COM SET IN A RETRO DINER.
IT CENTERS ON BRIDGET, A SERVER AND ASPIRING ACTOR WHO WAITS ON A ROTATING CAST OF QUIRKY REGULARS.
SIR, THAT'S NOT AN OMELET. IT'S A SLIPPER.
CLINK
DUU
WAH HA HA HA HA
AHA HA HA HA HA!!
THEY EVEN SHOT IT AT OUR FAVORITE DINER!
THE JOKES ARE SO CORNY...
YET SO GOOD...
WHAT'S THE MOST PALATABLE THING ON THE MENU HERE?
THE SPAM. AS WE DIDN'T COOK IT.
CLAP
CLAP
CLAP
CLAP
DUU
WAH HA HA HA HA

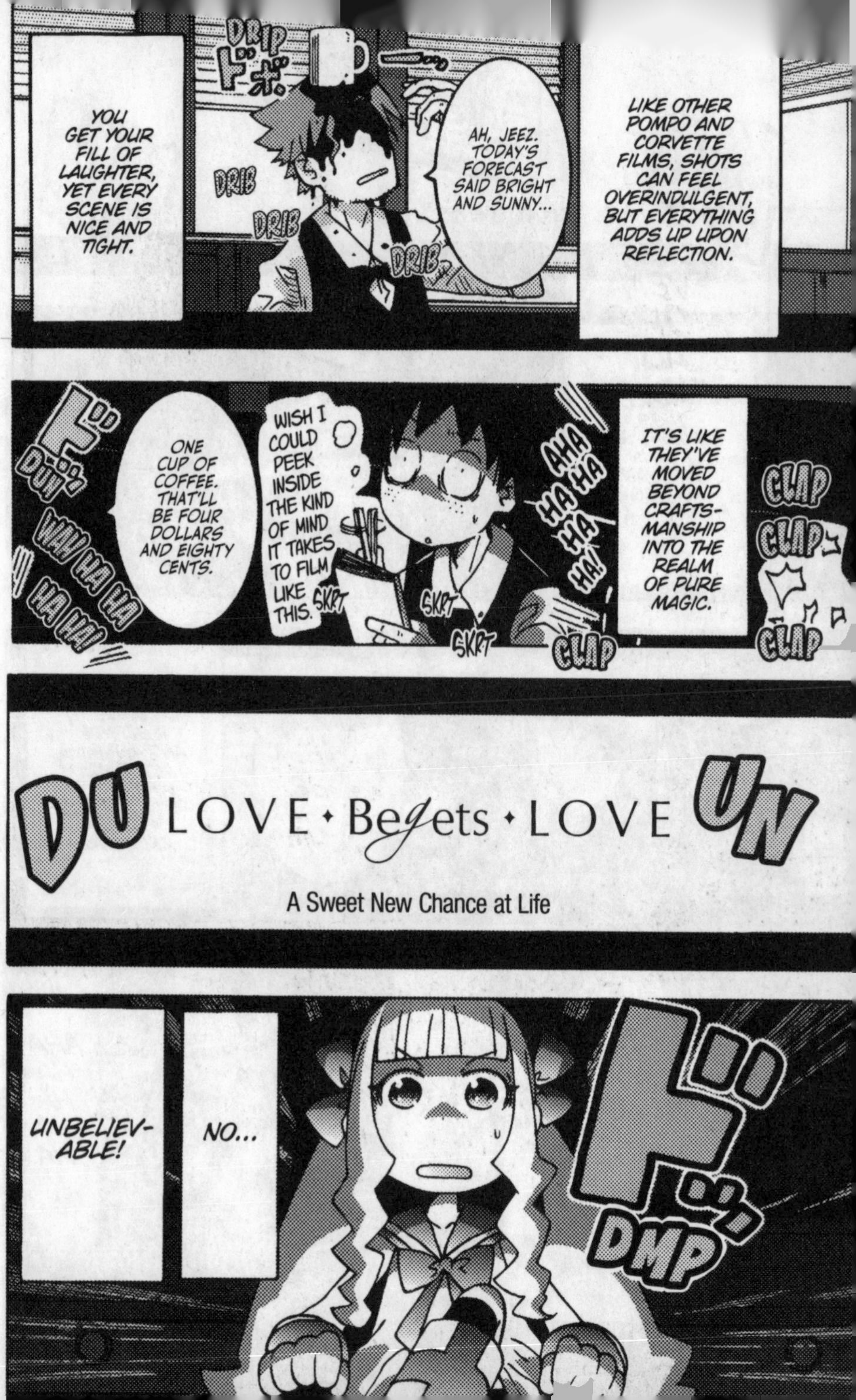
LIKE OTHER POMPO AND CORVETTE FILMS, SHOTS CAN FEEL OVERINDULGENT, BUT EVERYTHING ADDS UP UPON REFLECTION.
AH, JEEZ. TODAY'S FORECAST SAID BRIGHT AND SUNNY...
DRIP
DRIB
DRIB
DRIB
YOU GET YOUR FILL OF LAUGHTER, YET EVERY SCENE IS NICE AND TIGHT.
CLAP
CLAP
CLAP
IT'S LIKE THEY'VE MOVED BEYOND CRAFTS-MANSHIP INTO THE REALM OF PURE MAGIC.
AHA HA HA HA HA HA!
CLAP
SKRT
SKRT
WISH I COULD PEEK INSIDE THE KIND OF MIND IT TAKES TO FILM LIKE THIS.
SKRT
ONE CUP OF COFFEE. THAT'LL BE FOUR DOLLARS AND EIGHTY CENTS.
DUN
WAH HA HA
HA HA!
UN
DU
LOVE ✦ Begets ✦ LOVE
A Sweet New Chance at Life
DMP
NO...
UNBELIEV-ABLE!

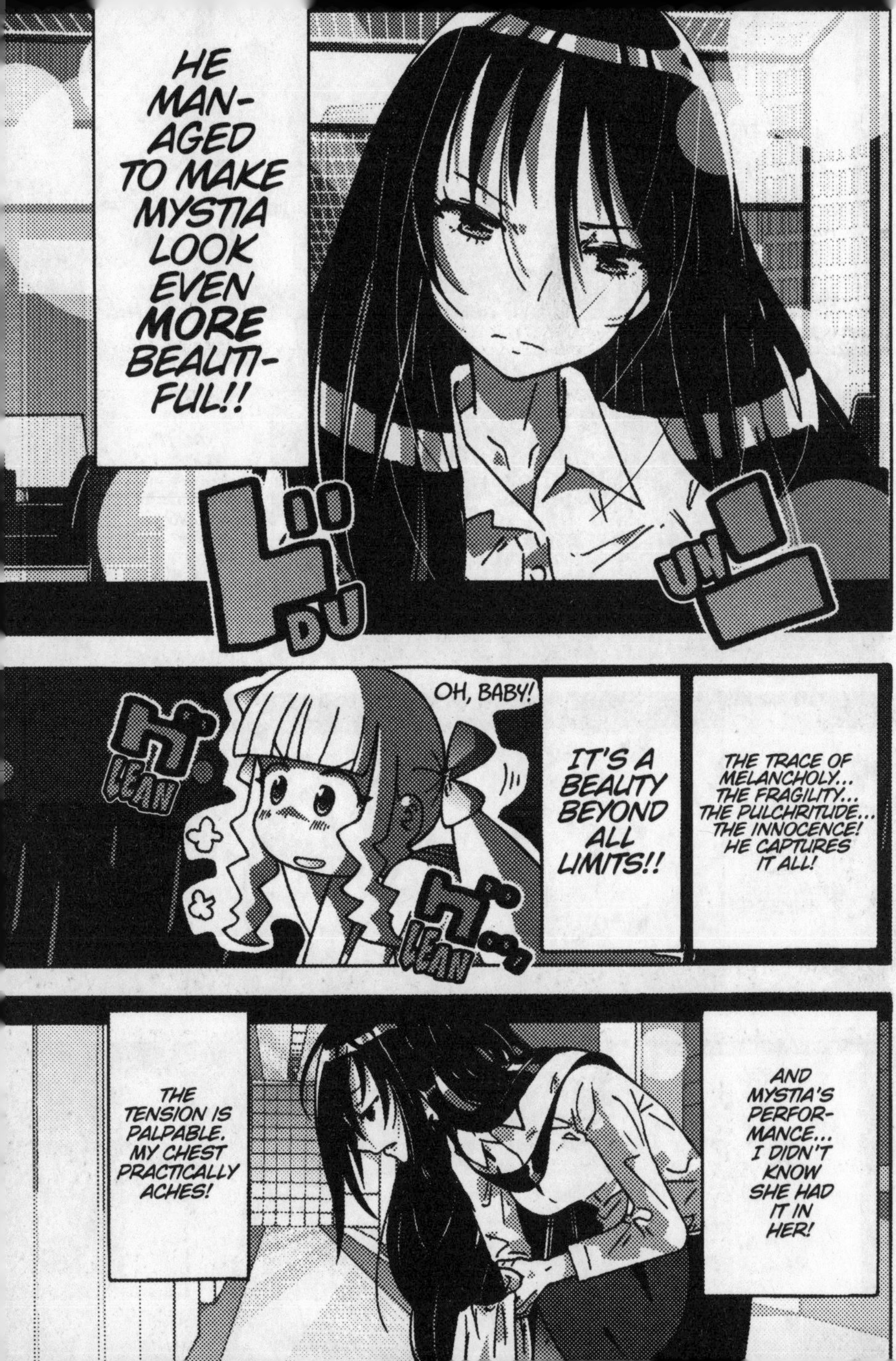
HE MANAGED TO MAKE MYSTIA LOOK EVEN MORE BEAUTIFUL!!
DU
UN
THE TRACE OF MELANCHOLY... THE FRAGILITY... THE PULCHRITUDE... THE INNOCENCE! HE CAPTURES IT ALL!
IT'S A BEAUTY BEYOND ALL LIMITS!!
OH, BABY!
LEAN
LEAN
AND MYSTIA'S PERFORMANCE... I DIDN'T KNOW SHE HAD IT IN HER!
THE TENSION IS PALPABLE. MY CHEST PRACTICALLY ACHES!

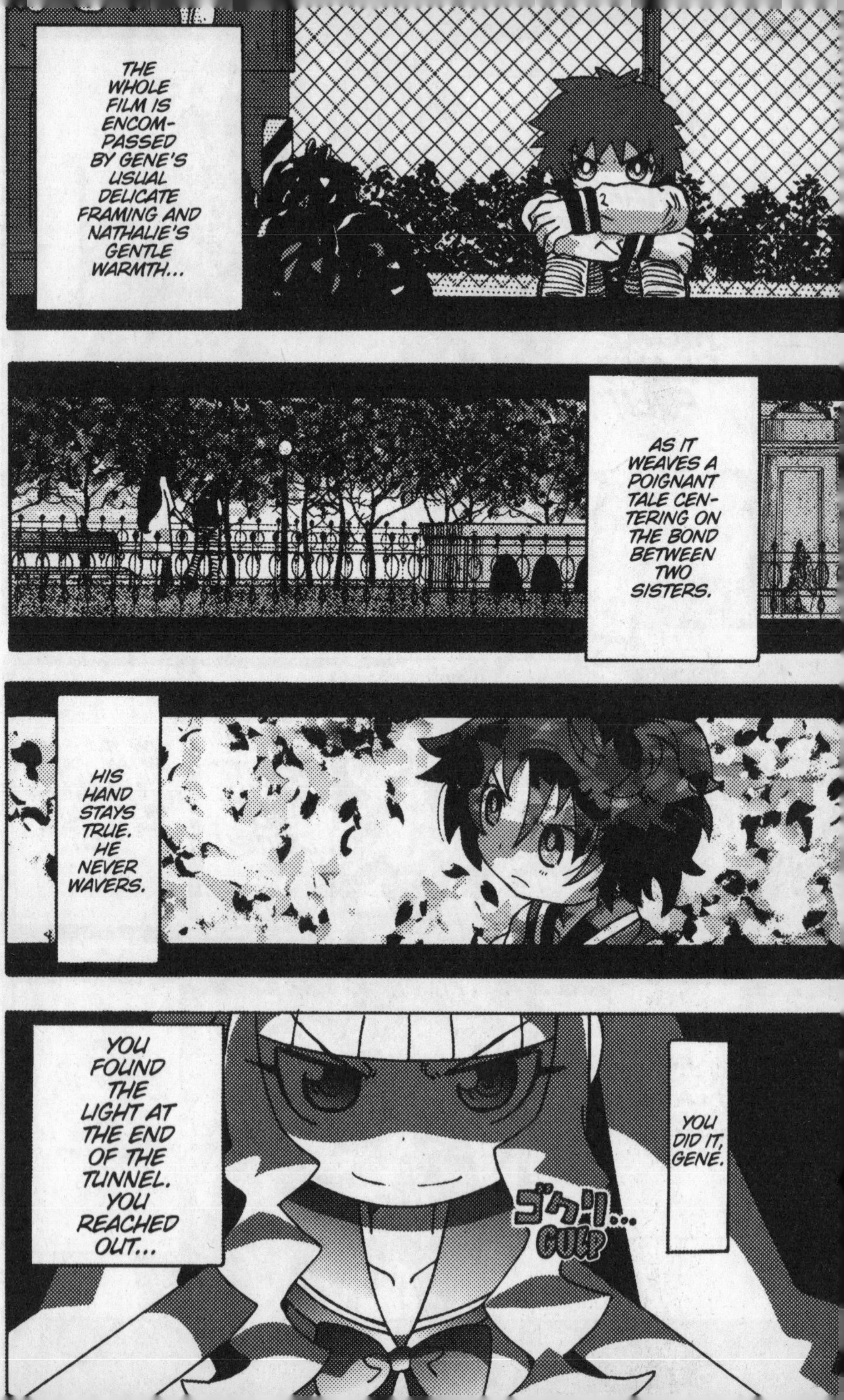
THE WHOLE FILM IS ENCOMPASSED BY GENE'S USUAL DELICATE FRAMING AND NATHALIE'S GENTLE WARMTH...
AS IT WEAVES A POIGNANT TALE CENTERING ON THE BOND BETWEEN TWO SISTERS.
HIS HAND STAYS TRUE. HE NEVER WAVERS.
YOU DID IT, GENE.
YOU FOUND THE LIGHT AT THE END OF THE TUNNEL. YOU REACHED OUT...
ゴクッ!!...
GULP

GRABBED ON, AND HELD TIGHT TO YOUR CREATION!!

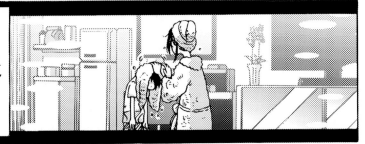

AND HERE IT IS!!

EVERYTHING I'M SEEING ...

THE IMAGES BEFORE ME NOW ...

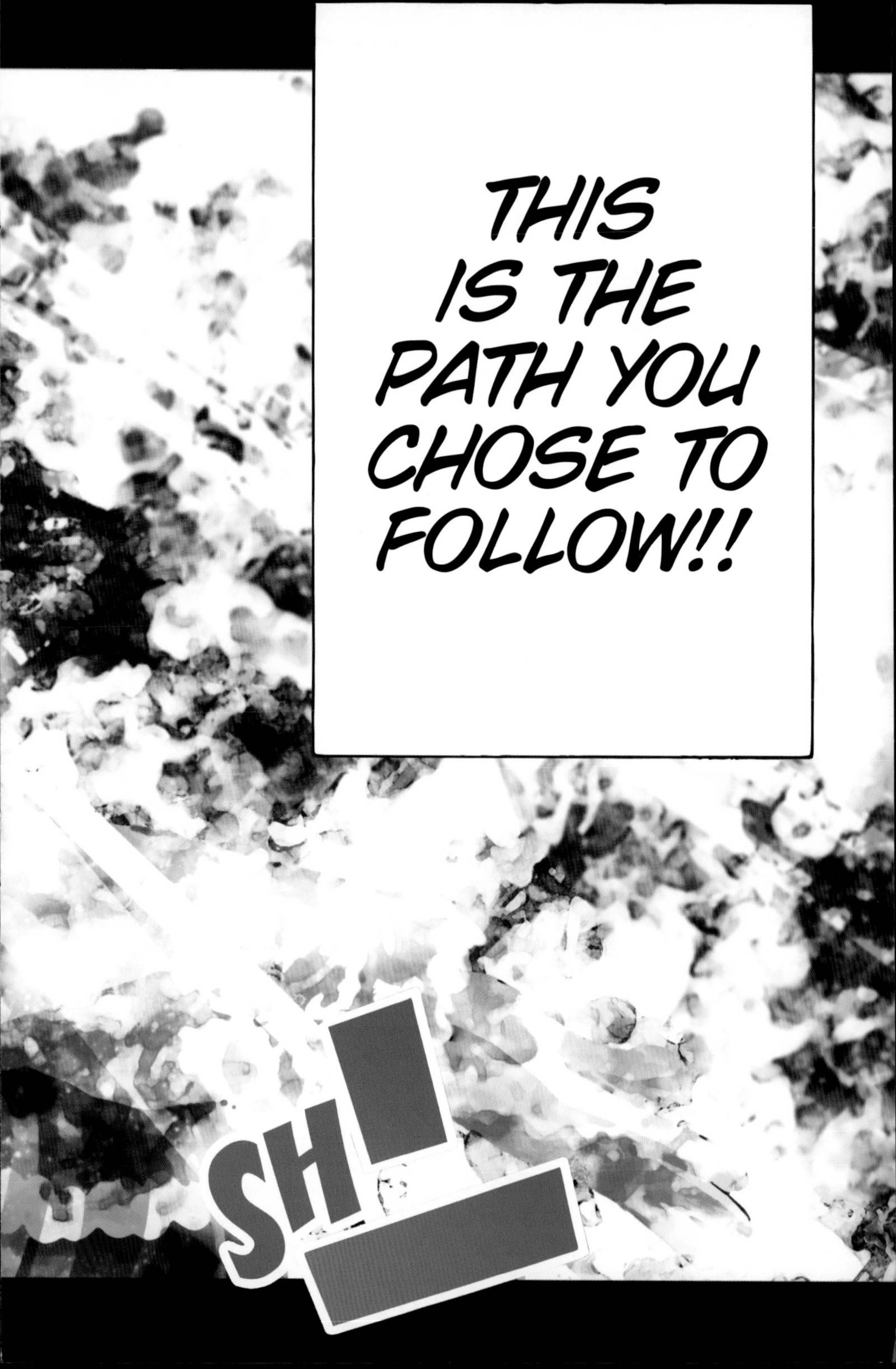
THIS IS THE PATH YOU CHOSE TO FOLLOW!!
SH

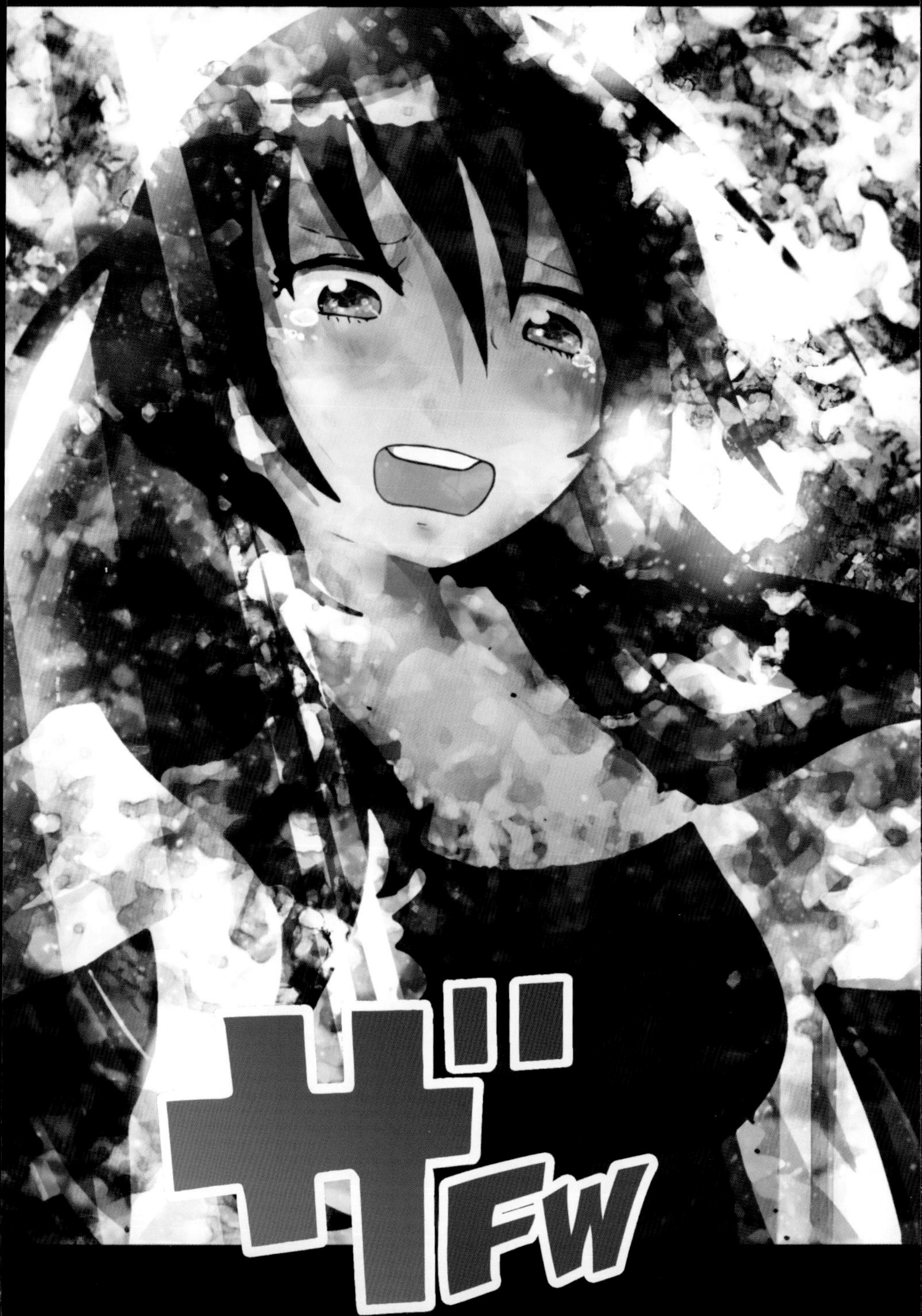

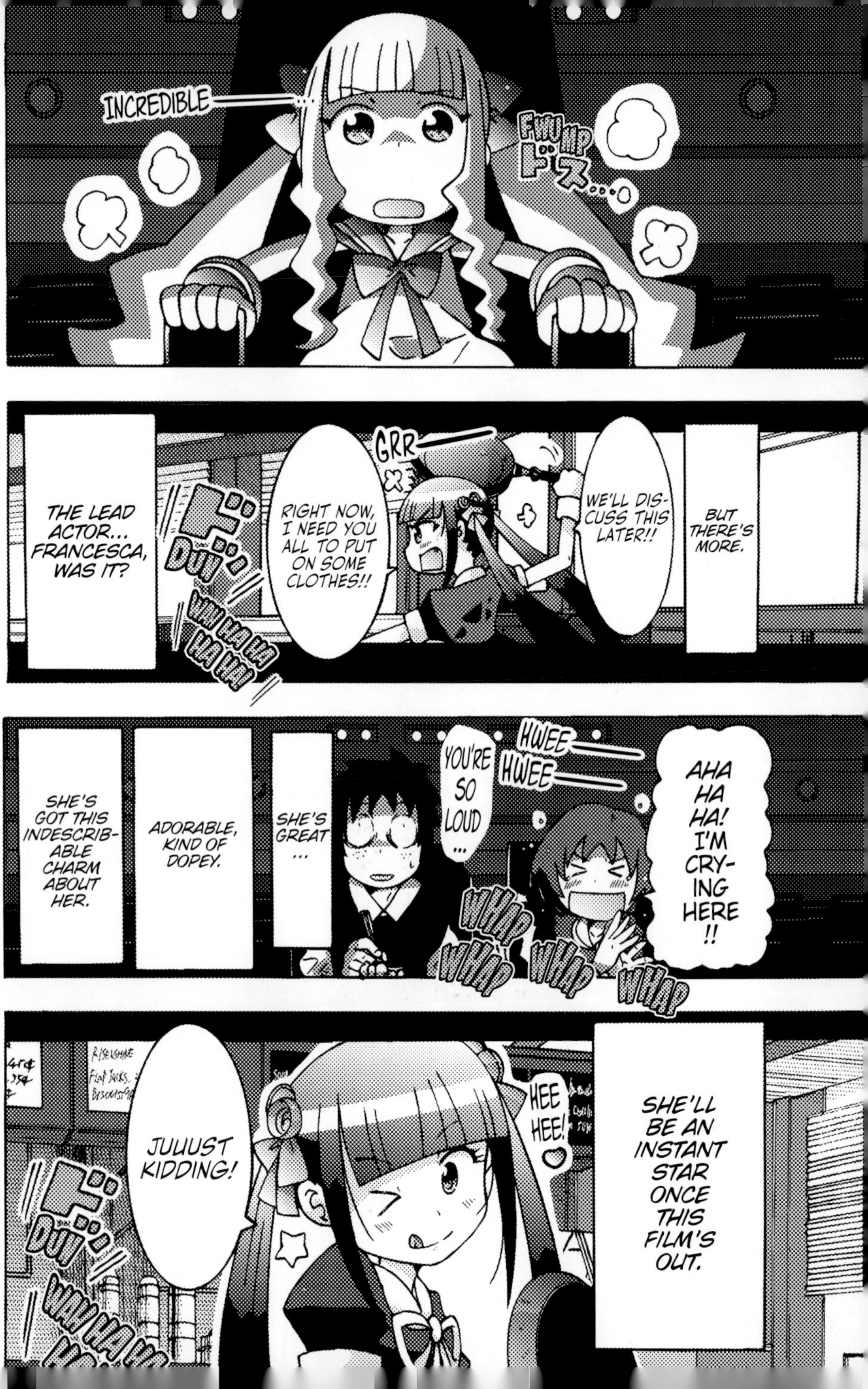
INCREDIBLE
FWUMP ドス…
BUT THERE'S MORE.
WE'LL DISCUSS THIS LATER!!
GRR
RIGHT NOW, I NEED YOU ALL TO PUT ON SOME CLOTHES!!
DUH
WAH HA HA HA HA
THE LEAD ACTOR... FRANCESCA, WAS IT?
AHA HA HA! I'M CRYING HERE!!
HWEE HWEE
YOU'RE SO LOUD...
WHAP WHAP WHAP WHAP
SHE'S GREAT...
ADORABLE, KIND OF DOPEY.
SHE'S GOT THIS INDESCRIBABLE CHARM ABOUT HER.
SHE'LL BE AN INSTANT STAR ONCE THIS FILM'S OUT.
HEE HEE!
JUUUST KIDDING!
DUH

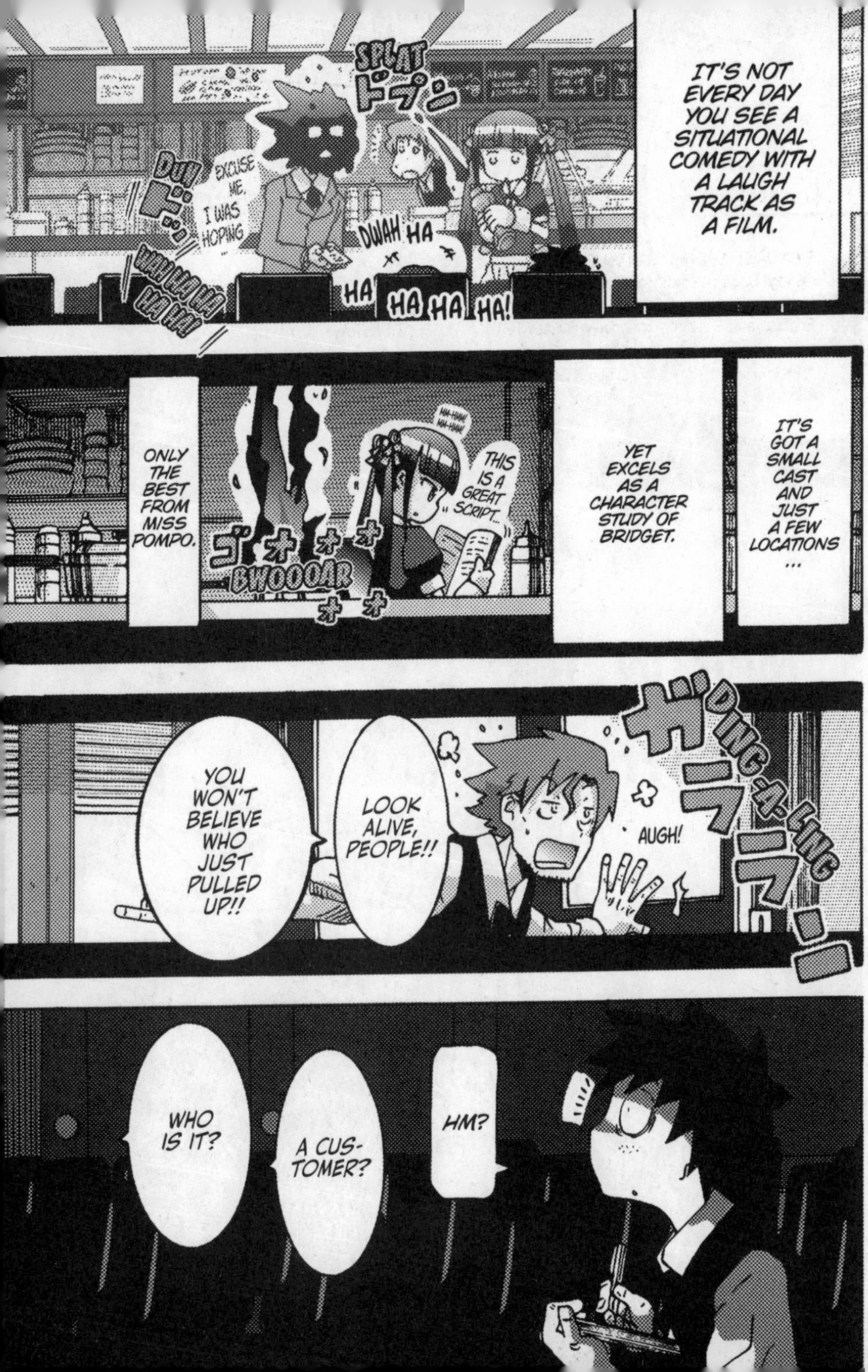
IT'S NOT EVERY DAY YOU SEE A SITUATIONAL COMEDY WITH A LAUGH TRACK AS A FILM.
SPLAT
EXCUSE ME, I WAS HOPING...
DUN
DWAH HA HA HA HA HA!
WAH HA HA HA HA HA!
IT'S GOT A SMALL CAST AND JUST A FEW LOCATIONS...
YET EXCELS AS A CHARACTER STUDY OF BRIDGET.
MM-HMM! MM-HMM!
THIS IS A GREAT SCRIPT...
BWOOOAR
ONLY THE BEST FROM MISS POMPO.
DING-A-LING
AUGH!
LOOK ALIVE, PEOPLE!!
YOU WON'T BELIEVE WHO JUST PULLED UP!!
HM?
A CUS-TOMER?
WHO IS IT?

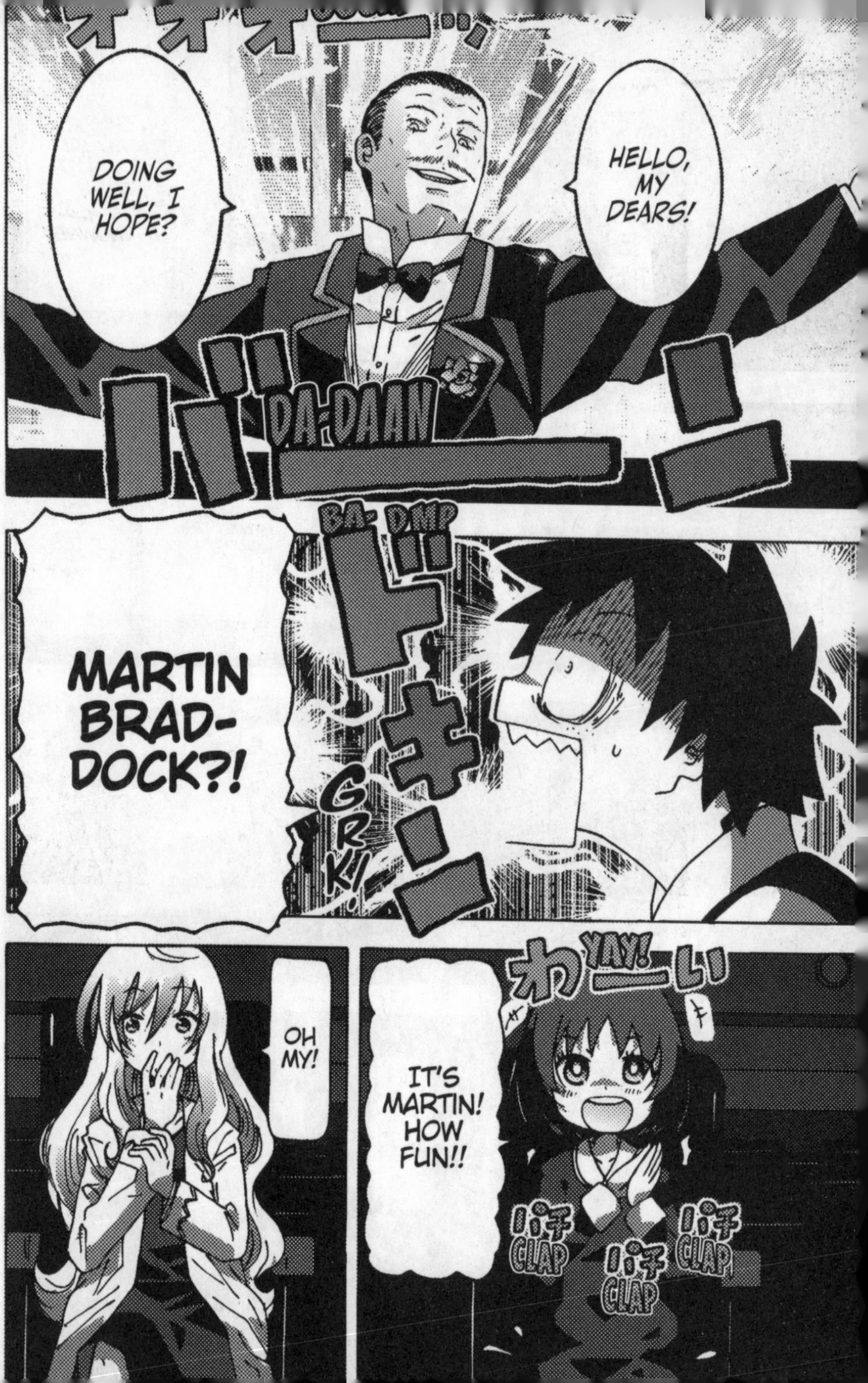
HELLO, MY DEARS!
DOING WELL, I HOPE?
DA-DAAN
BA-DMP
GRK!
MARTIN BRAD-DOCK?!
わーい
YAY!
IT'S MARTIN! HOW FUN!!
CLAP
CLAP
CLAP
OH MY!

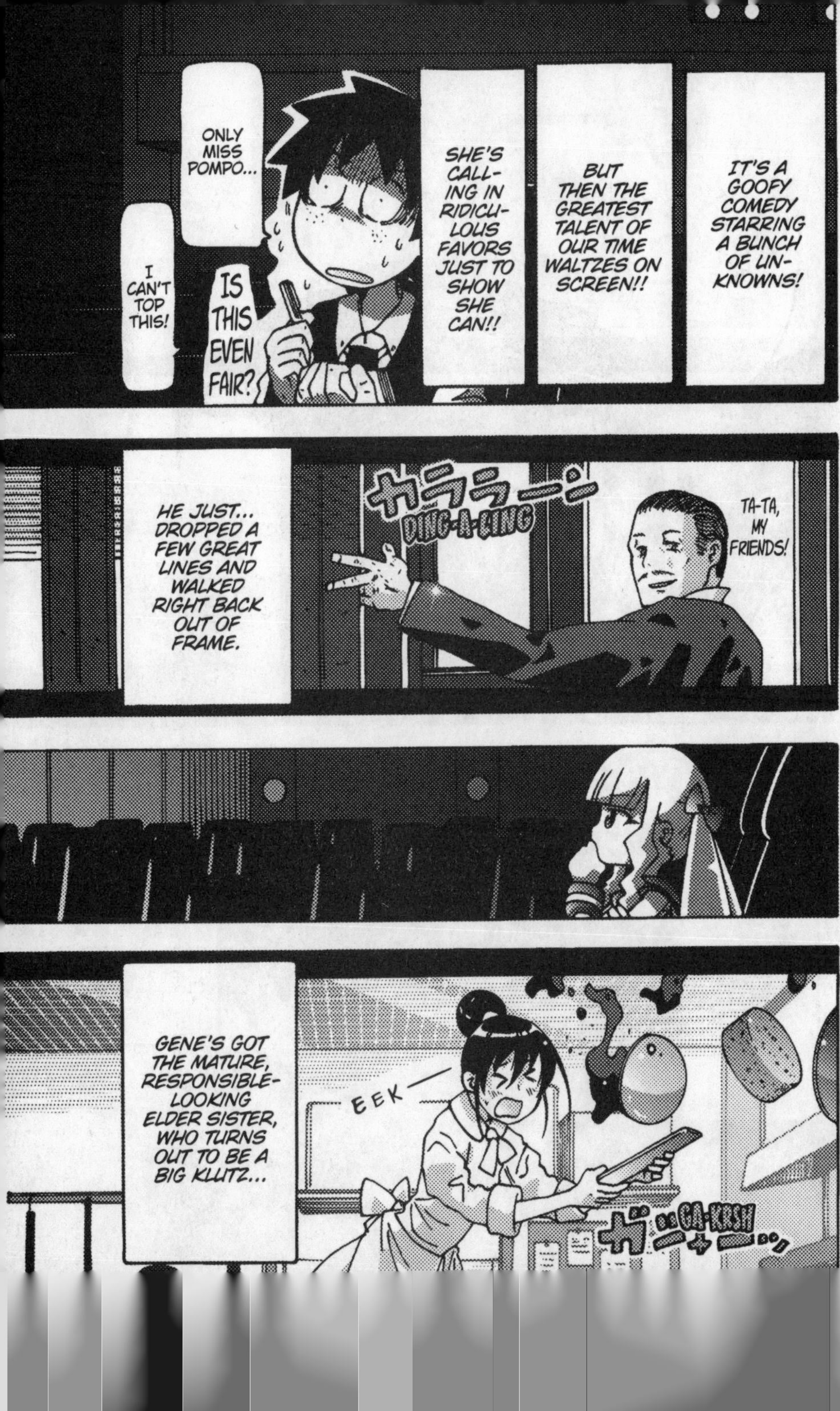
IT'S A GOOFY COMEDY STARRING A BUNCH OF UN-KNOWNS!
BUT THEN THE GREATEST TALENT OF OUR TIME WALTZES ON SCREEN!!
SHE'S CALL-ING IN RIDICU-LOUS FAVORS JUST TO SHOW SHE CAN!!
ONLY MISS POMPO...
IS THIS EVEN FAIR?
I CAN'T TOP THIS!
TA-TA, MY FRIENDS!
カラーン
DING-A-LING
HE JUST... DROPPED A FEW GREAT LINES AND WALKED RIGHT BACK OUT OF FRAME.
GA-KRSH
EEK
GENE'S GOT THE MATURE, RESPONSIBLE-LOOKING ELDER SISTER, WHO TURNS OUT TO BE A BIG KLUTZ...

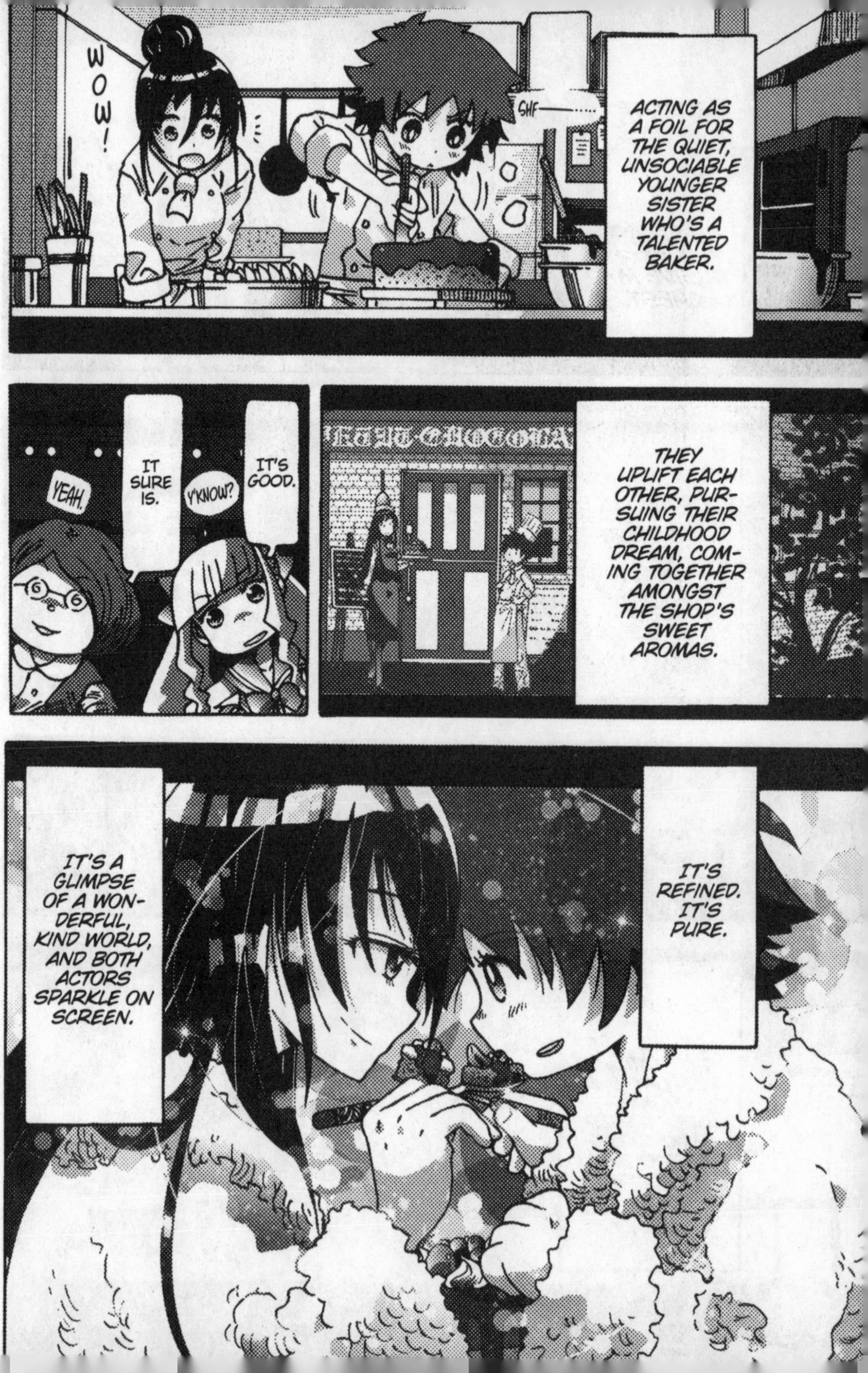
ACTING AS A FOIL FOR THE QUIET, UNSOCIABLE YOUNGER SISTER WHO'S A TALENTED BAKER.
SHF——......
WOW!
THEY UPLIFT EACH OTHER, PURSUING THEIR CHILDHOOD DREAM, COMING TOGETHER AMONGST THE SHOP'S SWEET AROMAS.
IT'S GOOD.
Y'KNOW?
IT SURE IS.
YEAH.
IT'S REFINED. IT'S PURE.
IT'S A GLIMPSE OF A WONDERFUL, KIND WORLD, AND BOTH ACTORS SPARKLE ON SCREEN.

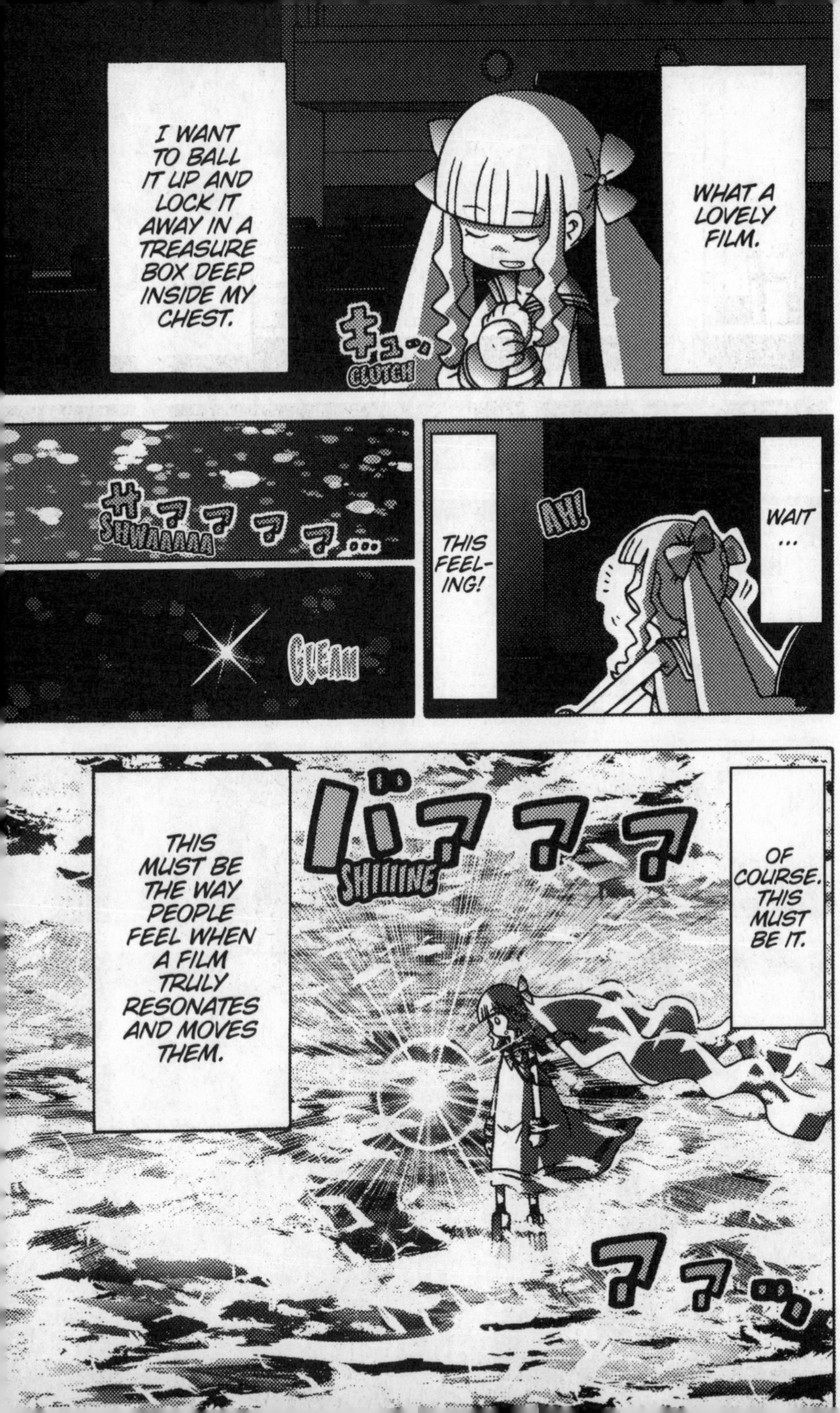
WHAT A LOVELY FILM.
I WANT TO BALL IT UP AND LOCK IT AWAY IN A TREASURE BOX DEEP INSIDE MY CHEST.
CLUTCH
WAIT ...
AH!
THIS FEEL-ING!
SHWAAAAA
GLEAM
OF COURSE. THIS MUST BE IT.
THIS MUST BE THE WAY PEOPLE FEEL WHEN A FILM TRULY RESONATES AND MOVES THEM.
SHIIIINE

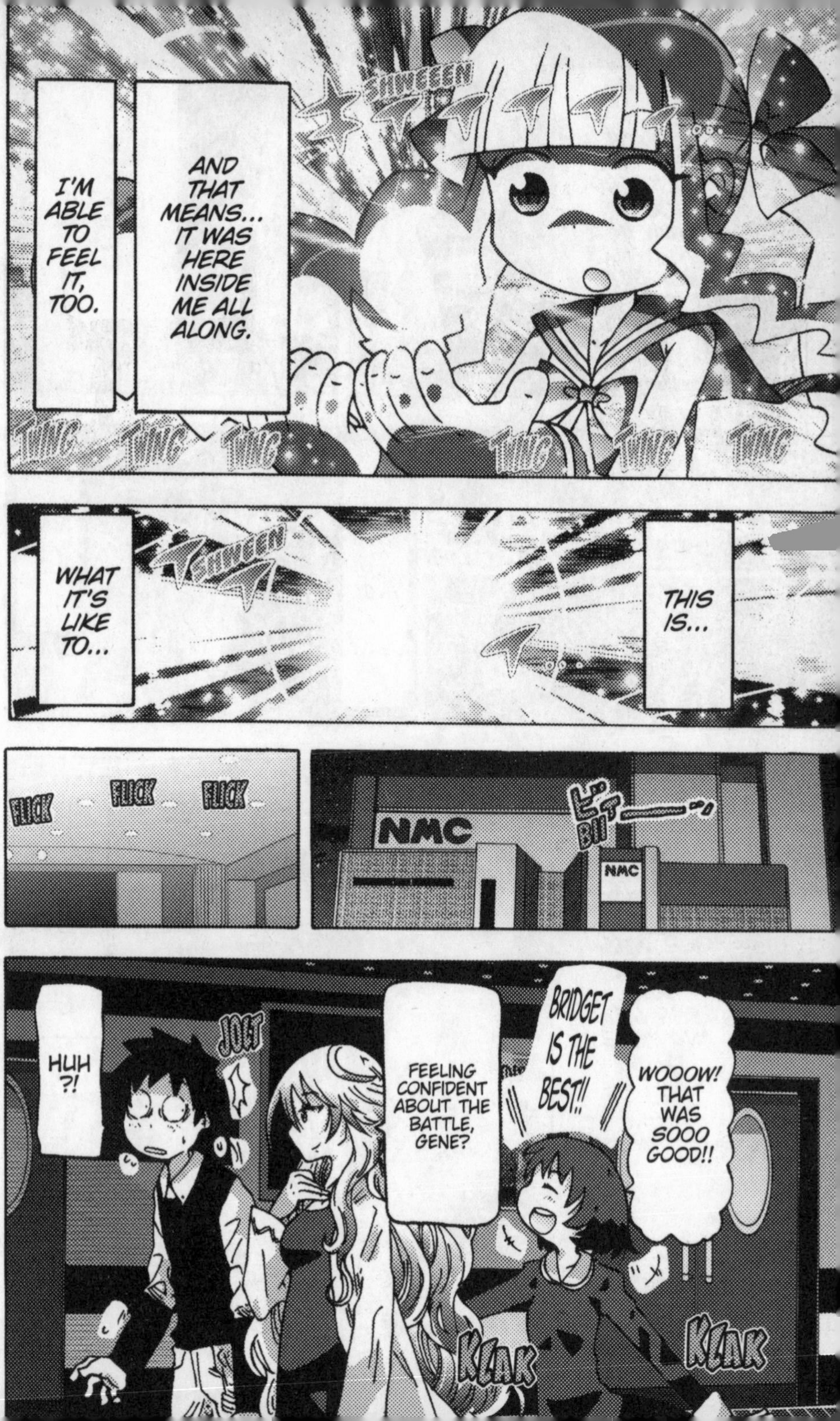
SHWEEN
AND THAT MEANS... IT WAS HERE INSIDE ME ALL ALONG.
I'M ABLE TO FEEL IT, TOO.
TWING TWING TWING TWING TWING TWING
THIS IS...
SHWEEN
WHAT IT'S LIKE TO...
ビー BII
NMC
NMC
FLICK FLICK FLICK
WOOOW! THAT WAS SOOO GOOD!!
BRIDGET IS THE BEST!!
FEELING CONFIDENT ABOUT THE BATTLE, GENE?
JOLT
HUH?!
KLAK KLAK

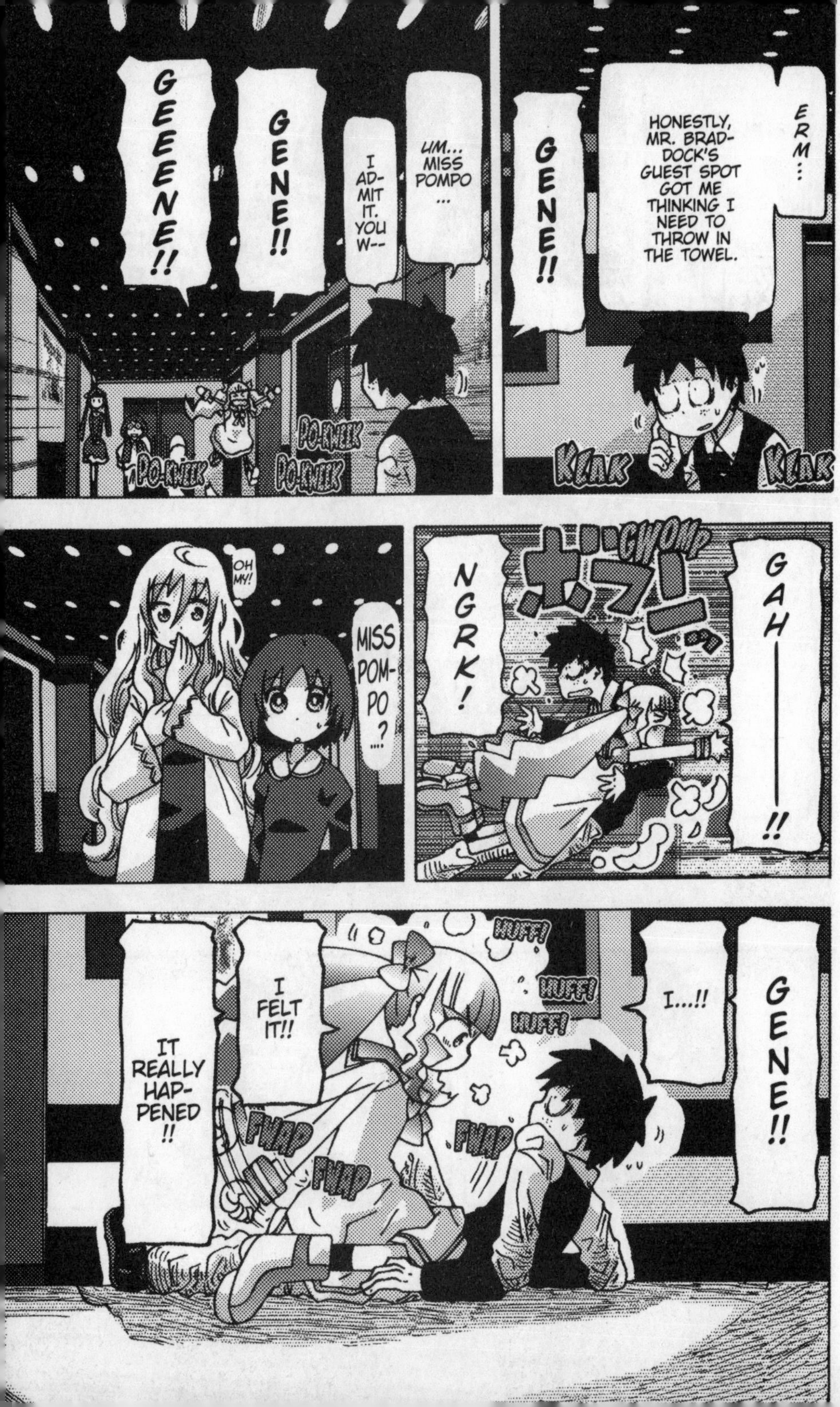

ERM...
HONESTLY, MR. BRAD-DOCK'S GUEST SPOT GOT ME THINKING I NEED TO THROW IN THE TOWEL.
GENE!!
KLAK
KLAK
UM... MISS POMPO...
I AD-MIT IT. YOU W--
GENE!!
GEEENE!!
PO-KWEEK
PO-KWEEK
PO-KWEEK
GAH——!!
GWOMP
NGRK!
MISS POM-PO...?
OH MY!
GENE!!
I...!!
HUFF!
HUFF!
HUFF!
I FELT IT!!
IT REALLY HAP-PENED!!
FWAP
FWAP
FWAP

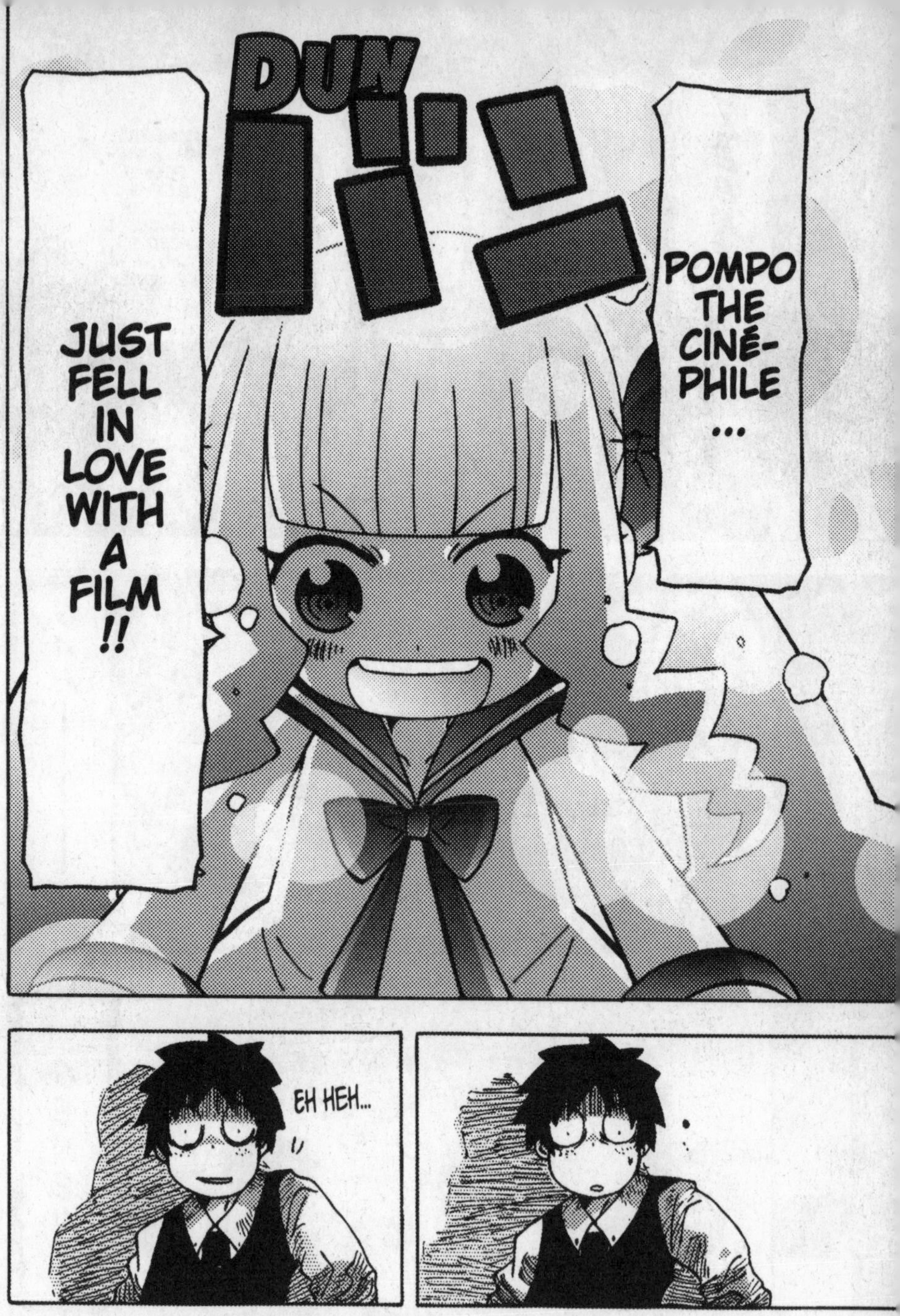
POMPO THE CINÉPHILE...
DUN
JUST FELL IN LOVE WITH A FILM!!
EH HEH...

POMPO: THE CINÉPHILE 2
END

McTiernan's Top 3 Films

Mr. McTiernan's three films are Hollywood masterpieces produced from the mid-1960s to mid-1970s, often starring either Robert Redford or Steve McQueen (two dashing silver screen personas whose names still resonate today).

When a film is produced by a big Hollywood studio, the director is on a tight leash. The producers lay out specific requirements and the director is expected to meet them. Normally, a producer's job only extends to securing investments, finding collaborators, assembling the cast and staff, generating cash with the release of the finished film, and turning a profit. But in the studio system, the producers rule all. Even legendary directors like Alfred Hitchcock and John Ford found themselves unable to overturn studio demands, watching as lead actors were pressured into performance decisions or carefully crafted scenes were cut entirely. Such drastic changes were justified as necessary to guarantee sales. In extreme cases, a director may only be involved in shooting the film, with final cut editing and other vital post-production duties left completely to the producers.

This culture is visible even today. A few years ago, during production of a certain spin-off film in a very well-known franchise, a second director was brought on and instructed to reshoot half the film. In Hollywood, that's just how things go. If one director leaves, another is quickly found, and the camera keeps rolling as scheduled.

Here in Nyallywood, Mr. McTiernan is the man who knows how to run a big studio. Though he shares a job title with Miss Pompo, he's working on a different scale, churning out one major blockbuster after another. Because of that, when Gene went to work on *Max Storm 2*, he found himself facing a slew of challenges unlike anything he could have imagined on one of Miss Pompo's sets.

Introduced Works

The Great Gatsby
1974 / USA / Based on the book *The Great Gatsby* by F. Scott Fitzgerald /
Directed by Jack Clayton / Starring Robert Redford, Mia Farrow, Bruce Dern

The Cincinnati Kid
1965 / USA / Based on the book *The Cincinnati Kid* by Richard Jessup /
Directed by Norman Jewison / Starring Steve McQueen, Edward G. Robinson, Ann-Margret

Three Days of the Condor
1975 / USA / Based on the book *Six Days of the Condor* by James Grady /
Directed by Sydney Pollack / Starring Robert Redford, Faye Dunaway, Max von Sydow

POMPO: THE CINÉPHILE 2

COLUMN 3

Leon's Top 3 Films

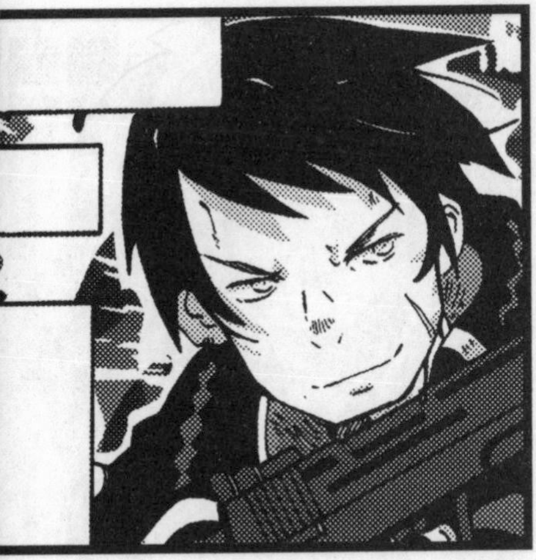

Each of Leon's choices is tied to a real-world conflict or revolution.

Kathryn Bigelow's *The Hurt Locker* takes place in 2004, during the height of the Iraq War. It's the story of an explosive ordinance disposal team, tasked with disarming landmines and similar threats. The film received high praise for drawing attention to the situation in Iraq, still mired in conflict at the time of the film's release.

Argo is a fictionalized retelling of the rescue of six US embassy diplomats during the Iranian Revolution. An elaborate ruse involving location scouting for an imaginary sci-fi film allowed a CIA operative to sneak the diplomats out of the country disguised as crew members. It's a story so fantastic, it's shocking to think it really occurred.

The Motorcycle Diaries takes viewers even further back in time to 1952, when a young Che Guevara took a life-changing road trip across South America. The film is a coming-of-age story, exploring the real-life experiences that set Guevara on his path to becoming the hero of the Cuban Revolution.

All three movies serve as excellent models for an actor committed to honing his craft while embracing stories of conflict, action, and chiseled physiques. Leon positions himself much like Mel Gibson, whose repertoire encompasses action series like *Mad Max* and *Lethal Weapon*, as well as historical dramas like *Braveheart*, for which Gibson received two Oscars (as both director and producer). Coincidentally, *Argo* is also a film in which the director, Ben Affleck, plays the lead role. Several years later, Affleck juggled an acting role as the iconic superhero Batman along with directorial duties in a separate project of his own. No doubt Leon hopes to someday branch out into directing to score a double Nyacademy Award for Best Director and Best Actor.

Introduced Works

The Hurt Locker
2008 / USA / Directed by Kathryn Bigelow /
Starring Jeremy Renner, Anthony Mackie, Ralph Fiennes

Argo
2012 / USA / Directed by Ben Affleck /
Starring Ben Affleck, Bryan Cranston, Alan Arkin, John Goodman

The Motorcycle Diaries (Diarios de motocicleta)
2004 / Argentina, USA, Chili, etc. / Based on the book *The Motorcycle Diaries (Diarios de motocicleta)* by Ernesto "Che" Guevara / Directed by Walter Salles / Starring Gael Garcia Bernal, Rodrigo de la Serna

Christia's Top  Films

Christia's choices represent a longing for the good old days. All three films tell stories of women living proudly or leading vibrant careers in times when gender inequality in the entertainment industry was far more visible.

Dreamgirls is a tale of trials and triumphs in the 1960s music industry based on actual experiences of Black girl groups. *Chicago* paints a picture of the city as it was in the 1920s, rife with gangsters and prospectors. It follows two women embroiled in scandal who are willing to go to any lengths to secure the public spotlight—including lies, bribery, and murder.

Both appeared on Broadway and received rave reviews. In the 2000s, they were remade as films. They gave new life to the classic musical genre, making it young and trendy once more.

The Artist deals with an actor who manages a sensational rise in popularity in the late 1920s as Hollywood transitions from silent films (with their intertitles and live musical accompaniments) to "talkies" (or contemporary film, with dialogue and music included on the reel itself). Opposite her character is a renowned silent film star who can't come to grips with the emerging technology and risks being left behind. It is shot entirely in black and white and in the fashion of a silent film (with the addition of background music). Only the bare minimum of dialogue is used, faithfully conveyed via intertitles. These are expressive techniques so old they may as well be fossils, but in reviving them, *The Artist* shows audiences of our century how rich the filmmaking of yesteryear truly was.

All three are also notable for their costume designers, wardrobe and makeup collaborating with the actors to display the fashions of these eras. Altogether, these choices suggest that Christia aspires to a charm that spans the ages.

Introduced Works

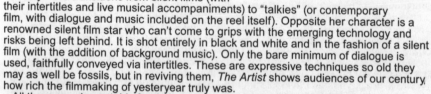

Dreamgirls
2004 / USA / Based on the Broadway musical *Dreamgirls* by Tom Eyen, Henry Krieger / Written and directed by Bill Condon / Starring Jamie Foxx, Beyoncé Knowles, Eddie Murphy, Jennifer Hudson

Chicago
2002 / USA, Germany, Canada / Based on the play *Chicago* by Maurine Dallas Watkins and the book *Chicago* by Bob Fosse and Fred Ebb / Directed by Rob Marshall / Starring Renée Zellweger, Catherine Zeta-Jones, Richard Gere

The Artist
2011 / France, USA, Belgium /
Written and directed by Michel Hazanavicius / Starring Jean Dujardin, Bérénice Bejo, John Goodman

COLUMN

José's Top 3 Films

José, the mysterious masked assistant, has chosen three substantial cult classics in the sci-fi horror genre that share a common theme of humanity teetering on the brink of disaster, often due to an extraterrestrial invasion or other mysterious lifeforms.

In one film, a massive, secret influx of alien beings is revealed to be deceiving the earth's populace *(They Live)*. In the remake of a 1958 film, a mysterious organism preys upon individual victims, growing larger and larger until it threatens to consume an entire town *(The Blob)*. And in the third, a single vagrant entity moves from host to host as it pleases, committing crimes ranging from simple theft to the violent murder of a record store owner *(The Hidden)*.

While the scope of each invasion differs, all three of these films left quite the impression on audiences, particularly thanks to the labors of their special effect makeup crews. Their gruesome, visceral displays would be taken for granted today, but were groundbreaking in the 1980s and contributed to a trend that propelled Hollywood into a new era in which special effects became a major selling point of films. Imagine glimpses of terrifying, slug-like tentacles slipping in and out of a victim's mouth, faces morphing and crunching into skull-like alien visages, and shots of bodies melting into horrifying, sticky ooze capable of slithering along the floor. Sickening scenes like these became and continue to be the object of endless, excited discussions among cult followings.

Incidentally, Gene, the man behind the mask, is a certified movie nerd. But his interests typically lean more toward film as high art. Films like these seem a little more in Miss Pompo's realm, considering her B-movie fixation. In fact...the caricature of José feels a bit like something right out of a Spaghetti Western.

Introduced Works

The Hidden
1987 / USA / Directed by Jack Sholder /
Starring Kyle MacLachlan, Michael Nouri, Ed O'Ross

They Live
1988 / USA / Based on the short story "Eight O'Clock in the Morning" by Ray Nelson /
Directed by John Carpenter / Starring Roddy Piper, Meg Foster, Keith David

The Blob
1988 / USA / Written and directed by Chuck Russell /
Starring Kevin Dillon, Shawnee Smith, Donovan Leitch

Fran's Top 3 Films

Fran works as a waitress at the Eggnog Diner, a restaurant frequented by Miss Pompo, and the three films she's chosen plainly convey her aspirations of stardom.

The Princess Diaries is a rags-to-riches story about a timid, unpopular high school girl who discovers that she is the sole heir to the throne of a tiny European kingdom. It was the dazzling cinematic debut and breakout role of Anne Hathaway, at the time touted as "the next Audrey Hepburn," rocketing the actor from obscurity to stardom like her character.

Fran's other films star noted child actor Freddie Highmore. In *Charlie and the Chocolate Factory*, he's one of five children in the whole world to secure a chance to tour a secretive candy factory. In *August Rush*, he plays a young prodigy who escapes an orphanage to search for his lost parents and hone the innate musical talents he inherited from them.

All three are stories of young lives changed forever thanks to a stroke of luck, underscoring Fran's strong desire to be chosen for greatness. Though the possibility of such fortune seems remote, Fran is onto something. One essential ingredient preceding stardom is being in the right place at the right time.

Eventually, every fairytale character outgrows the role. What defines the greats is how they proceed after the clock strikes midnight. Anne Hathaway shed her innocent, good-girl persona, stepping into a more mature role with a revealing love scene in *Brokeback Mountain*. And in the TV series *Bates Motel*, Freddie Highmore deftly handled the complicated role of a teenaged murderer, sheltered by and fixated upon his mother prior to the events of the classic thriller *Psycho*.

Does Fran possess the same steadfast soul that allowed these two actors to flourish and persist? Only time will tell.

Introduced Works

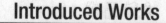

The Princess Diaries
2001 / USA / Based on the book *The Princess Diaries* by Meg Cabot /
Directed by Garry Marshall / Starring Julie Andrews, Anne Hathaway

August Rush
2007 / USA / Directed by Kirsten Sheridan /
Starring Freddie Highmore, Keri Russell, Jonathan Rhys Meyers, Robin Williams

Charlie and the Chocolate Factory
2005 / USA, UK, Australia / Based on the book *Charlie and the Chocolate Factory* by Roald Dahl /
Directed by Tim Burton / Starring Johnny Depp, Freddie Highmore, David Kelly

COLUMN

Jurgen's Top  Films

Jurgen doesn't own the Eggnog Diner, he just runs the place. It only takes a glance at his top films to realize he's got a quirk or two of his own. All three cater to the hard-core cinephile, though they have simple, clear-cut messages to convey.

Wings of Desire is about an angel with the appearance of a tired, middle-aged man. While observing a mortal woman, he falls in love and contemplates throwing away his immortality to be with her. It's a plain enough premise, yet arrives framed in ethereal shots overlaid with captivating recitations of original poetry.

Nostalgia, a film by the great master of Soviet cinema, Andrei Tarkovsky, is even more experimental—so much so that attempting to follow the plot is an exercise in absurdity. The sounds of the film merge with the beautiful images on screen, creating an expression that has to be seen to be understood. The work transcends the medium itself, becoming visual poetry. Some viewers find themselves glued to the screen, while others are entranced only insofar as it puts them to sleep. This is a movie for those who worship film, not merely enjoy it.

The Fisher King, in contrast, seems quite straightforward. Genius director Terry Gilliam departs from his usual eccentric playfulness to deliver a grown-up fantasy tale about a radio announcer who loses everything, only to be pulled back from the edge of despair by a pure, unassuming homeless man, poignantly portrayed by the great Robin Williams.

Jurgen, with his charming, ever-present stubble, would be right at home in any of these films. He has more than enough charisma for a side role, playing a character with a bittersweet past who still manages to retain his warmth and humanity. Given the right setting and theme, he'd be a fine lead as well. With any luck, audiences will get their chance to see him deliver the stories of redemption and peace we all long for.

Introduced Works

Wings of Desire (Der Himmel über Berlin)
1987 / West Germany, France / Written and directed by Wim Wenders /
Starring Bruno Ganz, Solveig Dommartin, Otto Sander, Peter Falk

Nostalgia (Nostalghia)
1983 / Italy, USSR / Directed by Andrei Tarkovsky / Written by Tonino Guerra and Andrei Tarkovsky /
Starring Oleg Yankovsky, Erland Josephson, Delia Boccardo, Domiziana Giordano

The Fisher King
1991 / USA / Directed by Terry Gilliam /
Starring Robin Williams, Jeff Bridges, Amanda Plummer, Mercedes Ruehl

Corvette's Top 3 Films

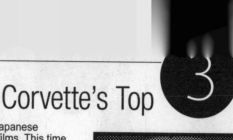

Director Corvette, ever fond of Japanese anime, has chosen three *new* top films. This time, he's focused on theatrical spin-offs of successful TV shows.

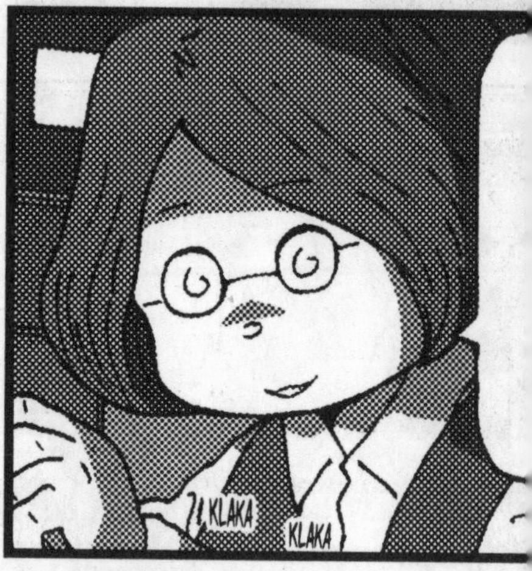
KLAKA
KLAKA

Nearly anyone who grew up in Japan will have some memory of watching the *Go! Anpanman* series. It's an immensely popular franchise, and one that has seen a new theatrical release every year since 1989's *Go! Anpanman: The Shining Star's Tear.*

The *Pretty Cure (PreCure)* series is another TV staple that has been bringing viewers joy for years. Aimed primarily at elementary school girls, it originated in 2004 with *Futari wa Pretty Cure*.

The films in both franchises stick to a tried-and-true formula: a guest character is introduced and shown to be facing some antagonistic force, and the series' heroes do everything they can to resolve it. The fact that this basic premise manages to stay fresh over the years is a testament to the craftsmanship in the Japanese anime industry. Each film makes use of innovative locations or new little twists to ensure continued enjoyment, no matter how familiar the plot.

As Director Corvette is noted for his own ability to reliably convey stories of others' design, it makes sense that he has a soft spot for these long-running standbys of Japanese cinema and the production challenges they pose. In effect, each film is an extended, cinematic episode of the TV series.

Corvette's third choice, *Girls und Panzer der Film*, ties to this theme in that its director, Tsutomu Mizushima, has for many years been involved in the production of TV episodes and films for *Crayon Shin-chan* (yet another long-running series aimed—for the most part—at children). *Girls und Panzer der Film* even shares some hallmarks in terms of story: it is the tale of a determined heroine leading her friends to victory when all seems lost. Viewers get to see characters they love band together for an epic all-star adventure that can only be done justice on the big screen. In a word, films such as these aspire to be the ultimate episode of the series they represent.

Introduced Works

Go! Anpanman: Nanda and Runda of the Toy Star
(Soreike! Anpanman: Omocha no Hoshi no Nanda to Runda)
2016 / Japan / Original series by Takashi Yanase / Directed by Jun Kawagoe / Written by Shoji Yonemura / Character design and animation directed by Minoru Maeda / Starring Keiko Toda, Ryusei Nakao

Kirakira Pretty Cure a la Mode the Movie: Crisply! The Memory of Mille-feuille!
(Eiga Kirakira☆Purikyua ara Mōdo: Paritto! Omoide no Mirufīyu!)
2017 / Japan / Original series by Izumi Todo / Directed by Yutaka Tsuchida / Written by Isao Murayama / Character design by Mari Ino, Katsumi Tamegai / Chief animation directed by Katsumi Tamegai / Animation directed by Kazuhiro Ota / Starring Karen Miyama, Haruka Fukuhara, Tomo Muranaka, Saki Fujita, Nanako Mori, Inori Minase

Girls und Panzer der Film (Gāruzu & Pantsā Gekijō-ban)
2015 / Japan / Directed by Tsutomu Mizushima / Written by Reiko Yoshida / Original characters by Fumikane Shimada / Character design and chief animation directed by Isao Sugimoto / Starring Mai Fuchigami, Ai Kayano, Mami Ozaki, Ikumi Nakagami, Yuka Iguchi

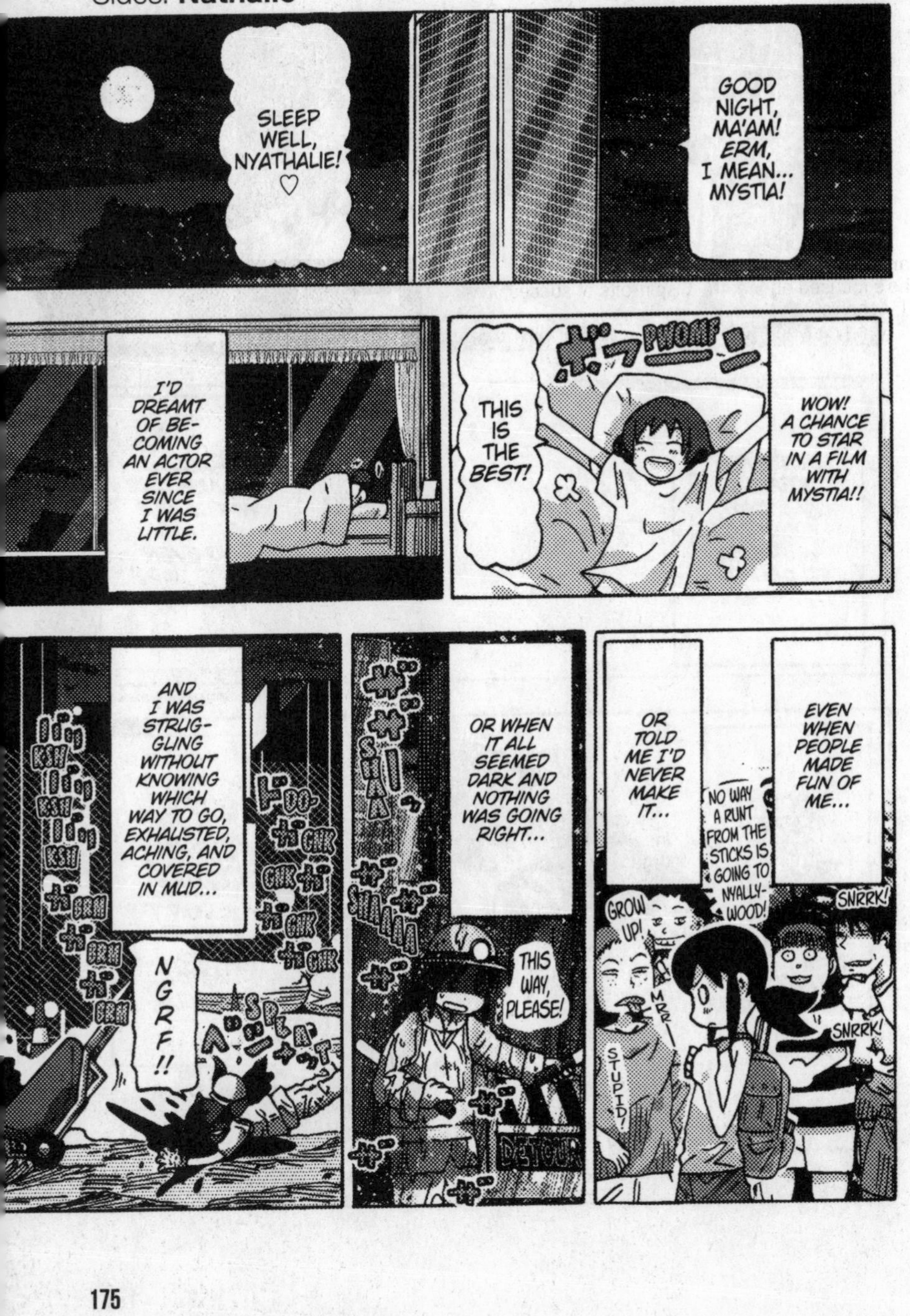
GOOD NIGHT, MA'AM! ERM, I MEAN... MYSTIA!
SLEEP WELL, NYATHALIE! ♡
WOW! A CHANCE TO STAR IN A FILM WITH MYSTIA!!
PWOMF
THIS IS THE BEST!
I'D DREAMT OF BE-COMING AN ACTOR EVER SINCE I WAS LITTLE.
EVEN WHEN PEOPLE MADE FUN OF ME...
OR TOLD ME I'D NEVER MAKE IT...
NO WAY A RUNT FROM THE STICKS IS GOING TO NYALLY-WOOD!
SNRRK!
GROW UP!
MRR
STUPID!
SNRRK!
OR WHEN IT ALL SEEMED DARK AND NOTHING WAS GOING RIGHT...
SHAAA
SHAAAA
THIS WAY, PLEASE!
DETOUR
AND I WAS STRUG-GLING WITHOUT KNOWING WHICH WAY TO GO, EXHAUSTED, ACHING, AND COVERED IN MUD...
KSH
KSH
KSH
DO-
GNK
GNK
GNK
NGRF!!
SPLAT

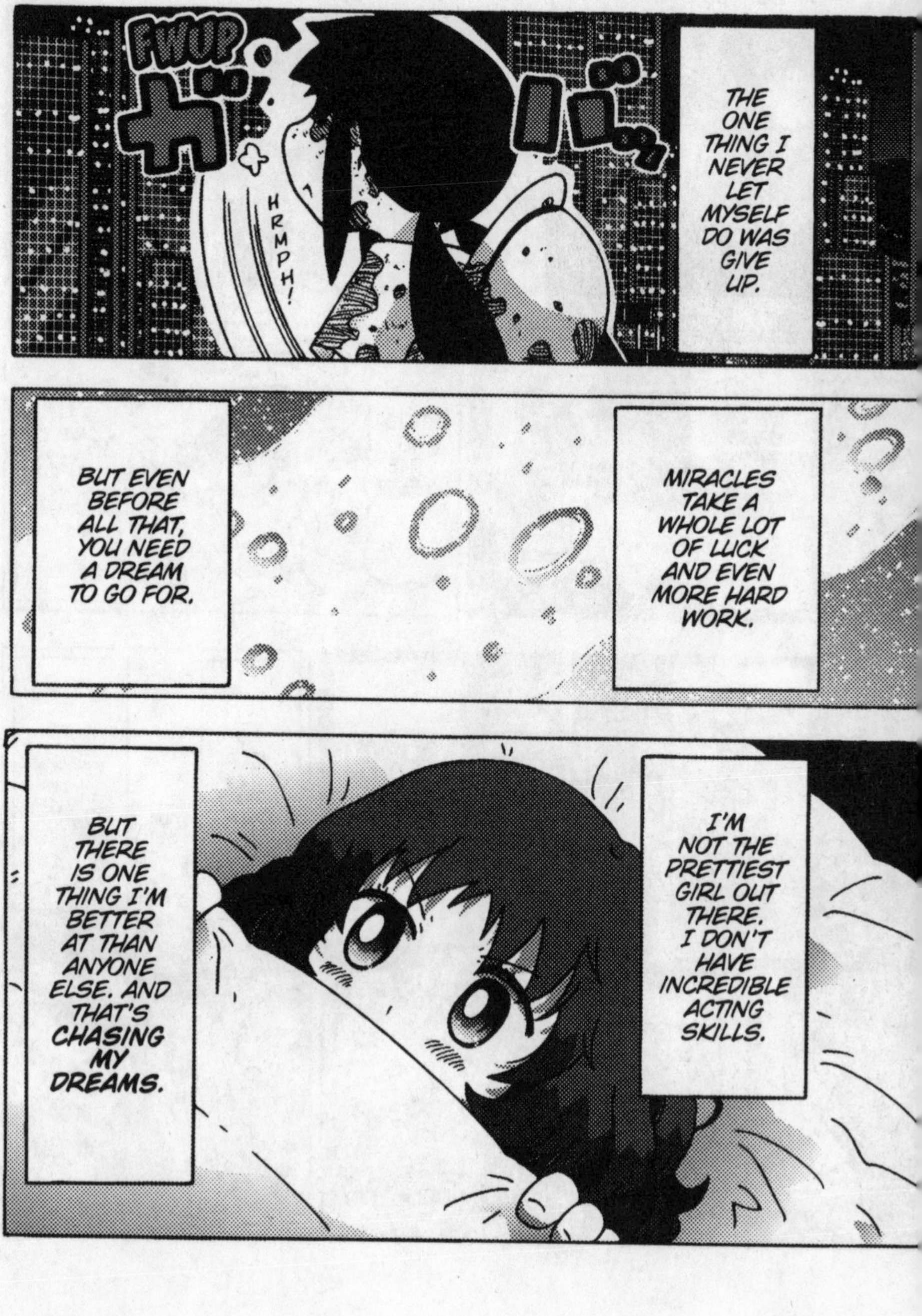
THE ONE THING I NEVER LET MYSELF DO WAS GIVE UP.
FWUP
HRMPH!
MIRACLES TAKE A WHOLE LOT OF LUCK AND EVEN MORE HARD WORK.
BUT EVEN BEFORE ALL THAT, YOU NEED A DREAM TO GO FOR.
I'M NOT THE PRETTIEST GIRL OUT THERE. I DON'T HAVE INCREDIBLE ACTING SKILLS.
BUT THERE IS ONE THING I'M BETTER AT THAN ANYONE ELSE. AND THAT'S CHASING MY DREAMS.

AND NOW, IT'S TIME TO CHASE ANOTHER!

WHERE WILL MY NEXT DREAM TAKE ME? WHAT WONDERFUL NEW THINGS WILL I DISCOVER?!

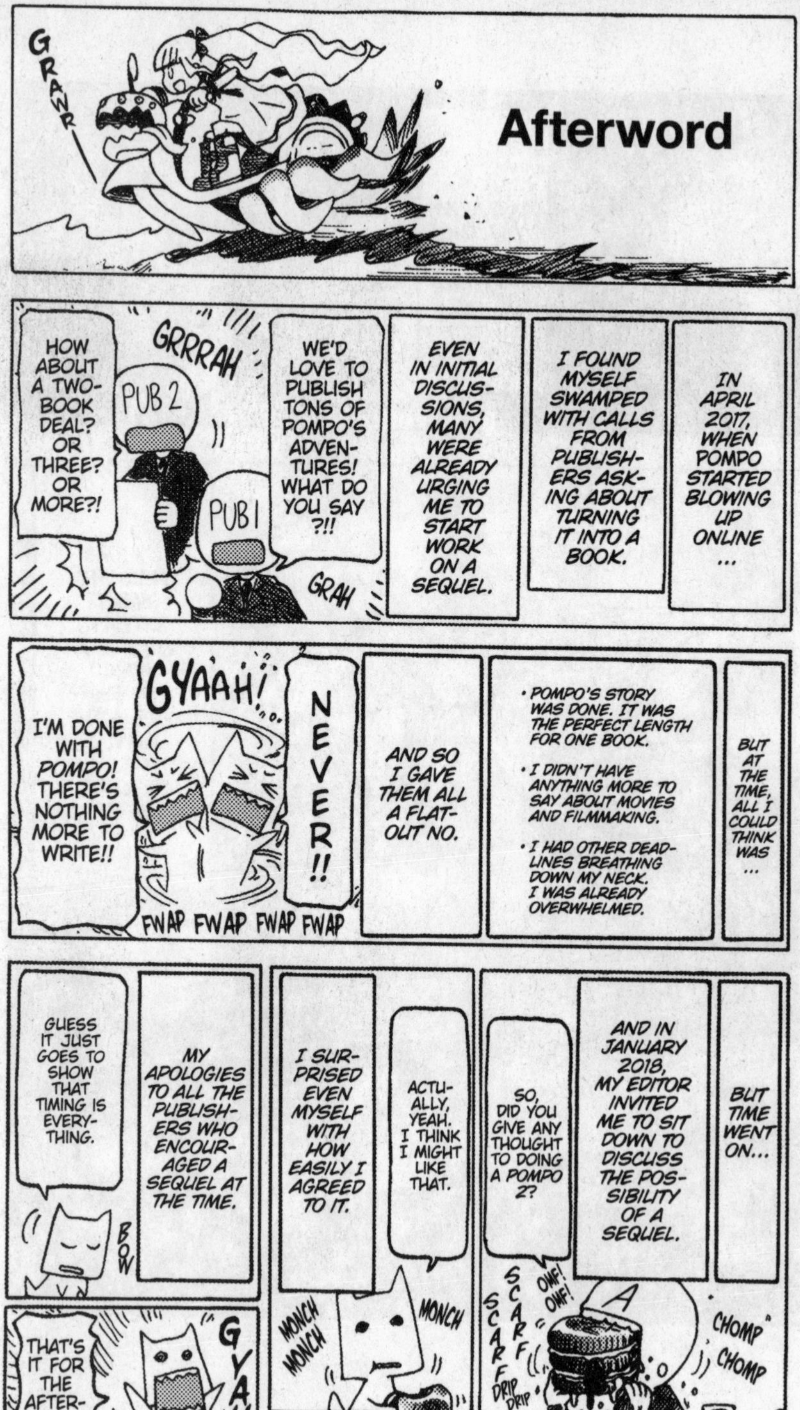
Afterword
GRAWR
IN APRIL 2017, WHEN POMPO STARTED BLOWING UP ONLINE...
I FOUND MYSELF SWAMPED WITH CALLS FROM PUBLISHERS ASKING ABOUT TURNING IT INTO A BOOK.
EVEN IN INITIAL DISCUSSIONS, MANY WERE ALREADY URGING ME TO START WORK ON A SEQUEL.
WE'D LOVE TO PUBLISH TONS OF POMPO'S ADVENTURES! WHAT DO YOU SAY?!!
GRRRAH
PUB 2
PUB 1
GRAH
HOW ABOUT A TWO-BOOK DEAL? OR THREE? OR MORE?!
BUT AT THE TIME, ALL I COULD THINK WAS...
• POMPO'S STORY WAS DONE. IT WAS THE PERFECT LENGTH FOR ONE BOOK.
• I DIDN'T HAVE ANYTHING MORE TO SAY ABOUT MOVIES AND FILMMAKING.
• I HAD OTHER DEADLINES BREATHING DOWN MY NECK. I WAS ALREADY OVERWHELMED.
AND SO I GAVE THEM ALL A FLAT-OUT NO.
NEVER!!
GYAAH!
I'M DONE WITH POMPO! THERE'S NOTHING MORE TO WRITE!!
FWAP FWAP FWAP FWAP
BUT TIME WENT ON...
AND IN JANUARY 2018, MY EDITOR INVITED ME TO SIT DOWN TO DISCUSS THE POSSIBILITY OF A SEQUEL.
SO, DID YOU GIVE ANY THOUGHT TO DOING A POMPO 2?
OMF! OMF!
CHOMP
CHOMP
SCARF SCARF
DRIP DRIP
ACTUALLY, YEAH. I THINK I MIGHT LIKE THAT.
I SURPRISED EVEN MYSELF WITH HOW EASILY I AGREED TO IT.
MONCH
MONCH MONCH
MY APOLOGIES TO ALL THE PUBLISHERS WHO ENCOURAGED A SEQUEL AT THE TIME.
GUESS IT JUST GOES TO SHOW THAT TIMING IS EVERYTHING.
BOW
GYAH!
THAT'S IT FOR THE AFTERWORD!!

STAFF

Author
Shogo Sugitani
—TOP FILMS: PART 2—
Tomorrow's Joe 2 (Ashita no Joe 2)

Producer
Toshitaka Mizobe
—TOP FILMS: PART 2—
Lupin the Third: The Castle of Cagliostro

Designer
Tomoyuki Arima
—TOP FILMS: PART 2—
Back to the Future Part II

Writer (Columns for McTiernan, Leon, Christia, José, Francesca, Jurgen)
Shinichi Manabe
—TOP FILMS: PART 2—
Spider-Man 2

Editor & Writer (Column for Corvette)
Satoshi Arima
—TOP FILMS: PART 2—
Home Alone 2: Lost in New York

Special Thanks
Yusuke Tomizawa
—TOP FILMS: PART 2—
Ghost in the Shell 2: Innocence

Special Thanks
Takayuki Hirao
—TOP FILMS: PART 2—
Dawn of the Dead (1978)

**Last but not least,
thank you to all my fans!!**

POMPO
THE CINÉPHILE

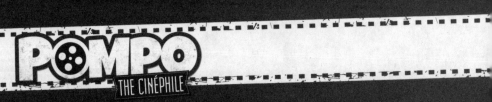

POMPO
THE CINÉPHILE

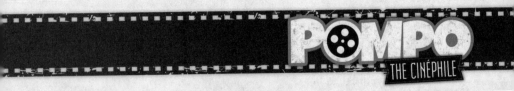

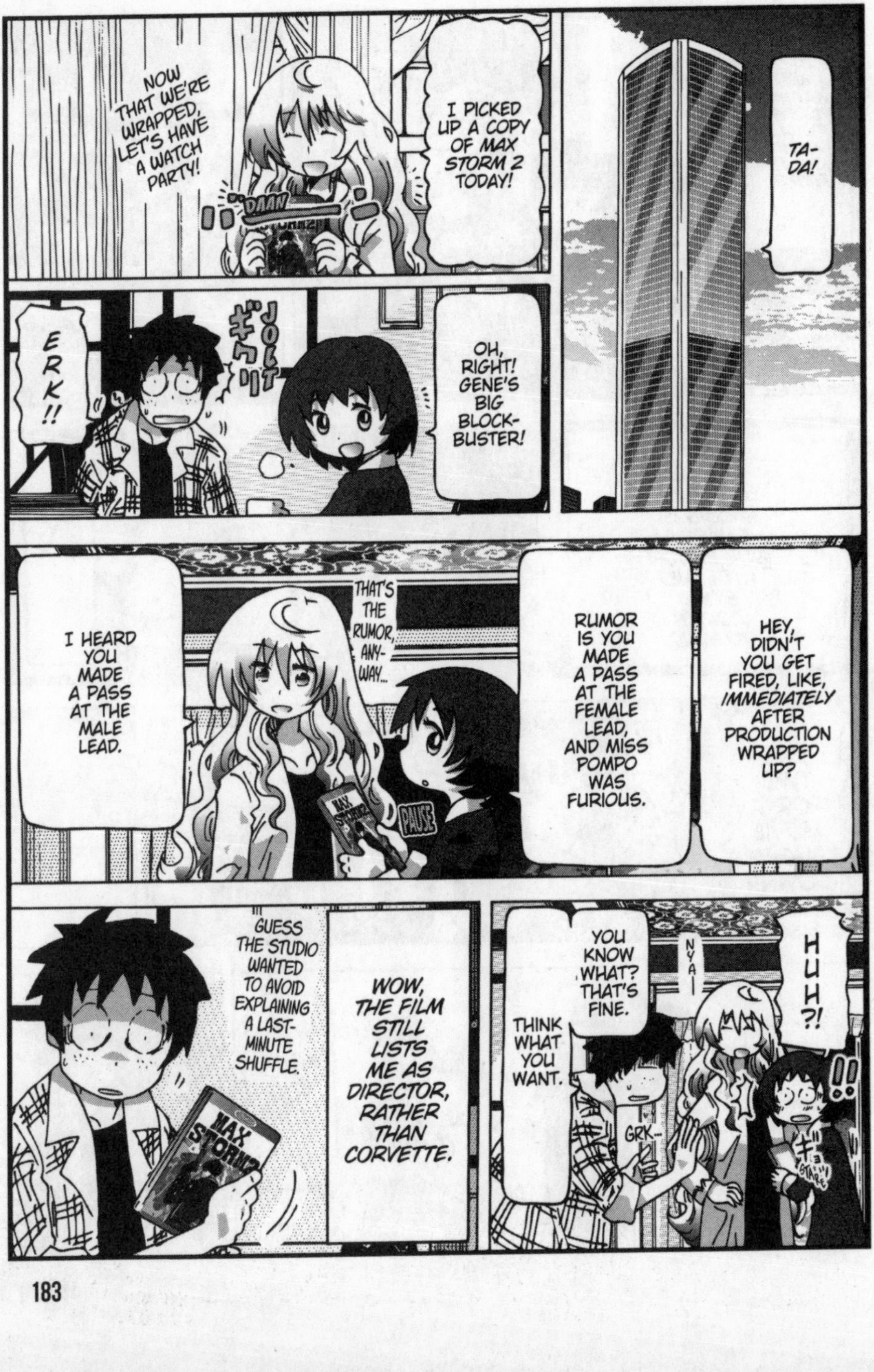
TA-DA!
I PICKED UP A COPY OF *MAX STORM 2* TODAY!
NOW THAT WE'RE WRAPPED, LET'S HAVE A WATCH PARTY!
DAAN
OH, RIGHT! GENE'S BIG BLOCKBUSTER!
JOLT
ERK!!
HEY, DIDN'T YOU GET FIRED, LIKE, *IMMEDIATELY* AFTER PRODUCTION WRAPPED UP?
RUMOR IS YOU MADE A PASS AT THE FEMALE LEAD, AND MISS POMPO WAS FURIOUS.
THAT'S THE RUMOR, ANYWAY...
I HEARD YOU MADE A PASS AT THE MALE LEAD.
PAUSE
HUH?!
NYA—
YOU KNOW WHAT? THAT'S FINE.
THINK WHAT YOU WANT.
GRK—
STARE
WOW, THE FILM STILL LISTS ME AS DIRECTOR, RATHER THAN CORVETTE.
GUESS THE STUDIO WANTED TO AVOID EXPLAINING A LAST-MINUTE SHUFFLE.

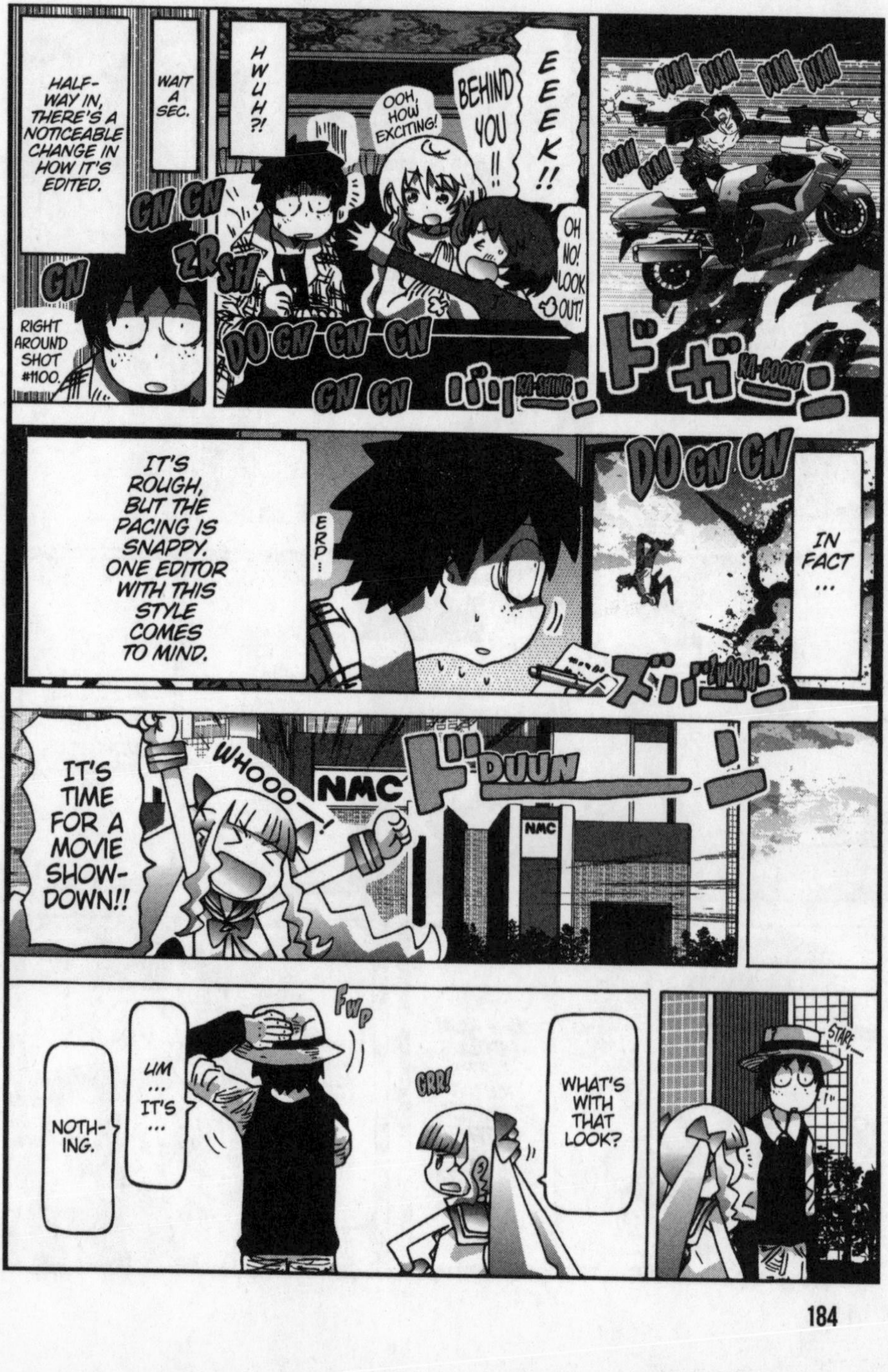
BLAM BLAM BLAM BLAM
BLAM BLAM
KA-BOOM
EEEK!!
BEHIND YOU!!
OOH, HOW EXCITING!
HWUH?!
OH NO! LOOK OUT!
GN GN
ZRSH
DO GN GN GN
GN GN
KA-SHING
WAIT A SEC.
HALF-WAY IN, THERE'S A NOTICEABLE CHANGE IN HOW IT'S EDITED.
GN
RIGHT AROUND SHOT #1100.
DO GN GN
IN FACT...
WHOOSH
ERP...
IT'S ROUGH, BUT THE PACING IS SNAPPY. ONE EDITOR WITH THIS STYLE COMES TO MIND.
DUUN
NMC
NMC
WHOOO—!
IT'S TIME FOR A MOVIE SHOW-DOWN!!
STARE
WHAT'S WITH THAT LOOK?
GRR!
FWP
UM... IT'S...
NOTH-ING.

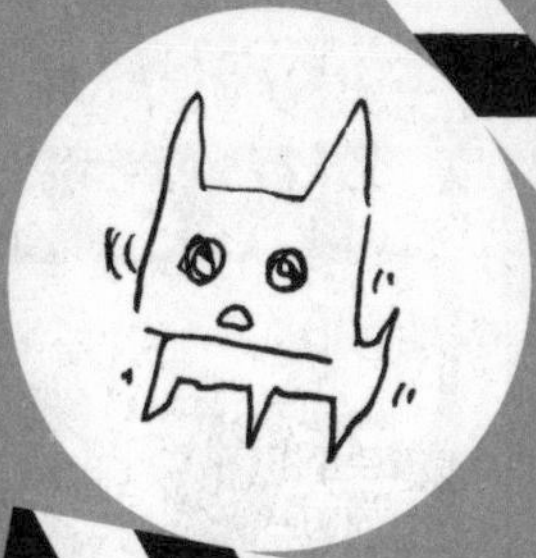

PROD. TITLE:

POMPO: THE CINÉPHILE 2

PRESENTED BY:

SHOGO SUGITANI

MANGA ARTIST PROFILE:

WORKS FOR PRODUCTION GOODBOOK

Production GoodBook

STUDIO KAGUR·A

Cover Design: **Tomoyuki Arima**

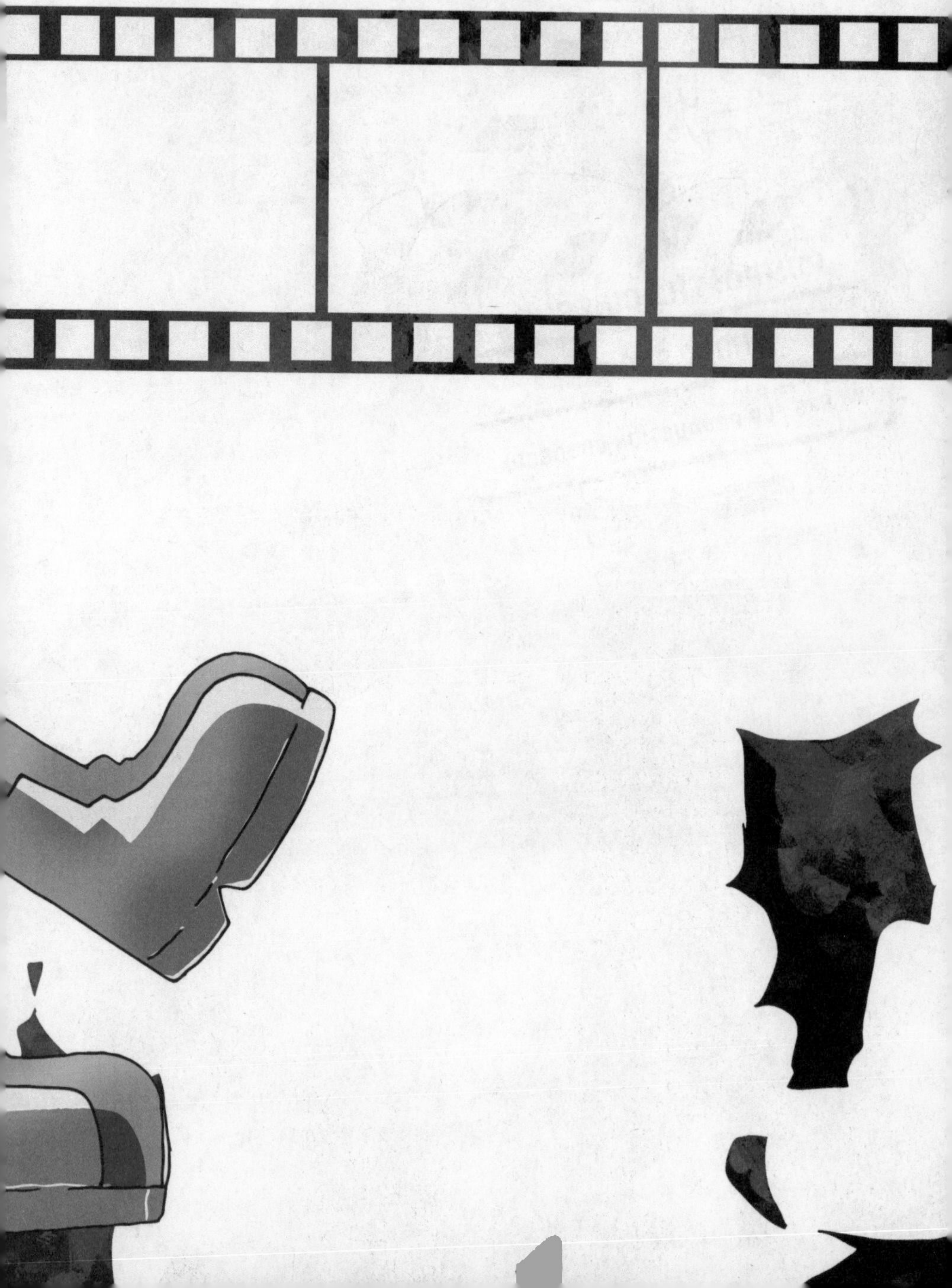

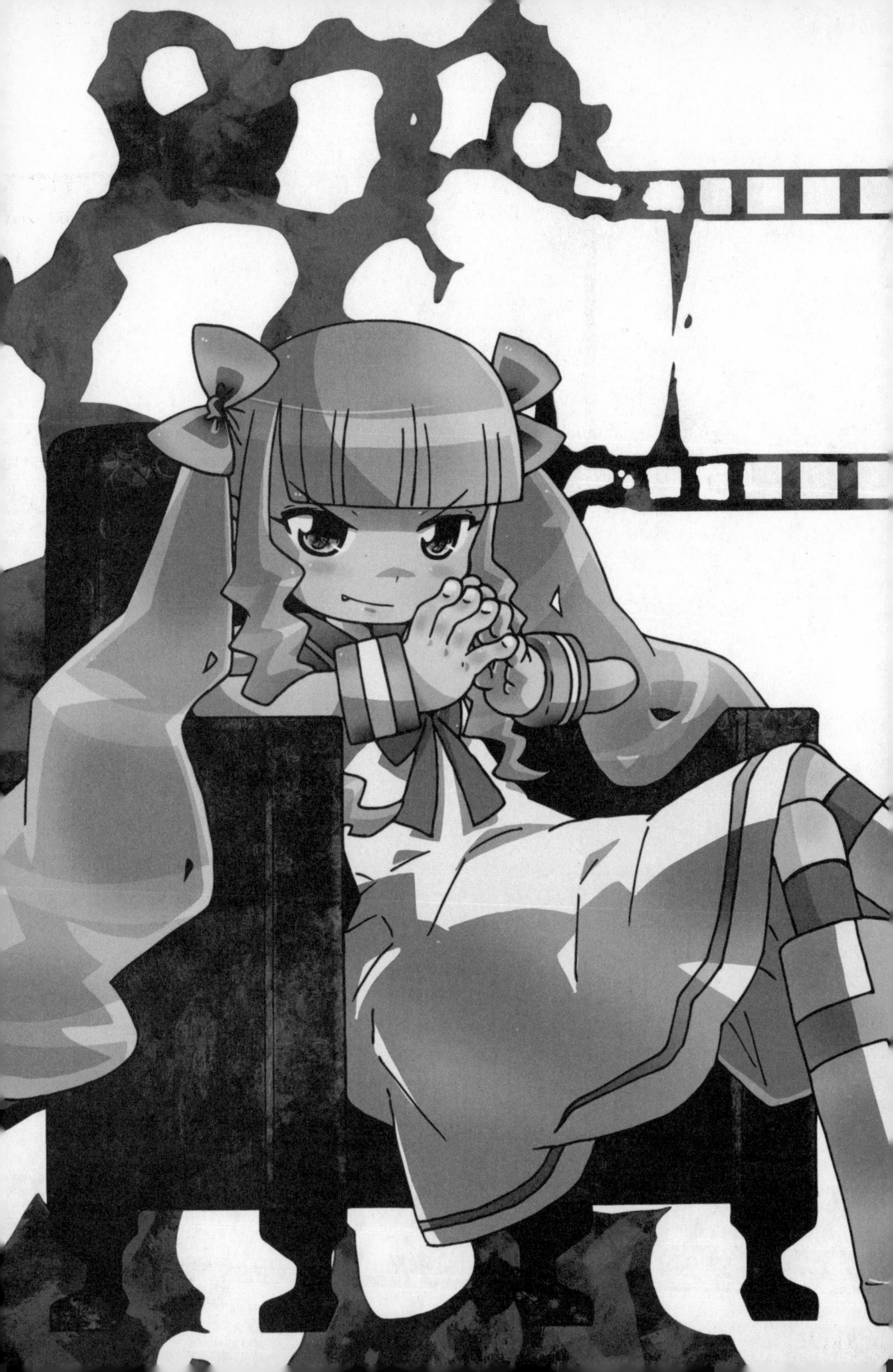

POMPO THE CINÉPHILE

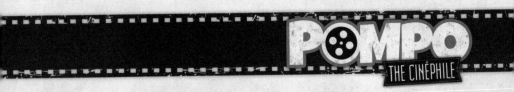

SEVEN SEAS ENTERTAINMENT PRESENTS

POMPO
THE CINÉPHILE

story and art by SHOGO SUGITANI

Vol. 2

TRANSLATION
Stephen Christenson

ADAPTATION
Jay Trust

LETTERING
James Gaubatz

LOGO AND COVER DESIGN
Hanase Qi

PROOFREADER
Kurestin Armada

COPY EDITOR
Dawn Davis

EDITOR
Jenn Grunigen

PREPRESS TECHNICIAN
Rhiannon Rasmussen-Silverstein

PRODUCTION ASSOCIATE
Christa Miesner

PRODUCTION MANAGER
Lissa Pattillo

MANAGING EDITOR
Julie Davis

ASSOCIATE PUBLISHER
Adam Arnold

PUBLISHER
Jason DeAngelis

EIGA DAISUKI POMPO SAN Vol. 2
©Shogo Sugitani, Production GoodBook 2018
First published in Japan in 2018 by KADOKAWA CORPORATION, Tokyo.
English translation rights arranged with KADOKAWA CORPORATION, Tokyo.

Seven Seas press and purchase enquiries can be sent to Marketing
Manager Lianne Sentar at press@gomanga.com. Information regarding
the distribution and purchase of digital editions is available from
Digital Manager CK Russell at digital@gomanga.com.

Seven Seas and the Seven Seas logo are trademarks of
Seven Seas Entertainment. All rights reserved.

ISBN: 978-1-64827-565-4
Printed in Canada
First Printing: November 2021
10 9 8 7 6 5 4 3 2 1

READING DIRECTIONS

This book reads from *right to left*,
Japanese style. If this is your first time
reading manga, you start reading from
the top right panel on each page and
take it from there. If you get lost, just
follow the numbered diagram here.
It may seem backwards at first,
but you'll get the hang of it! Have fun!!

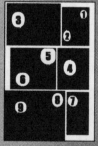